1001 Things
Your Kids
Should
See & Do

(Or Else They'll Never Leave Home)

LARRY H. HARRISON JR.

THOMAS NELSON PUBLISHERS
Since 1798

Table of Contents

Introduction

The purpose of childhood is training for adulthood.

All kids talk about how they are "so out of here" after graduation. They announce they're going to college, going to Borneo, traveling around Europe, spending time in New York City.

These are the same teenagers who get so turned around on their way home at night, they call you wondering if taking the highway to North Dakota was the right exit. And they know home means free food. Air conditioning. Nice bed. Mom's shoulder. Dad's money. And as long as they stay home, they can avoid the messy complications of adulthood.

That's when many start saying, "I'm so out of here after a year or two of junior college."

Later, "I'm so out of here after my MBA." Then, "You'll never see me again once I get my second PhD."

That's typically when parents resign themselves to reality, build a bedroom over the garage, and move into it.

There are over a thousand things every kid needs to see and do to have the faith and courage and skills and confidence to walk out that door when adulthood beckons. And you can either start preparing them for adulthood early in their life, or deal with a thirty-year-old waiting for dinner downstairs. In their pajamas. •

They Need to Visit Mister Rogers' Neighborhood

1. They need to see that you love them completely. The way they are.

•

2. They need to catch moonbeams.

•

3. They need to see you light up when they get home from school. Or when you get home from work.

•

4. They need to tell the truth.

•

5. They need to read. Fast. And remember.

6. They need to dig a hole to China.

•

7. They need to take
a nap with their dog.

•

8. They need to search
for the end of a rainbow.

•

9. They need to trust, at a very
early age, that home is safe.

•

10. They need to see your face in the
crowd at their soccer games and band
concerts. Cheering. Not yelling.

11. They need to build a birdhouse.

•

12. They need to develop
their curiosity about things.

•

13. They need to look at a leaf
through a magnifying glass.
And see wonder exists
out of ordinary sight.

•

14. They need to collect a jar
of lightning bugs at night.

15. They need to tell the difference between cicada and cricket sounds. They'll be hearing things all their lives that sound like one thing, but are actually another.

•

16. They need to play flashlight tag with their friends and discover the joys of summer nights.

•

17. They need to develop a sense of adventure. The younger the better.

18. They need to be assigned chores. Even if it's just cleaning their rooms.

•

19. They need to spend hours building a sand castle on the beach, then watch the evening tide wash it away.

•

20. They need to climb up the inside of a lighthouse.

•

21. They need to watch a chrysalis turn into a butterfly. You can buy them on-line.

22. They need to find
their way out of a maze.

•

23. They need to watch a windmill.

•

24. They need to see you
reading your Bible. At home.

•

25. They need to
learn proper grammar.

26. They need to know who they are: their full name, address, their mom and dad's full names, and phone number. (Ask them this all the time.)

•

27. They need to learn when to call 911.

•

28. They need to see you struggle with difficulties.

•

29. They need to go to camp. To learn they can live without you. And you, without them.

30. They need to listen to
a storyteller at the library.

•

31. They need to pray. First
with you. Then without you.
(And hopefully for you.)

•

32. They need to get along with their
brothers and sisters and other kids.
This will pay dividends in adulthood.

•

33. They need to ride a bike.
And fall down. And get up
and ride some more.

34. They need to conquer their fears.

•

35. They need to learn life
is not all about them.

•

36. They need manners. This will
carry them far in the adult world.

•

37. They need to go fishing. And learn
the mystery of anticipation.

•

38. They need to hear for themselves
that a Monster Truck Show just may
be the noisiest thing in the world.

39. They need to bait a hook. And take a fish off one. Learn that life is messy. Even some of the best parts.

•

40. They need to learn to not keep secrets from you.

•

41. They need to take care of another living thing. A goldfish is the beginning of responsibility.

•

42. They need to stand up for themselves.

43. They need to do the
hokey-pokey on Rollerblades.

•

44. They need to roll in the snow.
Even if they live in Florida.

•

45. They need to share
an apple with a horse.

•

46. They need to stare into
the eyes of a gorilla. Either
in Africa or at a good zoo.

•

47. They need to say nice things about
people instead of hurtful things.

48. They need to make a
best friend. And be one.

•

49. They need to sit on
the roof and get another
perspective of their world.

•

50. They need to sell cookies
for their team or club or band.

•

51. They need to sleep outside
and watch for falling stars.

52. They need to sit around a campfire and hear ghost stories that will keep them scared witless all night.

•

53. They need to listen to Mozart or Beethoven every morning before school.

•

54. They need to write to pen pals. Across the state. Across the country. Across the world.

55. They need to watch a tree grow from a seedling over several years. And see that pretty much describes the mystery of life.

•

56. They need to watch a colt find its legs.

•

57. They need to open a Kool-Aid stand.

•

58. They need to learn to say, "I'm sorry."

59. They need to develop
the courage to support a friend.

•

60. They need to grow a
vegetable garden. And battle
birds, grasshoppers, and bugs.

•

61. They need to eat
weird foods: Tofu. Miniature
corn. And dried bananas.

•

62. They need to spend time
with their grandparents.
To hear stories about you.

63. They need to see you at work.
(Right now, they think you
just read a newspaper all day.)

•

64. They need to respect their
"curfew." Television curfew.
Computer curfew.
Be-home-by-9-p.m. curfew.

•

65. They need to develop minor
culinary skills. Like the ability
to make a butter sandwich.

66. They need to sign
with a deaf person.

•

67. They need to learn how to cross a
stream. There will be plenty in life.

•

68. They need to learn to
dry their hands on towels.
Not the walls or furniture.

•

69. They need to learn what's
flushable. Tissue is. Root beer
bottles, dolls, and toy cars are not.

70. They need to develop the art of listening. Without interrupting. And remembering what's being said.

•

71. They need to change their underwear without being told.

•

72. They need to stop eating when they're full. Not when their plate is clean.

•

73. They need to see pictures of themselves when they were babies.

74. They need to see pictures of
you when you were their age.
Expect howls of laughter.

•

75. They need to
body-surf in the ocean.

•

76. They need to ride a train.

•

77. They need to leave
a hornet's nest alone.

78. They need to keep a journal as early as grade school. Both of you will love reading it twenty years later.

•

79. They need to catch butterflies.

•

80. They need to learn most barking dogs are just saying "hello."

•

81. They need to figure out time and direction by using the sun.

82. They need to see the moon, Mars, and Jupiter through a telescope.

•

83. They need to watch an eclipse.

•

84. They need to find books that keep them reading under the covers with a flashlight.

85. They need to stand up when meeting an adult. And shake hands while looking them in the eye.

•

86. They need to explore the attic. It's probably the most mysterious place they know.

•

87. They need to make cookies. This involves reading, hand-eye coordination, and self-denial when it comes to the cookie dough.

88. They need to learn how
to find their way home.

•

89. They need to see a sea horse
swimming underwater.

•

90. They need to turn off
the television.

They Need
to Grow Up

91. They need to overcome
disappointment and failure.
While you stay out of the way.

•

92. They need to use deodorant in
their armpits. Not room spray.

•

93. They need to use soap.
All over their body.

•

94. They need to clean up
a room before they leave it.

95. They need to get themselves organized. If you do it for them, they'll never learn.

•

96. They need to watch their language.

•

97. They need to take dance lessons. Probably not from you.

•

98. They need to see poverty. To understand its impact. And how education is usually the cure.

99. They need to have a cause:
baby seals, whales,
energy conservation.

•

100. They need to learn to
not take anything personally.

•

101. They need to be able to
talk to adults. Not just cross
their arms, stare at the floor,
and mumble something.

102. They need to eat without
food falling out of their mouth.
This usually requires swallowing
before stuffing more in.

•

103. They need to keep
their hands out of their
nose, mouth, ears, and hair.

•

104. They need to write a
letter to the editor. Any editor.

105. They need to give up their bedroom to visiting friends and relatives. It's good practice for future giving.

•

106. They need to baby-sit kids for money.

•

107. They need to learn to control their emotions.

•

108. They need to deal with the bully in their life.

109. They need to apply for a job at McDonald's. To see all the career options open to an uneducated person.

•

110. They need to take a mission trip with you to a Third World country. See how people in abject poverty have not lost their joy.

•

111. They need to do introductory algebra and a considerable amount of geometry.

112. They need to give away clothes they last wore two years ago.

•

113. They need to quit wearing their Christmas socks by March.

•

114. They need to think positive.

•

115. They need to store their Social Security card someplace besides their wallet.

•

116. They need to show gratitude.

117. They need to clean out
their closets. Pitch the useless
stuff that's just cluttering them.

•

118. They need to deal
with the flat tires in life.

•

119. They need the simple math
skills required to figure out
if they have enough gas to
pass up the next gas station.

•

120. They need to see someplace
so fantastic they can always return
to it in their mind to feel at peace.

121. They need to change their bed
sheets. Or they could study the
interesting forms of life that are
growing there under a microscope.

•

122. They need to see a utility bill.
To become aware there's a cost
for just sitting in the bedroom
staring out the window.

•

123. They need to see an old
person with an old tattoo.
You don't really need to comment.

124. They need to reset their clocks the night before daylight saving time changes. Not the week after.

•

125. They need to wash their underwear. Not wear their parent's.

•

126. They need to mow and edge a yard. In one afternoon. Stopping only for water. Without complaining.

•

127. They need to be able to discuss fine literature.

128. They need to wire up a DVD to a satellite TV and speakers. And not blow up anything.

•

129. They need to find authors they love to read.

•

130. They need to learn the secret to packing and organizing a school backpack. This is the only way homework makes it home and finished assignments make it back to school.

131. They need to write a short story about their life that lets you see them in a new way.

•

132. They need to write and shoot a thirty-second movie using a digital camera.

•

133. They need to clean the garage. And help you figure out what in the world all that stuff is for.

134. They need to disinfect their toilet. They'll gag and say they're grossed out. Stick a scrub brush in their hands anyway.

•

135. They need to turn off the iPod and listen to a thunderstorm.

•

136. They need to go to ball games with you. It's a chance to yell and scream, see friends, and occasionally ask about the score.

137. They need to learn what clothes go into the washing machine, what clothes go to the dry cleaners, and what clothes to give away.

•

138. They need to be home for dinner.

•

139. They need to use fabric softener sheets as intended, not as paper towels.

•

140. They need to hold the starch when ironing underwear.

141. They need to wash clothes with laundry detergent, not pet shampoo.

•

142. They need to bleach their hair without it turning orange.

•

143. They need to learn how to order a nonfat, decaf, double hot, white chocolate mocha latte. Whatever that is.

•

144. They need to find a favorite place to study. Not socialize, study.

145. They need to compare prices of fast food against preparing meals at home.

•

146. They need to develop excellent English language skills: to talk without using made-up words, foul words, or poor grammar.

•

147. They need to be conversational in Spanish or another foreign language.

148. They need to "RSVP."
It doesn't matter what it stands for,
it simply shows whether they
were raised by wolves or not.

•

149. They need to make friends
with people who don't look like
them. Or speak their language.

•

150. They need to know that
if they change their thoughts,
they change their lives.

151. They need to develop the habit
of brushing. Flossing. And mouth
washing. Really, for everybody's sake.

•

152. They need to eat if they
find themselves tired,
hungry, or in a bad mood.

•

153. They need to enter the
spelling bee. And only lose
on words like "ambidextrous."

•

154. They need to develop
great study skills: lights on,
phone off, and eyes open.

155. They need to dress appropriately for different occasions.

•

156. They need to start saving money. Some adults never get the hang of this.

•

157. They need to put lids back on everything.

•

158. They need to be on time.

•

159. They need to learn to go heavy with the Pine-Sol while cleaning the kitchen and bathrooms.

160. They need to organize, file, store, and somehow preserve their school papers, pictures, and memories.

•

161. They need to learn what SPF 15 means, before their skin is flaking off their back.

•

162. They need to give thanks. Every morning. Every night. Every meal.

•

163. They need to trace their family tree. Learn who the nuts are in the family.

164. They need to develop
the inclination to inquire.

•

165. They need to know
how to lift something heavy.

•

166. They need to avoid
self-deception. A little brother
or sister can help here.

•

167. They need to act like they're
happy. (Especially useful when there's
nothing to be unhappy about.)

168. They need to be courteous to other people. Start with family members.

•

169. They need to take a water life-saving course.

•

170. They need to develop the math skills to compare credit card offers with different interest rates and annual fees.

•

171. They need to read newspaper editorials. And voice an opinion.

172. They need to learn to make a point by looking people in the eye, without twitching or scratching. Or using the word "like."

•

173. They need to be up on current events: the energy crisis, global warming, and international terrorism.

•

174. They need to think for themselves. Even if they're spectacularly wrong.

175. They need to write thank-you notes. Even for the orange and green-striped puffy shorts their grandmother thought were so cute. Thank-you notes for even those.

•

176. They need to remember the appearance of their body is not as vital as the development of their mind.

•

177. They need to try new things even though they're afraid.

178. They need to see that their
friends will help shape
their life. So choose wisely.

•

179. They need to see that following
the crowd is pointless if the crowd
is headed in the wrong direction.

•

180. They need to get things
done without your help.

•

181. They need to stay away
from their friends when
their friends are acting stupid.

182. They need to defend
their position without yelling,
cursing, or name-calling.

•

183. They need to see that the
supermodel doesn't look
as good in person as she does
in a fashion magazine.

•

184. They need to realize
they're not sad or depressed.
They're tired. They need a nap.

185. They need to be able to live without TV. It could result in making the college dean's list.

•

186. They need to see what happens to people who throw up, starve themselves, or use drugs to lose weight. Bad things.

•

187. They need to see that change is inevitable. The popular girls will lose their looks, the jocks will get fat, the class clowns will become doctors, and the nerds will run the world.

188. They need to learn
memory techniques.

189. They need to collect their
thoughts before speaking,
especially in class or in stressful
situations. It's a way to keep
from babbling nonsense.

190. They need to practice the fine
art of not talking ill of anyone.

191. They need to learn to drive.
In rush hour. In the rain. On tight
roads. And if you can't ride with
them without stroking out or having a
panic attack, they need more lessons.

192. They need to pay for any
accidents or damages. They need to
know this is a condition of driving.

193. They need to watch you
buy a car to learn how it's done.

194. They need to see a Kelley Blue Book and learn to use it before they buy any car, new or used.

•

195. They need to buy liability insurance for their car. They'll discover the unique joy of being barbequed by an insurance company.

•

196. They need to learn how to get their car an inspection sticker and new tags. And then to do this every year. On time.

197. They need to take care of their car: get the oil changed every 5,000 miles, keep tires properly inflated, and throw everything out of the trunk once a month.

•

198. They need to wear their seat belts. This needs to become a habit.

•

199. They need to use the right grade of gasoline. Not to use premium in a car that takes regular. Or vice versa.

200. They need a game plan
for a late-night flat tire.

•

201. They need to know how
to pack and use jumper cables.

•

202. They need to make sure
the car is in "PARK" before they
pull out the keys. Or have a
tow truck number handy.

•

203. They need to get the name
of a good traffic lawyer.

204. They need to learn they're the ones responsible for the fees of their new friend, the lawyer. And any fines.

•

205. They need to read everything before they sign. And have a lawyer read it as well.

•

206. They need to file an income tax return if they made any money this year. On time.

•

207. They need to plan ahead. Start with lunch.

208. They need to develop
a firm handshake.

•

209. They need to learn the odds
of becoming a movie star,
celebrity, or rich athlete are greater
than being hit by a satellite.

•

210. They need to accept life isn't fair.
That mileage may vary.

•

211. They need to speed read
with comprehension. It's a trick
that will get them to law school.

212. They need to learn about delayed gratification. It's what can keep them studying while everybody else is partying.

•

213. They need to set goals. Start small—finish tonight's homework.

•

214. They need to learn how to checkmate in four moves.

•

215. They need to learn what to do with a cloth napkin. And it isn't blowing their nose in it.

216. They need to learn at
fine restaurants, they can order
a meal that isn't on the menu.
And have it prepared a certain way.

•

217. They need to take off the
corn shuck wrapper before they
eat a tamale. This is a food
that has stumped presidents.

•

218. They need to learn to not be
intimated by any waiter. Or be rude.

219. They need to just eat a raw oyster. And not look at it too long or comment on what it looks like.

•

220. They need to learn how to tip: 15 percent to waiters and cabbies, a couple of dollars a day to hotel maids, and a dollar or two to baggage handlers.

•

221. They need to talk softly. Especially in public places.

222. They need to learn how to crack
and eat shellfish. Before they're left
alone with a lobster and a nutcracker.

•

223. They need to let the other
person win the argument.
It's all about whether they would
rather be happy or right.

•

224. They need to learn to talk
to teachers in a different tone
of voice than the one they
use with their friends.

225. They need an opinion on things besides their curfew and appearance. And discuss them.

•

226. They need to pay attention. This trait will enable them to pay rent one day.

•

227. They need to form a well-read, well-thought-out opinion on evolution.

•

228. They need to be able to change even the best-laid plans when the situation changes.

229. They need to fix the relationship with the teacher they're fighting with. It's time to make up, kiss up, and button up.

•

230. They need to learn the rules. Especially if they intend to break them.

•

231. They need to learn to pay bills before their due date.

232. They need to be neat.
Neat in appearance, neat in
organization, neat in thinking,
neat in their actions. Neatness
will always beat the alternative.

·

233. They need to learn to deal
with corporate voice mails and
operators. They'll be dealing
with them the rest of their lives.

·

234. They need to be able to
order a nourishing meal in a
fast-food restaurant. It may be
where they eat for the next ten years.

235. They need to stay in contact
with friends. Even ones
they haven't seen in years.

•

236. They need to sharpen their
negotiation skills. With someone
other than their parents.

•

237. They need to resist high
pressure. Whether it's kids their
own age, salespeople, or adults.

•

238. They need to sell
something on eBay that doesn't
belong to their sister.

239. They need to hide a spare key.
And remember where they put it.

•

240. They need to be able to listen to
other people, especially adults,
without commenting until asked.

•

241. They need to remember silence
is golden. Especially if they don't
know what they're talking about.

•

242. They need to say
"hors d'oeuvres" correctly.
And know what they are.

243. They need to vacuum
their room. Regularly.

•

244. They need to use mouthwash.
People of the opposite sex
will sit closer to them.

•

245. They need to not compare
themselves or their possessions
or their accomplishments to
other people. This is a key
to happiness. And humility.

246. They need to learn how
to use saran wrap. It won't
be a pretty lesson.

•

247. They need to have good posture.
Especially around adults.
Nothing says "junior high" like
some kid slouching around.

•

248. They need to be able to
introduce themselves to strangers
in all situations: weddings, parties,
business affairs, college tours. This
ability is a mark of future success.

249. They need to check their teeth after a meal. There's usually something brown dangling from the bicuspids.

•

250. They need to get organized and plan ahead, instead of worrying.

•

251. They need to practice basic etiquette or people will think they just fell off the turnip truck.

252. They need to put a crease in
their shirts or jeans or pants
with an iron. On an ironing board.
Not while they're wearing them.

•

253. They need to wash their face.
It will help their zits go away.

•

254. They need to take CPR lessons.
Just have them use Listerine
before they practice on you.

255. They need to join the
debate team and develop the
ability to speak to a group without
breaking into hives and stutters.

•

256. They need to recognize
phish or spam when they see it.

•

257. They need to learn the dangers
of visiting gambling or sex Web sites.

•

258. They need to learn the
name of a good auto mechanic.

259. They need to learn a person's integrity is a mirror of their relationship with God.

•

260. They need to make a "to do" list. Every day.

•

261. They need to back off when a fight is likely to break out. This is called "maturity."

•

262. They need to fend off grubworms in a garden.

263. They need to live off cash.
Not a debit card or credit card.

•

264. They need to understand the
term "finite resources," especially
when it comes to oil in the ground,
trees in the forests, and money in
their parents' checking account.

•

265. They need to shake talcum
powder on their feet to kill
the smell. This could bring
the family back together.

266. They need to follow instructions. This is usually the deal killer to succeeding in the adult world.

•

267. They need to go bird watching with people who know what they're doing. Soon they'll be able to spot an olive-sided flycatcher.

•

268. They need to develop resilience.

•

269. They need to call a cab when the only other way home is with a drunk driver.

270. They need to learn
how to drive in the snow.

•

271. They need to gift-wrap a present
without it looking like it was a project
accomplished by a mental patient.

•

272. They need to get things done.
Homework assignments. Tasks.
Chores. College enrollment forms.

•

273. They need to buy only
those clothes that fit. No matter
the price, the label, or the store.

274. They need to do things well without expecting praise.

•

275. They need to accept blame. Not pass it on.

•

276. They need to win arguments through persuasion.

•

277. They need to know how to mail a letter. You think they know. They don't know.

278. They need to return their overdue library books. Even the ones three years past due.

•

279. They need to read *The Seven Habits of Highly Effective People*. Developing one good habit could be life changing.

•

280. They need to view themselves as a smart, ambitious leader who gets things done. Because how they see themselves is precisely how the world will view them.

281. They need to program
their cell phone. Then yours.

•

282. They need to pick strawberries
or apples or oranges or watermelons
at a nearby farm. And learn how the
earth supplies everything we need.

•

283. They need to figure out who they
want to be. And begin acting as if.

•

284. They need to learn what interests
them. By trying new things.

285. They need to learn the price of independence is rent, auto insurance, utility bills, groceries, cable, Internet access, car maintenance, commuting costs, and more. After computing all that, a curfew sounds like a fair trade.

•

286. They need to not be afraid of the competition.

287. They need to grasp the sacrifices their parents have made to get them this far.

•

288. They need to finish what they started.

•

289. They need to smile.

They Need
to Exercise

290. They need to run a 10,000-meter race. Even if they have to walk part of the way.

•

291. They need to see the men's and women's U.S. Olympic soccer teams in action.

•

292. They need to play on a team. (They run, they yell, they kick, they push other kids around, they get knocked down, then they get snacks afterward. Sweet deal.)

293. They need to keep a soccer ball in the air for a minute using only their head, legs, knees, chest, and feet.

•

294. They need to hit a nonreturnable serve.

•

295. They need to learn to swim. Before they can walk.

•

296. They need to jump off a high diving board without landing on their back. This will take several weeks of practice and a few sore backs.

297. They need to go to gymnastics class. So you don't have to demonstrate a cartwheel.

•

298. They need to excel at one sport. Archery, badminton, football, Ping-Pong—there's a sport waiting for them.

•

299. They need to deal with defeat and be humble in victory.

•

300. They need to hit a golf ball over a lake. This will require clubs, lessons, and many, many golf balls.

301. They need to take downhill ski lessons from someone besides you. And conquer the double black, double diamond course while they're still young.

•

302. They need to keep track of their own athletic and dance stuff. Not depend on Mom or Dad.

•

303. They need to find a cardio workout they'll stick with. Running, dancing, biking, swimming, even walking.

304. They need to be
able to pop a wheelie.

•

305. They need to train with
weights. And with somebody
who knows what they're doing.

•

306. They need to snowboard
down a half pipe. These are
not found in most states.

•

307. They need to push
themselves physically. And learn
to trust their body's strength.

308. They need to bike their age
in miles beginning at six years old.

•

309. They need to race
somebody. Using anything
but a car or motorcycle.

•

310. They need to climb. A jungle
gym. A tree. One day, a career ladder.

•

311. They need to dog paddle
at least five minutes in deep water.
(Tell them some people spend
their lives in deep water.)

312. They need to climb
a twenty-foot rope.

•

313. They need to be able to run
or do vigorous aerobics for an hour.
(A two-year-old can do this. Teenagers
might have to work up to it.)

•

314. They need to jump on
a trampoline. To feel the
thrill of being airborne.

•

315. They need to hit a fastball.
And realize fast balls will be
coming at them all their life.

316. They need to hold their breath underwater for sixty seconds. Not their brother's breath. Their breath.

•

317. They need to dribble a basketball with either hand. Failing that, they need to pass.

•

318. They need to be able to throw a baseball where they're aiming it. Without whacking anybody or breaking anything.

319. They need to shake
off bumps and bruises.

•

320. They need to eat less
junk food and exercise more.

•

321. They need to hit
a kill shot in volleyball.
And return one.

•

322. They need to swim
a quarter of a mile.
Without having to be rescued.

323. They need to water ski.
Everyone at some time in
their life finds themselves being
pulled around a lake by a boat.

•

324. They need to run a mile in
under six minutes. At least once.

•

325. They need to
hike up a mountain.

•

326. They need to climb a wall.

327. They need to ride
a horse. Without injuring
themselves or the horse.

•

328. They need to learn how to
disable an attacker. Karate
will give them confidence and
maybe save their tush one day.

•

329. They need to coach
younger kids. This is
great preparation for life.

They Need Culture

330. They need to develop
a personal vision.

•

331. They need to shape, fire,
and glaze a plate or a vase in
grade school that you'll proudly
display in your living room.

•

332. They need to visit museums
and galleries regularly. To see what
others believe is rare and beautiful.
Soon, they'll have their own opinion.

333. They need to take an
intensive, advanced arts class,
like 3D graphic design or animation.

•

334. They need to mix
colors on a palette.

•

335. They need to take a
photography class. Learn to
work with light, shadows,
film speed, and contact prints.

•

336. They need to sculpt a figure.
Out of clay or wood or stone.

337. They need to make a 3D model of a building.

•

338. They need to shoot and complete a Claymation film.

•

339. They need to write and produce a graphic novel.

•

340. They need to take piano lessons and bring the audience to their feet at the end of a recital.

341. They need to tour science museums. And let themselves be in wonder.

•

342. They need to feed the giraffes.

•

343. They need to learn why Michelangelo did all that religious stuff.

•

344. They need to take a drawing class.

•

345. They need to see live productions of an opera, a musical, a ballet, and a New York touring company. And bring binoculars.

346. They need to spend the summer in a museum camp. It's cheap, it's air-conditioned, and it can unlock the artist within.

•

347. They need to meet a writer or two. And see that second-period English just might have a purpose.

•

348. They need to recognize the difference between Impressionist and Modern paintings. Many adults have no idea.

349. They need to see DaVinci's art and learn he is not famous for his code.

•

350. They need to see MOMA in New York.

•

351. They need to visit the Louvre. Even if it's just on the Internet.

•

352. They need to be able to sing a few John Lennon songs.

•

353. They need to hear a symphony the way it's supposed to be heard. In a park. Over a picnic dinner. While the sun sets.

354. They need to try out for
the school play or musical.
Be a tree if that's all they can do.

•

355. They need to swim with a porpoise.

•

356. They need to dance with
a sidewalk-performing artist.

•

357. They need to cut down their
own Christmas tree at a tree farm.

•

358. They need to watch sharks eat.
And remember there are human
beings with similar characteristics.

They Need
to Be Good
in Science

359. They need to develop an understanding of the natural world: the seasons, plants, motion, energy, chemicals, and matter.

•

360. They need to chase each other through an arboretum. Over the years, they'll start noticing what they are running past.

•

361. They need to be able to answer the question, "Who was Galileo?"

•

362. They need to understand global warming better than most congressmen.

363. They need to learn
why the temperature is warmer
in the summer than the winter.

•

364. They need to recognize the
difference between a scientific
fact and a scientific opinion.

•

365. They need to hunt pecans. And
their success will increase when they
learn what a pecan tree looks like.

•

366. They need to identify the
Big Dipper, Orion, and Leo
without a sky map.

367. They need to enter the
high school science fair
with a project their parents
can't comprehend.

•

368. They need to learn about the
Human Genome Project. And figure
out if they are a human genome.

•

369. They need to appreciate how
Copernicus stood up to the church.

•

370. They need to enter the Invention
Convention at school. And create
something never seen before.

371. They need to stay up late
and witness a meteor shower.
This is how astronomers are born.

•

372. They need to see stars through a
planetarium telescope and realize
they've just traveled back in time.

•

373. They need to be able
to intelligently discuss
the big bang theory.

374. They need to calculate
how far away lightning is
by timing the seconds between
the flash and the thunder.

•

375. They need to take cover
when lightning storms approach
soccer fields, golf courses,
and baseball diamonds.

•

376.   They need to understand
the principles of electricity.
And not by sticking a nail file
into an electrical outlet.

377. They need to learn
how to use a compass.

•

378. They need to identify different
cloud formations. And know
which ones mean to take cover.

•

379. They need to spot poison ivy.
And then take another route.

•

380. They need to tell the difference
between tulips and roses.

381. They need to understand
all living things need water.

•

382. They need to learn which
berries are edible. And why
no one eats berries found
on the bottom of bushes.

•

383. They need to dissect a frog.
Without getting sick.
Think of it as a rite of passage.

384. They need to suck honeysuckle.

•

385. They need to understand where oil comes from . . . and how, until further notice, our world runs on it.

•

386. They need to trek deep into the earth to see stalactites and stalagmites. And wonder if this is what the earth looked like in the beginning.

387. They need to be able to tell the difference between a black widow spider, a stinging scorpion, and a cricket. The one that sprays dead bug juice everywhere is the safest.

•

388. They need to hear a coyote howl.

•

389. They need to see a bat cave. From a distance.

They Need to Learn to Cook for Themselves

390. They need to get in the
habit of eating three meals a day.
Most kids skip breakfast, have
a Coke for lunch, come home
famished, and eat all night. Not the
most recommended dietary plan.

•

391. They need to bake bread.
To learn that the best can't
be found in grocery stores.

•

392. They need to read
the ingredients.

393. They need to compare prices of eating out versus home-cooked meals. This alone could reduce their college loans by about a third.

•

394. They need to go shopping at the grocery store. Navigate their way around the vegetable aisles. Get stuck behind a person armed with fifteen coupons. And come home with change.

•

395. They need to fry some Spam. While suspicious looking, it can keep them alive in college.

396. They need to develop
a taste for fruit.

•

397. They need to see that store
brands are cheaper. And the
most expensive brands are
usually placed at eye level.

•

398. They need to learn how to
boil water. And then all the
amazing things you can do with it.

•

399. They need to preheat
an oven. And not get in a hurry
and just stick food in it.

400. They need to learn you can't substitute one "cup" for one "liter."

•

401. They need to roast a turkey. This includes yanking the neck parts out of the cavity and shoving stuffing back in. This has turned some teenagers into vegetarians.

•

402. They need to check the date on milk and eggs for freshness before buying or drinking it.

•

403. They need to compare the cost per ounce of food. Seventh grade math.

404. They need to be able to open
cans without slicing their hands.

•

405. They need to know
PAM isn't a room spray.

•

406. They need to intelligently discuss
fats, carbohydrates, and protein.

•

407. They need to learn a
healthy breakfast makes them
smarter. And curiously thinner.

408. They need to peel a potato. Slice it. Boil it. Mash it. And serve it to their mom.

•

409. They need to see that *Joy of Cooking* isn't a biography of some Chinese chef.

•

410. They need to make something using a recipe found in their grandmother's cookbook.

•

411. They need to learn they can't bake something at twice the heat for half the time and expect it to be edible. Chances are good even the dog won't be interested.

412. They need to ice a cake.
And not eat all the icing
before it gets on the cake.

•

413. They need to discover oatmeal
is truly a miracle food. And cheap.
And can be made not disgusting.

•

414. They need to shop at a farmers'
market. And sample the goods.

•

415. They need to develop skills
with kitchen tools: whisks, sifters,
pots, pans, spoons, and spatulas.

416. They need to baste a turkey or chicken without basting themselves or the oven.

•

417. They need to plan, shop, purchase, prepare, and serve dinner for the family at least once a month. Without Mom.

•

418. They need to prepare one pasta dish that doesn't involve spaghetti and red sauce.

•

419. They need to milk a cow. One time. And try not squirting themselves.

•

420. They need to learn how to grill a cheese sandwich.

421. They need to follow the recipe. In the kitchen. In life.

•

422. They need to make a salad. Lettuce? Good. Tomatoes? Okay. Fruit? Possibly. Peanut butter? No. Never.

•

423. They need to be able to use the microwave without blowing up the kitchen.

•

424. They need to learn how to fry, scramble, soft boil, and hard boil eggs.

•

425. They need to taste how bread and olive oil can make a complete meal.

426. They need to prove they know what to do with a roast. Besides give it to Mom to cook.

•

427. They need to see how leftovers are sealed and stored in the refrigerator. Not left in a pot on the stove.

•

428. They need to spit out anything that tastes remotely suspicious. Not just swallow it out of embarrassment only to hurl later.

•

429. They need to learn to turn off the oven and stove-top burners. Or enjoy a visit from the fire department.

430. They need to set a table. Understand the purpose of the salad fork. And learn to use the settings from the outside in.

•

431. They need to learn that eating with chopsticks is about the most fun you can have with food.

•

432. They need to give thanks to God for every meal. And remember that not everyone is getting to eat today.

They Need to Learn about Money

433. They need to invest part of their allowance and summer earnings. Even if it's only a few dollars a week.

•

434. They need to see the inside of a bank. Get an idea of what the system is about.

•

435. They need to learn to budget.

•

436. They need to start tracking where they spend their money. It's the easiest way to gain control over it.

437. They need to watch
the electronic ticker tape
in a brokerage office.

•

438. They need to learn how to write
a check and balance a checkbook.

•

439. They need to calculate
the charge for bounced checks.

•

440. They need to start using their
own money to change the world.

441. They need to see the magic
of compound interest.

•

442. They need to learn the
three keys to wealth: income,
discipline, and time.

•

443. They need to develop the fine art
of living without. A useful skill when
tempted to pay with credit cards.

•

444. They need to learn that
making the minimum monthly
payment on a credit card means
the credit card is never paid off.

445. They need to see what
makes credit cards radioactive: late
payment fees, inactivity fees, over the
limit fees, and balance transfer fees.

•

446. They need to learn how to
read and interpret a credit report.

•

447. They need to build a good
credit score. It can impact
the rest of their lives.

•

448. They need to use the words
Dow Jones, *NYSE* and
NASDAQ in a sentence.

449. They need to start buying stocks or mutual funds. A share at a time.

•

450. They need to meet with a successful investor.

•

451. They need to see your mortgage statement. To understand a thirty-year mortgage means paying two times the original loan.

•

452. They need to resist temptation when they walk into a mall.

453. They need to spend their time doing something besides shopping.

•

454. They need to save for something specific.

•

455. They need to tell the difference between a need and a want. A need is underwear. A want is $150 French silk underwear.

•

456. They need to start reading the financial section of a newspaper.

•

457. They need to comparison shop.

458. They need to get real: nineteen-year-olds don't live in their own condo and drive a BMW.

•

459. They need to buy a certificate of deposit. Even a small one.

•

460. They need to buy a savings bond.

•

461. They need to be able to calculate interest on any loan or CD. Second semester, seventh grade math.

•

462. They need to learn how matching 401(k)s are as close to free money as they may ever get.

463. They need to memorize the following sentence: "I will never invest in a restaurant, or a club, or a time-share condo."

•

464. They need to learn that when most people are buying stocks, it's probably time to sell.

•

465. They need to grasp the importance of owning property.

•

466. They need to cash their paychecks at a bank. Not at a check-cashing store that legally holds them up.

•

467. They need to set financial goals. Besides just spending all their parents' money.

468. They need to base financial decisions on the here and now. Not what could be.

•

469. They need to watch how much money the person they are dating is spending. It's a clear sign of their values.

•

470. They need to see you give anonymously.

•

471. They need to learn to give 10 percent back to God. A fair trade.

They Need to Be a Computer Geek

472. They need to become a whiz
with the computer. In the living room.

•

473. They need to develop great
keyboarding skills. To type
using ten fingers without looking.

•

474. They need to wire their
computer to a printer and
an Internet connection.

•

475. They need to learn how to do
research on the Internet. They're not
as good as they like to think they are.

476. They need to learn
what a Pentium chip is.

•

477. They need to load software
onto their computer. Without
maiming the hard drive.

•

478. They need to set up a log-in
name and different passwords on
their computer and various sites.

•

479. They need to develop a system
to remember all their passwords.

480. They need to create multi-media presentations using video, PowerPoint, text, audio, and slides.

•

481. They need to purchase and download songs off the Internet, then load them onto an iPod or other MP3 player.

•

482. They need to modify their own software.

•

483. They need to work with XTML, Perl, JavaScript, and databases.

484. They need to calculate their family tree based on DNA sequences.

•

485. They need to know how to use Photoshop, even if they're planning a career in the wrestling business.

•

486. They need to set up a blog and keep it current.

•

487. They need to remove anything stupid they may have posted on MySpace. College and job recruiters are looking there too.

488. They need to be suspicious of any download that comes from someone they don't know.

•

489. They need to install a good virus blocker before they have to rebuild their hard drive.

•

490. They need to create a personal home page.

•

491. They need to develop great skills with Excel, PowerPoint, and Word. These are the tools of business.

492. They need to create
a computer animation.

•

493. They need to learn how
to post photographs on-line.
And what kind to post.

•

494. They need to play 3D computer
games that strengthen problem
solving and spatial navigation skills.

•

495. They need to design and create
computer games. Not just play them.

496. They need to learn the locations of WiFi hot spots and be able to safely use a computer there.

•

497. They need to learn how to scan photographs or documents and then e-mail them.

•

498. They need to learn no Nigerian wants to give them 40 percent of $25,000,000 for helping him get money out of the country.

499. They need to store,
display, and analyze data.

•

500. They need to use a reverse DNS
lookup to find the domain name of
spammers. Then spam the spammer.

•

501. They need to learn that
fraudulent charges and ID theft
happen to people who visit
Internet gambling and porn sites.

502. They need to trash any e-mail asking for their Social Security number, their mother's maiden name, or their checking account number. Because the people who need that information already have it.

•

503. They need to learn any email that says "Your account will be closed in forty-eight hours" or "Dear Valued Customer" is probably from Russia.

They Need to Understand What Is Going on in Today's World

504. They need to study the history of Rome. To learn how a country that once ruled the world lost everything.

•

505. They need to be able to find the following countries on a world map: England, France, Germany, Spain, Israel, Russia, China, Vietnam, Brazil, Argentina, Egypt, Iran, Iraq, United Arab Emirates, South Africa, Nigeria, and the Sudan. Most kids can't even find Louisiana. The boot.

506. They need to study how
Jerusalem has been under
Muslim rule for some 1,400 years.

•

507. They need to learn France was
once more famous for its conquerors
and rulers than its fashions.

•

508. They need to identify the seven
continents. And know which conti-
nent they're currently standing on.

•

509. They need to study the Cold War.
And know who won.

510. They need to be able to identify where the Mississippi begins and ends

•

511. They need to have an idea what the Amazon is, and that it's not found in the United States. Or on the internet.

•

512. They need to visit Israel. In person. In books. They need to understand why the world is still fighting over this part of the world.

513. They need to learn the history of the Jewish and Palestinian people. Start with Abraham.

•

514. They need to visit a mosque and learn about Islam.

•

515. They need to find the Palestine territories on a map.

•

516. They need to read the Koran.

517. They need to make friends with Hispanic kids, Asian kids, European kids, Hindu kids, Muslim kids, and American-Indian kids.

•

518. They need to understand the illegal immigration issues facing the United States today. And that they'll be dealing with them tomorrow.

•

519. They need to walk along the Texas-Mexico border and ponder the forces that lead people to risk everything to come here.

520. They need to study Charles Darwin. And learn why we're still talking about him 150 years later.

•

521. They need to study how much Old Testament history occurred in Iraq ... once one of the most advanced civilizations in the world.

•

522. They need to learn why English is our native language, not Spanish or French. Or German.

523. They need to study the history of World War II and learn who the good guys were.

•

524. They need to see Auschwitz, Dachau, Treblinka, and Warsaw in person or in books.

•

525. They need to understand the term "concentration camp" does not refer to a camp for kids with ADD.

526. They need to
comprehend the holocaust.

•

527. They need to learn
terrorism led to World War I.

•

528. They need to talk to a veteran
who was there, in Vietnam.

•

529. They need to serve
dinner in a shelter.

•

530. They need to collect
money and food for Africa.

531. They need to stand on an oil rig.
Understand what goes into getting
a barrel of oil out of the ground.
And marvel how the earth
supplies everything we need.

•

532. They need to name five
countries that supply the world's oil.
Besides the United States.

•

533. They need to be able to
articulate the difference between the
U.S. government and that of China,
Russia, North Korea, and Cuba.

534. They need to identify
five Islamic countries.

•

535. They need to read how
Jerusalem is the holiest city to
Christians, Jews, and Muslims.
And wonder at God's plan.

•

536. They need to stand at the site of
the World Trade Center. And listen.

•

537. They need to see footage about
the Berlin Wall. And learn how it
couldn't keep freedom contained.

538. They need to watch old film
clips about the Atomic Bomb.
They'll then understand why
it must never happen again.

•

539. They need to read all sides—
David Brooks, Maureen Dowd, Helen
Thomas, Frank Rich, Bob Herbert,
George Will, and Ann Coulter.

•

540. They need to watch *Saving
Private Ryan* and *Band of Brothers*.
To understand that war truly is in
every sense of the word, hell.

They Need
to Know God

541. They need to ask God to direct their lives every day.

•

542. They need to make amends.

•

543. They need to study Proverbs. And see some lessons are thousands of years old.

•

544. They need to look for wonder in every situation.

545. They need to comprehend
the majesty of the universe.
Most kids can't comprehend
the size of their zip code.

•

546. They need to read the Bible so,
unlike a lot of people who argue
about religion, they'll know
what they're talking about.

•

547. They need to learn that anyone
who says all religions lead to the same
God has never studied any religion.

548. They need to do more than just believe in miracles. They need to rely on the One who performs them.

•

549. They need to celebrate others' successes.

•

550. They need to let go of resentment. It makes life way too heavy.

•

551. They need to pray for the people they despise.

552. They need to be restless
with the status quo. And believe
things can be better.

•

553. They need to bring
a date to worship service.

•

554. They need to help build a
home with Habitat for Humanity.
Even if all they do is fetch water.

•

555. They need to see you being
faithful. To your marriage, to
your faith, to your community.

556. They need to not take
life quite so seriously.

•

557. They need to do good deeds
without anyone finding out.

•

558. They need to know that
labels say more about the
wearer than they realize.

•

559. They need to practice self-denial.
Perhaps the most difficult spiritual
assignment in the teenage years.

560. They need to realize
other people are hurting.

•

561. They need to see the world
through compassionate eyes.

•

562. They need to start tithing.
With their own money. Even if
they only make $10 a week.

•

563. They need to regularly do
something for somebody for
which they cannot be repaid.

564. They need to show love to someone who is unworthy of being shown love. This will bring them in touch with Christ.

•

565. They need to be wowed by a sunset. And a sunrise if you can get them up that early.

•

566. They need to actually listen to sermons.

567. They need to serve as an acolyte. There's nothing like putting on a white robe, picking up a cross, and marching down the aisle with an entire congregation watching to make an eight-year-old take worship service more seriously.

•

568. They need to fast during Lent.

•

569. They need to live their life so their faith is obvious.

570. They need to become friends
with their own brothers and sisters.

•

571. They need to talk and joke
with the kids who aren't cool.

•

572. They need to remember they
are a child of God. Especially when
they are hanging around people who
would like them to forget that fact.

•

573. They need to ask the Holy Spirit
for the words to say when
talking to unbelievers.

574. They need to say grace before meals and actually feel gratitude for God's provision.

•

575. They need to pray daily to exhibit the fruits of the Holy Spirit: love, joy, peace, patience, kindness, goodness, faithfulness, gentleness, and self-control.

•

576. They need to know the "truths" stated in *The DaVinci Code*, and similar books, are pure hokum.

577. They need to
memorize Scripture.

•

578. They need to tell a friend
they'll pray for them.

•

579. They need to ask their
friends to pray for them.
And be honest about why.

•

580. They need to develop the habit
of sharing God's gifts. And experiencing the miracles that go with that.

581. They need to stop
blaming other people.

•

582. They need to forgive.

•

583. They need to understand
that while God seems to be
late, He is always on time.

•

584. They need to share
their story of their faith.

585. They need to have an answer for people who say, "Christ was a great prophet who did wonderful things."

•

586. They need to trust God's will. He will never let them down.

•

587. They need to see the suffering of other people. And not look away from it.

•

588. They need to visit synagogues and temples of other faiths. See the similarities. See the differences.

589. They need to do things that build up their faith. And realize there will always be people trying to tear it down.

•

590. They need to resolve to stay in their faith. And not lose it over a bad experience, an atheistic college professor, or a friend who's angry at God.

•

591. They need to meditate nightly on God's word and wonder.

592. They need to learn all
religions think they're right.

•

593. They need to keep a journal.
Especially during hard times.
And know God is there.

•

594. They need to pay attention
to their conscience. And know
if something feels wrong,
it probably is wrong.

595. They need to not be afraid to
question any part of the Bible.
And not be too lazy to seek the answers.

•

596. They need to join a group
like Campus Crusade for Christ.
Put their faith in front of people.

•

597. They need to smile more.
It will make their life more
pleasant. And others'.

598. They need to teach a youth group or Vacation Bible School or work with grade-school kids as a camp counselor. A high moment will be when they come home and complain about kids.

•

599. They need to stand up for the unpopular student.

•

600. They need to let gossip die with them.

601. They need to know the history of their religion.

•

602. They need to grasp that once they ask the Holy Spirit to take up residence in their lives, He will. Even if they can't feel Him, He's there.

•

603. They need to remove the fear of failure from their consciousness. But to step out in faith.

604. They need to thank God.
Especially when it's difficult
to be thankful.

•

605. They need to dream big.
The Holy Spirit specializes
in the impossible.

•

606. They need to remember
that another person may not
hear the word of Christ all day.
Except through them.

They Need
to Travel

607. They need to ride a horse down a Rocky Mountain trail.

•

608. They need to be sprayed by Old Faithful at Yellow Stone.

•

609. They need to stand in a freezing glacier lake near a boiling, steaming, too-hot-to-touch lava pot. And wonder.

•

610. They need to see a bald eagle up close. And an owl. They're beautiful and fascinating birds. And may disappear in their lifetime.

611. They need to see New York City from the top of the Empire State Building. And wonder how in the world such a thing could be built in 1931.

•

612. They need to see salmon running in a mountain stream. And smell them cooking over a campfire.

•

613. They need to learn how to stand in a strange city on a street corner with a map, and figure out where to find the embassy, their hotel, or the police station.

614. They need to learn where
to park their car at the airport
or train station. And remember
where they parked it.

•

615. They need to learn about
airport shuttles. How to get off
at the right terminal, not just
circle helplessly around the airport
while their flight comes and goes.

•

616. They need to learn to
make connecting flights at the
airport they're landing in . . .
not at the airport across town.

617. They need to stand in front
of an English church founded
in 600 AD to comprehend
how new the United States is.
(Of course, Roman ruins make
England look like a new suburb.)

•

618. They need to pack
mosquito repellent.

•

619. They need to decipher take-
off and arrival information posted
in airport terminals. And trust
it could be right half the time.

620. They need to learn what to do if a flight is cancelled. And that yelling is not going to solve anything.

•

621. They need to tour Washington D.C. Visit the White House, Congress, and the State Department. Get an understanding of the institutions behind our country.

•

622. They need to see the Lincoln bedroom.

623. They need to visit Arlington Cemetery. The Vietnam Wall. The National WWII Memorial. Get an idea of the price of freedom.

•

624. They need to stand on or read about the Great Wall of China. It says a lot about the country itself.

•

625. They need to look down at the sunken USS *Arizona* at the bottom of Pearl Harbor. And realize sailors are still down there.

626. They need to explore
the Smithsonian Museum.
It's the most fantastic history
lesson they'll ever have.

•

627. They need to tour an Indian
reservation. And discuss if reserva-
tions are doing anybody any favors.

•

628. They need to see London,
France, and Rome with you, so
when they go back, they won't be
wandering lost in a foreign land.

629. They need to walk to
a glacier. And learn it's always
further away than it looks.

•

630. They need to ice fish
on one of the Great Lakes.

•

631. They need to stand on a
mountaintop. Experience the thrill
of airplanes flying below them.

•

632. They need to ride Amtrak
from New York City to anywhere.
And be able to get back.

633. They need to watch the bears in Yellowstone Park. From their car. And know that teenagers who leave their cars to feed bears often wind up as bear food.

•

634. They need to take a picture of a moose. Not with a long lens.

•

635. They need to go to a state fair. Eat the corny dogs, ride the rides, and watch the people.

636. They need to volunteer
for an environmental conservation
project anywhere in the world.
Even down the street.

•

637. They need to pack an
electricity converter when
traveling outside the United States.

•

638. They need to stand
under a waterfall.

639. They need to buy a globe and refer to it, when they hear of a war in the Sudan or a crisis in Bolivia. Learn where these places are.

•

640. They need to have their breath taken away at the sight of the Grand Canyon.

•

641. They need to stand on the Continental Divide and watch rivers run in separate directions.

642. They need to walk around
Ellis Island. And realize the hope
it gave to millions of people.

•

643. They need to walk Paul Revere's
ride in Boston. And grasp how
a few determined colonists
defeated a world superpower.

•

644. They need to camp out in the
mountains. And not sleep in the car.

645. They need to know to drink bottled water if they're in a foreign country. And to think of water in any U.S. lake or river or stream as a foreign country.

•

646. They need to explore a rain forest with old-growth trees. And realize this is what the world looked like thousands of years ago.

•

647. They need to walk the Revolutionary War battlefields at Lexington and Concord. The world was changed forever there.

648. They need to tour the Civil War battlefields where 600,000 soldiers died. And discuss how Americans could do such a thing to each other.

•

649. They need to travel Eastern Europe and see the suffocating impact of communism and dictatorship.

•

650. They need to discover America off the Interstate.

651. They need to know how to use public transit systems: decipher bus routes, train routes, subway routes, connections, and schedules. This will get them through any city in the world.

•

652. They need to get themselves vaccinated against diseases in foreign countries. And learn how not to bring them home.

•

653. They need to learn what to take on a trip. That it's not everything.

654. They need to know that showing up on time at the airport is, well, late. They need to show up early.

•

655. They need to learn to use computerized check-in.

•

656. They need to figure currency conversions before arriving in a foreign country. This will keep them from running out of money the first two days.

657. They need to come home
with their passport.

•

658. They need to purchase a
phone card to call home if they're
overseas. Tell them you'll hang
up on any collect calls.

•

659. They need to be able to snag
a great deal on airfares
using one of the travel sites.

660. They need to scan their passport, driver's license, important documents, and travel agent numbers, and e-mail all of it to themselves. Before they lose their wallet in a London taxicab.

•

661. They need to be able to hail a taxi in any city. And figure out if the taxi is legit or not, and if the driver is ripping them off.

662. They need to prepare for taxi drivers unable to speak the English language or read directions. They also need to realize this will happen in New York City.

•

663. They need to walk in the Atlantic surf. The Pacific surf. And the Gulf of Mexico surf.

664. They need to be bilingual if they want to explore all of Canada. And that doesn't mean English and Spanish.

•

665. They need to fly fish in a mountain stream. And not hurt themselves or others with the fishing rod.

•

666. They need to catch and release a trout. Even though they spent all day in the water waiting for it to bite.

667. They need to watch a windmill generate electricity. And wonder how many windmills it would take to propel a neighborhood.

•

668. They need to ride a street car in San Francisco. And hear how, for some reason, most cities that had them dismantled them.

•

669. They need to be able to keep themselves amused on an airplane. Or learn to sleep on one.

They Need
to Prepare
for College

670. They need to attend a career camp. There are great ones all over the country in engineering, aerospace, computer science, arts, science, and more.

•

671. They need to leave high school with a copy of their transcript. They will be asked for one the next five years.

•

672. They need to learn to research and write a ten-page paper. In five days.

673. They need to use a
comma correctly. Or it will
haunt them all their lives.

•

674. They need to take
the time to write an outline.

•

675. They need to be able to find
the plot point. In a book. In life.

•

676. They need to study the history of
English literature. They don't have to
be excited about it. Just know it.

677. They need to be able to navigate any library in the world using the electronic databases or card catalogues.

•

678. They need to be able to stand up for themselves. University professors and admissions counselors don't really care what parents think.

•

679. They need to read history's most influential thinkers, like Aristotle, Plato, and Marx. Their head will be filled with wild ideas. Perfectly normal.

680. They need to be a foreign exchange student. This will change the way they see the world.

•

681. They need to run for student office. Give speeches. Glad-hand the voters.

•

682. They need to be conversant in Spanish. About 30 percent of the country already is.

683. They need music lessons. Musicians in piano, guitar, band, or orchestra make great students. No one really knows why.

•

684. They need to have an idea of what they want to be when they grow up. It really helps in choosing classes, picking majors, and so on.

•

685. They need to take at least four AP and college prep courses while everyone else is taking the easy way out.

686. They need to put aside childish notions of "doing what they love to do" in college. They're going to learn how to make a living, how to change the world, how to make a difference.

•

687. They need to do more than just study. They need to have a life.

•

688. They need to develop the habit of reading papers aloud before turning them in.

689. They need to be
proud of their mind.

•

690. They need to handle a large,
complex, diverse workload. In the
time allotted. Without complaining.

•

691. They need to take high school
math beyond Algebra II and three
classes in laboratory science
(biology, chemistry, and physics).
Do well here, and universities
assume they'll do well there.

692. They need to proofread
what they write. And at
least use spell checker.

•

693. They need to understand the
importance of structure—of words,
sentences, thoughts, ideas, books,
paragraphs, projects, institutions,
cultures, religions, even the universe.

•

694. They need to support any claim
with evidence. This means they must
know what they're talking about.

695. They need to apply to
Harvard. Who knows?

•

696. They need to visit at least
five campuses, two out of state.

•

697. They need to study
Western Civilization.

•

698. They need to pick a college based
on what they want to do in five years.

•

699. They need to fill out a college
application. They would rather stick
needles in their eyes than do this.

700. They need to make a file
with a copy of their birth certificate,
transcript, Social Security number,
and teacher references, then
guard it with their life until they're
out of college or until they're thirty,
whichever comes first.

●

701. They need to apply for
financial aid. No matter how
rich they think their parents are.

702. They need to call a college admissions office and confirm the price of a four-year education, with scholarships, before accepting. Get it in writing.

•

703. They need to register with CollegeBoard.com. Here they can register for the SAT, take practice SAT tests, and get information on over 3,600 colleges. This could impact the rest of their lives.

704. They need to price out graduating in four years versus five or six. Four is significantly cheaper.

•

705. They need to pick a major they can actually earn a living with, not just study "voice" in college.

•

706. They need to log onto Collegeboard.com to find graduation rates, costs, demographics, and just about every other fact about any college in the United States.

707. They need to learn about ramen noodles. At three dollars a day, this is what they'll live on for four years.

•

708. They need to take a "basic skills" assessment to identify potential major and career choices.
This is how someone with a head for engineering doesn't find themselves writing a thirty-page paper on feminist literature.

•

709. They need to develop the skill of taking lecture and class notes.

710. They need to listen and retain what they've heard. Any mother can tell you a teenager doesn't remember half of what they hear.

•

711. They need to develop superior memorization skills. Before they start cramming all night for a final.

•

712. They need to be able to prioritize things. This will serve them well at 3 a.m. while studying for two tests and a paper due the next day.

713. They need to score at least 1900 on their SAT to have a shot at a top school. (There are hard and easy schools, hard and easy teachers, hard and easy classes, and hard and easy tests. There is only one SAT.)

•

714. They need to read the *U.S. News & World Report* college rankings, based on the SATs and grade points of last year's admissions classes.

715. They need to develop solid time management skills so a report that takes fifteen hours isn't started three hours before it's due.

·

716. They need to use a daily planner. Not just carry one.

·

717. They need to learn how to handle themselves in a college interview. Eliminate the "you know"s and the drama, but look sharp and answer questions with more than one-word answers.

718. They need to schedule their initial interview at a second-choice college. Get a few practice ones out of the way.

•

719. They need to hang out with smart kids this summer attending "education camp" like the ones at Phillips Exeter or Mt. Hermon, as well as most every college campus. Topics include computer visualization, earthquake engineering, tissue engineering, plant genetics, and prescription drug discovery. Yes, these are subjects high school kids are studying!

720. They need experience in scouting. Great kids are molded here.

•

721. They need to join the Key Club. Or any other organization that promotes citizenship, academics, and charitable works.

•

722. They need to make the debate team. They'll learn to think and talk at the same time.

723. They need to work on the school newspaper. Combines writing, proofing, responsibility, time management, and maybe finding a cause.

•

724. They need to make the National Honor Society. The kids who make this aren't necessarily the smartest kids, but the hardest working ones.

•

725. They need to mentor an elementary student.

726. They need to learn to study in a group. Not talk. Study.

•

727. They need to not cheat.

•

728. They need to learn to argue without emotion, but with facts. This involves, of course, actually knowing the facts.

729. They need to realize that studying in bed just leads to falling asleep.

•

730. They need to ask every college admissions office this question: "How many of your students found jobs in fields relating to my degree six months after graduation?" In business, this is called the money question.

•

731. They need to gain cheap college credits using the College Level Examination Program (CLEP).

732. They need to go to class in high school. Works every time.

•

733. They need to understand that they'll have to take a minimum of four years of English, three years of math, two of science, two of social science, and two of a foreign language to catch a college recruiter's attention.

•

734. They need to excel at taking standardized tests.

735. They need to take a leadership role in extracurricular activities. Not just show up for credit.

•

736. They need to memorize a thousand lines of poetry. They've already memorized a thousand phone numbers. They can do it.

•

737. They need to write five short stories, ten pages or longer. This is a small homework assignment in college.

738. They need to participate in
an academic decathlon.
It's where all their competition
for a top college can be found.

•

739. They need to evaluate the
function f(x)=(x+3)(x+1) at x=-1.
Parents will look at this
problem and just go to bed.

740. They need to identify the archetype for Sherlock Holmes found on today's most popular detective shows.

•

741. They need to take hard classes. Colleges don't care too much if they get an A in Home Economics.

•

742. They need to graduate.

They Need
to Read One
Hundred Books

They need to challenge their mind and elevate their thinking with great literature. A ton of it. This is a starter list from CollegeBoard.com. But a lot of teens will double and triple this.

•

743. Achebe, Chinua
Things Fall Apart

•

744. Agee, James
A Death in the Family

•

745. Austen, Jane
Pride and Prejudice

746. Baldwin, James
Go Tell It on the Mountain

•

747. Beckett, Samuel
Waiting for Godot

•

748. Bellow, Saul
The Adventures of Augie March

•

749. Brontë, Charlotte
Jane Eyre

•

750. Brontë, Emily
Wuthering Heights

751. Camus, Albert
The Stranger

•

752. Cather, Willa
Death Comes for the Archbishop

•

753. Chaucer, Geoffrey
The Canterbury Tales

•

754. Chekhov, Anton
The Cherry Orchard

•

755. Chopin, Kate
The Awakening

756. Conrad, Joseph
Heart of Darkness

•

757. Cooper, James Fenimore
The Last of the Mohicans

•

758. Crane, Stephen
The Red Badge of Courage

•

759. Dante
Inferno

•

760. de Cervantes, Miguel
Don Quixote

761. Defoe, Daniel   *Robinson Crusoe*

•

762. Dickens, Charles
A Tale of Two Cities

•

763. Dostoyevsky, Fyodor
Crime and Punishment

•

764. Douglass, Frederick
*Narrative of the Life
of Frederick Douglass*

•

765. Dreiser, Theodore
An American Tragedy

766. Dumas, Alexandre
The Three Musketeers

•

767. Eliot, George
The Mill on the Floss

•

768. Ellison, Ralph
Invisible Man

•

769. Emerson, Ralph Waldo
Selected Essays

•

770. Faulkner, William
As I Lay Dying

771. Faulkner, William
The Sound and the Fury

•

772. Fielding, Henry
Tom Jones

•

773. Fitzgerald, F. Scott
The Great Gatsby

•

774. Flaubert, Gustave
Madame Bovary

•

775. Ford, Madox
The Good Soldier

776. Goethe, Johann Wolfgang von
Faust

•

777. Golding, William
Lord of the Flies

•

778. Hardy, Thomas
Tess of the d'Urbervilles

•

779. Hawthorne, Nathaniel
The Scarlet Letter

•

780. Heller, Joseph
Catch 22

781. Hemingway, Ernest
A Farewell to Arms

•

782. Homer   *The Iliad*

•

783. Homer   *The Odyssey*

•

784. Hugo, Victor
The Hunchback of Notre Dame

•

785. Hurston, Zora Neale
Their Eyes Were Watching God

•

786. Huxley, Aldous   *Brave New World*

787. Ibsen, Henrik   *A Doll's House*

•

788. James, Henry
The Portrait of a Lady

•

789. James, Henry
The Turn of the Screw

•

790. Joyce, James
A Portrait of the Artist as a Young Man

•

791. Kafka, Franz   *The Metamorphosis*

•

792. Kingston, Maxine Hong
The Woman Warrior

793. Lee, Harper
To Kill a Mockingbird

•

794. Lewis, Sinclair   *Babbitt*

•

795. London, Jack   *The Call of the Wild*

•

796. Mann, Thomas
The Magic Mountain

•

797. Marquez, Gabriel García
One Hundred Years of Solitude

•

798. Melville, Herman
Bartleby the Scrivener

799. Melville, Herman
Moby Dick

•

800. Miller, Arthur   *The Crucible*

•

801. Morrison, Toni   *Beloved*

•

802. O'Connor, Flannery
A Good Man Is Hard to Find

•

803. O'Neill, Eugene
Long Day's Journey into Night

•

804. Orwell, George   *Animal Farm*

805. Pasternak, Boris
Doctor Zhivago

•

806. Plath, Sylvia   *The Bell Jar*

•

807. Poe, Edgar Allan   *Selected Tales*

•

808. Proust, Marcel   *Swann's Way*

•

809. Pynchon, Thomas
The Crying of Lot 49

•

810. Remarque, Erich Maria
All Quiet on the Western Front

811. Rostand, Edmond
Cyrano de Bergerac

•

812. Roth, Henry   *Call It Sleep*

•

813. Salinger, J.D.
The Catcher in the Rye

•

814. Shakespeare, William   *Hamlet*

•

815. Shakespeare, William   *Macbeth*

•

816. Shakespeare, William
A Midsummer Night's Dream

817. Shakespeare, William
Romeo and Juliet

•

818. Shaw, George Bernard
Pygmalion

•

819. Shelley, Mary *Frankenstein*

•

820. Silko, Leslie Marmon *Ceremony*

•

821. Solzhenitsyn, Alexander
One Day in the Life of Ivan Denisovich

•

822. Sophocles *Antigone*

823. Sophocles
Oedipus Rex

•

824. Steinbeck, John
The Grapes of Wrath

•

825. Stevenson, Robert Louis
Treasure Island

•

826. Stowe, Harriet Beecher
Uncle Tom's Cabin

•

827. Swift, Jonathan
Gulliver's Travels

828. Thackeray, William
Vanity Fair

•

829. Thoreau, Henry David
Walden

•

830. Tolstoy, Leo
War and Peace

•

831. Turgenev, Ivan
Fathers and Sons

•

832. Twain, Mark
The Adventures of Huckleberry Finn

833. Voltaire
Candide

•

834. Vonnegut, Kurt Jr.
Slaughterhouse-Five

•

835. Walker, Alice
The Color Purple

•

836. Wharton, Edith
The House of Mirth

•

837. Welty, Eudora
Collected Stories

838. Whitman, Walt
Leaves of Grass

•

839. Wilde, Oscar
The Picture of Dorian Gray

•

840. Williams, Tennessee
The Glass Menagerie

•

841. Woolf, Virginia
To the Lighthouse

•

842. Wright, Richard
Native Son

They Need to Be Good Citizens

843. They need to be able
to make an informed vote in the
next presidential election.

•

844. They need to see the
Declaration of Independence and
the Constitution. And read them.

•

845. They need to visit or read about
Jamestown, Virginia. Learn how the
United States was born on that beach.

•

846. They need to understand the
meaning of July 4, 1776.

847. They need to explain the structure of the U.S. government.

•

848. They need to be aware of the timeline of American history. That the Constitution wasn't signed last month.

•

849. They need to learn what "due process" means. And appreciate that most of the world can't fathom it.

•

850. They need to know how to cast a vote in a voting booth.

851. They need to know more about George Washington, Ben Franklin, Thomas Jefferson, and Alexander Hamilton than they do about rock stars, movie stars, and basketball players.

•

852. They need to explain how a bill becomes law.

853. They need to write letters
to their state representative,
congressman, senator, and president
urging the passage or defeat
of pending legislation.

•

854. They need to campaign for
someone. Lick envelopes, distribute
yard signs, be part of the process.

855. They need to enjoy their freedoms: freedom of speech, freedom of religion, freedom to gather in groups, freedom to travel, freedom to choose one's work, and freedom to lie in bed all day.

•

856. They need to work in a food bank or serve food in a mission.

•

857. They need to respect the flag and honor their country.

858. They need to tell
a soldier "thank you."

•

859. They need to join other
students and paint over graffiti.

•

860. They need to learn the
purpose of the Bill of Rights.
It will help them understand
the magnificence of our country.

861. They need to read to children in homeless shelters.

•

862. They need to see reality: that whenever there's a group of people, there are politics.

•

863. They need to understand the differences between divine law, natural law, common law, statute law, and international law.

They Need
to Learn to
Handle Life

864. They need to get experience with a plunger. Dorm and apartment bathrooms are looming.

•

865. They need to learn how to pay rent. With a valid check. To the right company. On time. All kinds of issues here.

•

866. They need to memorize this question: "Does this prescription come in generic?" It will save them a fortune.

867. They need to learn that everything gets a loose screw: doors, windows, table legs, eyeglasses, even relationships. Every once in a while, you need to go around tightening stuff.

•

868. They need to adjust the thermostat and turn the lights off when they leave a room.

•

869. They need to learn what to do and who to call when water is pouring through a skylight or broken window.

870. They need to work on hammering a nail without smashing their thumb. And when they smash their thumb, not curse.

•

871. They need to paint their room. Without the furniture, the floor, or too many clothes getting painted.

•

872. They need to learn that a paint-brush can be used over and over again if it's cleaned and taken care of.

873. They need to observe the difference between a Phillips head and a regular screwdriver. And see one can't be substituted for the other.

•

874. They need to hang pictures and posters using the appropriate hardware.

•

875. They need to tell the difference between a dandelion and a periwinkle.

876. They need to practice killing weeds with poison while leaving plants and shrubs standing. Unfortunately, this could take a couple of lessons in your yard.

•

877. They need to plant a tree. Not a small tree. A tree that requires about an hour of shoveling.

•

878. They need to see how duct tape can salvage most anything.

879. They need to change a light bulb.
With one that's the correct wattage.
Or they might get another visit from
their local fire department.

•

880. They need to get experience
replacing air conditioner filters.
And learn when to replace them.

•

881. They need to learn that a bolt
is always turned to the right to
tighten. This knowledge they will
pass on to their grandchildren.

882. They need to translate
"some assembly required" into
"the weekend is shot."

•

883. They need to acquire
a tool chest. With tools.

•

884. They need to accept there is
no reason on earth someone living
in an apartment or dorm or
condo needs a power drill.

•

885. They need to recognize the
smell of gas in the house. And know
that isn't a time to light up.

886. They need to learn how to use a drain opener on a clogged drain.

•

887. They need to learn how to clean a carpet stained by Coke, blood, tea, or a pet. Apartment deposits are lost over this.

•

888. They need to learn how to use a wrench. And pliers. And a drill.

•

889. They need to develop the courage to try to fix something themselves before calling a plumber, carpenter, or electrician.

890. They need to be on a first-name basis with somebody at Home Depot.

·

891. They need to operate a washer and dryer without Mom's help.

·

892. They need to learn that everything breaks. Usually at the most inconvenient times.

·

893. They need to clean an oven at home. Before they try doing so in their apartment.

894. They need to experience changing a vacuum cleaner bag. Many kids will just keep vacuuming with a dirt-filled dust bomb.

•

895. They need to learn not to use anything on furniture that says "soft scrub."

•

896. They need to use coasters.

•

897. They need to learn paper towels are never substituted for toilet paper.

•

898. They need to practice the fine art of sweeping with a broom. Into a dustpan.

899. They need to take out the trash. Before it starts smelling.

•

900. They need to learn one solution to their allergy problems is to just dust.

•

901. They need to see pictures of what grows in a bathtub if it's never cleaned.

•

902. They need to learn how to use Pine-Sol.

They Need to Know What to Do in an Emergency

903. They need to stop cuts with something besides a dirty sock.

•

904. They need to learn that if two or three Band-Aids don't stop the bleeding, stitches are probably required.

•

905. They need to develop some survivor skills. Where to stand in an earthquake, what to do if power goes out for a week, where to go if a hurricane is coming.

•

906. They need to ice down a muscle pull with frozen peas. Reason enough to keep them around.

907. They need to know to evacuate if the mayor, the governor, the federal government, or the president says, "Go." That they don't want to be caught in a flooded city with no power, fresh water, or police.

•

908. They need to find where the nearest emergency room is. Before they need it.

•

909. They need to learn that running in the heat of the day can cause heat exhaustion and lead to heat stroke.

•

910. They need to learn how to take one's pulse. And know that a resting heart rate below 50 or above 100 is not a good sign.

911. They need to know a good doctor.

•

912. They need to get a checkup once a year—heart, blood pressure, cholesterol. This is the way adults take care of themselves.

•

913. They need to see an eye doctor the moment their eyes are red, leaking weird things, or blurry.

•

914. They need to learn basic first aid.

•

915. They need to learn to tell the difference between a cold, an allergy, and the flu. All will make them want their mother, but an allergy doesn't have a fever.

916. They need to be aware if they're allergic to peanuts, latex, drugs, or insect stings—and know what their mother would make them do in case of an exposure or reaction.

•

917. They need to call the police instead of responding to physical threats.

•

918. They need to get in the habit of watching or listening to weather reports before and during storms.

•

919. They need to lock their doors.

920. They need to learn what to do
if a tornado is on the ground.

•

921. They need to learn the danger of
flooded streets. Especially at night.

•

922. They need to make a plan in case of
a disaster or terrorist attack.

•

923. They need to learn how to stop
bleeding with a tourniquet and pressure.

•

924. They need to use their
common sense. Like not go to
the beach to watch a tsunami.

They Need to Know the Facts about Alcohol and Drugs

925. They need to breathe through a pillow. And realize this is what emphysema feels like.

•

926. They need to talk to an ex-smoker. Getting off cigarettes is as painful and difficult as getting off heroin.

•

927. They need to realize any mind-altering drug changes how the brain works. Change it enough and congrats—your brain is different.

•

928. They need to understand that stimulants like methamphetamines ruin a person's looks, causes them to sweat like pigs, and eventually leads to the grave.

929. They need to learn that even though crystal meth is often found at dance clubs and parties, not to touch the stuff unless their goal is to live in a trailer park.

•

930. They need to see that a sensible diet and exercise is a far better way to lose weight than methamphetamines.

•

931. They need to learn that snorting cocaine can damage the septum between the nostrils, causing a hole in the middle of the nose. Perfect for a nose ring.

932. They need to read about the athletes who have stroked out using cocaine for the first (and last) time.

•

933. They need to realize that once a person leaves the world on an acid trip, they don't return until the drug is out of their body. Users experience panic, confusion, sadness, and frightening images.

•

934. They need to understand that days after a hallucinogenic drug wears off, a user can suddenly freak out while driving or interviewing for a job. Or like, on a date.

935. They need to realize that even in heroin-growing countries, it is generally accepted that only an idiot would look twice at the drug.

•

936. They need to be aware that Ecstasy isn't the safe, legal club drug it's rumored to be, but chemically similar to methamphetamine and can lead to liver, kidney, and cardiovascular system failure. And 43 percent of its users become addicted. Party on, dude.

•

937. They need to read the studies about marijuana use. Most teens don't smoke it.

938. They need to study what marijuana smoke contains: 50 percent to 70 percent more carcinogenic hydrocarbons than tobacco.

•

939. They need to see the impact of steroids. Really gross acne scarring.

•

940. They need to realize alcohol is a drug and that getting drunk regularly is a sign of a greater problem. Especially in the teenage years.

941. They need to get the phone
number of a cab company.
And use it if they've had more
than two drinks and they're driving.

•

942. They need to understand that
neither food nor sleep magically
sobers up a person. Only time.

•

943. They need to learn that there's a
razor-thin line between passing out
and death-by-alcohol poisoning.

944. They need to be aware that binge drinking in high school is a strong predictor of binge drinking in college and early adulthood.

•

945. They need to guard their drink at any party or club. Things can be added to it.

They Need to Know More about Sex than They Think They Know

946. They need to talk
to you about sex. Often.

•

947. They need to understand
sex changes everything.

•

948. They need to establish
their own sexual boundaries.
And not move them.

•

949. They need to define
what sex means to them.

•

950. They need to learn about the
human anatomy and how
the human body functions.

951. They need to know
how a woman gets pregnant.

•

952. They need to learn about
birth control and the one
foolproof method. Abstinence.

•

953. They need to stay sober.

•

954. They need to date
someone their own age.

•

955. They need to know they're more
likely to get a sexually transmitted
disease than they are the flu.

956. They need to read about
Chlamydia and gonorrhea and
that teenagers have a higher
rate of these diseases than do
sexually active men and women.

•

957. They need to be aware that up to
15 percent of sexually active teenage
girls are infected with a type of HPV
that is linked to cervical cancer.

•

958. They need to look past what
movies and TV say about sex,
that it always has consequences.

959. They need to learn that a person can get an STD without intercourse.

•

960. They need to realize more people are talking about sex than actually doing it.

•

961. They need to visit with a person who has AIDS.

962. They need to understand that condoms reduce the odds of gonorrhea, urea plasma infection, pelvic inflammatory disease, and cervical cancer. But it's not 100 percent.

•

963. They need to talk to a teenage mother. Get an idea of how much fun she's having.

•

964. They need to hear what the church and Scripture say about premarital sex.

•

965. They need to wait.

They Need
to Become
Responsible

966. They need to take responsibility for their actions. Starting in grade school.

•

967. They need to work. After school. Weekends. Christmas break. And summer if they're not in some educational camp. They won't understand this, but it's important.

•

968. They need to make at least $4,000 in high school. This will give them their first real taste of responsibility and independence.

•

969. They need to not compromise their values.

970. They need to be trustworthy.

•

971. They need to learn the
best way to start the hardest
things in life is just to start.

•

972. They need to learn how to complete
a job application. Without Mom's help.

•

973. They need to earn at least one supervisory
job promotion sometime in high school. That
tells colleges and future employers a lot.

•

974. They need to finish what they start.
Homework, for instance.

975. They need to deal with pain and disappointment. Without you scrambling to "spare their feelings." This is a gift only the most loving parents can give.

•

976. They need to know that if they've run out of spending money, it's their problem.

•

977. They need to pay their own auto insurance.

•

978. They need to leave a party when kids start opening liquor bottles.

•

979. They need to seek out responsibility. Not avoid it.

980. They need to accept all Ten Commandments and not just the four or five they find easy to agree with.

•

981. They need to learn there is no right way to do the wrong thing.

•

982. They need to be told you're proud of them. For who they are as a person.

•

983. They need to not require praise for doing what's right.

•

984. They need to make a habit of doing the right thing when nobody is looking.

985. They need to not break their promises. And not make any promises they can't keep.

•

986. They need to be on time.

•

987. They need to help with the household chores. Every day. The earlier you start with this, the less complaining there will be.

•

988. They need to develop strength of character to do the right thing, even though everybody else is doing the wrong thing.

•

989. They need to give blood for a friend. Or even more astounding, for a stranger.

990. They need to not buy
everything they can afford.

•

991. They need to ask God to
help them make the right choice.

•

992. They need to understand
that the right thing to do is
often the hardest thing to do.

•

993. They need to stand up for their
convictions. Even if their friends
disagree. Even if you disagree.

994. They need to
become a role model.

•

995. They need to learn
to apologize first.

•

996. They need to understand
it is impossible to be
good without God.

They Need Encouragement

997. They need to understand
adulthood is inevitable.
But growing up is optional.

•

998. They need to know that
millions of really confused and
goofy teenagers before them
have become successful adults.
Their parents, for instance.

999. They need
to be told God is
going with them.

•

**1000. They need you
to hug them.**

•

1001. They need to fly.

Praise for the Vampire Files Novels

DARK ROAD RISING

"P. N. Elrod ups the stakes (pun intended) in this latest, and best, installment of the Jack Fleming saga. Chills, thrills, and dark doings in '30s Chicago, heralded by the arrival of a darkly fascinating new vampire character with a deadly secret. Elrod takes her universe into unexplored territory with *Dark Road Rising*."

—Rachel Caine, author of the Morganville Vampires series

"The book is as dark and decadent as blood and chocolate. The writing pops, and Jack Fleming is a narrator to die for."   —Caitlin Kittredge, author of *Witch Craft*

"The setting is captivating, the characters are original, and the plot will leave you hungry for more."

—Lori Handeland, author of *Doomsday Can Wait*

"*Dark Road Rising* kept me up all night. A satisfying, smart, genuinely savvy read—with a lot of bite."

—Lilith Saintcrow, author of the Dante Valentine series

SONG IN THE DARK

"Jack Fleming has proven to be the most enduring of the vampire detectives, and Elrod has managed to keep his story and circumstances interesting from volume to volume."

—*Chronicle*

"Elrod knows how to pace the action without resorting to caricature. These characters, including the vampires, are believable and—for the most part—a pleasure to know."

—*Library Journal*

continued . . .

"Interesting twists, good period detail, fine characterization, and snappy dialogue." —*Publishers Weekly*

"There are enough plot twists and turns to keep the reader entertained right up to the end and looking for more."
—*Monsters and Critics*

"Entertaining." —*Locus*

"There's plenty of action, betrayal, friendship, murder, and mystery, but [there are] also a lot of questions about the nature of man and our ethics, strengths, and weaknesses. You can read it for the mystery, but there's more to the story here if you want something to think about on a dark and lonely night."—*SFRevu*

"Another exciting vampire crime-thriller featuring an immortal but not invulnerable protagonist who suffers from panic attacks because of lingering psychological trauma . . . This long-running series just keeps getting better and better."
—*Midwest Book Review*

"Vampire noir blends with hard-boiled detective fiction for an effective, atmospheric supernatural mystery. Jack's voice calls to mind black-and-white movies, big band music, and Al Capone–like villains. Fans of period fiction and classic detectives like Sam Spade and Philip Marlowe will thoroughly enjoy this somewhat-twisted tribute." —*Romantic Times*

COLD STREETS

"An entertaining, violent mix of hard-boiled mystery and the supernatural, with enough new surprises to keep things fresh." —*Locus*

"Clever characterization, wicked wit, and palatable mayhem . . . [an] entertaining detective romp."
—*Publishers Weekly*

"Features a wonderful cast of characters and a great deal of suspense leavened with touches of humor. Recommended."
—*Library Journal*

"Filled with snappy action and sharp dialogue, and featuring a likable . . . hero, Elrod's latest is certain to be a hit with the fang-loving crowd." —*Booklist*

"Elrod crafts . . . some of the snappiest mysteries around that just happen to feature one of the most well-realized vampire characters in current fiction. The pacing never flags, and the plotting never disappoints." —*Crescent Blues*

LADY CRYMSYN

"Mix ruthless gangsters and tough broads with long-standing secrets at stake, and things get dangerous, even for a vampire. Several sordid pasts, numerous plot twists, and even a ghostly presence combine for an only slightly supernatural but altogether entrancing whodunit." —*Publishers Weekly*

"A good mystery wrapped in a fantastic premise." —*Chronicle*

"Elrod's Vampire Files series . . . may be unique in both mystery and fantasy annals for its consistently high quality and [Elrod's] steadfast refusal to repeat a plot or take the easy way out." —*Crescent Blues*

"A suspenseful detective story with just a bit of horror—[it] examines the good-vs.-evil conflict with a twist." —*VOYA*

THE DARK SLEEP

"Tricky plot twists, lots of humor, and plenty of tense action make this good fun, as well as especially revealing for fans of the series." —*Locus*

"Mixing genres is always a difficult task, but it is one P. N. Elrod has mastered in her Jack Fleming novels. She tells an exciting story with all the elements of a classic mystery and blends in the proper amount of vampiric fantasy, resulting in a good story that will keep readers going till the end." —*Tulsa World*

⊸ The Vampire Files ⊸

DARK ROAD RISING

RISING

P. N. ELROD

ACE BOOKS, NEW YORK

THE BERKLEY PUBLISHING GROUP
Published by the Penguin Group
Penguin Group (USA) Inc.
375 Hudson Street, New York, New York 10014, USA
Penguin Group (Canada), 90 Eglinton Avenue East, Suite 700, Toronto, Ontario M4P 2Y3, Canada
(a division of Pearson Penguin Canada Inc.)
Penguin Books Ltd., 80 Strand, London WC2R 0RL, England
Penguin Group Ireland, 25 St. Stephen's Green, Dublin 2, Ireland (a division of Penguin Books Ltd.)
Penguin Group (Australia), 250 Camberwell Road, Camberwell, Victoria 3124, Australia
(a division of Pearson Australia Group Pty. Ltd.)
Penguin Books India Pvt. Ltd., 11 Community Centre, Panchsheel Park, New Delhi—110 017, India
Penguin Group (NZ), 67 Apollo Drive, Rosedale, North Shore 0632, New Zealand
(a division of Pearson New Zealand Ltd.)
Penguin Books (South Africa) (Pty.) Ltd., 24 Sturdee Avenue, Rosebank, Johannesburg 2196, South Africa

Penguin Books Ltd., Registered Offices: 80 Strand, London WC2R 0RL, England

This is an original publication of The Berkley Publishing Group.

This is a work of fiction. Names, characters, places, and incidents either are the product of the author's imagination or are used fictitiously, and any resemblance to actual persons, living or dead, business establishments, events, or locales is entirely coincidental. The publisher does not have any control over and does not assume any responsibility for author or third-party websites or their content.

PRINTING HISTORY
Ace trade paperback edition / September 2009

Library of Congress Cataloging-in-Publication Data

Elrod, P. N. (Patricia Nead)
    Dark road rising / P. N. Elrod.—Ace trade paperback ed.
        p. cm.—(The vampire files ; 12)
    ISBN 978-0-441-01755-3
1. Vampires—Fiction. 2. Fleming, Jack (Fictitious character)—Fiction. 3. Private investigators—Fiction. I. Title.
    PS3555.L68D367 2009
    813'.54—dc22   2009022431

PRINTED IN THE UNITED STATES OF AMERICA

10 9 8 7 6 5 4 3 2

*With thanks to Rox, Jackie,
and Lucienne*

1

Chicago, February 1938

WHEN I set the brake and cut the motor, the dead man in the backseat of my Nash shifted, groaned, and straightened up to look around. He suppressed a cough, arms locked against his bloodstained chest as though to keep it from coming apart.

"You okay?" I asked.

"Peachy." His voice rasped hollow and hoarse. He was lying, but that's what you do when you feel like hell and don't want to give in to it.

His name was Whitey Kroun. He was a big bad gang boss out of New York who had come to town to oversee my execution.

That hadn't worked out very well.

He'd taken a bullet through the chest only a couple hours earlier and should be healing faster. He needed blood and a day's rest on his home earth, but that would have to wait; I had one more thing to do before either of us could have a break.

"What's this?" His dark eyes were bleary with fatigue and pain.

We were in a parking lot close to the hospital. "I gotta see a man about a dog."

He grunted and pushed up his coat sleeve to squint at his watch. The crystal was gone, and the exposed hands swung loose over the numbers. "Well, it's half past, better get a move on."

I slammed out of the car and hurried toward the hospital entrance.

The streets weren't awake yet. At this bleak hour they seemed too tired, unable to recover from the pains of an overlong night. The smack of predawn air felt good, though, and I consciously tried a lungful. Clinging to my overcoat was the smell of Kroun's blood. The scent had filled the car, but with no need to breathe I'd been remarkably successful at pushing away the distraction.

Dried stains smeared the front of the coat, but the material was dark, no one would notice. Even if someone did, I had more serious concerns. I needed to check on my partner. The phone calls made hours ago to the emergency room and later to the doctor in charge weren't enough, I had to see for myself.

After convincing a lone reception nurse that I was the patient's cousin she got my name and other necessary information before giving away Charles Escott's location. He was in the men's ward.

I made sure that would change. "He gets a private room," I said, pulling money from my wallet. From her shocked look the stack was more than she'd make in the next two months. "He gets whatever he needs before he needs it." I folded the cash into her hand.

She stared at the money, uncertain. "Mr. Fleming, I—"

"Consider it a personal thank-you. Do whatever you want with it so long as my friend gets first-class treatment. I have to see him now."

"He shouldn't have visitors."

"We're not gonna play cards. I just need to check on him. Please."

She read my mood right: determinedly polite but not leaving until I got what I wanted. She slipped the money into her clipboard, hugged it to her front, and led the way down the empty corridors herself. Maybe I couldn't hypnotize people anymore, but a goodwill gift in the right place can take you far in the world. It had worked well enough for Capone, up to a point.

The ward was clean, but still a ward: a high, dim room full of restive misery. Some of the bodies shrouded under their blankets were frozen in place by injury, others twitched, sleepless from pain or illness.

I had a brief flash of memory of a similar place in France back when I was a red-faced kid still awkward in my dough-boy uniform. There, the ward had been full of nuns gliding back and forth between the wounded. Some of the guys played cards one-handed, getting used to the new amputations, some groaned despite their doses of morphine, some slept, some wept, and one poor bastard at the end was screaming too much and had to be taken to a different part of the building. After twenty years, the picture was still sharp, but I couldn't recall why I'd been there. Probably visiting someone, same as now.

Escott was second in from the door, lying slightly propped up on the narrow metal bed. His face was puffy and turning black from bruising, his ribs were taped, his hands bandaged like an outclassed boxer who'd unwisely stayed for the full twelve rounds. He seemed to be breathing okay, and when I listened, his heart thumped along steady and slow as he slept. But he looked so damned frail and crushed.

That was my doing. My fault.

He shouldn't be here. I'd been an incredible, unconscionable fool, and he was paying for my lapse with cracked, maybe broken bones, pulped flesh, and slow weeks of recovery. God help us both, I'd come within a thin hair of killing him. He still wasn't out of the woods. If I'd broken him up inside, he could bleed to death internally.

Not recognizing my own voice, I asked the nurse about that.

She consulted the chart at the foot of the bed. X-rays had been taken, though how anyone could make sense of a mass of indefinite shadows was beyond me. She told me what was wrong and, more importantly, what wasn't wrong. It was cold comfort. I'd only *half* killed my best friend.

I wanted to help him, to do more than what had already been done, but no action on my part could possibly make up for such stupidity. This was true helplessness, and I hated it. My hand went toward him on its own, but I made a sudden fist, shoving it into a pocket. The nurse read this mood as well.

"He'll be all right," she said. "It'll just take some time."

It could take years, and still wouldn't be all right.

One of his eyelids flickered. The other was fused fast shut from swelling.

Guilty at disturbing him, I started to back out of view, but it was too late. He was awake, if groggy, and fixed me in place with his cloudy gaze, not speaking.

When I couldn't take the silence anymore, I said, "Charles . . . y-you don't worry. They'll get you whatever you want. It's taken care of. You just say."

His eyelid slowly shut and opened again, and there was an audible thickening of the breath passing through his throat. I took that to mean he understood.

"I'm . . . I'm sorry as hell. I'm so sorry."

He continued to look at me.

"I'm sorry as hell, I—I—" I would not ask for forgiveness. I didn't deserve it and never would.

He shook his head and made a small sound of frustration.

I understood. He was afraid for me . . . afraid I'd try to hurt myself. That had been the cause of the fight. My face heated up from shame. "I'm sorry for that, too. It won't happen again. I swear. On Bobbi's life, I promise you. Never again."

The corner of his mouth curled in a ghost's smile. His lips moved in the softest of whispers. *"Jack."*

I leaned in. "Yeah?"

"About damn time, you bloody fool."

He lifted a bandaged hand toward my near arm, gave my shoulder a clumsy pat.

Sleep took him away.

Men aren't supposed to cry, but I came damn close just then.

Whitey Kroun, the corpse I'd left waiting in the backseat of the Nash, now slumped on the front passenger side with the door open, feet on the running board. His left trouser leg was rusty with dried blood, and he cautiously unwound a similarly stained handkerchief from his left hand. He flexed his fingers, checking them. Whatever damage he'd gotten seemed to be gone. He threw the grubby cloth away, hauled his long legs in, and yanked the door shut. The effort made him grunt, and he went back to favoring his chest.

He didn't say if he wanted to be dropped anywhere, and I didn't inquire, just started the motor and pulled away, mindful of the shortening time until dawn. We'd have to go to ground soon.

Shadows caught, lingered, and slithered quick over his craggy features as we sped under streetlamps, his eyelids at half-mast from pain. In good light Kroun's eyes were dark brown with strangely dilated pupils; now all that showed were skull-deep voids, unreadable.

Life had gotten damned complicated lately. It happens sometimes; for me it started when I tried to be a nice guy and do a favor for a friend in need.

That favor, along with circumstances beyond my control, had put me in the short line for the gang version of the hot seat. Kroun's arrival in Chicago was to sort things out and put me to bed with a shovel. Or an anchor. Lake Michigan makes for a very big graveyard when you know the wrong people.

But after looking me over, Kroun decided against carrying out the death sentence.

Mighty generous of him, except at the time I didn't know the real reason behind his choice. Outwardly, I'm not special; I own a nightclub that does pretty well, have a wonderful girl, a few good friends—I'm worse than some, better than most. Average. Most of the time.

Not ten minutes after we met, Kroun figured out about my being a vampire—you heard it right—and in the nights to follow never once let slip that he was *also* a card-carrying member of the union. I'd been tied up too tight in my own problems to notice anything odd about him or even remotely suspect. It had been one pip of a surprise when the boom came.

I was still getting used to it, the topper of a very busy evening.

It began with one hell of a fistfight between me and Escott, which was what had landed him in the casualty ward. I'd done something really stupid and his attempt to knock some sense into me set me off. I hadn't meant to hurt him, but I woke out of my rage a little too late. Before I could follow his ambulance to the hospital, I'd been sidetracked by a phone call from my girlfriend, Bobbi. In so many words she let me know there was a man in her flat holding a gun to her head.

That confrontation had ended badly.

Bobbi was fine, thank God, but there'd been quite an ugly fracas before the dust settled. Kroun had been present, caught a stray bullet, and died.

Apparently.

The shooter was also dead, and I was left with a nasty mess: two corpses, a shot-up flat, and me desperately trying not to go over the cliff into the screaming hell of full-blown shell shock.

By the grace of God, Escott's right fist, and Bobbi holding on to me like there was no tomorrow, I did not fall in. It had been a near thing, though. I was still standing closer than was comfortable to the edge of that dark internal pit, but no longer wobbling. Given time I might even back away to safer ground.

As I'd sluggishly tried to work out the details of what to do next, Kroun picked that moment to stop playing possum. One minute he was flat on the floor with a thumb-sized hole in his chest, the next . . .

Well . . . it had been interesting.

It took hours to clear the chaos at Bobbi's. I saw to it she was driven to a safe place to stay, then arranged to disappear the dead gunman. For this, I got some reliable if wholly illegal help involving the kind of mugs who are really good at guaranteeing that inconvenient bodies are never found.

Before the cleaning crew arrived, Kroun made himself missing. Temporarily. He hid out in the back of the Nash until the fuss was over.

That I was no longer the only vampire (that I knew about) in Chicago hadn't really sunk in yet.

Since we each had secrets to keep, we'd formed an uneasy alliance out of mutual necessity, and there was no telling how long it might last. I had fish of my own to fry and didn't particularly want to be looking after him—but he needed a favor, and, God help me, I turned sucker yet again.

I didn't want to think just how badly *this* could end.

Kroun seemed to doze. He'd not asked about our destination. I took it for granted that he wanted a ride away from the trouble and a chance to get his second wind, figuratively speaking. He had some serious healing to do; it might as well be in the company of someone who understood what he was going through.

He took notice when I made a last turn and pulled into the alley behind the house. Escott and I hung our hats in an

elderly three-story brick in a quiet, respectable neighborhood. Not the sort of place you'd expect a vampire to lurk,
but I'm allergic to cemeteries.

"What's this?" asked Kroun, blinking as I eased the car
into the garage.

"Home. I'm all in. You'll have to stay the day." Maybe he
had plans, but I wanted ask a few hundred questions, but
later, when my brain was more clear. Right now it felt like
street sludge.

"There's no need. I found a bolt-hole for myself," he said.
"I got time to get there if you call a cab."

"At this hour?" I set the brake, cut the motor, and yanked
the key. The ring felt too light.

"Cabs run all the time now, Fleming. It's a big burg, all
grown-up."

"That's just a rumor . . . ah . . . damn it." I searched my
pockets.

"Something wrong?"

"The house key's back at my nightclub. Left so fast I
grabbed the wrong bunch." The wrong coat, too. Along
with the Nash—which was Escott's car—I'd borrowed his
overcoat. He wouldn't thank me for the bloodstains.

I cracked the door, careful not to bang it against the wall
of the narrow garage, and got out. Kroun did the same, moving more slowly. Something must have twinged inside, for
he paused to catch his breath, which was an event to note.
Like me, he wasn't one for regular breathing. His reaction
had to do with pain.

He'd left a dark patch on the center back of the seat, a
transfer from a much larger stain on the back of his coat.
It'd been hours; his wounds would have closed by now.
The blood he'd leaked should be dried. Must have been the
damp. The heavy air smelled of snow, but not the clean kind
out of the north. This had a sour, rotting tang, as though
the clouds were gathering up stink from the city and would
soon dump it back again.

Going easy on his left leg, Kroun limped across the

patches of frozen mud and dingy snow that made up the small yard, then stalled halfway to the porch. He began to cough, a big deep, wet whooping that grew in force and doubled him over. It sounded like his lungs were coming out the hard way. I started toward him, but there's nothing you can do to help when a person's in that state. The fit comes on and passes only when it's good and ready to go. Spatters of blood suddenly bloomed on the untracked drift in front of him.

I couldn't help but stare at the stuff. The smell had filled the car, but I'd successfully shoved it aside. This was fresh, dark red, almost black against the snow. He wasn't the only one with a problem. Mine was less obvious. I waited, holding my breath, unable to look away.

Waited . . .

But—nothing.

Nothing for a good long minute.

Couldn't trust that, though.

Waited . . .

And finally took in a sip of air tainted with blood-smell . . .

Dreading what must happen next . . .

But no roiling reaction twisted my guts.

No cold sweats.

Not even the shakes.

It was just blood. A necessity for survival, but nothing to get crazy over. No uncontrolled hunger blazed through my gut, not even the false starvation kind that scared me.

So far, so good.

I relaxed, just a little.

Cold, though . . . I was cold to the bone . . . but that was okay. It wasn't the unnerving chill that left me shivering in a warm room, but the ordinary sort that comes with winter. I'd thought I'd lost that feeling.

Kroun's internal earthquake climaxed, and he gagged and spat out a black clot the size of a half-dollar. He hung over the mess a moment, sucking air, and managed to keep his balance. My instinct was to lend him an arm to lean on while he recovered, but he wouldn't like it. I didn't know him well, but I knew that much.

He'd made a lot of noise, perhaps enough to wake a neighbor. I glanced at the surrounding houses, but no one peered from any of the upper windows. The show was over, anyway. Kroun gradually straightened, his face mottled red and gray. He kicked snow to hide the gore.

"You okay?" I asked. I'd have to stop that. It could get irritating.

"Still peachy," he wheezed. When he reached the back porch, he used the rail to pull himself along the steps. He looked like hell on a bad week. "No house key, huh?"

"Yeah, but—"

He fished a small, flat case from the inside pocket of his tattered, filthy overcoat. A couple of nights ago it had been new-looking, but an explosion and fire had turned it into something a skid-row bum would have tossed in the gutter. Kroun might well have been rolling in that gutter. His craggy features were gaunt now, his hair singed—except for a distinct silver-white streak on the side—and when I inhaled he still stank of smoke and burned rubber. He opened the case, revealing a collection of picklocks. "Lemme by."

"No need," I said—and vanished. Into thin air. I was good at it. Didn't think twice.

"*Shit!*" Kroun hadn't expected that.

His reaction was muffled to me. My senses in this state were limited, but it did have advantages, like getting me into otherwise inaccessible places. Damn, I felt smug.

"Fleming? You there?"

I'm busy. I pressed toward the door, sensing the long, thin crack at the threshold, and slipped in. Though I could have passed right through the wood, this path of least resistance was less unsettling. Going solid again on the other side, I unlocked and opened up, gesturing Kroun in.

He looked like he wanted to say a lot of things, but held back. I thought I understood his expression: an interesting combination of annoyance mixed with raw envy. It only flashed for a second, then he pocketed his case. "Nice trick."

"Just a way out of the cold. C'mon."

He stepped into the kitchen, and I locked the door again for all the good that would do. Even the dumbest of Chicago's countless thugs knew how to break and enter in the more conventional sense, though none of them had any reason to do so here. Quite the contrary. I'd gotten into the habit of thinking that way, though. Blame it on the scurvy company I kept.

"Phone?" he asked.

"The wall by the icebox." Actually, it was a streamlined electric refrigerator that looked out of place in the faded kitchen. I dropped my fedora on the table and shrugged from Escott's coat, folding it over the back of a chair. "But you can stay here. It's safe."

"I don't think so." Kroun wasn't being impolite, just preoccupied as he crossed the room, got the phone book from a shelf, and flipped through it looking for cab companies. He found a page, running a finger down the columns of fine print.

I flicked the light on. Habit. We could both see well enough in the dark.

He murmured an absent-sounding noise and stared at the listings. "How many of these companies have the mob on them?"

"They all pay dues. The hotels, too. Shocking, ain't it?"

"Cripes." He put the book back. "It's as bad as New York."

To his former associates in crime, along with everyone else, Whitey Kroun was supposed to be dead. Not Undead, which none would know about or believe in, but the regular kind of dead, and he wanted to keep it that way. He did not need a cabby remembering him and blabbing to the wrong ears. There were ways around that, but Kroun must have been considering the trouble and worth of it against the shrinking time before sunrise.

He was clearly exhausted. He'd barely survived getting blown up, gone into hiding God-knows-where for the day, and only hours before had taken a bullet square in the chest. The slug had passed right through, ripped up his dormant heart, maybe clipped one of his lungs before tearing out his back.

My last twenty-fours hours hadn't been even that good. We both needed a rest.

"Spare bedroom's up the stairs, third floor," I said. "All ready. Just walk in."

Kroun frowned. "Is it lightproof?"

"The window's covered. You'll be fine."

"Where do you sleep?"

"I have a place. In the basement."

He gave me a look. "What? A secret lair?"

That almost made me smile. "It's better than it sounds."

Not by much, but it sure as hell wasn't a claustrophobia-inducing coffin on the floor of a ratty crypt like in that Lugosi movie. Just thinking about a body box gave me the heebies. My bricked-up chamber below was a close twin to any ordinary bedroom, being clean and dry with space enough for a good arm stretch. I kept things simple: an army cot with a layer of my home earth under oilcloth, a lamp, a radio, books to fill in the time before sunrise, no lurking allowed.

"Room enough for a guest?"

"I can only get into it by vanishing." That was a lie. There was access by means of a trapdoor under the kitchen table, hidden by expert carpentry and a small rug. I just didn't want Kroun in my private den. Since he was unable to slip through cracks I was pleased to take advantage of his limitation. Just because we had vampirism in common didn't mean I should welcome him like a long-lost relative. He'd sure as hell not tipped his hand to me about his condition.

"You maybe got a broom closet?" he asked.

"Yeah, but you wouldn't like it."

"I could."

"C'mon, Whitey, no one knows you're here—"

"Gabe."

"Huh?"

"My real name's Gabe." His eyes were focused inward. "Mom's idea. Gabriel. Hell of a name to stick on a kid. Got me in a few fights."

Now why had he told me that?

He got a look on his face as though wondering the same thing. Maybe he was dealing with his own version of shell shock. Well, I wasn't walking on eggs for him. "Okay. Gabe. No one knows you're here, and no one's looking for you. The cops are still sifting through what's left of that car. By the time they don't find your body in the ashes, it'll be tomorrow night and you can start fresh."

He seemed to return from memory lane. "You get day visitors? Cleaning lady? Anyone like that?"

"Nobody."

"What about Gordy's boys? Strome and Derner?"

"They know not to bother me with anything until tomorrow night. No one's gonna find you." There was no point telling Kroun to lay off being paranoid; the kind of stuff he'd been through would leave anyone twitchy. I understood him all too well.

"That won't discourage my pals in New York. First Hog Bristow gets dead, then me."

"Chicago's rough," I admitted.

"They won't blame the city." Kroun frowned my way so I'd be clear on who would be held accountable. He had good reason. Bristow's death was the mug's own stupid fault, though at the end I'd done what I could to help him along. Anyone else would consider my actions to be self-defense, just not his business associates back East.

Whitey—or was I to call him Gabe now?—Kroun had been my ostensible guest and looking into the Bristow situation when another mobster tried to take him out with a bomb. Kroun's apparent, and very public, demise had happened right in front of me, on my watch, and that made me responsible. The big boys he'd worked with in New York were bound to get pissed and react in a way I wouldn't like. Maybe I should try faking my death, too.

"Will your pals be sending someone here to deal with me?" I asked.

"Count on it. Unless Derner or Gordy can head them off."

Derner was my temporary lieutenant when it came to the nuts-and-bolts operation of mob business. His boss, Gordy Weems—a friend of mine and the man usually running things in Chicago's North Side—was still recovering from some serious bullet wounds of his own. I'd been talked into filling his spot until he was back on his feet. He couldn't get well fast enough for me. I had to be the only guy west of the Atlantic who didn't want the job. "Gordy stays on vacation. Derner and I will look after things, no problem."

"If you say so, kid."

Kroun had a right to his doubts. Running a major branch of the mob was very different from bossing an ordinary business. For instance, firing people was murder. Literally.

Another coughing bout grabbed Kroun. He tried to suppress it, but his body wasn't cooperating. He made his way to the sink and doubled over, hacking and spitting. When it subsided, he ran the water to wash the blood away. There wasn't as much as before; he must be healing.

I inhaled, caught the bloodsmell . . . and again waited. Nothing happened, no tremors in my limbs, no urge to scream, no falling on the floor like a seizure victim.

Very encouraging, but instinct told me I was still rocky and not to get overconfident.

"Cripes, I hate getting shot," he muttered.

"It's hell," I agreed.

He cupped hands under the water stream and rubbed down his face. "You've been through this, too?"

"Not if I can help it. But whenever I catch one, I always vanish. When I come back, I'm tired, but usually everything's fixed."

"The hell you say."

"You didn't know?"

He gave no reply.

"Didn't the one who gave you the change tell you anything?" I was very curious as to who had traded blood with him, allowing him the chance to return from death. *When* had he died? How long ago? He'd dropped no clue as to how long he'd been night-walking. He could be decades older than me in this life or months younger.

That streak of silver-white hair on the left side of his head marked where he caught the bullet that had killed him. Who had shot him and why? How had he dealt with his dark resurrection? The lead slug was still lodged in his brain, and the presence of that small piece of metal was enough to short-circuit his ability to vanish. It also prevented rejuvenation, kept him looking the same age he was when it happened. Instead of seeming to be in his twenties like me, he outwardly remained in his forties.

But Kroun wasn't sharing confidences. Making no answer, he twisted the water tap off and dried with one of the neatly folded dish towels Escott kept next to the sink. In the harsh overhead light Kroun looked even more gaunt than a few minutes ago. The coughing fit had sapped him.

"You hungry?" I asked. He had to be. He'd lost plenty of blood tonight. It would put him on edge, maybe make him dangerous. That was what it did to me.

"A little, but I can hold out till tomorrow."

I went to the icebox. In the back were some beer bottles with the labels soaked off, topped with cork stoppers. The dark brown glass obscured what was inside. They represented an experiment that had worked out. I pulled a bottle and handed it over. "It's cold but drinkable."

He eyeballed it. "You're kidding. You *store* the stuff?"

"Only for a few days. It goes bad once the air hits. Like milk."

He took the cork out and sniffed it. "It's animal?"

"Yeah."

He shot me a look. Checking. Appraising. "Good."

Damn. *That* angle . . . and he'd thought of it first. "Hey, you don't think I'd . . ."

"What?"

The son of a bitch. "I don't take from people."

"Sure you do. Your girlfriend."

"She's not food." I felt myself going red.

"No. There have been others who were, though."

"Where the hell do you—" I nearly choked.

He tilted his head. "Yeah?"

I shut down, because I was within a hair of knocking his block off, and that wouldn't accomplish anything. He was guessing, goading me for information. And gotten it. "How do you figure?"

"The other night . . . in Gordy's office."

When Kroun first clapped eyes on me. "But you didn't know about me right away."

"No, I didn't. There was a point in the proceedings, though. You put on a face I didn't understand at the time, but afterward I got it. You were looking at me, at the whole room, and realized you were in charge."

My nape prickled at his insight. I remembered that moment and wasn't proud of it, yet the idea had bolstered me when I was in need and gotten me out of a death sentence.

He went on. "You'd just figured out you were the big fish, and big fish feed on little fish. Only with us it's a literal thing. The question is, do you make a habit of feeding from people?"

"I goddamn don't."

He made a "no problem" gesture. "That's fine then, fine."

"And you?" I'd once encountered a vampire who took human blood—often and any way he liked. I saw to it he came to a bad end.

"I'm not in the habit, no."

"That's not an answer."

"It's the only one I got." He scowled when I didn't respond. "Get off your hind legs, Fleming, I'm no menace to society. I'm retired now."

Time will tell, I thought.

He waved the bottle under his nose again. "You get this stuff from the Stockyards?"

I nodded.

"Pretty smart. Good for emergencies, but someone could find it."

"Who looks twice at an old bottle? Nobody but my partner is ever here anyway, and he's wise."

"That would be guy in the hospital? Charles Escott?"

"Yeah. This is his house." Kroun had never actually met him, but had gotten plenty of information about my life and hard times from long talks with Gordy, who was also wise. Escott knew Kroun by sight and reputation, the latter being very grim, indeed. Somehow the reputation didn't seem to match up with the guy in front of me. Lots of people were good at hiding their real sides, though. I was an expert.

"And he knows all about you?"

"Yeah. Everything."

"You *trust* him with this?" He lifted the bottle, not talking about blood, but rather the condition that required I drink it.

"Completely. He's been one hell of a friend."

Kroun shook his head. "You're nuts to leave yourself open like that."

"Guess I am."

"Well, I don't want him knowing about me."

"He doesn't. Last he heard you'd been blown up in the car. Killed."

"Keep it like that."

"No problem." Escott was in no shape to be told. I also wanted to have some space between him and potential trouble.

"That girlfriend of yours . . ."

"Won't talk." Some edge slipped into my tone. Kroun heard it and picked up the meaning. Bobbi was strictly hands-off. He got the message.

He had a sample sip from the brown bottle. From his grimace it wasn't perfect, but drinkable; the blood would cure his hunger quick enough and speed his healing. He suddenly tilted the bottle and finished it off in one quick, guzzling draft. The stuff must have charged through him like a bull elephant. Head bowed, he gave in to a long shudder as though it had been 180-proof booze and not cattle blood.

"Wow," he whispered, almost in awe.

I knew the feeling. Taken hot from a vein, the internal kick is astonishing. When cold from storage, the reaction isn't that strong unless you're on the verge of starvation. Kroun possessed one hell of a lot of self-control to be willing to stick it out going hungry. If I went too long between meals, I got crazy—tunnel vision, unable to think straight, a threat to people around me, nothing pleasant. I made sure to feed every other night, though lately I'd been overfeeding like a drunk on a binge. It was a considerable relief now not to have that tug of mindless appetite urging me to clean out the rest of the cache in the icebox.

"That hit the spot, thanks." Kroun handed the empty bottle over, and I rinsed it in the sink. He looked improved, even filled out a little. Blood works fast on our kind. The whites of his eyes were flushed dark red and would stay that way for a short time, iris and pupils lost to view. I tried not to stare.

"Another?"

"No thanks." He moved into what was originally meant to be a dining room, but Escott wasn't one for fancy eating, preferring the kitchen. His old dining table was a huge work desk decked with orderly piles of books and papers. There was a big sideboard along one wall, but it served as a liquor cabinet and storage for odds and ends. Kroun paused and peered through the glass doors at all the bottles.

"Your partner a lush?"

Once upon a time. Back then a very good friend of his got tired of the drinking and tried to beat some sense into Escott about it. It'd worked. "He likes to be prepared for company."

The next room was the front parlor with a long sofa, my favorite chair, and the radio. I didn't bother switching on a lamp; the spill from the kitchen was enough for us. It also wouldn't reach the parlor window and give away that anyone was home.

Newspapers were stacked so precisely on the low table in the middle that you couldn't tell if they'd been read yet. They were yesterday's editions, and Escott would have gone through them, it just didn't show. He was that neat about things.

I grabbed the one on top, which bore a headline about the mysterious deaths of nightclub singer Alan Caine and his ex-wife Jewel.

Damn it all.

The story itself was thin on facts, padded to two columns by biographical sketches for them both. The police were investigating what appeared to be a murder-suicide. The estranged couple had been seen arguing in public and so on and so forth.

Damn again. Removing the accusation of murder and stigma of suicide from Jewel's name would be impossible. The killer was on his way to the bottom of the lake by now. He had no direct connection to either of them that could be proved. Any stepping forward on my part would be a futile gesture that would pin me square under the cops' spotlight.

I couldn't risk it and felt like a coward by giving in to common sense.

But still . . . maybe I could fix something up . . . get some of Derner's boys to phone an anonymous tip or three to the rags while the story was still newsworthy, sow some doubt. A double murder was a juicier story to sell than a murder-suicide.

I'd have to talk to Derner about funeral arrangements for poor Jewel. She hadn't had two dimes; I didn't want her going to the potter's field just because her ex hadn't kept up the alimony.

I'd get things moving and hope it wasn't already too late.

The world spun on relentlessly. New disasters rose up to overshadow the old as I discovered when I quit the parlor for the entry hall and opened the front door. Several editions lay piled on the porch. I grabbed them up, kicked the door shut, and dropped them all on the parlor table. To judge by the headlines, the presses had been stopped in order to fit in something special.

They all had the same story.

The only event that could eclipse a nightclub headliner's murder was the shooting of a movie actor. It warranted larger, bolder type to convey the importance of a near-fatal assault on the life of Roland Lambert, onetime Hollywood matinee idol.

Roland would hate the "onetime" part, but ignore it with bemused grace. He and his ballerina wife, Faustine, did exhibition dancing at my club, working to raise grubstake money so he could go back to California in style for a return to films. Toward that end, he'd made the most of the free publicity, having apparently granted an exclusive interview to every reporter in the country.

Above the fold in one journal was a picture of Roland in his plain hospital whites, managing to look devil-handsome, gallant, brash, and charming, just like the sword-fighting heroes he'd played on-screen. Faustine sat bravely at his bedside, holding his hand, decked out in the best Paris could offer, exotic and erotic as always. He wouldn't be dancing much anymore, having been shot in the leg.

That was my fault. Sort of. Roland had been in the wrong place when a bad guy had cut loose with bullets meant for me. The shooter was dead now. Not my fault—for a change—and someone else had bumped him off in turn. Roland didn't know that part and never would.

He had quite another story to tell, though, and it was a pip.

He'd sold the reporters the malarkey that he had run afoul of some real Chicago mobsters, and the tale was developing a life of its own.

"SHERLOCK" LAMBERT TAKES ON THE GANGS!—no kidding, that was how they'd printed it—headed an overwritten four-column section of a sob sister's feature. It was long on emotion, purple prose, with damn few facts, but why let the truth get in the way of such thrilling entertainment?

According to that version of events, a mysterious underworld figure had imposed his unwanted attentions on an innocent bride—at this point it was noted that film legend Roland Lambert adoringly kissed the hand of his beautiful wife, the famous Russian ballerina Faustine Petrova. After a brisk bout of fisticuffs, the gangster had been sent off in round order by her valiant husband, but that wasn't to be the end of it. Strange threatening letters began to arrive, compelling Roland to investigate and deal with their source. He was making serious progress at tracking the bounder to his lair, which was too close for comfort for at least one of the miscreants, and resulted in the present small setback. Here Roland gestured ruefully at his dreadful wounding.

Oh, brother.

At the time of the shooting, I'd been in a blind panic that I'd gotten him killed. Nothing like a little rest and a lot of personal moxie to turn things on their head. With a trowel in each hand, he'd plastered it on thick. I had serious doubts that any of the mugs in the gangs even knew the meaning of *miscreant*, but had to admire him. Roland's eyewash was a great misdirection. He'd made himself into a crime-busting hero, and my name was never once mentioned. What a relief.

The sob sister went into grand and glorious detail about how Roland had rescued his lovely bride from conflict-torn Russia. Their daring escape culminated in the Lamberts' romantic shipboard wedding amid the threat of lurking German submarines. Somehow, routine lifeboat drills took on an ominous significance, and the fate of the *Lusitania* twenty years back was remembered as though it had occurred yesterday. If there was ever going to be another war in Europe, stories like this would be one of the causes.

The couple had actually met over cocktails at a cast party for one of Roland's London plays, but that didn't make nearly as exciting copy.

The next paper went one better and compared Roland and Faustine to Nick and Nora Charles, speculating that a movie of their real-life adventures should be filmed, something that would even top *The Thin Man* for popularity.

Sleuth away, old sport, I thought.

Below the fold were a few short paragraphs about the mystery explosion in Chicago's Bronze Belt. It was old news compared to the rest, but could still sell a paper. A stark photo showed a smoke-filled street and staring bystanders frozen in the moment, but the camera flash hadn't reached far enough to show what was burning. It was a good shot, though; the photographer must have arrived with the fire trucks.

"You see this?" I asked, showing the page.

My houseguest was also catching up on the news and shook his head. "Huh. Doesn't look like the same place."

"You saw it from a different angle."

"I didn't see much but smoke."

Kroun had hurtled from the bomb-gutted car and hidden behind some curbside trash cans before going to ground for the day, leading everyone to believe he'd been blown to hell and gone. Our kind is pretty damned tough, but there are limits. Kroun had only survived because of the car's armor plating and the devil's own luck. He'd gotten seriously hammered around and burned, though. It was really too bad he was unable to vanish and heal the way I could.

The story was little more than a thin rewrite of yesterday's edition, but this time had names. Someone had traced the car's owner. The police wanted to question underworld figure Gordy Weems about the incident. He'd love that.

Kroun read the piece through and snorted. "They don't know anything. This guy got it all wrong."

"It happens. For you it's better if they don't have the facts."

"You used to do that, didn't you? Reporting?"

"Yeah. About a thousand years ago." I dropped into my chair, putting my feet up on the table.

"I hope that's a joke."

It occurred to me that he didn't know my real age, either. I was thirty-seven, but looked a lot younger. I felt a brief, smug grin stretch my face.

"So how long have you been like this?"

Just the question I wanted to ask. "You first."

"Uh-uh. You." He went past me to peer out the front window, pulling the curtain open just a crack, perhaps checking for the first changes that marked the coming dawn. You couldn't always trust a clock.

"Happened a year ago last August," I said.

"When you came to Chicago?"

"Yeah. Slick Morelli and Frank Paco did the honors."

They'd murdered me—a slow, vicious process—but I'd gotten some payback in the end. Slick was dead and Paco raving in a nuthouse God knows where. There was a lesson in that mess someplace about picking your enemies carefully, but I didn't like thinking about it.

"Morelli *and* Paco?" Kroun sounded like he'd met them once upon a time. "What'd you do to get noticed by those two?"

"Nothing I want to talk about." And he would know it already. He'd spent time with Gordy, who knew all the dirt about my Undead condition and how it had happened. Kroun would have used hypnosis to pick Gordy's brain clean about my death, so what was his game asking me? Probably to see if the stories matched. Suspicious bastard. I could get annoyed, only in his place I'd have done the same. "What about yourself? How did you buy it?"

He didn't answer, closely watching something outside. The only reasonable activity at this hour might be someone leaving for an early job or the milkman making his round.

"What is it?" I asked.

"Car's stopped in front of the house."

Now what?

"You know a big colored guy? Well dressed? Drives a Nash?"

Oh, hell. "What about him?"

"He's coming up the walk. Looks pissed, too."

"Let him in."

"It's your door, and I'm no butler."

The man outside began ringing the bell and pounding. I tiredly boosted up.

Kroun stepped into the entry hall. "Oh, yeah. He's pissed. I'd stay to watch, but—"

"Upstairs. Third floor. Keep quiet."

He went quick despite the limp, not making a lot of noise, though I couldn't hear much over the racket. He ducked from view at the top landing, stifling a cough.

I got the door. "Hi, Shoe."

Shoe Coldfield filled a very large portion of the opening, his anger making him loom even larger. Before I could say anything else, a word of explanation, an invitation to come inside, he slammed a fist of iron into my gut.

2

HE had an arm like a train. All the breath shot out of me. I folded and staggered and kept my feet only by grabbing the stair rail with one flailing hand. It wasn't as bad as it might have been for anyone else. I didn't want a second helping, though.

Coldfield's dark face was darker than normal, suffused with barely controlled rage. "You know why I'm here," he rumbled. Volcanoes reach that kind of deep pitch before they blow.

Took an experimental sip of air for speech. "Oh, yeah."

"Why the hell did you do that to him?"

"How'd you—"

"I got people who work at the hospital. One of them saw Charles brought in looking like he'd been worked over by a bulldozer and called me. They wouldn't let me see him. Took one look and knew I wasn't a relation. I tracked down the ambulance drivers and got them to talk. What the *hell* did you do?"

I'd grown a thick hide over my ability to feel guilt over some of the more objectionable things I'd done in life, but it was no protection now. I was in the wrong, and there were consequences to face.

"Charles and I had a fight—"

"The hell you did! What about?"

The words got stuck long before the halfway mark. The situation was edging close to being a reprise of my fight with Escott. Sweat popped out on my flanks.

"What?"

I shook my head. There was no way I could tell Coldfield what I'd done that had infuriated Escott enough to beat the crap out of me—and then my going bughouse-crazy out of control and returning the favor. All I could do was thank God that I'd stopped short of murder. I couldn't remember much about the fight, but the aftermath was clear and sharp, especially those frozen-in-lead moments when I thought Escott was dead.

"*What?*" Coldfield loomed again.

"Charles was pissed with me about something and we got into it. It's not important now." Favoring my middle, I straightened, knowing what was coming. No way out.

"Goddammit, you put him in the hospital!" Coldfield piled in a rain of gut-busters, grunting from the effort. He was in on my secret. Had been for a while. He also knew about the ugly business with Hog Bristow, what the bastard had done to me. For all that, Coldfield didn't pull a single punch.

And I took it.

He finally knocked me ass flat on the floor. I stayed there, not quite keeling over.

"*Talk* to me, you sonovabitch!"

He wasn't going away. Come sunrise he'd probably continue beating on my apparently dead body to make sure I had more damage than Escott.

I raised one hand in surrender. Seemed like too much trouble to stand. He'd just put me back again. It hurt to draw breath to speak. Took a minute to get enough air inside to do the job. "Look . . . you once socked him for his own good . . . didn't you? You got fed up?"

Coldfield nodded slowly. "What about it?"

"This time it was my turn. He did his damnedest to pound some sense into me. Nearly took my block off."

"You don't look it."

"I heal fast, remember?"

"And then what?"

"I wouldn't listen. So Charles kept at me . . . until I hit him. That's where the ambulance came in. I'm sorry, Shoe. I didn't mean for it to go that way. I'd take it back if I could."

"You can't."

Bowed my head. "No. I can't."

He made no comment, but I could still feel his anger. He wanted to hurt me and make it last.

I used the stair rail to pull to my feet. Damn, but he'd caught me good and hard, without brass knuckles, either. If he was like that with bare fists . . .

He laid in again with enough force so I'd remember not to forget. I dropped all the way, curled, and stayed there, gasping. Pain. More than I expected. Wouldn't be surprised if he'd ruptured something. I wouldn't vanish to escape and heal, though. That'd be spitting in his face. I'd take what he dished out and like it.

He stooped into my view and his voice went low, and for a chilling instant I glimpsed what was inside him that made him the boss of one of the toughest mobs in the city. "You *ever* cut loose on Charles again, I will kill you." He knew exactly how to do it, too.

I believed him.

"We clear on that? You understand me?"

"Yeah," I said, talking sideways because my mouth was mashed against the floor. "Never again. Promise."

Coldfield left, slamming the door hard enough to shake the house. A moment later he gunned his car, shifted gears, and roared away.

Good thing he was a friend or we might have both been in trouble. I don't take this kind of crap from enemies.

Another moment or three passed, then the stairs creaked as Kroun came down. He squatted on his heels next to me, hands clasped loose in front of him, and tilted his head. "You okay?"

Now that was one goddamned stupid question. And he wasn't a stupid man. I eyed him. He was concerned, just not one for mother-henning. "I'm great. Tomorrow I sell tickets to the real show."

"Huh." He got the message. It was none of his beeswax, but he almost smiled. "And *he* knows about you, too?"

"Yeah."

"F'cryin' out loud, put it on a billboard, why don't ya?"

"Okay."

A moderately long look from him, followed by a dismissive headshake. "I can't find soap."

Soap? While I got pulped he was looking for soap? What kind of a loon was he?

"Try the second-floor bath," I mumbled.

His eyes went wide. "You got *two* johns in this joint?" My getting a beating was nothing to sweat about, but a house with two toilets knocked him right over.

Actually there were three. Escott had put in a bath all to himself just off his bedroom, which was overdoing things, but it was his house, after all. I didn't say anything as Kroun was already impressed, and mention of more would be pretentious. As a kid back on the farm in Ohio, I'd been told not to brag about our three-seater outhouse lest the neighbors think the Flemings were getting high-hat above themselves with extravagance.

"What was his problem?" Kroun asked, rising as I slowly found my feet again.

I checked my middle. Carefully. Oh, yeah, that hurt. A lot. At least Coldfield hadn't used wood. A baseball bat would have done some truly life-threatening damage on me, but then I'd have fought back. "Nothing to worry about."

"I'm not, but why'd you let him do it?"

"He had to work off steam. And he had a point to make. That was my way of listening."

Kroun thought that over, looking at me the whole time. "You," he concluded, "are crazy."

No reason to deny it. Tonight I happened to agree with him.

"Who was he? Looked familiar."

"Shoe Coldfield. Heads the biggest gang in the Bronze Belt. He's best friends with Escott. He was in that grocery store we walked through to visit Gordy the other night. You may have seen him there."

"Gordy said Coldfield was looking out for him. What's the angle?"

"It never hurts to have someone like Gordy owe you a favor."

"So I've heard. Is that what this is about? You wanting me to owe you a favor?"

"Huh?"

He stared a second. "Ahh, never mind." He went upstairs, dodging into the hall bath long enough to grab soap from the sink, then continuing up to the third floor. Soon water was running in the pipes, making its long journey up from the basement heater tank.

When I felt like moving again, I checked my ribs, but Coldfield had focused on the softer target of my midsection. He'd inflicted ample bruising and spared his knuckles. The man was a smart thinker when it came to his brand of mayhem. Everything still hurt, and I stubbornly held on to it as though that would somehow help Escott.

I hobbled into the kitchen to blink at the clock. If he rushed things, Kroun could get cleaned up and make it to bed before dawn. I could take my time.

I made sure the front door was bolted, checked the back again just because, then vanished, sinking down through the kitchen floor. Once solid again in my hidden alcove the bruising and pain were magically gone, but I was tired, very tired.

The small table light next to my cot was on, so I didn't reappear in fumbling blackness. I'm a vampire who's gotten really allergic to the dark. I didn't used to be that way; but, after the crap I'd been through since my change, anyone would want to leave a lamp burning in the window.

No windows were in my artificial cave, but that was fine, what with my allergy to sunlight. Kroun had a right to be concerned about avoiding it, but he could manage. Things had to be a lot better for him in this place than wherever he'd hidden after the big boom. Did he have a supply of his home earth with him? I'd not thought to ask.

Damn, I didn't want to think about him and what to do with him and all the attendant complications concerning his apparent death. But the problem would be hanging around like an unpaid bill when I woke again, no way out of it. The mess Kroun had come to town to clear up was worse than before.

Derner—following my orders—had the right story to give to the New York mob bosses about Kroun's demise, but the details might not satisfy them. They were told that Kroun had been killed in the car explosion, then the man who rigged the bomb was in turn killed by me in a shoot-out. Very tidy. Too much so.

"They won't swallow that goldfish," I muttered, shrugging from my suit coat and prying off my shoes.

It would get out that there was no body in the destroyed car. The bomb had been big, but not so much as to wholly obliterate its intended target. Unless Kroun did something, New York would only send another man to find out why and then bump me. I'd gotten myself noticed by the wrong people one too many times. The idea of getting clear of town for a while was tempting, but that would leave Gordy holding the bag.

My other option was just to get it over with and let the mob do the hit. Let them think they'd executed me, then they could go home satisfied. Easy enough. I'd survived such attacks before. The problem with that was I'd not be able to go back to my business again. Just getting the legal papers to a new name forged would be a pain in the ass. I had friends, family, a club to run, things to do, and I needed to be able to do them as myself, Jack Fleming.

I stretched flat on the cot, loosening my belt, and felt gravity tug me toward the center of the planet. Illusion. The pull was really from the spread of earth under the protective oilcloth. This was my portion of the grave I'd never gone to, a tiny scrap of peace in the red chaos, protection from the insanity of my subconscious. My body seemed to weigh a ton; the feeling was surprisingly pleasant.

If I could hypnotize that next mobster into forgetting his job all would be well, but even thinking about using one of my evil-eye whammies made my head buzz like a too-crowded beehive. The last time I'd employed that talent had damn near exploded my brain. Deep-down instinct said another attempt would kill me. My nights of pretending to be Lamont Cranston and clouding men's minds like the Shadow were over.

Kroun was not crippled in that area, though. I could probably talk him into fixing things, especially if it meant his own safety. If I were him, I'd be cooperative and willing to try.

Only he wasn't me.

Who the hell is he? I wondered—my last thought as the rising sun swept me into the dreamless abyss for the day.

KROUN

God, my chest hurts.

Not as bad as before, but it was like a hangover that wouldn't quite give up and leave.

The through and through Gabriel had taken was healed; he could tell that much because the itching deep under his knitted skin had almost stopped. It still felt as though pieces of himself had torn loose and were wriggling their way back into place again. What wouldn't fit kept trying to migrate up his throat. If he was careful not to breathe or move fast, it wasn't too bad. But just when everything seemed settled, the internal prickling would rise, crest, and set him off hacking like a lunger on his last legs. Gabe was damned bored with it.

He climbed the stairs slowly, hoping there would be no more visitors to make things exciting. He went to what Fleming called the guest bath, twisted the sink's left-hand tap, waiting, waiting, waiting until the water ran hot.

Gabe stared at the mirror over the sink. His faded, near-transparent reflection stared back. The ones like Fleming had no reflection at all. How did he get by without being able to see himself? Shaving must be an ordeal.

On the other hand, he could disappear and get well again anytime he pleased. Gabe would have given much to have that; it would have saved him a lot of pain the last couple nights.

Leaning close, he checked his tongue and eyes, didn't find anything of interest, then scratched his chin and neck. Yeah, a shave would be good, but have to wait. No razor. Did he need a haircut? If he could grab his hair in the back then it was too long. Gabe ran a hand over his head. Yeah, half an inch there at least. Time for a trim, get rid of the singed areas.

The ridge was still there of course—the one in the bone on the left side of his skull. It marked where the bullet that originally killed him had gone in. And stayed. That small piece of metal allowed him to discern a remnant of his presence in mirrors.

His head hurt. Not like when it first happened, but bad enough, aggravated by the latest calamities. People had tried killing him yet again, and he didn't like the violent reminder that not so long ago someone had actually succeeded.

He also didn't like thinking about how many other people wanted him dead. One fewer to their numbers, but still—

I'd trusted *him. Goddamned Mitchell. Goddamned bastard. I should have seen that coming.*

It wasn't as though Mitchell had intentionally shot Gabe tonight at the girl's flat, but he *had* planned the bomb for the car. What a dirty way to kill a man.

Too bad only Fleming got to have all the fun of beating the hell out of—

Jack Fleming. Now *there* was one crazy noodle. One minute trying to be helpful, the next letting himself get pulped flat in his own house. What kind of a screwball was he? He seemed to know all the ropes about being a—Gabe stumbled over *vampire*.

Ugly word.

He'd read up on it, of course, and other details had just come to him from God knows where. Northside Gordy had filled in more blanks, but getting the firsthand knowledge from a guy who'd actually been through the same mill was much more useful. Getting it without raising too many questions was the problem. Fleming was curious and had only begun to start with the snooping.

Reporters. They're incurable.

Gabe was inclined to shed him fast then get lost, but Fleming might come looking, full of good intentions. With the whole of Gordy's organization on the hunt, Gabe wouldn't stay lost for long. He'd have to handle this carefully, keep the man on his side until a real exit could be managed.

He had been lucky at surviving until now, until they sent him to Chicago to take out the piss-and-vinegar punk who'd iced Hog Bristow.

Having other errands to see to, Gabe had gone, hoping to figure a way to avoid killing anyone. Fortunately, the punk had been smart enough to save himself.

Finding out that he was in the same bloodsuckers' club— well, that had been a real distraction.

But while the company was interesting, Jack Fleming was too reckless about who he let in on his secret; sooner or later, he'd tell others about the new guy in town. Though he seemed all right for the moment, he could turn on a thin dime.

The man was *nuts.*

That was plain from their first meeting. It'd been damned hair-raising when Fleming had gone into that fit. Gabe couldn't recall ever seeing anyone acting like that before, the sudden uncontrolled shivering, the eyes rolling up, then the poor bastard vanished into nothing. He said he was better now, but if he forgot himself and tried to hypnotize anyone again . . . apparently that was what set him off.

Gabe felt sorry for what had been done to Fleming. Torturing a bystander had never been part of the plan to get rid of Bristow, and it was just as well Fleming didn't hold a grudge. For now. The guy was trying hard to keep himself together, but he was still loopy as a bedbug, and that made him dangerous to be around. Soon as Gabe was on his feet and able to make a good job of disappearing, he'd get clear.

For that he would need a car and money.

Lots of money.

There were ways to get it, but later, when he wasn't wheezing like a bad engine.

Moving with great caution to keep from coughing, Gabe stripped to the waist and ran a hot, soapy washcloth over his face and neck, going easy over the fresh scar on his chest. There wasn't enough time for a shower-bath. He would only have to put on the same wrecked clothes again. It felt like he'd worn these for a week. If this was what being dead involved then he should have planned it better.

God, what have I let myself into? Is this going to work?

Gabriel Kroun wasn't a nobody who could leave the party without a ripple. He'd been through that before, the first time he died and found himself trapped in his previous life. Things *had* to run differently this time, and he had to work it better to avoid the same problems. The boys back home either liked and feared him or hated and feared him, and there was at least one who couldn't let his very public death slide without doing something.

Fleming didn't seem to be too worried about that, and he should be; he was either an idiot or counting on Gabe to step in and help.

I might. But not if it ended with old enemies finding out he was still walking around. Gabe had gone through too much to waste the opportunity to get away from the mob life.

Some of them were okay guys, but then Mitchell had seemed to be an okay guy. With a hypnotic nudge for insurance, the man was made incurious about where and how Gabe spent his days, and that had been enough. Not once had Gabe thought to add, *Oh, by the way, don't try killing me.*

On no account was he going to go back to that. Somebody up there had handed him a new start on a platter. He was certain he didn't deserve it, and suspicious that it might be yanked away.

Money and a car. Have to figure out something . . .

The guest room was clean, but basic. There was a wardrobe, no closet. None of the rooms on the floor had closets. Except for spare blankets, the wardrobe was empty and too small to hide in. He pulled all the blankets out and spread them on the bed. Damn, that looked vulnerable.

The room had one tall, narrow window with curtains and a pull-down shade that would dim the full daylight when it came. Easing it aside he peered at the street below and each house within view. A few lights showed in windows. Early risers were getting ready for work, their wives making coffee, eggs, hotcakes, bacon. He could remember eating those things, but not their taste. It had been good. He was sure of that.

Bacon . . . greasy, hot, crisp when fried right, but was it sweet, sour, bitter, or salty? He just didn't know.

He put the shade back and yanked the heavy curtains together. The predawn light was strong, leaving painful afterimages on his eyes. Damn, his head got worse because of it.

He shucked his shoes and trousers, folding himself into a clean, soft bed. Not bad. Damned good, in fact. The sheets seemed too short for his legs, so he messed them around until they were loose enough to pull over his head along with the extra blankets. Black as a mine now, dark enough for—

Just a few seconds to go.

His head pounded in weary anticipation. The left side. Always.

Gabe slipped into absolute immobility swiftly, managing to shut his eyes at the last instant. He'd forgotten once and spent the day with them open. When night came, they'd felt like razor-edged rocks.

Images flashed over the inside of his lids. His own little movie show. He got to relive Mitchell's shooting him all over again. Several times. Even once was too many. Then memory swept Gabe back to that damn car and the explosion. He stayed there in the searing heat for a long, long while, tasting the smoke, feeling the blind panic, the pain, tearing his hands as he slammed out the door and rolled clear before hell could suck him in for real and forever.

He was trapped in that bad spot much too long, going through it too many times. After a very long, long eternity, it finally lost strength, like a storm wearing itself out. The inner lightning and thunder ceased, leaving only the wind.

That was a good sound.

When the nightmares faded, he dreamed of wind whirring through pine needles. It was hollow and haunting, sad, cold music; he thought he should be afraid of it, but just never seemed to feel anything but comfort. He was safe there. At peace.

The sound gradually merged with shapes, pale light, and shadows. He lay on his back under a black sky shot with stars. Raw bare ground chilled his body, the scent of pines and the bruised smell of fresh-turned earth filled his head. A pine tree loomed tall over him. Its boughs waved in the wind, restless, singing to the night. Theirs was the sweetest, most calming song he'd ever heard. He had never before felt so relaxed and content.

It lasted until a heavy wedge of damp earth slapped over his face.

What are they doing? Why are they doing this to me?

His face was soon covered, his body frozen, his mind screaming and impotent. He couldn't see, only hear: the grunt of a man, breathing hoarse as he labored, the scrape of metal in the dirt—a shovel?—somewhere in the distance a woman sobbed. Hers was the anguish of the heartbroken. It hurt to listen to that kind of pain. He felt sorry for her, grieving for him so hard. If he could just wake up he could tell her it was all right. There'd been a mistake. He wasn't dead. He tried to remember her face . . .

But a fire-hot flare sizzled through his skull, obliterating everything. When that faded, it was too late for anything but blank terror. He was completely buried. Earth clogged his eyes and ears. No more singing from the wind, only silence like death, but worse because he was aware of it, of being dead.

Other, much more fragmented, scenes shot past. Some were good, most were not. They flashed and flitted too quick to grasp and study. Green land, deep water, a sky so solidly blue it hurt to look on; a room stinking of blood, his own laughter sounding too open and happy for that place; a tall man standing over him, swinging the buckle end of a belt, face blank, eyes crazy.

He taught me to kill. Why?

The horrors rose and ebbed, and, in the pauses between, the soft deep rush of wind through pine branches gradually returned, offering a temporary ease. That never lasted, and he wanted it to; but in the end, at the very end, he would begin to shift and struggle and push at the earth until it crumbled away from his face and harsh, cold air dragged him fully awake.

Gabe pitched off the smothering blankets, yelling. Without air in his lungs no sound came out. There was a moment's absolute certainty that he was still buried, and then he drew breath, abruptly aware he was in Fleming's guest room. Sunset had freed him from the steel grip of the monsters in his head.

Somewhat. They'd retreated only as far as the shadowed corners in his mind, grinning, waiting for their next chance to come at him again.

He leaned over the side of the bed and coughed. A glob of blood and tissue splattered the floor.

Damn it.

Another night to get through, alive or dead or whatever the hell it was for him now.

At least his head had stopped hurting.

FLEMING

I woke instantly, my mind sharper for being rested, the question about Kroun still there, if no closer to an answer. Pulling on last night's clothes, I vanished and floated, going solid in the kitchen. The house was quiet, though I could hear Kroun stirring upstairs. He gave a groan and coughed wetly. I felt sorry for him, for not being able to heal faster. We needed a trip to the Stockyards to get him some stuff fresh from a vein. That would help.

The phone rang. It was probably Derner, following orders. I'd told him to call me only after a certain hour, keeping any mention of *sunset* out of the conversation. He just might be imaginative enough to put two and three together about my condition and didn't need more clues than he already possessed. Like most of the mobsters I dealt with, he knew I was uncannily tough and had earned Gordy's friendship, which was usually enough to keep them from asking awkward questions. Now more than ever, since I couldn't hypnotize people anymore, I had to be careful.

I finally answered. "Yeah?"

"Boss?" Derner's voice. Terse. Tense. He could pack a lot into a single word.

"Yeah. How'd things go today?"

"No hitches at this end. Everything went smooth on that job."

I took him to mean the cleanup at Bobbi's flat. Derner and I were both wary that the phones might be tapped. It was illegal, but that detail was not something J. Edgar was too particular about. So long as his name didn't come into things, and his agents didn't get caught, he'd turn a blind eye if it got him good headlines as a gangbuster. Thus ran the scuttlebutt I'd heard from others, especially Gordy. I wondered how he'd come to learn it.

"Anything else?" I asked Derner.

"There's some guys here. They're upset about their friend having car trouble."

That would be muscle from Kroun's New York mob, pissed about the bombing. "How bad is it?"

"Real bad. I told them what you said and that you'd talk to them here, but they went looking for you."

New York would know about my nightclub, Lady Crymsyn. The muscle would be waiting there. The sign tacked on the front door with its TEMPORARILY CLOSED—BACK SOON! wouldn't discourage them. "I'll just talk to them and—"

"Those guys who blew in were hopping mad. They won't be talking. No chance. You gotta disappear yourself. This is serious."

"They serious about the big guy, too?" I meant Gordy.

"Just you for now. They heard he wasn't involved, but you have to get out of town. I told them who was really behind it; but you were the boss at the time, so you get the blame."

"That figures." Doesn't matter what kind of job you've got, doctor, lawyer, Indian chief, when a disaster happens while you're running the show, it's your fault.

Derner said, "I can get you a ride out of town, money, too."

"No need."

"But—"

"It's all right. I'll deal with them." There was the sound of footsteps from the hall; Kroun had come downstairs. If I explained the situation to him in the right way he might be open to helping me out of this jam. He couldn't vanish, but was still able to make people change their minds to his way of thinking. If he wanted to stay dead to them, he could arrange it. "When the coast is clear, I'll stop by and fill you in."

Silence from Derner's end. He must be getting used to

how I worked. He'd been there the night I'd faced down Kroun and survived. Maybe he thought I could somehow talk my way out of this one as well.

"How many of them are there?" I asked.

"There's two of us, pal."

I jumped. The reply hadn't come from the phone, but from directly behind me. A stranger's soft voice. Something, probably a gun, prodded my lower spine, forestalling further motion on my part. People who interrupted calls in this manner always had guns. How long had he been here? Not long enough to have searched as far as the guest bedroom. Or maybe he had—and discovered what appeared to be Kroun's dead body. Oh, hell.

"Say you'll call him back." The man's tone was almost conversational and very confident.

"Boss . . . ?" Derner sounded odd. He must have heard.

"I'll call you back," I said and dropped the receiver onto its hook.

The man said, "Good boy. Put your hands on the wall. High up."

I did so, and he frisked me, making a fast, efficient job of it, finding nothing threatening. My gun was in the overcoat hanging over the kitchen chair, well out of reach.

"You Jack Fleming?' he asked.

"Yeah. You one of Whitey Kroun's people?"

"No. Whitey was one of *my* people."

Oh, hell, again. Kroun's boss. Not that this should be a surprise. He sounded calm, but I sensed otherwise. Some of them could do that, hold a relaxed front, yet be flushed with rage. I was better at dealing with the ones who lost control and gave in to their emotions. This steadier type was a lot more unpredictable.

He went on. "Mitchell was also one of my people. So was Hog Bristow. They're dead, and you're not. You understand why I'm here?"

"You gonna buckwheats me?" I asked. My mouth went dry, just like that, at the word.

It was how the mob dealt with some of their enemies. Buckwheats meant a slow, hideous death, lots of blood, lots of screaming. I'd been through it and would not suffer again. I would kill to avoid it, no matter the consequences. Despite this internal promise, cold sweat flared over my skin, over the lines of scars Bristow had carved into me. My gut gave the kind of fast light flutter that presages vomiting. I leaned hard on my hands and took a deep breath, trying to stifle the nausea.

"That was Bristow's hobby," said the man. "I heard he did some knife work on you."

"Yeah. He did." The long icy threads left by his blade pulled tight on my flesh.

"And somehow you're still walking? Whitey said as much, but I didn't believe him." The man spoke quickly yet with careful, educated articulation. He wasn't any jumped-up street mug.

"He told you right." God, I was sick. Dizzy sick. A wave of it went over me, cold as gutter slush. If I fell into one of those damned fits . . . no. Absolutely not. Too humiliating. Swallowing dry, I let out my breath and sucked air, tasting my fear. "Whitey decided I'd paid enough."

"I get that. It's paid. Whitey let you off for Bristow, but I can't let you off for Whitey. How did you arrange the bomb?"

"Not me. Mitchell. He was behind it."

"You got Mitchell to—"

"No, he was on his own!" My voice was high and harsh. I pulled it down, fighting my not-unreasonable panic. Jeez, when had I started trembling? "I didn't know or I'd have stopped him. He wanted Kroun's job. If it'd worked right, I'd have gone up as well. Mitchell got his for it."

"So you say." The pressure of the gun muzzle increased and I couldn't help but flinch. "All the same, Whitey got blown to hell, and you didn't, and that's what matters to me."

This bird had not searched the place thoroughly, else he'd have found Kroun upstairs, dead to the world, and this would be a different conversation. Where the hell was Kroun, anyway? If he'd just walk in . . . "You know I didn't kill him. It was—"

"Not my concern."

Screw it. I wasn't going to beg for a chance to explain.

"I came to do a job," he said. "That's all."

I stared hard at the black phone. "One thing," I said.

"Yeah?"

"Who else is on your list?"

"Why do you ask?"

"I don't want others to pay for what you think I've done." The muzzle shifted and now rested hard against the back of my head. It felt good. It's a bad night in hell when the prospect of a bullet in the skull seems to be the easy way to get clear of problems. No bullet, lead or even wood, could slow me for long, but I did think about that kind of total oblivion for a few seconds. I wouldn't go there, though. Not ever again. I'd play the cards I'd been dealt and see the game through . . . with a moderate amount of cheating. "So when you're finished here—"

"You're it, pal," said the man. "No one else."

But I couldn't trust him.

I let myself vanish. I'd been fighting the urge to do so, and now I went out like a light, but only for the barest second, long enough to shift and return with death's own grasp on his arm. The gun went off. Twice. Right next to my ear. I barely noticed, twisting and slugging hard, anger blurring my senses. He grunted and sagged but got a strong left in with his free hand. Tough guy. But my second punch took him out, and he suddenly weighed a ton. I let him drop, dragging the gun clear of his grip, and stifling the itch to kick him for good measure.

He said there were two of them. I vanished again before the second guy could come running. My hearing was diminished, but I'd know if anyone was close. Nothing stirred. I rushed through the downstairs quicker than wind—no one else around—then went solid to check on the fallen.

He was taller than average, with a hard-packed build under the expensive coat. Considering his high level of confidence, he was younger than I'd expected, not far into his thirties. Despite the winter, his skin was tanned and healthy, and he might have given Roland Lambert a good run for his money for film-star looks. Jobs in the gangs tended to age a man, but this bird seemed immune. Myself, I felt about a hundred years old, give or take a week.

The back door was unlocked. Damnation. I'd brick the thing over, but the bastards would probably just drop down the chimney like Santa. I turned the bolt (for all the good that would do) as Kroun came in, but I saw him as a corner-of-the-eye movement. I was startled enough to swing the gun on him.

He froze in place, genuinely alarmed, palms spread. "Easy there, it's me."

As if that was reassuring.

Kroun wore only socks, skivvies, and had dragged on his bloodied shirt in lieu of a bathrobe. He frowned at the man on the floor. "Cripes."

"Friend of yours?" I asked.

"Unfortunately for you, yes."

I put the gun on the table, within easy reach. "He was shooting up the place. I had to clock him."

Kroun took that in along with the holes in the wall. "Well, you both made a good job of it." There was no longer a rasp in his voice. The day's rest must have fixed that, but he didn't look happy. "Is he broken?"

"Not permanently. Now what?"

" 'Now what' what?"

"He's after me because of you. I'd have to kill him to stop him and then someone else will follow and someone else, and I've got enough goddamned dead guys on my hands."

He gave me a funny look. "You all right?"

"No, I'm—" I shut down, getting control. I still felt the gun's muzzle kissing the back of my head and couldn't believe I'd found that a comforting thing, even for a second.

Shoving away the memory, the anger at myself and the circumstances, and taking a breath, I began again. "I am not all right. I got mugs like him breaking into my place to kill me. There's at least one other waiting somewhere else for his chance, and I'm damned sick of it. If you've got any influence over these bastards, get rid of them. I want them off my back for good."

He just looked at me, pupils dilated and unreadable, but his mouth went tight. He didn't like being ordered around, but then who does? "I can't do that," he said.

"You're the only one who can."

"I—" He bit off the reply, then looked at the fallen man again. "If I do that, they'll know I'm alive. I don't want them to know I'm alive."

"Hypnotize them not to remember you."

"It won't last."

"Long enough to buy you a head start."

"Hell, kid, you're not asking much. You know what I went through to get dead?"

"Yeah, actually I *do.*"

That got me double take.

"Welcome to the club," I added.

"Cripes," he muttered again. "All that for nothing?"

"It's how the world works."

His next remark was back-alley foul.

"You'll be a hero for surviving it—and you can tell them who's really responsible. That lets Gordy off the hook."

"And you, too."

"What's the big deal? Fix this mess, then take a vacation. Retire if that's what you want."

Kroun stared like I'd gone around the bend. Retirement in his line of work nearly always involved a funeral.

"You'll have to do the fixing anyway," I went on. "Odds are they're already wise to there being no body in that car, and they've been asking questions. My way they go home alive. Your way, they either get killed or kill other people, making an even bigger mess, and—"

He held a hand up, forestalling further persuasion. "Yeah-yeah, okay, enough already. I'll put the fix in. But you are going to *owe* me."

I worked hard not to show too much relief. He'd made a choice I could live with. I'd worry about the debt later.

"But not like this," he added.

"Like what?"

He gestured at himself. "Looks are everything in this game."

What?

"You want me to play? Get me cleaned up first."

He had to be kidding.

"Use your noodle. I'm not going anywhere fast looking like a train wreck."

I got my mental gearbox shifted. Finally. He *did* look pretty ridiculous. He must have clothes back at his hotel or wherever he'd stayed before the explosion. We could go there and pick them up.

"What about him?" I pointed to Handsome Hank on the floor.

"You got rope, don't you?" Kroun turned and went upstairs.

3

I HAD rope, or rather Escott did, stowed in the basement. I helped myself to the whole coil and trussed up the guy after searching him. He had a wallet filled with twenties, a pocketknife, a fountain pen, three money clips holding wads of cash I didn't bother to count, wire-rimmed glasses in a hard leather case, keys, and a map of Chicago with the locations of this house and my club neatly circled. No identification, though, not surprising for his sort.

In another case, larger than the one for his glasses, I found a clean syringe and four small, unlabeled vials. Their dark amber glass effectively hid the color of the liquid contents.

I gave the guy a second glance. So, did he go in for morphine or cocaine? Maybe he had diabetes; he didn't look like a doper, but some people were good at hiding their secrets. I should know. The lack of a label on the vials gave me the idea that the stuff hadn't come from any corner drugstore.

Everything went on the kitchen table next to my hat. I blindfolded and gagged him with a couple of the dish towels and dragged him into the hall. In case he felt frisky when he woke, I tied him fast to the newel post at the foot of the stairs.

In the parlor, I edged open the front curtain and saw an unfamiliar Studebaker parked where I usually left my Buick. Some people have a lot of nerve.

The street seemed clear, but that didn't mean anything; might as well see if he'd brought friends. I unlocked the front and got the mail and papers, tossing things on the hall floor, then went outside to look at the car, offering an easily bushwhacked target. No one took the bait. Damn. I still had plenty of rope left, too.

The car's registration was to a rental garage by the train station. The paperwork bore an illegible signature. My prisoner and his absent pal must have been confident about getting in and out of town without trouble. Had they planned to disappear my body or just didn't think the cops were up to tracing a connection between us? Probably the latter. A lot of these guys were either stupid or brazen depending on how smart they thought they were. Unless someone in Gordy's mob squawked—and no one would—they'd do their job and walk away clean, simple as that. Maybe New York expected Gordy to do the mopping up for them. He'd have done so; those were the rules.

I phoned Derner, who picked up halfway through the first ring. He sounded a whole lot more tense.

"It's me," I said. "Everything's okay, and I'll be in later tonight."

"You sure? What's going on?"

Jeez, he was going to make me think he cared. Maybe he did. If I dropped out of sight, then he'd have to run things. "Expect me when you see me. Business as usual until then."

"Right, okay." Not a lot of confidence there, for which I couldn't blame him. "The cops have been by—it's about Alan Caine. They want to talk to you."

This was tricky. The lines were likely tapped, and Derner knew it. He was a smart man, so this could be a way of feeding the cops misleading information. Fine by me; I could play with the best of them. "They'll have to wait, I've got things to do tonight."

"They're wondering about Jewel Caine, too."

"What do you mean?"

"The way they were going on, she didn't kill herself like the papers said."

"She didn't?"

"Which means someone did her in as well."

"Maybe the same guy who bumped Caine?"

"Whoever that is," he said.

Oh, Derner was doing genius stuff tonight. "My money's on Hoyle. He's crazy. Didn't Caine owe him money?"

"I wouldn't know, but I wouldn't be surprised."

"Okay, see if any of the boys have seen Hoyle. I wanna know what he's been up to lately. If he's the one, we send him over. I don't want no trouble with the coppers."

"Right, Boss."

I hoped someone was listening in. "Another thing—see about making arrangements for Jewel Caine."

"What?" He sounded surprised.

"Arrangements—a funeral. Anyone claimed her? She got family?"

"Uh—"

"Look into it. She was a good egg, we can do right by her."

"Well . . . uh . . ." Derner hesitated. He'd be thinking about the money it would cost. The night's takings from just one of the slot machines in the Nightcrawler's back room would pay for a nice service. If necessary, I'd point that out to him. "What about Alan Caine?"

"See if he's got family, then ship him out. Jewel wouldn't want to share the billing."

I hung up, then dialed a number I'd scribbled in pencil on my shirt cuff the night before. There was a delay as I negotiated with a hotel switchboard operator, then Bobbi's voice came on.

"It's me," I said again, but my tone was a lot warmer. "You okay?"

"Are you?" she countered.

"I am now, sweetheart."

"Anything wrong?"

"All the time," I said cheerfully. "But I'm taking care of it."

Bobbi required a lot more convincing than Derner, and such convincing would require us to be in the same room so I could give her a hands-on demonstration. Hands, lips, skin to skin, I was more than ready to show her exactly how well I was doing. I was a little nervous about it, but it beat the previous mind-freezing terror I'd felt before. Escott's version of a pep talk had sorted out a lot of things.

I owed him, all right.

And . . . Bobbi didn't know about the fight yet, or she'd have—

"I'm glad you're better," she said shortly. "Now what the hell happened to Charles?"

Oh.

Damn.

Damn, damn, damn, *damn.*

Given a choice, I'd rather have Coldfield come back and make me into a sparring dummy for a few hours instead of trying to explain things to her. "Uh, we had a disagreement that got out of hand."

"Disagreement?" Bobbi rarely shouted. As a singer, she thought it might damage her vocal cords, but this was an unequivocal shriek.

I winced. "Look, it's just something we got into, and it's over now. We're friends again."

"You put him in the HOSPITAL!"

"I know that, but—"

"You could have KILLED him!"

"Yeah, but—"

Bobbi made more loud and shrill observations about Escott's condition and my responsibility for it. I tried a placating tone when I could get a word in, then noticed Kroun had put his head around the corner. He'd shaved and resumed his damaged clothes and had his palms over his ears, letting me know he could hear her end all too well. I refused to be embarrassed about it.

"Let-her-talk," he whispered, exaggerating each word so I could read his lips.

I didn't have any better ideas, and it was obvious that Bobbi had been boiling for some time, so I shut up. She was staying at the same hotel with Gordy and his girlfriend, being watched over by Shoe Coldfield. He must have let her know a thing or three.

As before, I stood there and took it, and in some ways it hurt more than a physical beating. When she asked for the why of the matter, I fell back on the disagreement excuse.

"Why won't you tell me?" she demanded.

"Because it's not important anymore, and I know that sounds like a load of bull, but it's over now, it really is. I've apologized to him, and we're copacetic again."

She made a low growling noise, thick with dissatisfaction. Her protective soft spot for Escott was the size of the Grand Canyon. Perhaps he could persuade her to calm down. It struck me then that everyone had assumed I was the bad guy in the matter. Granted, I was still on my feet and a lot faster and stronger than Escott, but he did throw the first punch. A lot of them. But I'd thrown the last and most effective, so I was the bully. Those were the hard-cheese rules; I'd just have to live with them.

Kroun moved to the table to check the stuff I'd taken off his friend. He opened the cases, didn't seem surprised by the syringe, looked in the wallet, and tossed it back. He went through the contents of the money clips. Each had five twenties on top, and the rest were fifties and C-notes. I lost track as he counted through them, but at least nine or ten grand was there. He pocketed the fortune without a blink.

"Listen, Bobbi," I said, "we'll talk to Charles, and he'll let you know he's all right. We can visit Roland at the same time—and how is he doing?"

That subject change got me another earful, but not nearly

as harsh. She knew I wasn't to blame for Roland's wounding. Not too much, anyway.

Kroun picked up the car keys, tossing them high and catching them one-handed, showing impatience. Nice to know that he was so well recovered, but I still had more peacemaking to conduct with Bobbi and put my back to him. She'd cooled down somewhat, hopefully to the point where she wouldn't take my block off when we did get together. Kroun cleared his throat, coughed, and spat something into the sink. He ran water.

"What's that?" Bobbi asked.

"My guest from the party you threw last night."

"I thought he'd be gone."

"We still have some loose ends to tie up. It's going to take a while."

"The last visiting hour at the hospital starts at eight. I'll be there, then coming back to this hotel again."

"I'll go as fast as I can, but you know how it is."

"Yes, I certainly do." Dry tone from her, very dry. Ouch.

There was no way to end this one on her good side, so I offered a weak bye-I'll-see-you-soon and hung up. I waited to see if the phone rang with a fresh emergency, but it kept quiet.

"You ready?" Kroun asked. He'd wandered into the hall. He watched the prisoner, who still seemed to be out.

"Not yet. I need a new shirt."

"Make it quick, I need one more than you do."

A hot bath and shave would have been great, but the most I had time for was a fast swipe with a wet towel, then jump into a fresh suit. Not my best one, nor the worst, but it went with the thickening chin stubble. Maniac killers lurking in dark alleys might think twice about taking a swing at me; I was less sure about the mugs at the Nightcrawler Club.

When I came downstairs, the man was no longer tied to the banister post, and rope ends lay on the floor. What the . . . ?

Kroun was in the parlor, feet on the low table, reading a paper. "Don't worry," he said, not looking up. "I just put him in the car is all."

"You—?"

"Carried him out the door in front of God and everyone, yes, that's what I did. No one's made a commotion about it. You ready?"

I couldn't wait to get rid of him. Them.

I went to the hall closet, shrugged on one of my old overcoats, then to the kitchen to get my hat, a spare house key from one of the drawers, and the gun from Escott's coat. The roscoe the intruder brought was gone, so it figured that Kroun was armed, too. Double-armed, since he'd had a gun last night. He'd left the other effects on the table. I scooped them into a pocket, noting the bullet holes in the wall above the phone. Those would have to be patched before Escott came home.

It hardly seemed worth the effort to lock the house, but I went through the motions. Kroun handed over the car keys and got in on the passenger side. After the barest hesitation, he slammed the door shut. I slipped behind the wheel, adjusting the mirror.

"Where is he?" I asked. The backseat was empty of mobster.

"Trunk," said Kroun.

"He'll freeze."

"Only if we keep sitting here."

Taking the hint, I started the motor. I'd driven a Studebaker once before when working on a case, and afterward read magazine ads with close interest. The car was supposed to have a setup so that when stopped on a hill you didn't have to dance with the clutch, gas, and brake pedals to keep from rolling backward before it went into gear. As we were in a flat area, there was no opportunity to test things, but it was a sweet ride all the same. I hoped the guy in the trunk had air and not exhaust fumes to eat.

"Which hotel?" I asked Kroun.

"Hotel?"

"Where your stuff is."

"Skip that, take me to a men's store. A good one."

What the hell? "You're going buy stuff? It'll take all night."

"Not if it's a good store."

"Longer than getting the stuff at your hotel."

"Just find a place and give me ten minutes."

Son of a bitch. I wasn't interested in arguing, though, so I drove a few miles and pulled up to a clear stretch of curb. There were plenty to spare for a change since this part of the Loop didn't do much evening business.

Kroun got out, moving easily. During the day his bum leg had healed. He reached the store's door just as some guy inside locked it. Fine, like it or not, we would swing by his hotel instead.

When Kroun rapped the glass, the man shook his head and made an exaggerated shrug of apology. He probably didn't like the looks of this scruffy customer. He suddenly froze in place. For a second I thought Kroun had done an evil-eye whammy. The guy glanced over his shoulder then stared at Kroun or rather at something in his hand. Not a gun. Kroun had pulled out one of the money clips and waved several of the C-notes temptingly back and forth. A second guy joined the first and also froze, but only for a moment. The power of raw cash galvanized them, God bless America.

The door magically unlocked, and Kroun walked in like he owned the place. For all intents and purposes, he did. I marked the time to see if he'd make his ten minutes, then quit the car, going around to the trunk. The other key on the ring opened it.

There weren't a lot of pedestrians, and they were in a hurry to get out of the cold wind whipping around the buildings. Privacy secured, I lifted the trunk lid to check on the guy. He was curled on his side facing away from me, hands tied behind him, not looking any too comfortable. He stirred a little, his movements groggy and uncertain.

I adjusted his gag so nothing covered his nose. He jerked at the touch. "Easy does it, pal. You breathing okay?"

He *mumph*ed something, pissed. Couldn't blame him.

"Glad to hear it. Want to tell me where your partner is?"

The next *mumph* I interpreted as cussing rather than anything cooperative.

"I'm betting he's at my nightclub. Want to put something on that?"

More cussing, and he started fighting against the ropes.

I slammed the lid quick as a group of office girls scurried past; a few of them giggled as I tipped my hat at them, nonchalant as Fred Astaire pretending to be a bum.

Someone had pulled the store's shades down for the night, but the lights remained on. I strolled slow up and down the walk to stay limber and kept my ears open for noises from the car trunk. If the guy drew attention, I'd have to clock him again. He didn't, so I walked and checked my watch.

This was ridiculous, of course. The other night I'd tried to make myself permanently dead, and when that hadn't worked out, I'd planned for a second, more extreme effort that would have succeeded. Right now I should have been on a slab in a morgue, not standing in freezing wind outside a store waiting while some lunatic bought himself a suit.

And yet, here I was . . . and, strangely, it was all right.

Which had to make *me* the lunatic.

I'd read stories about suicides, and knew of some who had gone through with it, and at the time the thought was *what a waste*, felt a little sadness, and that was pretty much it. Not until I saw the blind fury on Escott's face did I consider its harsh effect on other people concerned, the ones close to the victim. There was no understanding or forgiveness for my actions, no shred of sympathy, as I'd expected. He'd accused me of being a selfish bastard for doing that to Bobbi, to him, to everyone who gave a tinker's damn about me. He was right. It wasn't only about my pain. It was the pain my hurting myself would give them. Better to just spit in their eyes and walk away with no explanation. Only I hadn't had the guts to do that—or the guts to ask for help.

So, I had indeed been a selfish, cowardly bastard.

Wincing, I silently added in *stupid* at the beginning of the list. I should have it printed for a sign and nail it to the wall over my bed. The idea would be to do my best to disagree with it each night when I woke up.

Would Escott remember my hospital visit? Would he believe me when I told him I was better? What I'd done had left scars on us both. It had changed things. For good or for bad, the change would always be there.

We'd just have to deal with it. The deed was done, and I'd have to live with the consequences.

That—or spit in his eye.

I shook my head. No. I wouldn't be traveling that road. He'd once crawled out of his own private abyss. I could do the same.

In nine minutes, Kroun emerged, looking a new man entirely in a sharp dark suit and polished shoes. When I first met him, he had a way of filling a room all by himself. People noticed it; men stood up straighter, and women leaned closer when he walked past. It had faded with the explosion and shooting, but that quality was back in spades. The hired help must have responded, for he was getting royal treatment.

He buttoned up a heavy wool overcoat and pulled on leather gloves. One of the shop guys clipped the tag from a charcoal gray fedora and handed it over with a slight bow and broad smile. They moved out of the way for three guys rushing past with arms full of boxes. I obligingly held the car door as they took turns shoving everything into the backseat. Last to go in were two suitcases wedged on top, blocking the window.

Kroun politely thanked everyone, tipped them each a twenty, which was twice what they earned in a week, and got in the car. They enthusiastically thanked him, adding invitations to come back whenever he liked, day or night.

I got in and turned the motor over. He checked his new silver wristwatch. "Ten minutes, if this thing is right."

It looked too expensive ever to be wrong.

"Now *that's* how you buy stuff," he said, satisfied.

"Oh yeah?"

"Let them do the work. They know the territory."

"What about mirrors?" Those were the main reason I got clothes only after a store was closed. It was easier than hypnotizing the whole staff—which was no longer an option anyway. I just slipped in, picked what I wanted, and left money in the manager's office along with the tags. Unlawful entry I was good at, but I wasn't a thief.

"I just stripped and had them dress me from the skin out. Ben Franklins make it go fast. How do I look?"

He was in blacks and charcoals, with a faint pinstripe on the suit, his white shirt nearly glowing in contrast to a midnight blue silk tie. "Like a mob undertaker."

Kroun settled the fedora at a rakish angle. "Let's go arrange some services, then."

"The other guy's probably waiting at my club."

He gestured for me to proceed.

There was traffic, as always, so it took some time to get there. If the man in the trunk hadn't tried to knock me off, I'd have felt sorry for him.

Not long for him now, though. I circled Lady Crymsyn's block, alert to lurking toughs. Neither of us spotted the prisoner's buddy.

"Think he's inside?" I asked.

"Count on it," said Kroun.

No point in asking why his bunch was so allergic to an ordinary invited entry after a polite knock; he wouldn't understand the question.

I pulled into my reserved spot in the parking lot next to the club. Damn, this Studie drove smooth, but I wasn't ready to give up my Buick yet. It had gone into the shop for new tires, then some eager beaver decided to put in some extra work. I'd made it clear to Derner—who only thought he was doing me a favor—that I didn't want solid-rubber tires, armor plating, and bulletproof glass added on. It was a *Buick*, for God's sake.

Just as I set the hand brake another car suddenly bounced into the lot and stopped directly behind us, blocking our escape.

Kroun and I went alert at the same instant. I didn't want to be trapped and piled out on my side, turning to face the threat. Kroun mirrored me, hand dipping to his overcoat pocket. I resisted the urge to go for my own gun, having the luxury of vanishing if need be.

Then I saw the kind of antenna on the other car and recognized the driver. "Nothing to worry," I called across the car roof to Kroun. "It's just the cops. Relax."

He muttered so that only I'd be able to hear. "Relax? You kidding?"

"Nothing to worry," I repeated.

"Body in the trunk," he reminded.

"*Relax*, dammit."

I shut the door and sauntered toward the Studie's back fender. Watching, Kroun stayed put, but took his hand from his pocket. His shoulders eased down.

The two men got out of their unmarked car, standing in place long enough to give us plenty of time to recall and sweat over our most recent sins. Even an innocent person has that reaction when getting the eye from a cop. They do it to people on purpose. I've seen it. It goes together with the fact that a cop can say "come with me," and you have to go. I usually didn't have a problem with that so long as it wasn't aimed my way.

I remembered the driver from last night; he'd asked a lot of questions about Roland Lambert's shooting. Sergeant something-or-other. He must not have been happy with my distracted answers, and it was a cinch he didn't believe any of Roland's malarkey.

"Hello, Sergeant . . . uh . . ." I tried, but just couldn't pull his name from my mental hat. He was a tough-looking son of a bitch; I usually remembered that type out of self-preservation.

"Merrifield," he provided, apparently unoffended. "I'd like to talk to you, Mr. Fleming."

I rated a "mister"? Maybe that was to put me off guard, but the way they'd rolled in so fast was not reassuring. They must have been parked up the block on the lookout for any activity at the club. "No problem, what about?"

"How about we go inside?"

If there was a mug waiting to ambush me in the club, he might get nervous and shoot everyone. "Out here's fine."

Merrifield didn't like that answer but wasn't going to press. His partner eyeballed Kroun, who had somehow toned his personal magnetism down to show only a poker-bland face. "Who's your pal?"

"Old friend from out of town."

"What's his business?"

"Just visiting. What's it to you?"

"You got a lot of junk in the back, what is that stuff?"

"His luggage, see the suitcases? C'mon, Sergeant, what's the deal? You got some real questions, I'll be glad to answer 'em." I hoped he didn't want to look in the trunk. I doubly hoped the guy stashed there kept quiet. Maybe he'd heard me and knew there were cops at hand. In his line of work, they were the common enemy.

Merrifield wanted the story behind Roland Lambert's shooting. Again. I gave him everything I knew except the names of the shooters. "I didn't see them, they went by too fast."

"And why were they shooting at you?"

He got a reprise of last night's song and dance of useless information. "I wish I could help you, but that's all there is. I'm just glad nothing worse happened."

"Actually, it did."

I felt a sharp internal jab of fear, thinking some new catastrophe had surfaced, but Merrifield only wanted more about Alan Caine's murder. That was a relief, just not much of one.

He knew I'd been at the Nightcrawler where Caine was last seen alive. I confirmed that and again told him Caine had skipped out on the second show. The backstage talk was he'd claimed sickness and left, which I repeated.

"The guy was a real ass," I said. "Anyone could have gunned him down."

"He was strangled."

"Damn papers never get anything right." One of them had indeed swapped the facts, claiming Caine was shot and his ex-wife Jewel was strangled.

"Then what is the right story?"

"You're asking the wrong guy." I wanted to put him straight about Jewel's not killing herself, but you can't say something like that and not have to explain the why and how of it.

"Where were you when Northside Gordy's car blew up?" he asked.

"In my club minding my own business."

"What are you doing being such good pals with a mug like Gordy?"

"You know, my granny asks me that every Sunday after church. I'm still trying to figure it out."

Merrifield was the patient sort. Usually my lip would have me in more trouble by now. "We know you've been running the show for him lately. You were at the Night-crawler for Caine's swan song, and you were sniffing around that little dancer he was cozy with. Then Gordy's car blows up, Lambert's shot, your limey Sherlock pal lands in the hospital, and two mugs associated with the Northside gang have their heads bashed in . . . shall I go on?"

"What mugs?" I thought I sounded convincing.

"You know them. We've talked to people, and the one connection they've given for all of it is *you*, Fleming . . . you're up to your eyebrows and sinking. Either you're doing this for Gordy or covering up for him while he does the dirty work. He'll hang you out to dry when he's done, too. Don't think he won't. Where is he?"

"Taking a vacation. I heard he's got a girlfriend keeping him busy."

"I'll bet he has. Why have you got a bounty out for Hurley Gilbert Dugan?"

He caught me by surprise. Only the guys in the mob were supposed to know about that. The cops had plenty of stoolies, though. "I was just doing my part as a concerned citizen by putting up a reward. Dugan kidnapped that poor girl, murdered those people—don't you think he should be off the street? Anyway, I withdrew it."

"Why? Is he dead?"

"Not that I know, but I wouldn't be sorry if he was."

"If he is, we'll talk to you about it first."

"I can't help you. He's probably dusted out of town for Timbuktu by now. Sweat those mugs who helped him out. They still locked up, or did a fancy lawyer spring them so they could disappear, too?"

Merrifield looked ready to shove my nose to a different part of my face. "Who's this bird again?" He jerked his chin in Kroun's direction.

"An old buddy from the army. We used to loaf in a bar and play footsie under the table, but don't tell his wife."

Kroun shrugged modestly at the other cop. "What can I say, he's crazy about me."

"Oh, yeah, real cute," said Merrifield. "I've had enough. Fleming, you and him get in the car. You can hold hands on the way to the station."

"You charging me with something?"

"No, I'm throwing a tea party so you can give me all the gossip. Come on." He took my arm, and I stifled the urge to pull away, or he'd say it was resisting arrest. I'd spend the night in the tank with the drunks. If I was lucky. "Garza . . ." he called to his partner.

But Garza was busy talking with Kroun. Listening, rather. Listening hard. Kroun had him fixed in place and was speaking low and intense. The wind carried away his words. Garza's face was blank, his jaw beginning to sag.

It was creepy seeing the process from the outside, and I wondered if I'd looked like that when doing my evil-eye parlor trick.

I had learned fast to rely on it, respect its power over others, and finally to fear it. Use it again, and the internal explosion would punch my ticket fast enough. But I'd gotten on without the talent for thirty-six years prior to my death and return; I could do all right in the future.

So long as I avoided situations like this, dammit.

"Garza!" snapped Merrifield. He still had my arm and drew me around as he turned.

Kroun kept up the patter for a few more words, probably telling Garza to stay put, then swung his gaze on Merrifield.

It was the reverse of a searchlight. Instead of a bright beam blinding you, it was like getting sucked into a hell pit of pure darkness. You were just as blind and falling, to boot.

I felt the dizzying tug like a physical force. That was wrong. I should have been immune to the influence of another vampire. If he'd thrown that directly at me, I'd have gone under the same as any human. I stepped back and to the side, as though to get clear of his range of fire.

Merrifield stopped in his tracks, not moving as Kroun stalked closer.

God, his eyes were unnerving. I'd seen them like that the night before when he'd taken aim at Mitchell, ready to kill. Kroun's soul was gone, well and truly gone.

In the vacated space I glimpsed something looking out from inside that made my flesh crawl. Sit in a pitch-black room, hear a noise, and ask "Who's there?" and of course there's no answer. What was behind Kroun's eyes was the thing that stands quiet and unseen just a few inches in front of you, aware of your growing fear, not answering your question.

Waiting.

It looked at me, blinked, and suddenly Kroun was back. Just that quick.

I'd not imagined it. I wanted to think so, but it *had* been there, and I was certain he was unaware of what was inside him.

Was it just him, or were we *all* like that?

Merrifield got back in his car, not saying anything or even seeming to notice me. Garza followed. The motor caught and rumbled, coughing when Merrifield shifted gears and backed out of the lot. Another metallic cough, and they drove off, blending with the rest of the traffic.

"Nice friends you've got," said Kroun.

"What'd you tell him?" I asked, voice faint.

"Didn't you hear?"

"Wind in my ears." Which was partly true. It had kicked up a lot and was colder than before. I'd been too spooked to hear. Was still spooked.

"I told him you couldn't help with his case, and he should go looking for a guy named Hoyle since he did all the killings. That was the one who helped Mitch, right?"

"Yeah." I didn't like thinking of Hoyle. I get that way about people who are shot right in front of me. The aftermath of his death had been even worse, and I wasn't going to think about that either.

Kroun lifted his hat and brushed a hand along the left side of his head, grimacing.

"You okay?" I said.

"Huh?"

"Does it give you a headache? What you did to them?"

"The eye-to-eye gag? As much as anything else. I can't take aspirin for it, either."

"Crush the pills up and mix them with blood."

"Really?" He seemed perfectly normal, wholly unaware of his quiet passenger. Not much I could do about it. He wouldn't believe me if I mentioned what I'd seen.

"Couldn't hurt to try."

He settled his hat into place. "C'mon, let's get this over with."

The front of the club was dark, but lights showed through

the windows. My sign about being temporarily closed was still in place, barely. The wind and damp were having their way with the cardboard, and it would tear free before the night was out. Standing so I wouldn't be framed in the opening, I cautiously opened the door, letting it swing inward.

"Not too smart of him," Kroun observed. "He should have relocked it after breaking in."

"That's my doing. We left so fast the other night I forgot."

"Huh. Hope you said good-bye to all your booze, it'll be gone by now."

Maybe.

"Why would he put the lights on?" Kroun asked. "He might as well have a brass band announce he's here."

"That's Myrna."

"Who's she? Cleaning lady? You got someone in there?"

"No nothing like that." I doubted Kroun was ready to meet the club's resident ghost. Myrna had been a bartender killed during a gang war some years back. She liked to play with the lights. The fact that the place was blazing like New Year's Eve was meant as a warning to me.

"You first," said Kroun, gesturing, very polite.

"Why me?"

"You got the vanishing trick. Check the place out. Find him."

"You know who he is?"

"I think so. The guy in the trunk usually travels with a mug named Broder. Muscle. He's big and a lot faster than you'd think—"

"I'm glad to hear it, but I'm not going rounds with him."

"You might if you surprise him the wrong way."

"I'm not surprising him at all. The only reason they want to kill me is because they think you're dead. He knows you, just go in and tell him to lay off."

"Oh." He seemed nonplussed about the reminder. "Yeah. I'll do that then."

I held back, and he went first, calling Broder's name and identifying himself. After a few long minutes he returned.

"Copacetic."

"Sure?"

"Yeah."

I wasn't so confident, but followed him in.

Broder was damn near as big as Gordy and didn't look nearly as friendly and gregarious. I'd have tagged him for a wrestler, but he lacked the thick paunch around the middle most of them had. Football, then, and his teammates would nickname him "Bulldozer." He looked more maneuverable and a lot harder to knock over. He regarded me with hooded, unfriendly brown eyes.

"Broder," said Kroun, "this is Jack Fleming, the guy you're not going to kill after all."

Broder grunted; his voice box must have originally been dug out of the ground somewhere and replanted in him, the tone was that deep. He didn't offer to shake hands, and I was glad of it.

"Okay, that was nice," said Kroun, who could see this was as chummy as we'd ever get. "Fleming, if you'd bring in the last member of the party, we can finish this up."

At the mention of the other guy, I was sure Broder growled. It was so low it might have been the rumble of a diesel engine from two streets over.

The light behind the bar flickered. Myrna was letting me know she was on watch. Kroun and Broder both looked at it.

"You should change that bulb," Kroun said.

"I'll make a note," I said, and went outside.

The wind had a nasty bite. I rarely noticed the cold, which meant it must be a really bad night for regular folks. Because of it, I expected the man in the trunk to be half-frozen and in need of a blanket and something hot to drink.

I expected, but didn't count on it, and drew my gun as I lifted the lid.

Good thing, too. He came out swinging. He'd gotten free of the ropes and had a tire iron in one hand and a long screwdriver in the other. I jumped back as he lashed hard with the iron in a lethal backhand. He missed breaking my knee by a gnat's whisker.

"Hey!" I yelled, which didn't do a damn bit of good. He boiled out, staggered for balance, then went for me, mad as spit. I moved a lot faster to get clear. He was too far gone to notice the gun. When he did see it, he made a determined swipe with the screwdriver.

Damn. I couldn't tell if he was nuts for real or gambling I wouldn't shoot. A gun's only good if you intend to use it.

He had me there. Time to cheat. I pocketed the revolver, ducked around the bulk of the car, and vanished. Almost immediately I reversed, knowing he'd been right after me.

Yeah. He was just *there*, probably realizing I wasn't where I should have been. He hesitated a second, which was all I needed to get behind him. Reappearing, I put him in a full nelson. He was no shrimp, but I had a supernatural edge in strength. I aimed sideways toward the building and launched us against it—only I vanished an instant before impact. Momentum did the rest.

He hit it pretty hard, to judge by the thump and grunt. I went solid. He'd lost the screwdriver and was wheezing, having had his breath knocked out. I dipped in before he could recover and plucked the tire iron away. He started for me again, but his energy was gone. I sidestepped like a matador and grabbed the back of his coat collar as he passed, hauling him around so he fell forward across the hood of the car.

"Settle down, pal, we're just going to talk," I said, catching and twisting one arm behind him.

"Go to hell," he puffed, struggling.

I pushed until his face was mashed against the metal and lifted his arm a few notches. Any more would break or dislocate it depending on where I put the pressure. He still struggled. "I've already been there, thanks to you and Hog Bristow."

At that name, and the emphasis I placed on it, he paused.

"We *talk*," I said quietly. "And maybe have a drink. You wanna get out of the cold?"

He thought it over, then nodded. I let him up easy, ready for another round. He rubbed his arm instead, his gaze sharp. "This is your club."

That was a quick recovery. He knew how to land on his feet. "Broder's waiting for you."

His eyes flickered. How did I know the name? Then he figured it out. "Where is he?"

"In the bar. Great guy. I want him to meet my sister."

That got me the kind of glare I was used to; nobody likes a wiseacre. "Is he all right?"

"Just peachy," I said, mimicking Kroun. "C'mon and see for yourself."

I tossed the iron and screwdriver in the trunk, slammed the lid, and walked toward the front of the club. The man followed, alert to trouble. His hand went to the inside of his coat, a familiar gesture for those used to a shoulder rig. He'd certainly know his gun was gone; it was an unconscious habit, like looking at your wrist whether the watch is there or not.

I opened the door to Lady Crymsyn and motioned him in. He gave me a fierce once-over. In the brighter light, his eyes were a very startling blue, like honest-to-God sapphires. I'd have to keep him away from Bobbi. She had a weakness for blue-eyed guys. Those peepers and the film-star looks could keel her over.

He stepped in and halted. The club's décor was impressive: black and white marble, chrome trim, a high ceiling, and enough red to justify the name. Over the entry to the main room hung the larger-than-life portrait of Lady Crymsyn herself. She didn't really exist, but a lot of men wanted her phone number all the same.

My new guest was focused elsewhere, gaping and suddenly white-faced at the sight of a nonchalant Kroun standing next to the bar. "Gabriel," he whispered. "Son of a bitch."

"You keep my mother out of this, Michael," said Kroun, without humor.

I glanced speculatively at Broder. If his first name was Raphael, we could move this to a church soup kitchen and have a quick prayer service.

He glared back, and I thought better about asking.

4

THIS bunch did not indulge in a tearful reunion over Kroun's miraculous return from the grave. Not that I expected anything in even distant view of the maudlin, but maybe at least a handshake traded between acquaintances. Michael had been willing to kill me over Kroun, after all, but that business must have been more to do with restoration of mob honor than revenge for the mobster himself.

Michael got over enough of his shock to speak. "What the hell happened to you?"

Kroun leaned against one end of the lobby bar, Broder anchored himself solidly at the other, and Michael stood slightly distanced, able to see them both. Occasionally, his gaze cut to me, but without hostility, just including me in the proceedings. He didn't have to bother; this was their business, not mine.

While Kroun related his escape from the jaws of death, I eased past Broder and checked behind the bar. Everything was normal, not a bottle out of place. Despite the unlocked front door, no one had burgled the joint, and I didn't think it was just good luck. Maybe I needed to thank Myrna for looking after things. She was quite a good guardian angel.

I noticed I stood on the permanently stained tile that marked the spot where she'd bled to death. No matter that the tile had been replaced several times, the stain just kept reappearing. I moved off it.

Broder watched me as though I might plan to slip arsenic into the gin and offer him the bottle.

"Like anything?" I asked.

"No."

That earthquake-deep growl would take getting used to, and I'd had more than my share of experience at dealing with intimidating types. He shifted his attention back to Kroun, and though his face was impassive, Broder's body was tense. From the look in his eyes, I got the idea that he actively hated the man.

"*Mitch?*" said Michael, all stunned disbelief. His reaction looked and sounded sincere, which meant he'd not believed anything I'd said back at the house. "But Mitch was—why the hell would he take the chance?"

Kroun did more explaining about his homicidal henchman. I wondered when he'd get around to hypnotizing them so they'd go on their merry way. I had to get to the hospital before visiting hours ended.

"Why didn't you call me, send a telegram?" Michael wanted to know.

Kroun explained that as well. He'd shrugged from his coat, placing it and the new fedora carefully on the bar, and eased onto one of the stools as though we had all night. I concentrated on being invisible without actually disappearing. The other two remained in place, sponging up his every word. He made it sound plausible. Hell, I knew the real story, and he had me believing the eyewash.

But Michael didn't like what he heard. "We came all the way out here, nearly killed *him*"—he jerked a thumb at me—"and that's *it*?"

"It's enough," said Kroun. "Don't go blaming Fleming, either. I told him to keep shut until I knew the score."

Told, I thought. Nicely chosen, having it seem like I was one of the boys following orders the same as any other soldier in their line of work. Fine, whatever it took to get rid of these two.

Counting Kroun, make that three.

He continued. "Fleming's off the hook for my murder and whatever else you can think up. Call Derner, tell him everything's squared, and take the next train back, we're done."

"They still made a try for you. I can't let that pass."

"There is no 'they.' Mitch was my man, and Hoyle was already on the outs here. No one else is responsible for their shenanigans. I know that, the question is why you can't get it through your thick skull."

Michael's eyes sparked and narrowed. Broder shifted.

Kroun didn't seem to notice. "C'mon, Mike. If it'll make you feel better, sock Fleming in the jaw a few times, call it payback, and have done already."

It wouldn't have hurt me much, but that wasn't going to happen this side of hell. Michael didn't bother looking my way, just shook his head at Kroun.

"Okay," he said. "I get it. Mitch was a bad apple, he's gone—and you're ready to forgive and forget?"

"Yeah."

"That's not like you."

"What can I say? People change."

"Sure they do. See it all the time."

I'd long picked up on a deeper tension between them. Though Kroun was one of Michael's people, he behaved like the man in control. Michael made him work for it, though. Come to think of it, Michael could have been disappointed about Kroun's surviving.

"Maybe good old Mitch was acting on *his* orders," I said to Kroun. Not smart of me to provoke a fight, but I wanted him to start convincing these guys to leave.

He turned my way. "Ya think? What about it, Michael? You want my job?"

"Go to hell." Michael's reaction was instant, right on the surface. He made no effort to mask his disgust.

Kroun's relaxed expression remained the same, but he went utterly still. His friend had crossed a line. Maybe they both had. Oh, crap. Kroun was armed. If his eyes got empty again, I'd have to try and stop him. This was my place, and it had seen enough blood.

Myrna must have agreed. All the lights suddenly flickered, dimming, but not quite going out. This went on for maybe ten long seconds, then they steadied up normal again. It successfully broke the mood, creating a new one.

Michael snapped around at me, suspicious.

"Electrical short," I explained.

"Who else is here?"

"Nobody but us chickens."

He didn't believe me. "Broder."

Broder nodded, pulled out a revolver big enough to stop a charging rhino with one shot, and headed toward the main room. The curving hall leading into it was dark.

"Wait," I said.

He paused.

"You might need this." I tossed him a flashlight. There were a dozen of them scattered throughout the club, Myrna was that playful. He caught it one-handed, neat and solid. "But it's just a short. Electric panel's over there." I pointed to a spot on the wall next to the lobby phone booth. The utility was hidden by a red velvet curtain. Michael crossed to check on it, then motioned for Broder to continue. His footsteps faded.

It got quiet enough that I could hear Michael's heartbeat. A little fast. He shouldn't be so nervous.

"Drink?" I suggested.

"No, thank you."

"At least a short beer." I drew one and put it on the bar.

"You gotta be thirsty after that trunk business, which I'm sorry about, by the way."

His focus shifted from Kroun, finally, and he came over for the beer. "You got some nerve."

"That part was my doing," said Kroun.

Damn. I wanted him to shut up so I could keep his pal's attention divided. Kroun seemed hell-bent on thinking up new ways to be fatally irritating.

Michael downed half the beer. Booze would have been better for such a cold night, but he didn't strike me as one who went for the hard stuff. I'd hung out in my share of dives and had learned a little about other drinkers.

"I got your stuff," I said. I pulled out the spoils I'd taken from him, spreading them on the counter.

He went first for the glasses case, opened it, and put them on. The gold wire-rims reflected the lights, making it harder to see his eyes. He looked less like a film star and more like the kind of brainy guy who lived in the college library. Neither image was in keeping with the reality that he was a big wheel in the New York mob.

He checked the wallet, put it away, then gave me a hard stare, mitigated quite a lot by the specs. It was difficult to take him seriously while he had those on.

"What?" I asked.

"The money," he said with a pronounced frown.

Money? Oh.

"I've got it," said Kroun, casually. He was messing with his handkerchief, his attention wholly on it. He shook open and refolded it so four points spilled over the top of his breast pocket like a tired flower.

"Hand it back," said Michael.

"Hm . . ." Kroun pretended to think, then shook his head. "No."

"That's my money, dammit."

"You found where I hid it in my hotel room. I recognize the clips. Next time I'll trust it to a safe."

"I thought you were—"

"Dead? That's a good reason to take it. I forgive you."

"One of those is mine."

"Huh. You're right." Kroun searched, produced the cash, and removed the money, tossing the empty clip to Michael.

He caught it reflexively, scowling. "Funny."

"You can spare it. You must own a bank or three by now. I bet you've made more in the last ten minutes than most guys see in a lifetime."

Glowering, Michael finished his beer and turned down my offer for a second. I washed the mug, stacking it with the others under the counter, just your friendly neighborhood barkeep.

We all jumped when something big crashed in the next room. I recognized the sound: chairs clattering, hitting the floor, lots of them. Kroun's hand went to his pocket, but he glanced at me. I shook my head to signal "don't worry" and he eased off, doubtful.

Michael was just to the curved entry hall when Broder appeared, nearly running into him. For a big guy he had speed, but he hauled up short, as though he'd been caught in an embarrassing act.

"What is it?" Michael demanded.

Broder scowled. He was good at that. "Nothing."

No one bought it.

"The lights were out," he went on. "I bumped a table in the dark. Knocked things over. The batteries are dead." He threw the flashlight. I caught it less neatly than he had earlier but spared the bottles behind me from breakage.

Under the counter, I clicked the light's button. The thing worked just fine now. It would be unwise to point that out to anyone, so I quietly put it away. Myrna was expanding her activities. What a gal.

"Find anything?" asked Michael.

Broder holstered his cannon. "A lot of dark. Heat's off back there. Cold as hell." For all that, he was sweating, a sheen covered his broad face, and beads gathered at his temples. The heating was the same throughout the building. I'd not turned it down. He had a tan similar to Michael's, but under it, his skin had gone muddy. When he approached the bar, I tried catching a whiff of his scent and was rewarded with the unmistakable tang of fear.

Looked like Myrna had found a new playmate for the evening. What had she done? Maybe it was better not to know. I poured Broder a whiskey without being asked, and this time he accepted, downing it quick.

"You okay?" I asked.

That got me a suspicious look; he knew I knew something about what had spooked him. "I am fine."

"Are we done here?" Kroun asked.

"Yes," Michael said shortly. "There's a late train back to New York tonight—"

"Enjoy the trip."

Michael visibly steamed. "You're coming, too."

"Uh-uh. I've got unfinished business."

What the hell? The three of us glared at him, waiting for the rest. Kroun spread the handkerchief out flat, refolded, and tucked it back so two neat triangles showed over the pocket.

"Which one's better?" he asked. "This or the other way?"

"Like that," I said. "What unfinished business?"

"Don't get your feelings hurt, but I had other things to do out here besides bumping you off." He flicked at his pocket with one finger. "You sure? I liked the other way."

"So do floorwalkers. What other things?"

"A floorwalker? Nah . . . not in *this* suit."

"Whitey," said Michael. "We're going back to New York. You don't have any more business here."

"Actually, I do. It's none of *your* business, and it's going to take a while, so don't expect me back any too soon."

Michael's tanned face went muddy like Broder's. "No. We're all leaving. Don't cross me on this."

"Come on, Mike. I nearly got blown to perdition and back, then had to put Mitch down like a rabid dog. I'm taking a rest. You've got guys who can fill in for me."

"No."

"I'll hang around here, see a few shows, maybe do some fishing—"

"*No!*" There was angry force behind that, far more than the situation warranted. Not knowing Michael, I couldn't tell for sure, but his anger was covering up something else. It was . . . fear. No such vulnerability showed on his face, but I could smell it. I remembered a moment when, with no small shock, I realized that Gordy was afraid of Kroun. Gordy didn't know about the vampire angle; it had been fear of the man himself. He and Michael had that in common. So, why were they afraid of him, and should I be worried?

Kroun's eyes were darker than before. His voice remained low and level and deadly patient. This was Whitey Kroun, not the more affable Gabe. "I'm not getting on that train. If I go back to New York, who's to say the next guy I run into won't try to finish what Mitch started? No, thanks. I'm staying here until you've done some housecleaning."

Michael recovered his self-control. Quickly. Throwing his weight around wouldn't work. His tone shifted, became the reasonable one of a man willing to compromise. "Okay . . . come and help me, then. Only you know who you've pissed off lately."

Kroun barked a short laugh. "That would be everyone."

"I'll make sure you're protected. No one's getting another chance at you. I guarantee that."

"Thanks very much, but I'm staying—until further notice."

Michael's hand twitched, reminding me of the gun no longer under his coat. Broder didn't make a move, just watched and listened. Apparently he'd seen this kind of thing before. I tried to read him for a clue as to how it might end, but would have had better luck with a brick wall.

"It's the old bastard, isn't it?" Michael asked. "You're here to see him."

"Yeah," Kroun admitted, after a moment.

"It's no good, he's crazy, you'll only stir him up. Stay away from him."

Kroun made no reply. Making an effort, I kept my yap shut, wanting to know more.

Michael glanced at Broder, who did not react.

Kroun poked at the handkerchief, pulling it out again. A quick refold and he put it back, this time showing a razor-thin edge of white. He looked at me for an opinion. I gave a thumbs-up.

"I'm gonna look up an old friend or two," he said. "No one you'd know."

"And do what?"

"None of your damn business, kid. I'm not repeating myself."

"Whitey—"

"Mike." Kroun raised one hand in a sharp "back off" gesture and met his gaze square and granite-hard. "Enough."

Silence stretched, but not to a breaking point, and the lights remained steady. Michael continued, body tense, but his voice was calm. "All right, fine. But since you're worried about people taking potshots, you'll have to have a bodyguard. Someone who will be the first person I hold responsible if anything goes wrong."

"Not him," Kroun nodded at Broder, who again did not react.

"No problem." Michael looked at me. "He'll do."

"Forget it," I said instantly.

"I can take care of myself," Kroun said.

Michael's mouth tightened, not in a smile. "You've got a point about being a target. Anything happens to you again, and I break this town like an egg—and Fleming knows it. You've vouched for him plenty tonight. He'll bust heads to keep you safe."

I'd also be motivated to get Kroun to leave as soon as possible. That might not be in keeping with his plan to retire from the business. I threw him an expectant look. Now was the time to put them both under and make them leave.

"Cripes," Kroun muttered.

"It's him, or Broder and I tag along."

"Go ahead," I put in. "I don't want the job."

"Gee, thanks," said Kroun.

"You can get out of this," I reminded, knowing he'd catch the meaning.

He shook his head once, surprising me.

"Come on . . ."

"No. Drop it."

Damn him. The crazy son of a gun wasn't going to do it. I snorted, turning to Michael, framing an appeal. "Look—"

Kroun broke in. "Won't work, Fleming. He's made up his mind. I know what that means, you might as well learn it now."

I already did and didn't like it. He *could* force a change in Michael's views, but it wouldn't stick. Depending on how strongly a person felt, the hypnosis might last for weeks or just a day or so. It was worth the effort to me, though. However difficult to influence, once Michael and Broder were on their way out of town, they might think twice about coming back again.

Yeah, sure.

I'm often a victim of my own optimism.

"It's just for a couple days," Kroun went on. To him I was hands down the lesser of two evils, giving him good reason to cave in so fast. "This place is closed, what else have you got to do?"

"Plenty," I said.

If I'd been *asked* instead of appointed, it would have been different. I'd been my own boss too long to go back to being pushed around by a bunch of murdering bastards. Yes, I was one myself by now, but . . . they all looked at me, hostility, assured expectation, and cynical resignation parceled out between them.

Oh, what the hell. I wanted to keep an eye on Kroun anyway.

He read my face easily enough. "That's settled. When's that train leaving?"

"Never mind the train." Michael held his glasses up to the

light. He rubbed at a lens with the end of his tie. "Broder and I are staying in town."

"Why?"

"None of *your* damn business."

"You want to see how it turns out with the old bastard."

"Among other things."

God, were they going to start up all over again?

"Fleming watches you, Broder and I watch Fleming. Everyone's happy."

Except Fleming, I thought.

"You—" Michael pointed at me, then gestured me over to the side.

I hated being ordered around by anyone, especially in my own place, but put up with it in the interest of getting them out more quickly. From the signs, Michael wanted an off-the-record talk. He couldn't know that Kroun would be able to hear it from across the room.

"Yeah?" I said.

He put the glasses in their case and looked me up and down. "You understand how we do things?"

"I'm wise."

"We'll see. You look after Whitey, and when I ask about what he does, you will tell me."

"No problem." *Look after?* That was a funny way of saying it, like Kroun needed a keeper.

"Lie or leave anything out, I'll know about it."

Threats were easy to drop, but I had the feeling he was giving me a legitimate warning. "Okay. But tell me why you're so anxious to know what he's up to."

"You like him? Think he's a friend?"

"I like him. The jury's still out on the other." I didn't mind Kroun knowing that.

"Smart of you. It's okay to like him, but don't trust him even if he tells you the Pope's Catholic."

"Why?"

"He came here to kill you, and you have to ask?"

Good point.

"It takes a certain kind of man for such work. He's one of them."

"You, too. You were ready to pull the trigger on me."

"Yes, that's true." He tilted his head. "But I would have felt really, really bad about it."

"You'd have felt bad?"

"For a long time. Yeah."

He'd had me fooled.

"Whitey doesn't have a conscience, he never did. He's amusing, can be very charming in fact, but killing is no more to him than driving a car is to you."

"You're worried he'll kill someone while he's here?"

"I don't want him stirring up trouble."

"Who's he after?"

"I wouldn't know. You get a hint of it, you call me."

If he knew, he'd probably tell me, and my job would be easier, but that wasn't going to happen. Admitting his ignorance would be weakness, and he'd never show that to the hired help. I hated games. "Where you staying?"

"Whitey's hotel. Derner has the number. This is important, Mr. Fleming. Important." He looked almost comically intense.

Kroun had him on edge, and it would be stupid to dismiss that. I nodded.

"What I hear from the crowd at the Nightcrawler is you have scruples," he said. "You don't like it when people die."

"I'm old-fashioned that way."

"Good. You watch him, keep him out of trouble, keep him from *making* trouble. Do whatever it takes."

"What do you mean by that?"

"That—despite what I said about you being the first to get the blame—I guarantee there will be no reprisals."

What the hell? I went cold inside. "Oh, now, just a damn minute—"

"You don't know him or you wouldn't balk." Michael sent me a long, level stare. He was smart enough to see past my third-best clothes and chin stubble, reading that I was a cut above the usual mugs in his line. For all that, he'd still misjudged me, and I resented it.

This smelled to high heaven. It could well be another version of what I'd just avoided: Kroun gets bumped—preferably by someone expendable like myself—then they bump me. "Fill me in."

"Get him to tell you. He seems to like you. He just might. As I said, do whatever it takes to keep him in line. If his stay here is quiet, you won't have to do a thing. When he's ready to leave, Broder and I will go with him."

Sounded great, except for going against Kroun's plan to retire. If he wanted Michael to know, he'd have mentioned it by now. It wasn't my place to bring it up.

"This is business, Mr. Fleming," Michael added, with a meaning to the phrase that was familiar.

I'd heard it from Gordy enough times to get the message loud and clear. Great, someone else to be on guard against. What the hell, it couldn't hurt to pretend to go along with him.

Well. Actually, it could.

"We're done," Michael pronounced. He should have told me not to repeat this conversation to Kroun, but hadn't. Did that mean he trusted me to keep shut, or he didn't care if Kroun knew?

Damn, I hate games.

Kroun snorted, eased off the barstool, and pulled on his new coat and hat.

"What the hell is that?" asked Mike, gaze fixed on the fedora.

Kroun took it off, checking it carefully. "Looks like a hat. What are you seeing?"

"It's black."

"Charcoal gray," Kroun corrected, putting it on.

"You always get white."

"People change. I have mentioned that, I know I just did." He must have noticed my expression. "Right?"

I shrugged, wanting to stay clear. "Who wears white in the winter?"

Mike seemed puzzled. "Whitey does, always has. It's how he got the nickname."

"I thought it was from the—uh—" I made a vague gesture on the side of my head.

"A white hat," said Mike. "Always. Since he was a kid."

How far did these two go back?

"It's the end of an era," Kroun pronounced. "C'mon, Fleming, close the store."

The clothing talk reminded me of something. "Minute. I'll be right back." I started toward the curving hall.

Broder got in my way.

I looked at Michael.

"What is it?" he asked.

It is infuriating to have to get permission to walk around in one's own place. I really missed my hypnosis, for then I'd have had the two of them out in the street dancing a fox-trot till dawn.

Pain like red hot railroad spikes in both eyes, followed by my brain exploding . . . but maybe worth it.

"Business," I said, deadpan.

Michael waved dismissively, and Broder made a slow nod. He wasn't moving, so I had to go around him.

In his low rumble—not directed at me—he said, "He'll be fine."

It's amazing what you can infer when your mind's working right. Michael must have signaled to him to follow me, and Broder had refused. He wasn't about to take a second trip into the main room. It was creepily dark in there. I'd not bothered with the lights, nor taken a flashlight, and couldn't blame him for hanging back.

There was enough glow coming from the high, diamond-shaped windows for my eyes. One thing I noticed right away: every chair and table was in place. There was no sign of what caused the big crashing noise that had chased Broder out.

"Myrna . . . you're the pip," I said at a conversational level.

No response. Maybe she was tuckered out from all the fun.

I crossed the dance floor, hopped onto the stage, and passed through the wings to the dressing area. There I did flip a light switch, as it was quite black with no windows, and went into one of the rooms.

Some of my clothes lay on the floor where I'd dropped them. That night, the damage Bristow had done to me wasn't healing and seemed to be getting worse. I'd come here hurting and afraid and had tried to wash it off my soul in one of the showers. When that hadn't worked, I'd tried to kill myself.

I snagged things up quick and piled them on a chair. Bloodsmell floated up, rusty and stale. That came mostly from my overcoat. It would need a good cleaning—if I could bring myself to wear—

No, definitely not. A dead man's blood was all over it, invisible against the dark fabric. I'd not killed him, but had drunk deeply from his twitching corpse.

Yeah. I'd done that.

Not something one can forget, not anything I wanted to remember, but there it was: insanity.

I was ashamed. Ashamed I'd lost control, crossed a line. If I was lucky, I would wince over that one for decades to come and learn from it.

If unlucky, I might do it again.

Face flaming, I rifled the pockets and found an address book, a plain thing in thin brown leather. It had belonged to the late Alan Caine. I'd taken it from his hotel apartment on the night of his murder on the off chance that it might prove useful in finding his killer. The problem had resolved itself, but now I had an idea for using the book to get the cops out of my hair. Derner could help, and it wouldn't cost a nickel in bribes.

Halting in midturn for the door, I realized I couldn't leave this stuff. If the cops ever decided to search the place . . . no . . . such complications I did *not* need. I spread the overcoat flat, threw all of the clothing on it, then rolled it into a bundle, ready for dumping.

I hurried out, bundle under one arm and the book in my pocket.

"What have you got there?" Michael wanted to know.

"Laundry."

"*That* was your business?"

"Yeah. I'm short on clean shirts."

He snorted. "Let's get out of here."

"Car keys," Broder said, his hooded gaze traveling between me and Kroun, not knowing which of us had chauffeured.

I handed them over. It never occurred to me to argue about who was to drive. He stood by the front door, making it plain we were all to exit first.

The leather case with the syringe remained on the bar. I got it and quietly passed it to Michael. He shot me a sharp look, but I wore my blandest "I don't give a damn" face. He shoved the case deep in his coat pocket and moved on. If Kroun noticed, he didn't show it.

I locked the front door. As we walked toward the parking lot, the outside lights winked on and off. The others saw and looked back; I kept going.

"It's just a short," I said to no one in particular.

At the Studebaker, Michael turned and smiled. "It's been a pleasure meeting you, Mr. Fleming. I'm very happy I didn't have to kill you. Tonight."

Some guys enjoy being cute. Michael and Broder quickly got in the car first, locking the doors. They moved fast, as though rehearsed.

"What's this?" Kroun asked, pitching his voice to go through the rolled-up windows.

One hand cupped to his ear, Michael mouthed an unconvincing "*What?*" and met our irritation with a good-natured, innocent smile. Broder started the motor, shifted, and backed out.

"He's stranding us?" I stared as Michael did the kind of playful bye-bye wave usually reserved for small kids.

"That's what it looks like," Kroun just shook his head. "Payback for the money I took off him. Michael's a big one for payback."

"I'll remember that."

"Huh. He's got my new stuff," he added.

"He said he was at your hotel."

"I heard. I'll pick it up later. Where to now? This hospital?"

"Yeah. There's an el stop just up the street. It'll take us. Cabs don't like this area much when the club's closed."

I turned, walking into the wind. My hat tried to fly off, so I carried it. Kroun jammed his on tight and kept his head down. He muttered unkindly about the cold and folded his coat lapels over his chest, turning up the collar. Maybe he felt it more than I. That slug in his brain might make a lot of things different for him.

"So," I said, "*is* the Pope Catholic?"

"Mike doesn't know things have changed. I'm not the man I was. He wouldn't understand that, even if I gave him the whole story—which I'm not."

"Doesn't anyone know about you?"

"Hell, no. Just you and your girl. There's no need for it to go any further. I survived the car exploding. The exact how of it stays with us."

"What about the other stuff? You heard everything. Michael as much as said I should kill you if you got out of line."

"You can try."

"Don't give me that. He was serious."

"Yeah. He was."

"Well? Why?"

Kroun shrugged. "I couldn't say."

"You could have asked. And gotten an answer. Why didn't you?"

"Because I learned more by letting him run off at the lip. If Michael makes a real nuisance of himself, I'll deal with him. You stay out of it."

What constituted being a real nuisance? Apparently the threat of getting killed wasn't enough for Kroun. Of course, he was already dead—Undead—and it might have changed his perspective on that point. Mine had certainly shifted considerably since my demise.

I tried another angle. "Who's this guy you want to see?"

"The old bastard," he said, with a finality that meant there would be no further elaboration.

"Where is he?"

"Not far away. It's my private business. I don't want you along."

"My hands are tied. I keep tabs on you or get in a bad spot."

"Yeah-yeah."

Kroun could give me the slip easy enough, which we both knew. He seemed disinclined to run off just yet, though.

There was a drugstore open near the el platform. He turned into it. I followed to get out of the wind. We must have looked like suspicious characters, what with Kroun being dressed so sharp and me so ratty. The clerk behind the cash register straightened, his hand going out of sight under the counter.

Kroun ignored his apprehension and pointed to the goods behind the glass. "Cigars, please," he said. He pulled a ten from one of the money clips. "The del Mundos will do. The whole box. Thanks. Keep the change."

He put the box under one arm, leaving the guy to gape after him.

"A seven-dollar tip?" I asked as we took the stairs up to the platform.

"I can afford it."

"Thought you didn't smoke." The other night he'd expressed surprise that I indulged. My habit was infrequent and mostly for show; I could only puff, not inhale. Maybe I should try cigars.

"I don't. They're a gift. You'll find out soon enough. Now when's the next damn train due?"

The hospital was busier than the previous night, though things were slowing down. A different nurse was on duty at the front, and she gave me directions to Escott's room, along with that of Roland Lambert.

Her eyes sparkled at the mention of his name. "You're his friend?"

"One of them."

"Are you in the movies, too?"

Behind me Kroun stifled a snort, turning it into a throat-clearing noise.

"Only when I buy a ticket."

"I got his autograph," she said. "He was so *nice* about it."

"Yeah, he's a smooth one." In another day he'd be running the place. I led off down a hall, then toward an elevator. The lights were brighter here; I crushed my bundled clothes into a smaller wad.

"Laundry, huh?" said Kroun. "Like hell. I can smell the blood. Whose is it?"

"Hoyle's. I was standing too close when he bought it."

"Ain't life sweet? You're not sentimentally attached to that stuff, are you?"

The elevator doors parted, we got in, and I asked the operator where the hospital's incinerator might be. He didn't like my looks and wanted to know why.

"My cousin's got mumps, and I'm supposed to burn his clothes." I offered the bundle to him.

He dropped back against the wall and held his breath. No grown man wants to deal with mumps. He kept his distance and took us to the basement, no stops.

Kroun grunted amused approval when the doors slid shut behind us, then got distracted by our surroundings. He looked around the nondescript area as though we were in an art museum and not some man-made concrete cave. Further directions from a passing janitor got me to where I needed to be.

Hospital incinerators are pretty impressive in terms of size and noise, but the door was oddly small. I had to use a long steel poker to push my bundle through the little opening, shoving the clothes deep into the roaring fire. I watched, fixed in place as the blaze attacked and began to eat the fragile fabric, then I slammed the door shut.

Until then I'd no idea just how heavy the bundle had been. I instantly felt better.

"You did more than just burn evidence," Kroun said when we were back up in the hospital's public area looking for the right corridor.

"Getting rid of a bad memory."

"That easy, huh? What do you do about keeping the good ones?"

I shrugged. "Pictures, I guess. Keep a diary."

"What about regaining good ones you've forgotten?"

This was a screwy subject, but I was getting used to his being screwy. His fussing with that handkerchief while important stuff was being discussed was a good dodge to gain thinking time. Only I had the suspicion his main concern had indeed been the handkerchief. "Talk over old times with family."

"Huh." He gave that one more consideration than it deserved, keeping quiet for the trip up to Escott's floor.

His room was at the opposite end of the hall from some kind of commotion. A lot of people were gathered around one of the doors: doctors, nurses, curious visitors carrying flowers and candy boxes. There was a party mood in the air, and I was sure it had to do with Roland. For a man who'd come close to bleeding to death, he knew how to land on his feet.

The atmosphere was considerably more subdued at the other end. The only activity was one old bushy-haired janitor arthritically pushing a mop around. He wore a hearing aid that must have been switched off and paid no mind as we approached Escott's door, but someone else was alert. Bobbi was just within the room, keeping an eye on the hall. She spotted me and came hurtling. I almost braced for a well-deserved smack from her purse, but instead she nearly knocked me over with a hug.

That was nice, really nice. Then she pulled abruptly away, her face like a thunderstorm. "You—you . . ."

I put my hands up, offering full and humble surrender. "You . . ."

Damn, she had a cute scowl. Even when really serious, she was stunning with her big hazel eyes, platinum blond hair, and a face that always made my stilled heart leap. By some strange miracle, she loved me. How had I forgotten that? My death *would* have ripped her apart. Escott had called me a selfish, unthinking bastard. Guilty as charged. Again.

I still couldn't tell her what had been behind the fight.

"Jack?" Her storm clouds wavered. Maybe she'd expected more from me than hangdog silence.

"I'm sorry, baby. I mean that. It's my fault he's here, and I'm sorry as hell. Won't happen again." I meant it. She had my number and could always see right through me. Anything less than total honesty she'd throw right back.

"I don't have to yell at you any more about this?" she asked.

"Not about this. Anything else, I'll take my licks."

She nodded, still looking at me with wary deliberation, hopefully getting over being mad.

Without thinking, I raised one hand and gently brushed the side of her face, half caress, half reassurance. Suddenly I wanted to tell her I loved her, but you don't say such things in public. Touching her like this was the closest I could come.

Damned if she didn't get it. Her eyes blazed up, and I felt like she'd just kissed me.

My little corner of the world shifted an inch in a direction with no name, settled into place, and suddenly felt *right* again. How long that would last I didn't know, but I'd try to keep it that way come hell or high water.

"How are you?" she asked. There was a lot more to the words than their surface meaning.

"I'm fine, sweetheart. Believe it."

She got that as well.

"And I'm fine, too," put in Kroun, who had a ringside to our interplay.

Bobbi turned and smiled, which was usually enough to knock most men off their feet. "Aren't you trying to be dead?"

His expression warmed as he flipped his charm switch on. "It turned out to be impractical."

"Why are you here, Mr. Kroun?"

"Call me Gabe. Please."

"I thought it was Whitey."

"Not for ladies who try to stop my bleeding all over their floor. I'm just along for the ride. Your boyfriend needs a keeper."

He should talk.

"Keeper?" she asked me.

"It's business."

That was the wrong thing to say, and I'd said it one time too many. Her lips tightened; the storm gathered again, frighteningly fast. Her voice was low, but every word had the force of a thunderclap. "I've had enough, Jack."

I couldn't pretend not to know what she was talking about. No placation I could think of would make things better. Not after the horrors of last night. She was the toughest woman I'd ever met, but had limits. "I know. And it's over. I'm winding this circus up."

"What do you mean?"

"I'm turning the show over to Derner until Gordy's on his feet. Tonight. After I leave here, we're going to the Nightcrawler to fix things. Gabe said he'd help." I shot him a look.

He kept his face on straight and shrugged agreement. "Figured I owed him."

"No more 'business'?" she asked.

"Just Lady Crymsyn, nothing else," I said. "I'm a tavern keeper, not Al Capone." I meant that as well.

"And if trouble comes up again?"

That was the tricky part. "If it's to do with me and mine, I take care of it, but anything else can take a hike."

She knew how the world worked and that I might not be

able to prevent mob business from horning in on my life. But she also knew I'd give it my best to steer clear. To my vast relief, that turned out to be sufficient. She smiled. Not a big one, not the kind that was like a sunrise in my heart, but it did the job.

"You're really okay?" she asked, one hand brushing my coat lapels and thus my scarred chest.

I had her meaning. After Bristow's handiwork, I'd not gone near her out of fear of losing control and hurting, even killing her. He'd given me something far worse than a few surface scars. The damage inside my head, my soul . . .

Was *healing*.

In reply, I pulled her close and held her tight. She didn't need to know why I'd been distant, only that it was past. "Yeah, baby," I whispered. "I'm really okay."

She abruptly relaxed and melted against me. It was a perfect moment, and those never last long enough. Had we been alone, it might have progressed to something even more perfect, but we were limited to a long hug in a hallway.

With people watching. I became aware of Kroun and the old janitor looking on. The latter sociably blew his nose, wiped his house-sized mustache, and adjusted thick glasses. Kroun wore an "ain't that cute" smirk on his lean face.

Just inside Escott's room stood Shoe Coldfield. He was scowling and stepped forward. The janitor quickly went back to his mop work.

Bobbi picked up on my shift of attention and self-consciously pulled away, patting her hair and smiling.

"Visiting hour's about over," growled Coldfield. He filled most of the doorway. I wouldn't be getting through unless he allowed it. Then he noticed Kroun. "What the . . ."

"Shoe Coldfield, meet Gabriel Kroun," I said.

Coldfield didn't move. "The guy in Gordy's car. The car that blew to hell and gone."

Kroun shrugged. "Hell doesn't want me yet."

They cautiously shook hands. I was glad for the distraction, not putting it past Coldfield to bust me one again just to make sure I knew my place. He stood aside to allow me in, then fixed his attention back on Kroun. Clearly he wanted more details, and Kroun would give him the same eyewash he spilled earlier. I passed up a second helping and went into Escott's room, halting short just inside.

Damnation, he looked *worse*. He'd been bad last night, but this . . .

His bruises had had all day to mature. The idea of beating someone black-and-blue was no abstract concept on him. Much of his face was nearly as dark as Coldfield's and the rest was a gray tone that put my hackles up. His eye was still sealed shut, but the open one blinked sluggishly at me.

"How are you?" he asked, barely above a whisper.

What the hell? "Charles, I—"

"No more bloody apologies."

"What?" Was he drugged? Feverish?

"You've done that already. Accepted. Now—how are you?"

"You remembered last night?"

"This morning. You were inconsiderately early. How are—"

"I'm fine, just fine."

"No more thoughts about pistols at dawn?"

I got his meaning. He was still worried that I'd try shooting myself again. I checked behind to make sure no one was hearing this and stepped closer. "No, Charles. No more. Word of honor, hand on my heart, I promise. On Bobbi's life, I promise."

He made no reply, and with his face so banged up I couldn't tell what he was thinking. He grunted. "Some water, please?"

A tumbler with a glass straw was on the bedside table. His private accommodation came with a tiny washroom with a shower. I made use of its sink for fresh water, then held the tumbler for him until he drained most of it. This close it was too easy to pick up the sickroom smell. He wouldn't be coming home anytime soon. "How are you?"

"Bloody awful. Can't sleep in this place. I want my own bed. And a beer. Something dark and a little sweet. Cool, not cold."

"Maybe Shoe can smuggle in a bucket for you."

"He won't. Stickler for hospital rules. I may have talked him into rye bread, though."

"Rye bread?"

"I don't understand why, but I've developed a craving for some. Fresh. A very thick slice. With lots of salted butter. But it's no good without the beer."

Okay, that was odd, but a hospital stay can make you crazy for the damnedest things.

"Jack . . . about Shoe . . ."

"We're okay," I said quickly, not wanting to talk about it.

"I don't believe that."

You couldn't get anything by Escott, even when he was doped and wrapped like a mummy. "He's a little sore at me. He wants to know why this happened. I can't . . . I just can't tell him."

"Yes. It's private. I've said it's been resolved. He's not one to back down."

"I'll stay out of his way."

"Most wise."

"Has Vivian been in?" I'd expected to see Escott's girl-friend here. After we'd saved her daughter from some brutal kidnappers, he'd gotten very close with the widowed Vivian Gladwell. Because of her, he'd lately drifted into the state of wearing a sappy smile for no good reason.

"I've not told her."

I was surprised at that. "You should."

"Why?"

He had me there. "Don't want to worry her, huh?"

"Precisely. And it would upset young Sarah to see me like this."

Sarah was in her teens, but mentally would always be a child. Escott had come to dote on her as had most of the people who'd met her, me included. She was a sweet thing, forever unspoiled by the adversities of growing up.

"Did you at least phone them?"

"Yes. Said I'd be out of town for a few days on a case."

It would take longer than that for his bruises to fade. I hoped there'd be no scarring under his bandages. My face went red again, and I had to work to keep from bumbling out with another inadequate apology.

He spared us both with a question. "Who's that with you? I heard another voice."

"Whitey Kroun."

Escott gave me a good long stare with his working eye.

"He survived that bomb."

More staring.

"Yeah. Surprised the hell out of me, too."

"Would you mind very much catching me up on events?" He still whispered, yet managed to pack in an acerbic tone.

"Didn't Bobbi say anything?"

"No."

To be fair, Kroun had asked her to keep shut about himself. "Well, it went like this . . ."

I was hampered, since Kroun didn't want others to know about the vampirism part. I had to respect that, even with Escott. In this case what he didn't know wouldn't hurt him. Leaving it out and keeping things simple, I told him what had happened to Mitchell, how Kroun had helped, and that a couple of his friends were champing to hustle him back to New York.

"Why does he not leave?" Escott asked.

"Says he's still got business here. I'm supposed to keep an eye on him till he's done."

"Then perhaps you should encourage him to waste no time concluding his errand. By all accounts, the man is dangerous."

"I'll do what I can. He's got his own mind." And more. I'd glimpsed Kroun's dark side and didn't like it. Other than that, he seemed friendly, but why take chances?

"A small favor?" said Escott.

"Name it."

"Please get everyone to go home. I think they may stay the whole hour, but this is as long as I can—"

"It's done. Go to sleep."

"Thank you." He relaxed into his pillows, looking completely exhausted and a lot older than his years. It struck me afresh just how awful he looked.

My fault. And he'd wanted to know how *I* had been.

I resisted the urge to ask if he needed anything. He'd have mentioned it already, like the beer and rye bread. I backed out, shutting the door.

"What's the matter?" Coldfield demanded. No doubt about it, I was on his shit list until further notice.

"He's tired. He asked for us to go home. He needs rest."

Bobbi touched Coldfield's arm before he could object. "Jack's right. Charles will be better tomorrow. You saw how he was fighting so hard to keep awake for us. We can come back in the morning."

Her magic worked. Coldfield unbent for her and agreed to leave, but muttered about returning later. If he wanted to keep an eye on Escott through the night, he'd damn well do it, everyone out of the way, especially me.

Saying good-bye to Bobbi provided an excellent reason to kiss her, and I made the most of it. My God, but it felt good.

More than good. It felt *right* again.

"Will you be by the hotel later?" she asked. She was staying at one of Coldfield's business investments while her flat was being scoured clean of violent death.

"Not tonight. I have to—"

"Tomorrow then." That was final.

"I'll have bells on."

She started to say something, then shook her head. Kroun was within earshot. She gave me a last peck on the cheek, squeezed my hand, then went off with Coldfield, who had driven her over.

Kroun and I still didn't have a car to get to the Night-crawler. It seemed wise for the moment not to ask Coldfield for a lift. A cab then, unless . . .

The ongoing commotion outside Roland's room brought something to mind. I'd called in mob muscle to bodyguard him; chances were someone would still be on duty. I wanted to look in anyway.

"Gabe? One more stop."

"The movie star?"

"Five minutes. Gonna rustle us a car."

He liked that idea and found a wall to hold up. He still had the box of cigars tucked under one arm. Gift, huh? Not for Gordy; they weren't his brand.

Roland Lambert was a popular man tonight. I recognized newspapermen from their pencils and steno pads. Photographers also stood by, ready to record anything that a headline could make important. They glanced my way, took in my clothes and hobo beard, and dismissed me just that fast. Men who looked like me really were a dime a dozen in the street; I was just taller than most.

I'd spotted one of the bodyguards, didn't remember his name, but knew his face, and he knew mine. I waved him over. He pushed through with no real effort.

"Yeah, Boss?"

"I'm calling off the watch on the actor."

"You sure?" He looked troubled.

"Yeah, what's the problem?"

He shrugged. "It's just he's a regular guy, y'know? Treats me like I'm some kind of big shot. And that Russian doll, what a lady . . ."

If I left him here any longer, he'd be ironing their sheets. "You get his autograph?"

"First thing. He was great about it, even thanked me for askin'. What a guy."

"He's a sweetheart, but I need you to—"

"*Jek Flem-ink! My heeeeeerrrrrrrro!*"

No mistaking that accent. The crowd parted, and Faustine Petrova enthusiastically flung herself at me.

I love Bobbi, but there's much to enjoy about a jubilant Russian ballerina jumping on you and using her lips all over your face like a machine gun.

5

To keep from toppling, I had to grab Faustine bodily. Staggering back, I hit a wall, but she didn't seem to notice, rattling on in Russian between the loud wet smooches she planted all over. I found out firsthand why the front of one's head is called a kisser.

Wow. Something began coming loose inside. I had no need to breathe, yet desperately sucked air, but it wouldn't stay in. For a second I didn't understand what was going on. I thought it was a bad cough or some strange hiccups, then it was both at once. The strangest damned choking noise clawed its way out of my throat.

Laughter. I was laughing.

Hadn't done that in a while.

Faustine laughed as well, a very full one, happy.

I couldn't stop. It felt good.

We were lunatics, much too loud for a hospital, but for a few moments we just had to cut loose. I hugged her, and I laughed.

Making a *mwah-mwah* noise she kissed each of my stubbled cheeks in turn then yelled, *"Godt blezz Am-er-i-ka!"*

Flashbulbs exploded, blinding, disorienting. Faustine posed with both arms around me, a big smile showing all her white teeth, except when she planted another kiss. Right on my mouth. My lucky night. This inspired hoots of encouragement from the audience and some applause.

In the back of my mind, I knew the cameras could have mirrors in their works, which meant no catching of my image on film. That could be trouble somewhere down the line, but I couldn't bring myself to worry about it. It just wasn't important right now.

She pressed me forward into the crowd. It was easier not to resist. A few strangers thumped me on the back, others shook my hand, an eager young nurse tried kissing me, too, and managed to bruise my ear in passing. Apparently they were willing to ignore my scruffy exterior so long as Faustine liked me.

What the hell had they been told?

Just inside the room stood a tall, round-bodied guy in a pale blue tropical suit and a melon orange shirt that had to have been custom-made because I'd never seen anything like it before. He grinned and grabbed my hand, pumping away as though I'd just flown over the South Pole.

"Hiya, hiya, name's Lenny Larsen! I wanna talk with you about a movie script!"

"Sure, first thing tomorrow!" I said, matching his hearty good cheer. It worked, and I got my hand back, albeit with his business card pressed to my palm. Faustine pushed us farther into the so-called sick room.

Roland looked just like his pictures in the paper, but more so. Cameras loved his handsome face, and he was sharply turned out despite the pajamas and hospital trappings. His thickly bandaged leg was elevated by a sling, wires, and a pulley device, the rest of him lounged comfortably against half a dozen pillows. Along with more well-wishers he was surrounded by a greenhouse of flowers and a shop's worth of fancy chocolates in ribboned boxes. Except for the pale cast to his skin, he seemed to be having a great time and smiled broadly.

"Jack! Welcome to the party. Toss me my wife back, would you?"

At no urging from me, Faustine flew to his side, managing to make it look effortless despite the people in the way. The Lamberts had already suffered some rough patches in their new marriage, but all seemed forgotten. She leaned in and kissed his forehead, then thoughtfully brushed at the red lip color she'd left behind. "My poor da'link," she murmured. "Doz et hurt steel?"

"Just a twinge when I laugh, m'dear."

The members of the press made notes.

I knew what was coming; there was no stopping it. Better to play along, then get out.

Roland introduced me as the man who'd saved his life.

More pictures. I wished them luck in the darkroom.

Floods of questions. They wanted to know who was gunning for Roland Lambert, did I have any leads, had the cops caught the shooters, was I in the mob . . . that one made me twitch.

I held my hand up, mouth open to make a statement, which brought a temporary hush. "Sorry, folks, I am just as puzzled as you, but I know that Chicago's finest—" Some goof in the back, who probably covered local crime, snorted loudly. "That Chicago's *finest* are on the job and will no doubt make an arrest."

That was the kind of statement I'd heard often enough while on their side of the fence. We all knew what it meant. I got hit with more questions but shook my head and waved them off. "I'm just glad Roland's going to be fine." So I assumed from the circus; I'd had no chance to ask.

"Is it true you've sold your nightclub to the mob?"

That was a new one. "No. It's just closed until my star act is back."

Taking the cue, the Lamberts beamed. More flashbulbs died.

"What about your gangster friends?" asked another wiseacre.

"Don't have any, sorry to disappoint you. Why don't you come by the club when it's open and see for yourself—first round's on the house!"

That turned the tide. There's nothing like an offer of free booze for distracting the Fourth Estate from the scent of a story. Faustine, a most canny woman, passed a big box of chocolates around the room, further distracting them and at the same time drawing attention back to herself.

"Jek iz Am-er-i-kan he-rrro, joost like my da'link huz-bendt. Jek doez not like the geng-sterz, they do not like heem. When they shoot, my brafe Rrrolandt throwz heem-self een way! He savez Jek's life, Jek rrrushes heem to hoz-peetle."

Pencils scribbled more slowly than usual as their owners dug their way past Faustine's accent. It seemed heavier to-night, whether from the excitement or by design. Faustine glowed as they peppered her with more questions.

"Yez, I am Amer-i-kan by the marry-ink of Rrrolandt, but I vish to be *more* Amer-i-kan and take tezt for eet. I *loff* thees con-drrry!"

That went over well.

The guy in the orange shirt loomed next to me, big teeth in a tanned face. "That's right folks, you can call Faustine Petrova our own little Miss Russian America! You never saw a more patriotic dancer, and you'll see more of them both when we make the movie! The name's L-A-R-S-E-N, Lenny Larsen!" He passed out more cards. I pocketed mine and hoped never to see him again.

Faustine and Roland were clearly in on the details. I went along with them, figuring it had to do with Roland's Holly-wood comeback. He'd left some years ago—too much drink-ing got in the way of his career—but he was on the wagon and might be worth something at the box office again after this debacle.

I waved to let him know I was leaving, eased into the hall, and found myself next to a doctor. I asked him about Roland's health.

"He'll be able to go home in a few days," he said. "We took out the slug. It's just a question of watching for infection. So far, he's clean."

That was good. When I'd been in the army, more often than not it was the blood poisoning that took a man, not the bullet.

The bodyguard didn't want to meet my eye. He looked forlorn. "You sure they're safe, Boss? I mean, ya never know."

"You're right. Stick around, then. I want you to keep an eye on Charles Escott, too."

"Who?"

"The guy in 305. He's with Gordy's outfit." Damn, but I really was getting better at lying, and the name-dropping tipped things. "Look in on him, make sure things are copacetic, send up a flag if they ain't. But I need your car."

"Sure! No problem!" Happy as a puppy with a new bone, he dug out a key, told me what kind of car and where he was parked. I said I'd be at the Nightcrawler Club, then got clear.

Kroun was still holding up the wall and shook his head. "That's quite a rash you got there."

"What?"

"The crazy dame who jumped on you. You're smeared with more war paint than she is."

I got my handkerchief and rubbed my face. It came away covered with Faustine's deep red lip color. "Jeez."

"You said it. So . . . how do I get your job?"

The only parking at the Nightcrawler was in the alley behind the club. There was a guy hanging around to shoo away anyone who didn't belong. I eased into a spot. There wasn't a lot of space; Kroun had to slide across to the driver's side to get out, grimacing more than the effort required. After what he'd been through, I gave him credit for just being able to get into a car, period.

The man on watch at the back door nearly swallowed his cigarette when we climbed the steps. He'd apparently heard the news about Kroun's demise. I asked if Derner was in, knowing he would be; he was always in. This was my way of letting the guard know it was business as usual.

Don't think he bought it.

The kitchen staff was too busy to pay notice, but a couple of mugs in the rear hall exchanged looks and quickly got out of the way.

Kroun grunted, putting in a note of disgust. Coming back from the dead clearly annoyed him.

We got a similar reception walking into Gordy's office upstairs, but more of it. Derner was on one of three phones now on the big desk. He glanced over, then did one hell of a double take.

"I'll call you back," he said into the blower then hung up, missing the first attempt, knocking the phone over on the second. He stood up, eyes big as he threw me a *what the hell?* look. "Boss . . . ?"

"Good news. Mr. Kroun's back," I announced cheerfully.

Kroun snorted and went past to drop himself into a deep, overstuffed leather couch. He kept his coat and hat on, cigar box balanced on one knee, telegraphing that this better not take long.

"Gee, that's great," said Derner, his voice faint. "What's goin' on?"

I gave him as much explanation as he needed to pull himself together, then tossed the ball to Kroun. Leaning back, ankles crossed and feet on a table, he issued a number of succinct orders, most of them to do with taking me off everyone's execution list and putting forward Mitchell as the ringleader of all the trouble. Derner had gotten that from me the night before, so it was no surprise, but he wanted to know why.

"Tried to give himself a raise the hard way," said Kroun. "He's in the lake, right?"

"Yeah, sir. Couple of the boys took him over to the meat packers and—"

Kroun raised a hand. "No details."

Couldn't blame him for that. I didn't like thinking what the cleaning crew had to do to distribute a man's body into several fifty-gallon drums along with enough cement to keep it all on the lake bed.

"Get New York on the phone, and I'll put the fix in," he said. "This should be Mike's job," he added, aiming that at me.

"I think people are more scared of you," I said.

He gave a grunt. "Good point."

In ten minutes, regardless of whether the lines might be tapped, Kroun got me cleared of trouble with everyone else who mattered. He shot me a look as though to say, *Happy now?*

Relieved was the word.

Kroun got up, went to the desk, and just stood, looking down. Derner quickly relinquished the chair to him. Kroun switched on the desk radio, searched the phone book, and made a call. He kept his voice lower than the music and scribbled something on the inside of a matchbook. Derner and I exchanged looks; neither of us knew what was going on. I could figure it had to do with the kind of stuff Michael wanted to know about.

Hanging up, Kroun arranged to have someone pick up his carload of new clothes. He informed Derner that Broder and Michael would be staying on for a few more days and might be dropping in. Derner took it in stride. Entertaining the big bosses was easy enough. Booze, girls, gambling, and more booze usually did the job.

"We still got a problem about Alan Caine," he said. "Should they know about it?"

"No," said Kroun, moving back to the couch. "I'll handle them."

Caine's murder had had the cops sniffing around the club. The latest news reported that Jewel Caine's death had not been suicide after all. Small comfort to her family, if she'd had any. Derner had found out she didn't.

"Okay," I said. "Get something organized on services for her. She was friends with the girls here, make sure they show up and give her a good send-off. Tip the papers. Find people to say nice things about her."

"The cops will want to know why we're paying."

"An anonymous cash donation to the funeral home. I'm sure you can find one that understands what's expected."

He started with another objection. Kroun cleared his throat. Loudly. Derner nodded and went back to the desk to make phone calls.

"That's the only good part of this job," Kroun muttered. "I say frog, and they have to jump."

"Thanks," I said.

"Why do you let him argue like that?"

"He brings up things I need to remember." I had more to do before calling it quits for the night and told him as much.

"What else is there?"

I showed the leather address book, not quite taking it from my pocket. "This belonged to Alan Caine, I have to leave it in a spot where the cops can find it and solidly link Hoyle and Mitchell to the murders. Should take the heat off the club and send it Mitchell's way. We can put a rumor out that he ran off to Havana after killing Hoyle—"

"Who?"

"The guy who rigged the bomb. The clothes I burned . . . that was his blood . . . remember?"

"Who killed him?" he asked.

"Doesn't matter, I just make sure the cops blame Mitchell. He'd have bumped Hoyle anyway to cut a loose end about the car bombing. No one's found the body yet, but it's only a matter of time. This book on him might suggest to the cops that Hoyle killed Caine for gambling debts." It was thin at best, but better than nothing.

"Did you kill Hoyle?" Kroun's voice was conversational.

"No." I had the impression he wouldn't care if I had, he just wanted the facts straight.

"And this Hoyle *is* dead?"

"Yeah." Thoroughly. What was bothering Kroun? Did he have any reason to doubt my word on it?

"He's not going to surprise you the way I did?"

That was straight out of left field and right between the eyes. "Uh."

"You never know," he said, matter-of-factly.

Damn. The possibility never occurred to me. There had been no blood exchange, no chance that he'd rise again. I'd drunk from Hoyle only after he was dead. There was also *no* way that Kroun could know what I had done. Even Escott didn't know, no one ever would.

For a bare instant I'd been thrown off-balance, but decided Kroun was just stirring things up for the hell of it. He was damned good at that. He had a point, though.

"What do you know?" I asked.

"Enough to not take anything for granted."

"But what do you know?"

"I'm only trying to get you to think, kid. You've been lucky and done okay for yourself, but one of these nights it'll catch up to you."

I thought of Bristow. "It already has."

"If we're here, there can be others." He cast a glance at Derner. The radio was still on, masking our low voices. "You think you'd have run into more like us by now? Not if they're more careful than you. You didn't get my score because you weren't even looking."

Another good point, but I couldn't agree with him on the rest. I'd always kept my eyes open at the Stockyards on the chance of spotting another member of the club. Nothing had come of it yet. "Why think that about Hoyle?"

"Why not?"

No arguing with that. "Okay, I'll be more paranoid."

"The only way to live," he said. He went on. "So how does that book connect Hoyle to Mitchell?"

"Mostly it connects Hoyle to Alan Caine, who owed money to Mitchell. The cops can ask stoolies all over town and get the same story of Hoyle and Mitchell having a falling-out over who knows what. Derner will see to it."

He shook his head. "Needs more. Gotta cover the 'who knows what' part."

"I'm listening."

"Caine gambled. You need markers. With the right dates. Mitchell's name on some, Hoyle's name on others, and Caine's signature on them all to clinch it."

I got him. "Plant 'em where they'll be found."

"So the cops figure Hoyle killed the Caines, one for not paying his debts, the other to shut up a witness. This shorts Mitchell out of his marker money. Mitchell kills Hoyle for shorting him. It's not what happened, but it's reasonable. Cops like reasonable, don't they?"

"Son of a bitch."

"Glad you agree."

Derner earned his keep that night. He contacted a specialist and had the guy in the office thirty minutes later. Samples of Caine's writing came from the address book, and we kept it simple. On various types of plain paper and using different pens the forger wrote several IOUs, signed Caine's name, collected a fee, and left. I don't think he said ten words and never once asked a question, the perfect mob employee.

Hat over his face, Kroun stretched on the couch and pretended to nap until it was done. "Ready to go?" he asked, standing.

I'd hoped he would stay at the club waiting for his clothes to arrive while I finished things. Despite orders to babysit him, I didn't want company. "This won't take long," I said.

"Good."

He left the cigars on the table and strode out. I had to follow.

Derner had called in additional help for this last errand. As I rolled to a slow stop up the street from a battered parking garage, another car turned the corner and pulled in behind me. Kroun went alert, maybe thinking it was cops again, but I told him it was okay, and we got out into the icy air.

Strome, the stone-faced guy who'd been my lieutenant since I'd taken over for Gordy, got out and stood ghost-quiet. He had shot Hoyle the night before, thinking to save my life, and I couldn't fault him for that. Of course, given the right circumstances, he'd shoot me without a second thought; it was just another job to him.

He glanced once at Kroun and left it at that; apparently Derner had filled him in. Strome gave me a hard look, though. "You okay, Boss?"

That surprised me. "Yeah."

He nodded, just the once. Granted, the last time he'd seen me—sprayed with Hoyle's blood and brains—I'd fallen into a seizure, and it had left one hell of an impression.

Best to change the subject. "That girl who was down there . . ." Hoyle had kidnapped a little cutie who had been in the wrong place at the wrong time during a murder. She'd been in need of a rescue. It was just her hard luck Strome and I were the ones to do it. "Did he hurt her?"

Strome understood what I meant. "She didn't say, but I don't think so."

"How is she?"

He considered, then shrugged. "Blubbed a little, then made me buy her supper and take her home. Guess she's okay. Dames." Clearly he found women to be a vast, if not-too-troubling, mystery.

"Let's wind this up," I said, taking the lead.

The garage had a tin roof that bucked and banged in the wind. The place was mob-owned; chances favored the vehicles inside were, too. Hoyle had chosen it as an emergency bolt-hole to hide from the world, and it had almost worked. The whole area was empty of foot traffic, and cars passed it by. The surrounding small factories and shops were closed tight. Every city had deserted pockets like this. They look dangerous and lonely after dark, but are often safer than a bank vault simply because no one's around to make trouble.

We crowded down a short flight of concrete steps to the basement entry, and Strome handed me a set of keys. On our last visit he'd picked the lock to get in.

From the doorway you could see a light on at the far end of an otherwise black basement. I'd not expected that. It was as though Hoyle were waiting for me to return.

Strome hung back to watch the street. I was highly aware of the bloodsmell tainting the freezing air and tried not to take any in as I entered. There was decay in it and the strong odor of something else unpleasant. Kroun followed, looking around and frowning. He'd caught the scent, too.

Ducking to avoid the low ceiling, I trudged the length of the basement to the curtained-off room at the end. Harsh illumination came from a mechanic's light hung on a nail. The too-bright bulb hurt my eyes and made the shadows just that much blacker. I cast around, trying not to be nervous about it, but no one was hiding anywhere. It felt like we had company, Hoyle's ghost perhaps. If that was the case, he wouldn't be a nice one like Myrna.

I told myself to shut the hell up.

One of the mystery smells was from an electric heater I'd left running. It had burned itself out. The rest was from Hoyle when his bowels and bladder had given way in death. He wouldn't be coming back. The smell of his advancing decay confirmed it. He lay facedown, a hole in the back of his skull. There should have been more blood, but I'd—

"You waiting to sell tickets?" Kroun asked. The top of his hat brushed the low ceiling. He hunched to avoid problems.

There was an old cot against one wall. I shoved the book under the thin pillow.

"Fingerprints," said Kroun.

Damn. He was right. I'd been careful about wearing gloves so only Alan Caine's prints were on the brown leather, but it wouldn't sit right if Hoyle's were absent.

Hoyle's left arm was flung wide. It'd have to do.

Even with gloves on I didn't want to touch him, but it was unavoidable. His arm was heavy and stiff as I lifted it. Rigor would have worn off by now; this was a result of the cold seeping down from outside. If he stayed here, he could freeze right through.

I pressed his fingers to the book and the IOUs, hoping something would stick. He'd not washed since going on the run. I got a few greasy smears no one could miss. Good enough. I left the book on the floor, dropping it so the papers would spill out, sufficiently obvious to catch attention.

Then I backed away, grateful Hoyle's face had been hidden. Dying was bad enough, but to peg out in a dank, deserted basement where only your killer knew where to find you . . .

"C'mon, Jack." Kroun's voice jarred the silence. His tone was different. Was this his version of concern?

"Yeah, okay." I followed him out, leaving the light on. No need to look back; that tableau would be in my head for a long, long time.

Strome would make a phone call to the cops sometime in the morning. He'd ask if they wanted to know where Mitchell stashed Hoyle's body. The question would make sense to Merrifield and Garza.

Soon after, the cops would give the place a good going-over, find what I wanted them to find and more that I didn't. Along with the bullet entry and exit holes, the coroner would certainly note the ripped flesh on Hoyle's throat and wonder at the lack of blood in the corpse. I'd been clumsy and crazy with hunger, but if the guy was good at his job, he might determine the damage had been caused by something akin to human teeth. There was nothing I could do about it. Hoyle's body was needed to set up a false trail to Mitchell, and that was more important. The authorities would be more inclined to think "mad-dog cannibal killer" than "vampire." When working as a reporter, I'd seen stranger things while covering the crime beat.

I emerged into the fresh air, thankful to be clear of that claustrophobic tomb. What I'd done there was shameful and would always be with me, but I had gotten good at distracting myself from the darker memories swarming in my skull. In time, the worst of them would fade.

That was what I told myself.

Kroun and I headed back to the Nightcrawler. Strome went off to God knows where to do God knows what. I did not care to inquire.

I drove slowly, certain that Derner would have more minutiae requiring a decision from me. When I'd taken over this branch of the mob, the arrangement was for me to be just a figurehead until Gordy got better, but somehow it had turned into real work. I figured I should get paid for services rendered, and the sum should be offensively high. Derner would squawk, but that was chump change compared to what the Nightcrawler raked in from the gambling in the private club. Gordy would shrug it off and call it a bargain.

Once I had the cash in hand I'd turn the reins over to Derner. Bobbi would be happy. That was all I wanted.

Derner, again on a phone, hung up when we came in. His hands weren't shaking this time so his aim was better.

"Your car's back from the shop," he told me. "It's parked out front."

That was good news. I'd had it towed to get new tires and some eager beaver decided it needed to be fancied up. I tossed the keys to my borrowed ride on the desk. "Have someone get these back to the guy on watch at the hospital. I got another car to fix." I told him about the bloodstains on the upholstery in Escott's Nash that needed to be cleaned off. No need to explain to him how they got there; this was a messy trade.

"They'll just replace everything, it'll be easier," Derner said. "Like another color?"

"Just match what's there and have them put on a new steering wheel. The old one's bent."

He did not ask how it had come to be damaged either, only made a note. "Your girl's hotel flat is clean. She can go back tonight."

Somehow I didn't think Bobbi would want to do that just yet. "Thanks. I'll let her know." I'd tackle the details about my getting paid when Kroun wasn't around. He might not care, but then again, he might. "Anything else?"

"Everything's copacetic." That meant all other business was under control, no immediate problems, but Derner glanced at Kroun as though expecting a cue, mindful there could be more. Kroun just stood in place and looked back steadily, which was confusing until I caught on. He was doing the same thing that the cops had done to us earlier. Stare long enough, and you'll get the other guy feeling guilty about something.

"My new clothes?" Kroun prompted.

Derner looked relieved. "Yes, sir, got 'em downstairs in a dressing room. The costume lady's in tonight, I told her to get the stuff packed for you—if that's okay?"

"Sure, fine. Which dressing room?"

"Uh, not that one." He meant where Caine had been strangled.

"Good. When she's done, have a guy put them in Mr. Fleming's car."

My, weren't we formal? On the other hand, he'd just let Derner know I was back up on my rung of the ladder. However temporary, I was to get respect, same as Gordy.

Remembering something I should have asked Bobbi hours ago, I gave an internal wince. "How's Gordy doing? Any news?"

Derner's usually gloomy face brightened a little. "I talked with him on the phone for a minute today. He sounded good."

"You sure?" I knew Gordy could put up a front. There wasn't a poker player born who could beat him at a bald-faced bluff.

"Yeah, Boss. His girlfriend said he'd be resting for another couple weeks, maybe more, but he was feeling a lot better."

Okay, Gordy could lie, but Adelle would not. "That's great." I'd risked myself, pushing right to the edge to impart one last hypnotic suggestion to Gordy so he'd stay in bed until fully recovered. I'd come that close to blowing up my brain from the inside out, but it was worth it if it kept him alive.

"We're done, let's go," Kroun announced. He'd reclaimed the box of cigars—no one had dared touch them—and resettled his hat.

Fine with me.

Outwardly, my Buick looked exactly the same, just cleaner. The paint and chrome gleamed as though fresh from the factory. There wasn't a scratch or dent to be found, and I knew there'd been more than a few scars in place the last time I'd seen her. The windows were different, the glass thicker, but that was the only other sign of the special tinkering.

Kroun's suitcases were on the backseat, and the keys were in the ignition. Just like the cigars, no one had dared touch the car, not while it was under the eye of the club bouncers.

We got in, I tried the starter, and damned if the motor wasn't running more smoothly than before, and the gas tank was full. I could get used to being the boss with stuff like this as part of the job.

Shifting gears, it took a firmer foot on the accelerator to get her to move the extra weight. Just how much armor plating had they put in? She rode heavy; I had to haul the wheel to make the corners and put the brakes on sooner with more force. The solid-rubber tires gave off a different sound against the pavement, and despite the special shocks, I could feel the change in how they handled the bumps. No improvement there.

I'd just have to get used to things unless I wanted to buy

a new ride. That Studebaker came to mind, but there were still plenty of miles left in the Buick. It didn't make sense to spend the money.

"Wanna stop at the Stockyards?" I asked. If Kroun had further business tonight, he'd made no mention of it.

"Why? You hungry?"

"I could be. You have to be."

He appeared to think about it. "Guess so. But find a butcher shop instead."

"Risky."

"How so?"

"There's only so many times you can tell the counter guy your wife's making blood pudding."

"Huh." That amused him. "I'll take the chance."

"It won't be fresh."

"Fresh enough."

"But—"

"I just got these clothes, and I'll be damned if I'm going to slog through a stinking stock pen just to get a meal. I'll make the counter guy forget."

All right, put it that way.

Only I wasn't sure where to find a shop. I knew every angle about getting in and out of the Stockyards, but not much about where to buy their end products. "There's a place near the house. Charles goes there when he wants to cook something." Which was almost never. The butcher's was next door to a Chinese restaurant, and Escott was their chief source of income. He loved his chow mein.

Behind us, a car horn blared. I checked the mirror. The vehicle's headlights flicked on and off. The driver hammered the horn again, rapidly.

"What the . . . ?" If it was a hit, they'd have pulled up even to us without warning. I slowed and stopped at the next corner.

Kroun shifted slightly. The cigar box was on the floor, and he had a gun in hand instead.

"I think I know 'em," I said.

"Make sure."

If there was a problem, I did not want to be trapped behind the wheel. I put the car in neutral, pulled the brake, and got out.

The other driver did the same, trotting quick to meet me. He was one of the bouncers from the Nightcrawler. "Derner sent me," he called.

"What's wrong?" Something like this could only mean trouble.

The man's face screwed up with thought, apparently recalling specific instructions. "He said to say your girlfriend said to come to the hospital right away."

"What's wrong?" I repeated, my gut going hollow.

"She said to say your partner's gotten worse, and you're supposed to—"

I dove back into the Buick.

Kroun at my heels, I charged past the hospital's main reception. When the elevator didn't open fast enough, I tore up the stairs to the third landing, finding the right hallway in the maze.

Bobbi stood a few steps from Escott's door, her posture tense, arms tightly crossed as though to hold herself in one piece. Coldfield had his back to the wall opposite. There was no anger in him. Anger would have been normal, welcome. Instead, he seemed lost, punch-drunk. More than anything, that scared me.

Bobbi turned, tears brimming in her eyes. She didn't move, just waited for me to come up and took my hand in both of hers. I couldn't speak. The look on her face . . .

"What's happened?" Kroun asked.

"They won't say," she whispered. "Relatives only."

That said just how bad it was.

A nurse inside the room heard and came out. "Are you the family?"

I remembered putting myself down on paper as being

Escott's cousin. "Me. It's me. Is he okay?" It was a damned stupid question, but the kind that pops out when you desperately want a positive answer. Of course he wasn't okay, not with so many people in white uniforms milling around in there. They were busy, which was hopeful. It was when they stopped work and didn't meet your eye that— "What's going on?"

"The doctor will tell you." She went back in.

I could feel it swelling, a mix of rage and terror growing too quick and too strong. I flinched when a hand dropped on my shoulder.

Kroun. He shook his head once. That was all. Then he took his hand away.

It was enough.

One instant I was ready to hit the roof, and the next a chill calm replaced the anger. I still wanted to punch through walls, but that wouldn't help. That was why Bobbi and Coldfield were so pulled in on themselves. They had to be, to keep control. Kroun, on the outside of things, took up a post next to Coldfield.

"Tell me?" he asked softly.

Coldfield blinked. "It . . . uh . . . it was Gordy's man, the one watching the actor. He checked on Charles, didn't like what he saw, got the nurse, started things moving. When they couldn't find Fleming, they knew to call my place. Bobbi called the Nightcrawler, and we drove . . ."

The guard himself came up. "Boss?"

"What'd you see?" He didn't hear me the first time; I had to say it again.

"I looked in like you asked. His color wasn't so good, and he was breathing funny, sweatin' bad."

But Escott was all right. Just hours ago he had been weak, bruised, and tired, but otherwise all right. *A good night's sleep and he'd be better in the morning . . .*

"I seen it before," the man went on, shaking his head, not meeting my eye.

"Seen what?"

"Mr. Fleming?" This from a doctor. He looked—I didn't want him to look like that.

"Yeah, what's going on?"

I didn't want him to say what he said: his words came out in a low sympathetic tone, words that said my friend was dying.

The words washed past. I just stood there. It was someone else doing the listening. Some other guy was going through this, not me.

"Can't you do anything?" Bobbi asked the doctor.

"We're doing what we can."

"But he was *fine* earlier."

"I'm afraid septicemia can work very fast. Once an infection's passed into the bloodstream . . ." He went on, not pulling punches. The odds were against Escott. Six out of ten people died from blood poisoning, died quick and ugly. I grabbed at the hope that he might get lucky and be among those who threw it off and recovered.

They finally allowed me in to see him.

One look.

I knew he wouldn't make it.

But I wasn't a doctor. I could be wrong, desperately wanted to be wrong. I found myself in a chair by the bedside, looking at Escott's face. His skin had a blue cast; he was sheeted with sweat yet shivering, jaw clenched, his breath coming fast and shallow, eyes sealed shut. He didn't react when I said his name. I got a whiff of his sweat when I spoke, and that took me back twenty years to some nameless hospital in France where young men who had survived gas and bullets and shelling and disease succumbed to infections just like this one.

The stink was the same, exactly the same. My friends had died then, and my friend was dying now.

I'd put him here. I'd killed him.

Bobbi slipped up next to me. "He's going to be all right, Jack."

"They're gonna do something?" Maybe they had better

medicine now. Twenty years was a good long time. Someone must have figured out how to cure this.

She made no answer.

"We just need get his fever down," said Coldfield, who seemed to be talking to himself. He'd come in to stand on the other side of the bed. His sister was a nurse; he might know more. But all he did was put a damp cloth on Escott's forehead. "We need some ice in here, that's all. A little ice."

The doctor was out in the hall talking to Kroun. I didn't bother listening. Only one nurse remained; the others had vanished. The old janitor from earlier worked his way slowly past, pushing his mop around an already clean floor.

"Some ice, please?" Coldfield said, his voice mild. He used another cloth to dab at Escott's face and neck.

The nurse nodded and left, not hurrying, and she should have. If Escott had had any kind of chance, she'd have moved faster.

Eventually she returned with a bowl of ice and a full ice bag. Coldfield took them both and thanked her. She backed off to stand by the door.

It was my fault. I did this.

Coldfield shot me a murderous look, and that was when I realized I'd spoken out loud. "You're goddamn right on that," he whispered. "And you know what's going to happen next."

Coldfield would kill me.

I didn't care.

"Stop. Both of you," said Bobbi. Her fingers dug into my shoulder. She was trying to keep her balance. Tears spilled steadily from her eyes. She couldn't have been able to see through them.

I got up and made her sit. She gently took Escott's near hand and bowed over it, bowed until her cheek lay on it, her face turned away from me.

That smell again, the rapid rasp of his breath, his shivering—he wasn't going to wake up. They wouldn't even try to wake him. Better that he just slip away in his sleep, that was what they'd say.

The room went blurry.

My hands closed hard on the cold, white-painted iron of the bedstead, and I held tight to keep on my feet. Something was wrong with my knees; I couldn't feel them or anything else except the nausea slithering in my gut. A knot of it clogged my throat, high enough to choke on, but too low to swallow.

I couldn't take this. I couldn't stay here and watch.

But I'd have to. Somehow.

He'd stay for me.

6

As the night crept by, the nurse periodically checked Escott, making notes on a clipboard for whatever good that would do. Coldfield kept up with the compresses. The doctor came again, but didn't have anything new to say, just looked tired.

Escott got worse, sinking as we stood by. The sound of his fast, shallow breathing filled the little room. It was the only sound in the world. I hated it, and I didn't want it to stop.

I thought about calling Vivian Gladwell. Escott hadn't wanted her to know he was in the hospital. Would he want her here now? Would it help? I couldn't work it out, couldn't decide, couldn't do anything.

Faustine came in. Gordy's man had gone off, maybe to get her. She'd shed the reporters. I hardly noticed when she hugged me, then moved on to speak to Bobbi. Couldn't hear what she said, but after a minute the two of them left. Bobbi held herself together until they were in the hall. Soon as she was out of my sight, she broke down sobbing. I went to the door. Bobbi wept and clung hard to Faustine, who slowly took her toward Roland's room, speaking in Russian. The words didn't matter; the soft, caring tone in them did.

Kroun was still out there holding up the wall, hat in hand, overcoat draped over one arm. He watched Bobbi, frowning.

"Hitting her pretty hard," he observed. "Must really like him."

"They're close friends, yeah."

"Friends with a dame. How 'bout that?"

I'd heard him say it before. "It can happen. Like me and Adelle Taylor."

The mention of her name caused Kroun to crack a brief, pleased smile. When it came to Adelle, he was starstruck. "She's friends with your pal in there?"

"Yeah. She is. Listen, you don't have to stay."

He shrugged. "When you gonna do something?"

I shook my head. "They can't do anything."

"Yeah, I got that from the doc. What about you?"

"I can't—I . . . what?"

"Give him some blood."

Must have misheard him. "What?"

"You know what I mean."

I did. I'd thought of it. A lot. But I couldn't decide; I just didn't know what Escott would want. "It might not work. He might not change. It hardly ever—"

Kroun gave me an odd look, then went in the room. The nurse was writing a new entry on the clipboard. He walked around her to the bedside. Coldfield straightened to glare first at him then me.

"He looks like hell," said Kroun, his attention on Escott. "Why haven't you done anything yet?" This was directed my way. He dropped his coat and hat on the chair.

"Done what?" Coldfield rumbled.

"He wants me to do an exchange on Charles." There was only so much I could say with the nurse present. I closed the door to keep things private.

"An exchange?"

"The kind that made me . . . like I am."

"Like you?" That shook him. "He *knows?*" Coldfield straightened to face Kroun.

"Yeah. He's in the same club."

"What?"

"Hey!" Kroun hadn't wanted that news spread.

"What's it matter?" I said.

Coldfield pointed at Kroun. "He's like *you?*"

"That a problem?" Kroun asked.

"I donno yet."

"An exchange," I said again with enough emphasis so the meaning was clear. "You know Charles best, what would he want?"

Coldfield visibly fought to focus. He must have gotten details from Escott at some time or other about how vampires are made. I take in blood, let it work through me, then give it back again. After death, Escott might return, but it rarely worked, or there'd be a lot more vampires in the world. He might not come back as I had done. "It would make him like you?"

"It probably won't work. Long odds, Shoe. Real long. Against."

It was a lot to take in, a lot to think about. He looked at Escott, then at me.

"What would Charles want?" I asked.

"To *live*, goddammit! What the hell you waiting for?"

"I can try, but you've got to understand that—"

"Cripes," said Kroun, disgusted. "Stop wasting time and just give him blood before it's too late."

The nurse had picked up that something out of the ordinary was afoot. "A transfusion?" she said.

"Yeah, sweetheart, one of those."

"Let me get the doctor." She sidled toward the door.

"Ahhh, *cripes.*" Kroun slipped his suit coat off and unbuttoned one shirt cuff, rolling it up.

"Sir, you can't just—"

He ignored her. The tumbler with its glass straw was still

on the bedside table. He took the straw and snapped it in half, then dumped the leftover water on the floor and put the tumbler back but nearer the edge.

"Sir? What are . . . *stop!*" Her voice shot up.

Kroun let out a few ripe words as he swiped the jagged end of the straw hard across his exposed wrist. Blood suddenly flooded out. He held his wrist over the glass to catch the flow.

We stood rooted—me, Coldfield, and the nurse—too shocked to move or speak while Kroun freely bled.

He grimaced and cursed some more and finally grabbed up a discarded compress. Shaking it open he wrapped it tight on the cut. The bloodsmell hit me hard.

"Gabe . . . ?"

"Not now." Kroun tapped Escott's face with the back of his hand. "Hey. Hey, pal. Wake up. Come on!" He hit harder, once, twice, and Escott's eyelids fluttered. He made a protesting moan. He wasn't awake, but could respond a little. Kroun held the glass to Escott's lips and tilted it.

The nurse screamed and surged forward. I caught her and kept her back. I didn't see what good this might do, but Kroun seemed to know his business.

"Come on . . . drink up, pal," he murmured. "That's it."

Some of the blood trickled down one side of Escott's mouth. The rest made it in past his clenched teeth.

Coldfield gaped at me, out of his depth. I shook my head.

The nurse got to be too much of a struggling handful, so I swung her toward the door. She pushed it violently open and kept going, shouting for help.

"Gabe?"

"He got most of it," said Kroun, putting the glass on the table. "Didn't choke." He went into the washroom. He twisted the sink spigot and carefully undid the cloth, holding his cut under the stream of water. "Damn, that stings."

He'd heal quick enough, but Escott . . .

Bobbi rushed in. "Jack?" She froze, seeing the blood that

smeared Escott's face and pillow. "My God, *what are you DOING?*"

The doctor, arriving with what seemed like half the hospital, asked the same thing and almost as loudly. While he checked Escott, he also instructed several heavyweight orderlies to escort us from the building. Things might have devolved to a fight, but Kroun caught the doctor's eye for a moment. I was too busy to hear, but the eviction was abruptly canceled, and the orderlies and everyone else were kicked out of the room instead. Confused, they hung close, peering in with other bystanders attracted by the commotion.

I shut the door on them, leaving me, Bobbi, Coldfield, and Kroun inside with the oblivious, hypnotically whammied doctor.

Kroun sat the man down and told him to take a catnap. Things fell quiet except for the fast, labored saw of Escott's breathing. He was fully out again.

Bobbi started up. "What did you do to Charles?" She'd aimed both barrels in my direction.

"It was me," Kroun muttered. "Just trying to help." His bleeding had stopped, leaving a hell of a red welt on his wrist. He frowned at it.

She put that together with the blood on Escott. "How? How does that help?"

He didn't answer, just shook his sleeve down, buttoning the cuff.

I stumbled out with a half-assed account of what he'd done.

Bobbi looked at Escott, then at us. "*Will* it help him?"

Kroun shrugged. "Maybe. Left it late. Have to wait and see."

"Jack, will this turn Charles into—"

"I don't know. Gabe?"

He shrugged again, pulled on his coat, buttoned it, checked his handkerchief. If he started fiddling with it again, I'd knock his block off.

"C'mon . . . talk to us. How did you know to do that? I never heard of it."

"Well, it's a big world, you learn something new every day."

"Not something like this!"

"Hey! Sickroom! Pipe down!" Hat on, he slung his overcoat over his good arm and started for the door.

"You gotta talk, dammit."

He paused, back to us, head half-turned, considering. Then, "No. I don't."

He went out.

"Son of a bitch," rumbled Coldfield. "The son of a bitch is crazy as a bedbug."

"You're all crazy," said Bobbi. She went to Escott, found a clean, damp cloth, and dabbed at the blood. It took her a while; her tears were back.

I went to her, but she didn't want to be held.

Someone ventured to open the door. It was Faustine.

"Things go-ink how?" she asked, gently easing inside. A damn good question. "Bob-beee, poor da'link. You let me help, yesss?"

"I'll be all right, I need to stay."

Faustine looked hard at the doctor, who was still out for the count. "Zen I find coffee. Yesss?"

No one turned her down. She swept out. I heard her dealing with the crowd in the hall, telling them to leave, all was well, all was fine. I recognized the nurse's voice raised in challenge, but Faustine wouldn't let her by and kept asking about coffee.

Hours of hell later I went looking for Kroun.

He was in a dark waiting room at the far end of the hall, feet up, nose in a magazine. The glowing spill from the corridor was more than enough for our kind to read by, but it looked odd. I turned the light on.

He squinted. "Ow. Too bright."

"Too bad."

"How's your friend?"

It was hard to speak. Almost too hard. I had to swallow, and my mouth was cotton dry. "His . . . his fever's down. He's breathing better."

"That's good."

"Is he going to need a second dose?"

"Nope." Kroun turned a page.

"The doctor woke up."

"He remember much?"

"Not a lot."

"That's good, too."

"He checked Charles out, took a blood sample, did some other stuff. The infection's . . . Charles seems to be throwing it off. The doc said it's a goddamn miracle."

Kroun shrugged. "Maybe it is. Thanks for telling your big friend about me. Next time use a megaphone."

"He had to know."

"No, he didn't."

"Coldfield won't say anything. Who'd believe him?"

"That's not the point—"

"Where'd you learn *that* angle on the blood? Who told you?"

"Doesn't matter." He continued to read.

"The hell it does. The one who made me didn't know, and neither did the one who made her. Who did your initiation?"

"Drop it, kid."

Was he ashamed? Granted, such things could get embarrassing. "You don't have to go into detail."

"I'm not going into it at all."

"Where'd you meet her? When?"

"You deaf? I'm not—"

"Or was it a man?"

That netted me a beaut of a "what the hell did you just say?" expression.

It lasted about two seconds.

I blinked at dark green linoleum, disoriented. I was face-down on the floor with no understanding of how I'd gotten there. My jaw hurt and hurt bad. I tried moving it, and some dim insight—along with a sudden burst of agony and the taste of my own blood—told me it was broken. Shattered maybe. In several places. The rest of me wanted to vanish, and I didn't fight the urge.

When I resumed solidity, everything was in working order again, though I still drew a blank on what had happened. I found my feet, taking it slow.

Kroun sat in his chair as before, but leaning forward, rubbing the knuckles of his right hand. They were raw and red. His expression was calm. "Are you anywhere near the point of backing off, or do you want your face rearranged more permanently?"

I stared at him, wiping leftover blood from my mouth with the back of one hand.

"Well?"

"I'm thinking."

He snorted and picked the magazine up from the floor. "And the man said *I* was crazy. I heard him." He flipped pages filled with pictures about hunting and fishing. "I need to get out of this town."

"Thought you still had business."

"I do. Tomorrow night. 'Till then, I got nothing else."

"No need to hang around here."

"Some babysitter you are. Forget about Michael and Broder already?"

"You could say."

"Word of warning: don't. Mike looks nice, but he isn't. Broder looks dangerous, and he is."

I'd figured that out already; Kroun just wanted a change of subject. "I'll keep that in mind."

"Smart boy. I'll need a ride tomorrow night."

"No problem." I could guess that it had to do with those cigars. It seemed a good idea to not try any more questions. I'd goaded him enough for one night. "Lemme tie things up here then we'll go. Thank you."

"Mm?"

"Thanks for what you did for Charles. I owe you."

He grunted again and found a page to read.

Bobbi looked up when I came in. She smiled—a small, sleepy one—but my world tilted another notch back toward its proper place once more. I could deal with anything so long as she smiled like that.

"Faustine's left?" I asked.

"She's bunking in Roland's room," she said. "If there's more excitement she doesn't want to miss it. You got more waiting in the wings?"

"Not that I know of."

I checked Escott over again for the umpteenth time, looking for changes. His heartbeat was strong and steady, no longer racing fit to tear itself apart.

"It's getting late for you," she said.

"You, too."

"I'll be fine. Shoe and I are staying."

Coldfield didn't speak, but his expression was eloquent. Yes, Escott seemed to be safe now, but that did not mitigate the fact that I'd nearly killed him. If not for Gabriel Kroun and the devil's own luck, Escott would almost certainly be dead by now. However matters had turned out, I had been stupid, and Coldfield did not forgive stupidity.

We were very much alike on that point.

The blue tinge to Escott's skin had faded. His color was nearly normal except for the bruises, and he looked to be in a natural sleep instead of deeply unconscious. That death smell was still present, but it was old air not yet cleared by the ventilation. What I got from him now was ordinary sweat, and that more than anything reassured me that he was truly recovering.

It'd happened extremely fast. In a tiny span of hours he'd drifted back from the brink. I'd *watched* the process and hardly dared to hope. The doctor had muttered about a miracle and recorded it on the clipboard. The nurses would glance at me and whisper to others, and on down the ladder went the story. Even the deaf old janitor must have gotten word; he kept his back to the commotion, clearly not wanting any part of it.

What the consequences might be later for Escott I couldn't begin to guess. Bobbi—all of us—wanted to know if it would change him in some other way.

I only knew of one means to turn a person into a vampire and just how rarely it worked. A blood exchange takes place, but with a normal human donating first, *then* taking in the vampire's blood; *that* was how it was done.

Kroun's variation was new to me, only he wasn't talking, which was nuts. What harm was there in telling?

Would Escott recall anything about drinking Kroun's blood? Perhaps as a fever-induced dream?

Coldfield might tell him. I wouldn't know where to start.

Bobbi promised to phone me at sunset tomorrow. I kissed her good-bye, nodded at Coldfield, who did not react, and left.

I drove to the Stockyards.

Snow sifted down, cheerful as Christmas. It was pretty until the window wipers began to clog. The milk trucks were out, as were the newspaper trucks, not a lot of cars. We made good time.

Kroun was pale as paint, though he wouldn't admit to being hungry. I was, mildly. Before Hog Bristow put me through hell, I'd gotten into the habit of never letting my hunger go beyond the mild stage. I found a place to park under a broken streetlamp and we got out.

"Cripes, what a stink," he complained.

"Don't breathe."

"Huh."

A high fence separated us from the source of the stink. Not a problem for me, but he'd have to climb get in. He studied the fence and shook his head, apparently mindful of his new clothes.

"It's not that bad," I said.

"Yes. It is. You have more of those bottles in your icebox?"

"Yeah, but—"

"I know. Not fresh. I'll get by. Hurry it up before we're under a drift. I'll be in the car."

He had a hell of a lot more self-control than I did. By now I'd have been crazy-starved, shaking, and suffering tunnel vision. Maybe the bullet in his skull had something to do with it. Kroun sauntered back to the Buick and shut himself in.

I vanished, passed through the fence, and re-formed on the other side.

After my resurrection, it'd taken months for me to get used to my new diet. The profound physical satisfaction I got was one thing; it was the part about biting into a living animal's vein and feeding from it that had bothered me for a long time. The benefits outweighed the unpleasant details, though, and eventually I reached the point of not thinking much on them.

Getting blood while it was still flowing and hot might not have the same importance to Kroun. Some people demanded bread straight from the baker's oven while others were happy enough with two-day-old leftovers. Others wouldn't even notice a difference. Maybe he was like that.

These nights I had to be cautious about choosing a four-footed victim. My hypnosis had been handy for soothing skittish animals; now I had to find ones that were already calm. Not easy. Cattle could be deceptive: one second lethargic, the next trying to trample you. Horses were easier prey; they were used to being handled. The shorter hair on their hides was a bonus.

Three tries to find an animal that allowed me to do what I had to, then I rushed the process. Things were getting damned cold. The snow swirled and fell more thickly, caking on my shoulders. Kroun's idea of going to a butcher shop was looking better by the minute.

The cattle in the next pen over abruptly stirred, restless and noisily fretting. They might have smelled their impending death on the freezing air, but if not, then something else had bothered them. Kroun's advice about being more careful was still fresh in my mind.

You can't be paranoid if someone really is after you.

I broke off feeding and looked around, listening hard, but I heard only lowing and the wind. Sight was limited because of the falling snow. The cattle could have been reacting to the weather or one of the yard workers. I'd learned to avoid them, but sometimes got spotted. Usually a man would shout, which was my cue to vanish, leaving him with a mystery. I was sure stories were circulating about a dark-clad specter haunting the stock pens.

Had it been a worker, he'd have yelled by now. My neck prickled the way it does when you think you're being watched. Most of the time we're wrong, and no one is around, but I paid attention to such warnings. The instinct is there for a reason. The last time I'd felt it, Hurley Gilbert Dugan had stepped out of the cold shadows and shot me.

He didn't seem to be around, which was just as well for us both. I'd have killed him on sight. Not a lot of people inspired that kind of reaction in me, and I wasn't proud of it. On the other hand, given the opportunity to bury *him* in the lake, I'd do it and no second thoughts.

I had come a long way down my private road to damnation.

Sparing my shoes further damage, I vanished and floated out, not re-forming until I was close to the Buick. If anyone saw, then their view would be as impaired by the snowfall as mine.

I took a last gander at what I could see of the empty street, got in, and wasted no time flooring it.

"What?" Kroun asked. "Something wrong?"

"Not much. It's been a hell of a night."

No disagreement from him on that.

The house had been broken into, again.

Any other time, I'd have gotten somewhere a few miles beyond mere anger, but it was late, and I was tired. I should have a revolving door installed so the next wave of housebreakers would have an easier time of it.

Instead of picking a door lock, someone had let himself in the hall window at the back with a brick, smashing out the glass near the top so he could twist the catch, lift, and climb in. The front door looked straight down the hall, and right away I noticed the curtains fluttering. The window was wide open, and glass shards gleamed from the melted snow that had blown in. It overlooked the alley behind the house. The neighbors had missed the noise, else the cops would be waiting.

"Your friends were here again," I said, disgusted.

Suitcases full of his new clothes in hand, Kroun put them down by the stairs, balancing the box of del Mundo cigars on top of one. He walked to the window and studied smears left by the intruder's wet shoes. "Don't think so. Michael can open any door, and Broder would just kick it in. They're not this sloppy."

Yeah, maybe. I did a quick search of all three floors, attic, and the basement, but no big bosses from New York lurked in the shadows. Sweeping outside, I looked in the garage, but Escott's Nash was safe. I found footprints in the snow by the house, but the fresh fall had nearly filled them in—not that I was an expert tracker. The intruder had pushed a garbage can under the window and used it to boost himself up; ignoring the locked doors, he'd left the same way. His prints led toward the alley entry and the street beyond.

"Michael's got no reason to return," Kroun said when I came back. "If he wants to know more about you, there's other ways for him, like talking to Gordy."

"What if they were here for you?"

"Then they were disappointed, but this doesn't smell like either of them."

"They're trying to shake me up."

"Why should they bother?" He shut the front door, cutting down on the cold cross draft from the broken window. "Anything missing?"

"Don't know." I made a second search of the place. Escott and I didn't have much in the way of valuables. He had an old gold pocket watch, but kept it in a safe hidden under the basement stairs along with his petty cash. I had a few cigar boxes stuffed with money there, too. Neither of us trusted banks much. The safe hadn't been broken into, but throughout the house someone had rummaged around in the drawers and closets. Nothing seemed to be gone, though.

"Not a burglar," said Kroun. "A reporter after dirt? There were plenty of them around when that Russian dame was all over you."

"Maybe. Faustine wasn't shy about naming names. But if anyone wanted to know about me, he could ask for an interview. No need to do this."

"What about the FBI?"

I didn't like that one. "I'm not important enough for them to bother with."

"Don't be so sure. That Hoover is crazy. He tells his boys to do something, and they do it, whether it's a good idea or not. Like me with Gordy's bunch."

"But—" I broke off.

"You think of something?"

"It's nuts."

"But worth considering?"

"Gilbert Dugan—that society bum behind the kidnapping I worked on? He was going to send anonymous letters off to a lot of places, the cops, the FBI, the tax people, to let them know that I was a suspicious character they should investigate. I got rid of those letters, but he might have written more."

"They'd pay attention to mail from some lunatic?"

"Probably not, but it'd only take one guy having a slow day to set a ball rolling. Maybe the G-men would burgle a joint, but this doesn't make sense. They'd pick me up for questioning first."

"Who else has it in for you?"

"Hand me a phone book."

"Don't stay here then. I'm not." He went into the kitchen and opened the icebox. He pulled out a brown bottle and yanked the cork. I'd seen drunks guzzle a beer that fast, but not often. As before, it hit him like a jolt of hard booze. "Wow. That's good stuff you keep there. Thanks for the hospitality." He left the empty in the sink and went toward the front hall. He looked at his suitcases a moment, shook his head, and walked out the front door without them.

"Hey, I'm supposed to keep an eye on you," I called from the porch.

"I'll stay out of trouble, I promise."

"Where you going?"

"Don't know yet. Safer that way."

"You need a ride there?"

"Nope."

"You coming back?"

"Tomorrow night, first thing. Still need to wind up some business." He moved briskly down the sidewalk, ignoring the snow.

No point asking what the business might be. He would return, if only to get his clothes.

I shut the door and muttered unkind things about the ass who'd broken the window. The place wasn't secure for me, not during the day.

My secret room under the kitchen . . . well, someone had found it.

The heavy kitchen table and the rug under it were slightly out of place. Escott was meticulous about keeping one of the table legs squarely over a small cigarette burn he'd made on the floor. He'd put it there on purpose, claiming it was a kind of burglar alarm, and damned if it hadn't worked. The burn was visible now. I was seriously spooked.

The intruder had not made it down into the room. A normal human could drop in but needed a ladder to get out. I had a folding one kept out of sight under my cot, and it was still out of sight, unused.

The intruder chose to avoid getting trapped in my basement lair, but he'd still seen it. What had he made of it? I didn't keep any secret diary or important papers there, just my attempts at writing lurid fiction for dime magazines. One close look, and he'd probably laugh himself silly.

A sense of violation, shaken confidence, and rage—I had the whole list of what it feels like when an unknown threat invades one's supposedly safe castle. This was far from the first time I'd been through the experience, but you never get used to it. If I found the guy . . . he wouldn't be happy. With both arms broken, it's hard to climb into people's houses.

I scavenged scrap boards in the basement that were long enough and got the hammer and nails. Fastening the boarding to the sash, I stuffed layers of newspapers in the gap between them and the remaining glass. If anyone wanted to get in again, he could do it; this was just to keep the weather out. As a repair it stank, but I felt better for the effort.

It was too dangerous to sleep the day here, and there wasn't time to drive to Lady Crymsyn and hide out in its hidden sanctuary—if it was indeed still hidden. The bad guys might have found it as well. I thought of calling the Nightcrawler and having a couple of the bouncers come over to watch the house, but for all I knew they might be in on it. Maybe it had been an overeager reporter looking for dirt. Maybe it had been those two cops, Merrifield and Garza.

Locking the front and back doors—including shoving a chair under each knob—I inspected all the windows, pulling shades, seeing to it the catches caught. It was more habit than expectation of keeping anyone out. I worked my way upstairs.

The clock on my dresser showed I had enough time to take care of some much-needed details so long as I was quick. One scalding-hot shower and a close shave later put me in an improved state of mind. I dressed to be ready for tomorrow night, intending to waste no time getting back to the hospital to see Escott. Yes, he was better, but a relapse could happen. Hope and worry chased themselves around inside my skull, each feeding and exhausting the other turn on turn, no end in sight to their insane race.

Grabbing two spare blankets from a cupboard and an oil-cloth packet of my home earth, I went up to the attic.

A determined break-in artist could still get in despite a heavy trunk I'd dragged over the trapdoor, but I wouldn't be sleeping there. Stooping to avoid rafters, I walked to the far end of the narrow space where a small window with cloudy glass peered at a similar window across the alley. Vanishing, I sieved through, floated over, and re-formed in the neighbor's attic.

I got my bearings, went semitransparent, and drifted to a dark corner behind some junk that hadn't been moved in years. Solid again and moving quietly, I put one blanket on the dusty floor, lay down, and wrapped up in the other. Very cozy. I'd done this before for a little peace of mind. The packet of earth was snug under the small of my back. It was cold, but nothing I couldn't handle. I'd rest well for the day, as safe as could be improvised, and not too worried the neighbors would find me. Spring cleaning was weeks away.

What arrangements would Kroun make? Perhaps something similar. With those picklocks he could walk through most any door. He could also hypnotize people into forgetting his presence. He'd look after himself well enough, hopefully without hurting anyone along the way.

That gave my conscience a pang. He was supposed to be a bad guy, same as his friends. Michael had specifically warned me to beware of him. But Kroun's reputation wasn't matching up to the side he'd shown tonight. If he was that bad, then why had he saved Escott? So that I'd owe him twice over? Maybe, but he had looked genuinely concerned at the time.

Why wouldn't he talk?

Wh—

Sunrise.

KROUN

Cold town. Damn cold town.

Gabriel felt a lot better with a bellyful of blood, but even that wasn't enough to take away the heavy weariness that had crept up on him over the last few hours.

He needed rest, the kind he only ever got from sleeping on soil, but that was a luxury he'd just have to put off. Leaving himself open to having the dreams, nightmares, night terrors in the day, whatever they were, was more important.

Mixed in with their horrors was information . . . memories.

Bad ones, like the bomb ripping through the car, but if they also led to something useful—like how he'd known his blood would help that man—then Gabe would take the bad with the good and get through it.

Fleming was getting too pushy with his questions.

Gabe hadn't enjoyed busting the kid, but sometimes you have to make a point when the other guy's playing dumb. Fleming wasn't dumb, not for damn sure, but he had a hell of an instinct for getting under the skin. No wonder Hog Bristow had . . .

Gabe's shoulders jerked. No, better not to be thinking about *that* mistake just before bedtime. The memories he courted had to be his own, not imaginings about another man's run of bad luck. He did not need to dream about being skinned alive. How the hell had Fleming survived the ordeal? Even Gordy didn't have those particulars.

Looking over his shoulder more than a few times, Gabe checked to see if anyone followed. Whoever had gotten into

Fleming's house might have been watching from a distance, waiting to come after one or the other of them.

No one showed himself on foot or in a car; what could be seen of the street through the thick snowfall was clear. Fleming was the target, then. Presumably he would find a safer haven for the day than that drafty brick barn.

Not my problem.

Long strides eating up the pavement and the snow filling in his tracks, Gabe left the rows of houses, entering the beginnings of a business area. This was where the neighborhood wives bought their groceries, where their husbands worked, where their kids ran errands. A good life when you could find it. Gabe's life before his change had not been so tranquil, he was certain of that.

He found the shop he wanted, one that Fleming had driven past on the way back to the house. On second look it still seemed suitable. The dingy window fronting the street was obscured with sheets of yellowed newspaper to discourage the curious from peering in, and a faded CLOSED sign hung crookedly on the door. The alcove entry was littered with minor trash, indication that no one had been there for months. Make that years. The papers dated from '33.

Good enough.

The picklocks got him inside.

It might have been some kind of store before things went bust on Wall Street. There were a few long tables, shelving, and a single counter for the clerk and cash register, but no other indication of its history. The dust was thick and the stale air cold, but Gabe had known worse places to spend the day.

He found a small storage closet in the back. Solid door, no windows. Good. No room to lie down . . . not so good, but he'd live with it. He scrounged around the shop and found a spindly wooden stool that would serve. A few swipes with a forgotten rag cleaned the dirt off the seat. Gabe took it in the closet and positioned it just right. He sat, back against the closed door, legs braced so he wouldn't fall over. No one could sleep like that, but then his bout of daylight immobility couldn't really be called sleep. Better this than sitting on the floor in his new clothes.

Gabe let his head droop forward, shut his eyes, and waited for the sun to smother his conscious mind for the day.

The dreams did not disappoint.

The monsters that had retreated into the shadows hurtled free again. There was no losing them, not when they called the inside of his head home.

His trip through hell began with the exploding car. He felt the fire, the ripping within his chest as the smoke seared him from the inside out. Close, too close. He could have died there. Died again. The changes in his body prevented that, but the awful recovery . . .

He was swept farther back and heard the wind threading through the pine needles again. How he loved that sound. Peace, pure peace. It did not last. The soothing music cut off as earth, wet and icy cold, was heaped over his inert body.

Yes, it was bad. One of the really bad memories.

He'd been buried and would stay there, deep in his grave.

No ending to this one. Death was like that. It was forever. He was dead and aware of every grinding moment, every second passing him by.

Aware of the loneliness.

Never mind the soul-killing panic, the weight crushing his chest, the dirt clogging his mouth, nose, and ears, the absolute paralysis, the cold; he was completely *alone* in the blackness. No angelic choir, no hell's chorus, no afterlife at all, only infinite, unrelieved isolation. He'd go mad from it; anyone would.

No. Not for me.

He had to get free, somehow.

The earth was heavy, but he could shift it if he tried. Maybe.

Some shred of will returned to what was left of his consciousness and transferred to his dead limbs, generating feeble movement.

He struggled and squirmed, gradually working upward. He hoped it was up. There had been stars framed by pine branches above him before that first shovelful hit his face. He just had to dig toward them.

Hard going, though. The hardest thing he'd ever done. Had they heaped rocks atop his body? He pushed at whatever it was, shoving it to one side rather than lifting—

His frozen hands clawed air.

More effort, and he worked his torso free, then his legs, boosting himself upright but dizzily swaying. He grabbed at a tree trunk and held on, spitting dirt, blinking.

Woods. Darkness. A small cabin not fifty feet away through the trees. No lights. No sound but the wind and the soft lap of water. A lake . . . no, a river. He came here to do his fishing. That, and . . . and . . . what was it?

He was filthy, and he stank. Smells were painfully sharp: the clean cold wind, the scent from the pine trees, the muddy earth, the blood. His clothes were soaked with it.

And God in heaven, his head *hurt*. He pressed palms to his temples and tried not to whimper like a sick dog. Take a lifetime of headaches all at once, triple their pain, and it might come close to what he felt. It rushed over him like a lightning storm.

It hurt the most . . . there . . . some kind of bump . . . no, a ridge, right in the bone. As he touched it, the pain exploded. He dropped in his tracks, unable to bite off the scream. He writhed on the broken earth of his grave and shrieked until his air was gone. Not replacing it seemed to help. Strange as it was to go without breathing, he understood it was all right. He was dead, and things were different now.

Dead. Just not a ghost. Something else.

He'd remember when the agony eased.

Only it didn't.

After a long, long time he realized it wasn't going away.

He swiped dirt from his eyes. His vision blurred and failed for a few moments, then returned. *Blinding* pain: he had the firsthand meaning of that now. He'd just have to get through it. He was in danger from . . . something . . . the sun. It would rise soon. He had to find a place to hide from it.

Back under the earth?

His grave? No. Not there again. Not ever.

Besides, there was . . . no, that couldn't be right. For a tiny instant he forgot his pain, trading it for curiosity.

Gabe touched an oddly familiar shape half-submerged under the loose clods and rust brown pine needles.

His numbed fingers slid over a layer of grit, brushing it off.

When he realized what it was, he yanked his hand back as though from a fire.

Gabriel shot awake, one hand twitching up to the left side of his head as though to keep his brain from bursting through the bone.

He had no comparable pain, but remembered what he'd felt then. How the hell had he gotten through it?

Where was that place? Not near Chicago. It was . . . the cabin . . . and it was . . .

Gone now. The sunset took it from him, damn it.

The thing he'd found . . . *what* was it? He could almost feel it again under his fingertips . . .

The sunset took that as well.

Damn.

His raised hand was a fist now, and he considered punching a hole in the wall, then thought better of it. This deserted and forlorn old shop wasn't his property to damage. He made himself relax and stretched out of his braced posture.

Not too bad, just a little stiff. He'd lose that on the walk back to Fleming's house. Gabe wasn't fully rested, but he would make up for it later.

Patience. Another day's worth of dreaming might get him everything.

In the meantime he'd talk to the old bastard and see if that would help.

7

FLEMING

THE neighbor's attic had some heat seeping up from the lower floors, but it was still cold. It took a few minutes to get myself moving again. My usual sanctuary was fairly close to the basement furnace, and I missed its comfort.

After floating back to the house, I made sure that no one had moved the trunk from the trapdoor, then descended through the floor and down the stairwell to the front hall. The kitchen phone was ringing as I materialized.

It was Bobbi, calling as she'd promised.

"How's Charles?" I asked.

"He's fine, sweetheart, just *fine*. It's a miracle." The jubilation in her voice flowed through me, warm and reassuring, and I sagged as the worry fell away. I knew she was smiling, and the spark would be back in her eyes.

"I'll be right over."

"Don't go to the hospital. He left."

I thought I'd not heard her right. "Come again?"

"He was well enough to check out this afternoon. The doctor wanted him to stay, but Charles insisted on leaving."

"What the hell? But last night—"

"He's *better*, I'm telling you."

Miracle, indeed. This I had to see.

"Shoe brought him to the hotel. The one I'm at."

"I'll be right over."

She made no reply.

"Bobbi?"

"You should wait a while, Jack."

"But—" Oh.

"Shoe's still upset by what happened."

"You are, too."

"Darling, I know that Charles getting blood poisoning wasn't your fault, but Shoe doesn't see it that way."

"He's right. It was my fault. If I'd . . . oh, never mind."

"What did you two fight about? Shoe won't tell me."

"He might not know. It was between me and Charles, and it's over now. Please, believe that." My tone begged her to drop it.

She grumbled something away from the receiver that I didn't catch, but it did not sound kind. Time to change the subject. I asked after Roland and Faustine. They were both fine and making plans to leave for Hollywood as soon as Roland was on his feet again. Things were happening, it seemed.

"Does it have to do with that guy who was there?" I asked. "The fast talker in the funny shirt?"

"Lenny Larsen? Yes, he's got a deal for them. A real movie deal!"

"He's crazy."

She went indignant. "For getting them work?"

"No, he's just a crazy guy. He's too slick by half."

"Jack, you only saw him for a minute."

"It was enough. Don't you let him spin you around, okay?"

"What do you mean spin me around?"

"Con you. The guy's got to be a con man."

"Well, of course he is. They're like that in Hollywood. You just have to make sure he's working for *you* when he's giving others the business."

Oh, God. She sounded as though she knew what she was talking about.

"What was that?" she asked.

"Nothing. Look, I've got to see Charles. I could find a way in if you tell me which room, which floor."

"The same floor as mine and Gordy's—he's better, too, by the way. He found it's easier to just rest than to argue with Adelle."

"That's good. I'll want to see him."

"Am I on your list?"

"You're first up, baby."

"That was the right answer."

I told her Derner's news about her apartment being clean and ready for her. She didn't exactly turn handsprings. "I'll go with you if you like," I added.

"You certainly will. I'm not sure I want to see the place yet. I'd like to stay another night here."

"At a noisy hotel?"

"It's about the same as my place, only I know everyone. I feel safer here with them around. How nuts is that?"

After what she'd been through in the last few days, it sounded perfectly sane to me. "It's a vacation. Not nuts at all."

"There's more."

"Oh, yeah?"

"It can wait. When do you plan to sneak in?"

"Uh."

"Thought so. You've got business, right?"

"Has to do with Gabriel Kroun." I braced for a touchy reaction.

"Oh. That's okay, then."

What the hell? "Hey, you're not—"

"Mad? Jack, he saved Charles's life. If it wouldn't make you jealous, I'd give him one lollapalooza of a big kiss."

"Uh . . . um . . . uh."

"Oh, relax. He's safe. I'll just shake hands."

"Uh-nuh . . . um." I cleared my throat next. It seemed the best response. "Well, uh, if you really want to thank him—"

"Yes?"

"He likes Adelle, seen all her movies. Maybe she could autograph a picture, put his name on it so it's specially for him?"

Bobbi thought that was a great idea. She wanted to know more about Kroun, but I didn't have much to say since I didn't know much. Telling her about the run-in with the cops, with Michael and Broder, the burgling of the house would just throw a cold, wet blanket on her high spirits.

We moved on to other topics, such as when Lady Crymsyn might open again and how to replace Roland and Faustine's big dance number. As always, I thought Bobbi should do the whole show, but her instincts were better on what to put on a nightclub stage. While I never got tired of hearing her sing, the customers might have other ideas.

Someone knocked on the front door, loudly rapping out "shave-and-a-haircut" but skipping the "two bits."

Bobbi heard the noise. "That your friend?"

"Not exactly friend, but I think so."

"Bring him over. Shoe won't have problem with you if he's along."

Optimistic of her. "Maybe. I gotta go, don't know how long it'll take. Expect me when you see me?"

"Don't I always?"

We hung up.

I moved a chair from under the doorknob and let Kroun in. He had a few smears of dust on his new overcoat and declined to say where he'd spent his day.

"What put you in such a good mood?" he asked after giving me a once-over.

"My girlfriend."

He glanced around. "She's here?"

"She phoned." I told him about Escott's recovery. "He's at Coldfield's hotel—the one where Adelle Taylor is staying with Gordy." As I'd hoped, the mention of her got Kroun's attention.

"Maybe we should go over, say hello," he said. "Ya think?"

"You got anything else to do?"

He grimaced. "Unfortunately, yes. I've an appointment and need a ride."

"Where? For what?"

"Later. I need a shave first."

He took one suitcase upstairs to the guest room and soon had water running in the bathtub. He might be a while.

With little to do but kick my heels, I gathered up the day's papers from the porch and brought in the mail. Nothing in the latter was for me, but the papers were full of re-worked angles on Roland Lambert's escapades as Chicago's newest gangbuster. Fresh pictures of him grinning or looking devotedly at Faustine were below the fold but still on the front page. Speculation was again raised about Hollywood doing a movie based on their exploits. No pictures of yours truly being affectionately assaulted by Faustine were there, though a couple papers mentioned me as a nightclub owner involved with the mobs. In one they called me "Jim Flemming." I was almost used to people spelling the last name wrong, but they could at least get my given one right.

The Alan Caine murder had moved to page two, small photo, with the cops apparently following a new lead. There were hints they had a suspect and were close to capturing him. Hoyle had been found. On page four was a two-paragraph filler about a man's body in a basement under a garage, foul play was suspected. No name, no mention of the address book I'd planted, no connection to the Alan Caine investigation. The cops were playing it close to the vest there.

Back on page two the header on another column read, SINGER'S SUICIDE WAS MURDER! with a quote from the coroner about Jewel Caine's autopsy proving she had not taken her own life. Cold comfort. Very cold. For a few seconds I wished Mitchell alive again so I could kill him, then discarded it. If I had a wish, then better to use it to bring back poor Jewel instead.

Though the cops were still on the hunt, tomorrow the story would be considered a dry well by most editors and passed over for other news. There might be something in the obituaries about Jewel's funeral, but no more, a sad and unfair end to a tough life. What was the point in trying if this was all a person had to show for it: a few lines in a paper and a headstone no one would visit. Some people didn't get even that much.

I tried to shake it off, as this was just the kind of thinking that would annoy Escott. Better come up with a distraction . . . like the damned broken window at the end of the hall. Despite my makeshift patch, there was quite a draft blowing through.

Taking advantage of being the boss once more, I called Derner. He knew someone who knew someone who could fix the glass after hours.

"I'll be by the club later," I said, "to drop off the house key."

"He won't need no key, Boss," he assured me.

The surprise was that I wasn't surprised.

By the time I'd worked through the rest of the papers, Kroun came downstairs, ready to leave. His singed hair and eyebrows had filled out sometime during his day sleep, and he looked better for a shave and a fresh shirt.

"Where to?" I asked, resigned to playing chauffeur for the time being.

He gave me a matchbook from the Nightcrawler. There'd been some scattered on the office's big desk. This was the one he'd scribbled on during his one private call.

I opened the matchbook. An address was written inside. I knew the street, but not the number. "What's this?"

"Let's go see."

We didn't have much to talk about on the drive over, so I switched the radio on and listened to a comedy show to fill the time. It had me chuckling in the right places, and Kroun snorted now and then. He wasn't the type to go in for a full belly laugh, though he clearly had a sense of humor. When the show was over, he turned the sound low and asked how long I'd known Adelle Taylor. I filled him in and told some harmless tales about her work at the Nightcrawler.

"She's a real humdinger," he said, drawing the word out, looking content.

I grunted agreement and pulled my heavy Buick to the curb, having found the address. It was some sort of a rest home and private hospital in one, to judge by the discreet sign attached to the iron driveway gate. An eight-foot-high brick wall with another foot of iron trim on top ran around the entire block. The trim ended in sharp spearpoints poking up through the latest layer of snow, giving me an idea of just what kind of patients were inside.

Kroun had his box of cigars in hand. He tucked it under one arm and led off.

The gate was locked, and a sign posted visiting hours with a warning no one would be admitted without an appointment. Kroun pressed an intercom buzzer, gave his name, and the gate rolled open along some tracks as though pulled by an invisible servant. It ground shut once we were inside. I thought they only had stuff like that in the movies.

A paved walkway that someone had shoveled clean wound to the main building. It was red brick like the wall, three stories, and on the plain side. The fresh drifts of snow softened its lines, but it didn't seem too friendly. Most of the windows were dark, with their shades drawn.

A large man in an orderly's white shirt and pants unlocked the door for us, locking up again. He gestured toward a reception desk in a small lobby where a nurse sat. She was busy with a stack of papers, but left them to deal with Kroun. He took off his hat, switched on his formidable personal charm, aimed it right at her, and damned if it didn't work. She warmed up, acting like he was an old friend she'd not seen lately, and conducted us down a hall and up some stairs to one of the rooms. The big orderly followed.

He had the keys and opened doors along the way.

It was that kind of hospital, all right, where the patients are shut inside for their own good and everyone else's. Who the hell did Kroun know here?

I kept my yap shut.

The orderly unlocked the last door and stood back.

The nurse gave Kroun a sympathetic smile, told him to check in at the desk before leaving, then went off.

Kroun cut the charm soon as she was gone. Face grim, he put his fedora on a small table just outside the door. He paused—hesitated more like—before reaching for the handle. I'd never seen him unsure of himself.

"Be careful," said the orderly.

"Hm?" Kroun looked at him.

"We cut his nails today. They're gonna have sharp edges."

Kroun nodded, then went in. He didn't tell me to stay out, so I followed. Quietly. The orderly hung by the open door.

Pale green paint on the brick walls, a cage over the overhead light, and the tile floor was layered with newspapers. Most lay open with uneven holes torn from the middle of their pages as though someone wanted to save an article. The biggest thing in the room was a hospital bed. It had thick leather restraint cuffs at the corners. Next to it was a reading chair, which looked out of place, so it must have belonged to the room's occupant, who was in it.

He was a big-boned, lean old devil, seemed to be in his eighties, and ignored us as we came in. He had a newspaper spread over his knees, peering at it through double-thick horn-rimmed glasses. The lenses must not have been strong enough; he hunched low to read. He had things open to a department store's full-page advertisement for an undergarments sale. Drawings of female figures in girdles and brassieres had his full attention. Carefully, he worked a hole into the sheet, his ink-stained fingertips and recently cut nails outlining an illustration.

On the bed next to him were a number of torn-out pictures, some like the one he was working on, others were photographs. All women. No portraits, he preferred them full length, matrons at charity events, debutantes, mannequins modeling the latest fashions. Painstakingly trimmed of their backgrounds, they lay in uneven piles, limp and ragged paper dolls.

Kroun took it in, his expression unreadable. "Hello, Sonny."

The old man grunted and continued his task. When he had the drawing torn free, he studied it under the harsh overhead light, then added it to one of the stacks on the bed. He had large hands, once powerful, but his fingers were twisted with arthritis, reduced to knobby joints and tendons. He had to work slowly to get them to do the job.

"Sonny."

He looked up. His mouth was a wide straight cut with hardly any lip, and he had the big nose and ears that come with age. His skin was flushed a patchy red, mottled by liver spots. White hair on the sides, a shock of gray on top, it needed cutting.

The glasses magnified his blue eyes to larger than normal. They were blank for several moments, then sharpened as an ugly smile gradually surfaced.

Something inside me writhed; it was the kind of instinctive warning that says run like hell even when you don't see the threat. This old man couldn't possibly hurt me, but the feeling was there and damned strong.

"What d'you want?" he asked Kroun in a gravelly voice full of venom.

Kroun pulled an institutional wood chair—sturdy with a

lot of dents—from a corner and sat almost knee to knee with him. He held up the box of cigars.

"Give," said the man, quickly shoving papers from his lap. He was in faded striped pajamas and shapeless slippers.

Kroun opened the box. "They're all for you, Sonny."

"My birt'day or som'tin'?"

"You want a smoke or not?"

Sonny grabbed a cigar, biting one end off, spitting it to one side. "You forget a light? G'damn jackets here won' lemme have no matches."

Kroun produced a lighter, a new silver one he must have gotten when he bought his clothes. He helped Sonny get the cigar going. I was glad I didn't have to breathe.

"Now that's a smoke." Sonny puffed, eyes narrowed to slits by satisfaction. "Who're you again?"

Kroun didn't show it, but he seemed thrown by the question. "Don't you remember?"

"I see lots of people. Which one are you?"

"Look at me. You'll know."

Sonny puffed and stared, but no recognition sparked in his distorted eyes. "What's wit' the hair?" He pointed the cigar at Kroun's white streak.

"Accident at my job, nothing much."

He nodded my way. "Who's the creep inna corner?"

"Just my driver."

"Fancy-schmancy, you gettin' all the drivers in town. Come here to high-hat me?"

"Thought I'd see how you were doing."

Sonny snorted and blew smoke into Kroun's face. "*That's* how I'm doin', you g'damn bastard. Locked in like a dead dog waitin' to be shoveled inna ground. You know how they treat me? No respect! You get me outta here!"

"I'll see what I can do."

"Liar. Everyone lies to me here."

"When you get out, where would you go?"

A slow, evil grin spread over Sonny's face. "*You* know."

"The fishing cabin?"

Sonny chuckled. At length. He sat back in the chair, his spine not quite straightening. The hunched-over posture was permanent. "Yeah . . . fishin'. I had some good times there. When you listened to me, you had a good time. You goin' up?"

"I don't know how to get there."

A scowl replaced the grin. "You're *stupid*, you know that? G'damn *stupid*. The g'damn place is still in g'damn 'Sconsin 'less some g'damn bastard moved it."

"Probably not," Kroun allowed. "I'm just not sure where in Wisconsin."

"Jus' over the state line, y'stupid dummy."

"And then where?"

"Hah?"

"It was a long while ago, Sonny."

"You're g'damn stupid. They got me shut in, treat me like shit, but I know how *long*, so don' go pissin' on me wit' that. You was here two mont's back—"

"No, I wasn't."

"You *was*! Lying li'l shit! Sat right *there* jus' like now, an' y' had 'nother bastard like him out inna hall an' you had *her* over where *that* bastard's standin'. Nice li'l twist, but you can afford 'em to be nice, can't ya? Brought her in, then went off and never come back. You were gonna come back and you din'. 'Stead you show up two mont's late in a fancy coat and nothin' to say but a lotta g'damn *lies*!"

Kroun held himself still as a statue as Sonny's voice beat against the painted brick walls. "Guess I lost track of things at that."

"Puh!" Sonny drew on his cigar, threw me a murderous glare, then seemed to relax. "So . . . how'd it go wit' her?"

"How do you think?"

The ugly snigger was back. "I bet. Picked a good 'un. She was a real humdinger." He drew out the word.

Kroun went dead white.

Sonny leaned forward. "Well? How'd it go? Tell me, g'dammit!"

Kroun swallowed and continued to hold very still. His tone was conversational but tighter than before. "Remind me how to get there, and I'll show you. I'll spring you from this dump, and we can both go fishing again."

Sonny laughed out loud, then stopped, his gears abruptly shifting. "You liar. No sharin' wit' you. Y' too good to have me along. Too good! Now y' won' even tell me nuthin'.'"

"Wouldn't you rather I show you?"

"Puh! Teach yer granny to suck eggs, g'damn li'l bastard. There's still things I can show *you*."

"Sounds good. I want that, Sonny. We can do it again. Wouldn't you like one more trip?"

The old man's eyes blazed. One of his big hands dropped to his crotch. He chuckled and rubbed himself. "I still got juice in me. What d'you think?"

Kroun nodded. "Yeah, sounds real good. You tell my driver how to get there. We'll sit in the backseat and smoke cigars like a couple of big shots while he does the work."

Sonny abruptly rattled off directions fast as a machine gun. Belatedly I found a pencil and scribbled on my shirt cuff. He thought that was funny and took pains to repeat everything. His cigar died. Kroun got the lighter working and held it out again.

His hand shook.

Sonny noticed. He relit the cigar, puffed blue smoke in the air, and smirked. "Got you excited, huh? Jus' thinkin' about it?"

"Yeah, Sonny. Just thinking about it." Kroun snapped the lighter shut and pocketed it. He rested his trembling hand on one knee. His other hand gripped the chair arm hard, his knuckles white.

Then Sonny shifted gears again and glared. "You ain't springin' me! I see that. You 'n' your fancy ways. Think you're too good, huh?"

Quick as a striking snake, Sonny threw an open-handed slap at Kroun's face. The impact of palm on flesh cracked loud. Another crack—Sonny connected again, backhanded.

Kroun didn't try to duck or block, just sat there and took it.

Sonny's mouth worked, and he spat. It hit Kroun's chin, then dripped to his coat.

Kroun still didn't move. He stared at Sonny. Stared long enough that Sonny's gears shifted once more. He pressed back in the chair and showed teeth. "You stay away from me. The jacket out there ain't gonna let you touch me, tha's his job, so you get out."

When Kroun stood and turned my way, I understood the old man's reaction. Kroun's eyes had gone blank, all pupil and no iris. Hell pits. When they leveled in my direction, I again felt like running, but he blinked and was himself. I was no more superstitious than the next guy, but this . . . it made my skin crawl.

The normal-seeming man that I now saw jerked his head toward the hall. Time to leave.

I got out. Sonny's curses and threats poisoned the air until the orderly closed and locked the door. It did a lot to mitigate the noise.

"You okay?" he asked Kroun. "He nick you?"

Kroun felt his cheek, checking for blood. "I'm fine." He got his handkerchief and wiped spittle from his chin and coat, then collected his hat, putting it on. He wasn't shaking as badly as before but was still ghost white. "The nurse wanted to see me." His voice was calm, soft.

We followed the orderly downstairs. Kroun had to deal with some paperwork, sign a couple of things. I stood by the exit next to the orderly, ready to leave as soon as possible.

"Crazy old guy," I muttered.

"Yeah," the big man agreed. "Those cigars helped. Got him in a good mood. He's usually a lot worse with visitors. Not that he gets any."

"No one else comes?"

He shrugged. "Just two guys that I know of. Haven't seen the other for a long time, but I'm night shift."

"What's he look like?"

"Like a doctor. The bills get paid."

"Know anything about this fishing cabin?"

"If I listened to their baloney, I'd be locked in one of those rooms myself, so no I don't. That bird's right out of his head most of the time. Nothing he says is gonna be up-front. You point at a horse, he'll call it a dog."

Kroun put the charm on again with the nurse, but from my vantage it seemed brittle. He glanced my way once, indicating he'd heard my questions and the orderly's replies. The somber and sympathetic nurse pointed at something on a clipboard, and Kroun signed it.

When the time came, the orderly let us out of the booby hatch. The clean, cold winter air was sweet. Kroun and I breathed deeply, then headed for the electric gate. Someone must have been on the lookout; it opened as we approached.

Kroun paused on the sidewalk, watching the gate roll shut as though to make sure it locked properly. Only then did some of the tension leach from the set of his shoulders.

"You got those directions clear?" he asked.

"Yeah."

"I remember most of it, but put 'em on paper for me, would ya?"

"No problem." What did he want with that fishing cabin? I had an idea and it wasn't pleasant.

"Leave it with Derner. I'll be by the Nightcrawler tonight."

"Where you going?"

"Gotta take a walk, clear my head. I'll cab over later."

"Gabe, I'm supposed to stick with you. If that guy was the old bastard that Michael—"

"Yes. Yes, he was. You heard some stuff."

"And I'm wondering why I heard it. You didn't have me in there just to take down directions."

"Actually, I did. But I figured if I had you wait in the car, you'd go invisible and sneak in anyway to listen."

"You figured right. What was he talking about?"

Kroun closed his eyes briefly and shoved his hands in his overcoat pockets. "Nothing I want to discuss. He's nuts. Didn't know me, my name. Lot of stuff comes from him that doesn't make sense."

"Made sense to you."

He turned away. "I'm going to get some air and think."

"Gabe—"

He snapped around. "And forget the goddamned watch-dogging for a couple hours! If Michael calls you on it, say I gave you the slip. He'll believe it."

"Okay, but—"

"*What?*"

"Who's the crazy guy?"

That got me a scorching glare. "Mike will tell you."

"Uh-uh. You."

More glaring, then his anger suddenly faded. His shoulders didn't ease down so much as shrink. He seemed older. He took the handkerchief from his pocket where he'd absently stuffed it after wiping off the spit. Kroun studied the crumpled fabric a moment, then threw it away. The wind caught the white square, swept it a few yards, then it nose-dived into a snow-clogged gutter, merging with the trash already there.

"Gabe?"

"Yeah, sure. Why not?" He lifted his fedora, rubbed a palm along his streak of white hair, then resettled the hat again. "The son of a bitch is my father. Now ain't that a kick in the head?"

He walked away, moving fast.

Kroun had his thinking to do, and so did I, but mulling things on my own wouldn't do the job this time; I needed to see Gordy. Working hard to avoid going over what I'd seen and learned, I drove straight to the Bronze Belt, not quite crossing into the territory, and parked a couple blocks away. It didn't take long to leg the remaining distance to the residence hotel where Shoe Coldfield had obligingly given safe shelter to Gordy and just about everyone else I knew.

I took it for granted that one of the countless lookouts in the area had spotted me, but with my collar up and hat low, they might not know me from any other lost white guy. Soon as I had the building in view, I vanished and floated the last hundred yards—not easy with the wind—and sieved through an upstairs window.

Damned if I didn't get it right the first time. I partially materialized on the third floor, or so the door numbers declared once I was solid enough to see. The place was pretty active; I went invisible again and bumbled down the hall, careful not to brush close to anyone. Coldfield knew that an inexplicable chill might mean I was hanging around.

I passed rooms where people talked and radios played. Gordy was somewhere halfway down on the left, so I drifted from door to door, hoping to hear his voice. No such luck, but I did catch one that surprised me. I slipped under the threshold crack and hovered out of the way in a ceiling corner.

Michael, and presumably his tough friend Broder, were there.

"I don't like this guy you picked," Michael said. "He doesn't have what it takes."

It was Gordy's room, and his response sounded confident. "He does when it's needed. The boys are used to him. The trouble's over. I'll be back soon enough."

If I'd had ears, they'd have been burning.

"There shouldn't have been trouble in the first place. Your kid put his foot right into it with Bristow."

"That was me. I'm the one who took Bristow to the kid's club. It wasn't his fault Hog didn't like his face and decided to go buckwheats on him. That was out of my hands. Besides, Hog jumped the gun. He put me here. And that's your fault. You're the one who sent him."

I could almost hear the steam coming out of Michael's ears.

Gordy continued, "But the trouble's over. The kid's got things running smooth. That's all that matters."

Michael gave him the point. "All right. I get you. If he screws up again, it's on you both. You got that?"

"Yeah. No problem."

"We'll see. Next is Whitey. I want him on a train back to New York."

"He's your man. You make him leave."

This resulted in a long silence. It was Michael's night to paint himself into a corner. "You know he could be more trouble."

"It's part of the business. You said you got Fleming watching him. Nothing's going to happen."

"You sound very certain about that, why?"

"The kid has a way with people."

"Like he did with Bristow?"

"Bristow was nuts. If you're saying that Whitey would—"

"No, not the same thing. But he's dangerous."

Gordy sighed. "Still your problem. You ordered him home, and he wouldn't listen. Right?"

Michael made no reply.

"If he won't listen to you, what chance have I got? I'm thinking he'll leave when he's good and ready. You want him out faster, offer to help him do what he wants done."

Another long silence. Then, "C'mon, Broder."

Footsteps passed close below me, then the door shut. I waited. If anyone else was in the room with Gordy, they would say something, but it continued quiet. Drifting down, I slowly took on form.

Gordy was propped up in bed, and his eyes went wide. He was wise to my peculiar talents, but it didn't make them any less alarming to witness. "That's some cute gag you got, Fleming."

"It's handy. How are you?"

"Better. A lot better."

He looked it. His color had improved since my last visit. The sickroom smell was gone. One of the windows was open an inch. He'd apparently convinced someone of the benefits of fresh air.

"Was Michael here for long? I just caught the tail end of things."

"Couple minutes. He ain't one to socialize with the help. You heard he don't like you much?"

"I'm used to it. He's right. I don't have what it takes, but I'll keep swinging at the ball until you say different."

"Good enough. Have a seat."

I pulled up a chair and took off my hat. "Where's Bobbi and Adelle?"

"Down having supper. They'll be a while. Dames. Always talking. Coldfield's been looking after 'em good. Lookin' after us all. I owe him."

"Is he here?"

"Went off with Escott. Donno where. Heard your pal had a close one."

"Yeah. He did."

"Bobbi told me. What had you and him fighting?"

"Nothing important. But Coldfield's blaming me for nearly killing Charles."

"Bobbi told me that, too. She told me everything." He let that hang.

My mouth dried out.

"Think Michael knows about Kroun being like you?" he asked.

Oh, crap. "Gordy, you're not supposed to know that."

He waved a large hand. "I'm not supposed to know a lot of things, but I do anyway. If Kroun's got a problem with that, he can make me forget, can't he?"

"He'll have a problem with it all right. Bobbi shouldn't have told you."

"It wasn't only her. Coldfield put in a few words."

"Jeez, at this rate the whole city'll have the headlines in the morning, and Kroun's gonna blame me."

"Nah. It stops here."

"What about Adelle?"

"I won't tell her if you won't."

"Deal." I sat back in the chair but didn't relax. Some part of me was alert for trouble. I heard the doorknob being worked. It was enough warning; I instantly vanished.

Hinges creaked. "You okay, Gordy?" It was one of the guards belonging to Coldfield's hotel fortress.

After a pause Gordy said he was fine. My disappearance must have startled him.

A scraping sound as the man moved the chair. "Those two guys are gone. Didn't say where."

"No big deal. I'm gonna take a nap now."

"Sure. Lights out?"

"Leave that one in the corner on."

"Sure."

A click, steps, then the door was closed.

I went solid. The room was much dimmer than before.

Gordy's eyes remained wide. "Real good trick, kid," he said, his voice low. "You don't want no one knowin' you're here?"

"Coldfield's that sore with me. It's better I keep my head down for a while. You serious about that nap?"

"Nah. Siddown."

I gently returned the chair to the bedside. "I won't be long, just a couple questions. On Kroun."

He nodded as though he'd expected as much. "You didn't answer—does Michael know about him being like you?"

"Kroun said no, and he wants to keep it that way. Take that how you like. Whether he's wise or not, Michael's got a hell of a worry going about him."

"Must have a reason."

"Yeah. I may have the why behind that."

I told about the visit to the nuthouse and Kroun's talk with Sonny. I told about the newspapers and how Sonny tore out pictures of women from them. I told about the hospital bed and its heavy cuff restraints. I told about the things Sonny said and Kroun's reaction to them.

Gordy didn't reply, just looked at me a long while. I'd

given him something he hadn't known before. Something pretty big.

"Is that crazy old man really his father?" I asked, to break the silence.

"I can check into it and find out."

"Without anyone else catching wind?"

"No. If I was on my feet, maybe. Not now."

"Hold off then. I don't want Kroun to know I've talked to you."

"He'll figure you will."

"Yeah, and he won't like it. Why did he let me in on it, though?"

"Donno." Gordy's face was always hard to read, but I could tell this had thrown him.

"What do you know about this cabin? The other night Michael pitched a fit when Kroun said he might do some fishing. Putting that with what the old man said . . ."

"Don't sound so good, no. Sounds like he takes girls up there, gives 'em a rough time."

"Maybe worse?"

He shrugged.

"You never heard anything?"

"If there was anything to hear, I'd have gotten it. Whitey comes over from New York now and then, does whatever business needs doing, has himself some fun, but I never got nothing on him visiting any old man, nothing on that cabin."

"What do you know about Kroun's past? Where's he from?"

"He came out of nowhere, worked his way up in New York. Only got to be a big noise in the last few years. Lotta boys are like that. Nothing on them their whole life, then suddenly they're running things. Happened to me."

That happened because Gordy's boss had been killed. Promotion in the mob was often the result of inheritance. "He knock off his boss to move up?"

"The guy before him was skimming off the top, then—

for a guy who didn't hunt—he went on a hunting trip and never came back. That's the story I got. Whitey was in the right place at the right time and slipped into the empty spot. No one argued with him."

They probably didn't dare. "What about Michael?"

"He's the one who figured out the skim. He's got schooling, but keeps out of sight. He looks after the books, squares the deals, does the thinking. He runs stuff, keeps the money moving, but Whitey sometimes has the last word. For some it *is* the last word."

I asked more questions and got everything Gordy had stored in his file cabinet of a brain. Such history was not easy to hear.

Kroun had ordered at least a dozen executions over the last few years; those did not count however many he'd personally carried out himself on the side. Gordy had been present at three, twice as a witness, once as a participant.

About two years ago, when Slick Morelli had been the big boss, Gordy had helped get a man down into the Nightcrawler's basement on a pretext, then held him in place. Kroun put a gun muzzle in the man's mouth and took the top of his head off just that quick. The thick walls and the club band playing upstairs covered the noise. The whole process had taken less than half a minute. Kroun hadn't cracked a sweat, hadn't even blinked. Right afterward, he'd gone up to the club and danced with the chorus girls as though nothing had happened.

No, not good to hear at all.

I considered Gordy a friend, but that dark side of him was part of the package. When it was necessary, he could kill and not think anything of it. He didn't like the killing, but he'd still do it.

I found myself squirming inside, knowing I'd gotten that way myself, it just bothered me more. How long would that last if I stayed on this road?

"What had the man done?" I asked.

"Kroun never said. Just gave the orders, and we did what

we did. He's good at that kind of job. Those mugs never knew from Adam when their number was up. He pals with 'em until it's time, does the job, then goes back and pals with their friends a few minutes later. Not a lot of guys are able to pull that off."

Michael had warned me. He'd said Kroun had no conscience. I'd met a few similar types, and you can usually tell there's something wrong with them even if you don't know exactly what it is. It's enough to make you cautious. Being able to hide it so well made Kroun different from them, and a hell of a lot more dangerous.

Gordy added, "When he came to town for you, I figured he'd do the same as always. Instead, he has you up to the office to hear you out. That never happened before."

"He always been called Whitey?"

"Yeah. Used to wear a white hat, winter and summer. The streak of white hair is new. Says he got skull-creased by a jealous husband who was a bad shot."

"Where'd that happen?"

He shook his head. "I heard it was in New York. But maybe that cabin?"

"And what happened to the husband? To the wife?"

A shrug. "You'd have to ask Kroun."

"I doubt he'd say."

"To you he might."

"Oh, yeah?"

"You got plenty in common. He didn't try to keep you out when he talked with the crazy guy. If Kroun didn't want you to know this stuff, you wouldn't."

"Carelessness in his old age?"

"Don't count on it. He'll have a reason. And don't trust him."

No. I would not do that. "But how did he get to be like me? You'd think he'd tell me of all people."

But Gordy had no answer to that, either. Instead, "Derner phoned today. Said you did a good job dousing the fire on Alan Caine and the rest of it."

I shrugged. I'd done what was needed but wasn't proud of it. "That fire won't be out until they find Mitchell, only they never will. Someone could still get burned."

"It's the best you can expect, kid. The heat's off our bunch, that's what matters. Derner told me you didn't like the fix job on your car."

I managed a short grin. "It's okay. If I'm being the boss, I might as well have an armored car. The wheels—I just wanted them changed, not swapped for solid rubber."

"Rough ride?"

"My eyeballs bounce so much I can't see the road."

That amused him.

"I'll swap for pneumatics once Kroun's gone home."

If he went home. He struck me as being sincere about getting away from the mobs. How would he do it, though? Fake his death again? That hadn't worked too well for him.

"Any idea where Coldfield went with Charles?" I asked.

"Said something about checking his mail."

"Then they'll be at Charles's office. I'll drive over and see. Maybe if Charles plays referee, he can calm Shoe down."

"Don't count on it," Gordy repeated.

8

KROUN

THAT sick bastard should have kicked off years ago.

Gabriel walked quickly despite the snowdrifts on the sidewalks, despite the ice hiding underneath. He wanted distance between himself and the venom-spitting monster locked away in that nuthouse.

And Fleming with his damned questions.

I should have had him wait in the car.

Too late, he knew the worst of it now.

"Not the worst," Gabe muttered aloud.

He missed a step, skidding on one heel before gaining his balance. Where had *that* come from? He glanced around, but the street was empty. No one had heard him. God, he should not be talking to himself, even when he was alone; he couldn't take that chance. Only crazy people did that, and he wasn't going to end up like Sonny.

Before that happened . . . well, he didn't know.

Maybe I should back off on this.

Tempting. He had money, easy enough to buy a cheap

car and get clear of Chicago. He could disappear himself in Minnesota or Canada, find a place to live and . . . do what?

He didn't know that, either. But it would probably take care of itself.

Fishing would be good, but after what Sonny had said . . . there was now a taint on that pleasure.

Gabe couldn't kid himself, he had to find the cabin and get things settled. The last time he'd been there—wherever it was—he'd gone up with a driver and some woman. Had she been the one weeping over his death? His driver back in November had been a mug named Ramsey, who'd dropped out of sight. If he'd been the one to put a bullet in Gabe's skull, then making himself missing was the smartest thing to do.

What had happened there? Even if Gabe found the cabin, he had no guarantee it would convey anything useful. Backing off now would leave him with unanswered questions, but he could live with those . . .

No, he would not. Good or bad, bad or worse, he had to find out.

The goings-on Sonny had implied made Gabe's stomach turn. Those pictures so carefully torn from the papers . . . disgusting, sick. How could they allow that?

The old bastard's crazy, that's why he's locked up.

One of the reasons why, anyway. Gabe didn't want to think about the others and kept walking.

The street, a nice one with big trees on either side, opened to a wider road with businesses and more traffic. A hotel took up a sizable portion of a block on his side. There were a couple cabs out front. He opened the door of the nearest and got in, giving the driver an address. The phone work he'd done in the Nightcrawler's office had paid off, giving him two leads to check out. This second one promised to be considerably different.

The driver was apparently familiar with the number. He smirked when Gabe paid him off.

Gabe went up the steps of a large, prosperous-looking

brick house similar to the other two-story houses along the street. Each had a small yard, some protected by iron-barred fences or painted wood pickets. Driveways had cars in them, walks were shoveled. The Depression seemed to have passed this area by, which could mean that mob money was all over the block. The big shots didn't always hang out at the bars and pool parlors. Even Capone had parked his family in that sweet place over on South Prairie.

No need to ring the bell. A bouncer on duty opened the door. His eyes flashed wide in recognition, then he shifted from surprise to stone-faced neutrality. His body tensed.

Gabe was almost used to it. He took his hat off and waited with the bouncer in the small entry until a pleasant-faced woman wearing a soft print dress and a long rope of pearls came. She also underwent a not-so-subtle transformation of expression, going on guard.

"Hello, Mr. Kroun," she said.

"You have anything for me?" he asked, radiating affability. He couldn't remember her name, but so far as memory served, most madams were alike. He thought she'd been pretty once, but life had a way of eroding one's assets.

She hesitated. "We're very busy tonight. It will be hours before anyone's available."

He looked past her into the parlor beyond where a radio played dance music. "Seems to be plenty available."

"I mean anyone suitable for *you*."

He was in strange waters now. Gabe knew in this area his appetite—there was a word as loaded as a set of crooked dice—had undergone a major change. He'd not availed himself of the services of the houses in New York, playing things safe. Out here in Chicago he felt better about indulging himself—except for the madam's manner with him.

He put on one of his best smiles. "Let me be the judge of that."

He started in, but she halted him with a hand on his arm. "Listen, Mr. Kroun, I got a business to run. You hurt my girls, and they can't work, then you gotta pay extra."

Gabe didn't know how to react to that so he went stone-faced, too. It clearly frightened the woman, but she stood solid. He put his hand over hers, patting lightly. "I'm not here to hurt anyone. Let's go in." He kept hold, taking her along.

Several young women sat around the parlor, some in Oriental-style silk robes, others in evening dress, one in a pale blue slip and nothing under it. They looked good; the place was high-class enough to have very presentable merchandise for the clients. None seemed too enthusiastic, though. A couple of the girls clearly recognized him. They whispered to the uninformed, who avoided his eye.

The madam pulled free and pointed to a thin, angular girl by the radio. "That one," she said. "She doesn't mind your games."

He managed to not inquire just what those games might be and focused on the girl. Nice, but with an edge that had nothing to do with her lean frame. He'd slice himself up on those bones and suspected she used morphine. She wasn't his type. He wasn't sure what his type was, but she wasn't it. He checked out the rest. A shorter, more rounded one caught his eye. She wore her dark hair almost like Adelle Taylor, though the face and figure were different. She'd been one of the girls who recognized him.

He smiled and nodded. "She'll do."

The madam opened her mouth, but he looked at her. No need to put any special weight behind it. Early on he'd come to understand that people were afraid of him. He made use of it. She backed down from voicing whatever objection she had.

The girl flinched when called over and avoided his eye. He could get around that. What he could see of her arms showed clean of needle pocks. Good, he didn't want a doper. He couldn't understand why people did that to themselves. It had to hurt.

However fancy the place, it was payment in advance. He settled with the madam, then went upstairs with the girl.

Her room was much as he expected: a big bed, satin pillows, a few bottles of booze on the dresser, a curtain partway open to a closet full of clothes, heavy curtains over the window so she could sleep during the day. A small sink was in one corner, a lamp with a red silk scarf over it stood in another, imparting a rosy glow to things. She had a radio and a record player. Not too bad. The mirror on the dresser was thankfully tilted away from him.

Soon as he shut the door she dropped to her knees and started unbuttoning his pants. Her hands shook.

"Hey, slow down, sweetheart," he said, catching her wrists. She flinched again, going pale. He drew her upright. "What's the rush?"

"No rush, but the others said you was a busy man."

Probably said a few more things besides. "Not that busy. How about we have a drink first?"

"I'm not allowed. Mrs. Temple marks the bottles. It's only for guests." She stumbled over the word. He thought she'd nearly said "customers."

"How about you have one and I'll say it was for me?"

She thought a moment, then nodded. "Vodka. Straight."

A good choice, it wouldn't leave much of a smell on her breath. He went to the dresser, poured a double. The damn stuff was strong, nearly made his eyes water. He took it over to her, but didn't release the glass as she reached for it.

"Look at me, honey," he said.

They were close, she had to raise her head up quite a bit.

"Well, don't you have beautiful eyes? How do you like mine?"

She gave no opinion, but he had her full attention now.

"What's your name, honey?"

"Lettie."

"Okay, Lettie, I don't know what you've heard about me, but I'm not going to hurt you. I want you to relax and"—he recalled one of Fleming's quirks—"just pretend we're old friends. You like me a lot, and we're going to have a good time, got that?"

She nodded.

He shut it off and gave her the drink. Her manner changed just that quick. She was suddenly at ease and even dug out a smile for him, a sweet one. Then again, he'd paid well for it.

He looked at the bed, but wasn't quite ready to start. It reminded him of the one in Sonny's room. Fine thing to think of now.

A soft creak from the hall froze him. Someone was coming up to their door, being stealthy, but like a herd of elephants to Gabe's hearing. Either the madam or the bouncer was checking on things. What the hell had happened on his last visit?

He opened the door. The bouncer loomed tall, solid, unapologetic.

"We're okay here," said Gabe.

The man remained.

Goddammit, I can't do anything with him listening. Gabe focused on him. "I said we're okay. Go downstairs and don't bother us again. Everything's fine."

That worked. The man left. Gabe shut the door.

"Lettie?"

She'd quickly finished the vodka and even washed the glass in the little sink. She came up to him and put both hands on his waist in the front, fingers slipping inside his pants. Very friendly. Her robe was open. Under it she wore red satin step-ins with lace around the legs. Nothing else. Her breasts were nicely rounded, more than enough for . . .

He cleared his throat, backed off a step, and put his hat on the dresser. His overcoat went on a chair next to it. The gun he'd taken from Michael weighed heavy in one of its pockets. He took care to not let it bump anything. "Uh, tell me, you know anything about cutting hair?"

Her smile faltered. "W-what?"

"Can you give me a haircut?" He rubbed a hand over his head so she'd know just where he wanted the trim.

"You serious?"

"Yes, I am. Another day, and I'm gonna look like one of those English sheepdogs. If not you, then one of the other girls . . . ?"

She laughed, a small one. "I used to cut my brother's hair. He didn't like it much, though."

"Hey, brothers are put on this earth to not like things." He took off his suit coat, watchful for her reaction to the gun he wore in a shoulder rig. She made no comment, didn't even seem to notice it. He slipped free of the leather straps, flexing his shoulders. "I bet you did a good job."

"You sure?"

He undid his tie, then the buttons of his shirt collar. "Yeah. Where do you want me?"

Bemused by now, Lettie took charge. She moved his overcoat to the bed, put some newspapers on the floor and the chair over the papers. Again, a reminder of Sonny's room. That had to stop, or he wouldn't enjoy any of this. He took his shirt and undershirt off next, but was strangely shy about his trousers. Damn fool way to be at his age, but he couldn't help it.

"Come on," she said. "You don't want to get hair on them; they'll itch."

He let her talk him out of his pants, socks, and shoes, then sat, feeling vulnerable in just his skin and skivvies. The room was warm, but goose bumps whispered down his arms as she pushed his head forward and started work on the back of his neck with scissors.

"You really needed a cut," she said. *Snip-snip-snip.* "I'll try to get it even, but you should have a barber with one of those electric-shaver things for this."

"Lettie, when I have a choice between you and some guy talking baseball, you'll get the job every time."

She snickered. "Short back and sides?"

"Yes, please, and some off the top."

"Yeah, I know how to do that. I never had anyone want a haircut, lemme tell you. The others'll think you're crazy."

"You girls talk about us?"

"Sure, not much else to do."

"Remember the last time I was here?" The snipping ceased, and he was acutely aware of a stranger standing behind him with something sharp in hand. He hoped his suggestion about being old friends was still strong. "It's okay, Lettie. I want you to tell me everything. Who did I see then?"

"Nelly Cabot."

He held off on further questions, letting the name sink in, waiting for something to come to him. Nothing. "She have dark hair like you?"

"I guess. She went blond though. They get picked more often. She went blond. You know. *All* over. The men really like that."

Not the kind of information he sought, but interesting nonetheless. "And I liked it, too?"

"You liked the things she . . . didn't mind doing."

Gabe wasn't ready to go into that just yet.

Lettie resumed trimming. He kept quiet while she navigated the critical areas around his ears, then started working the top. She used a comb in some way that yanked at his scalp. No wonder her brother had complained. "What's this white patch?" she asked. "You didn't have it last time."

"Accident at my job, nothing much. Did I take Nelly out?"

"Don't you know?"

"I tied one on that night. It's fuzzy. I thought we went out."

"Yeah, you did. For the weekend. You made a deal with Mrs. Temple. Nelly put on her best dress, got a bag, and you went off in a big car."

"I had a driver?" Ramsey, perhaps?

"Sure did. Other girls was jealous, but Mrs. Temple said to shut up and not talk about it."

"I made her nervous?"

"She didn't let on, but we could tell she was scared."

Yes. He did that to people. Some of them. "And then what?"

"I donno."

"Yes, you do. Tell me, Lettie." He stared straight ahead and would have held his breath had he a need to breathe.

"Next morning Nelly showed up real early. Woke the whole house, carried on like it was the end of the world, screaming and crying. Scared me good."

"What had happened to her?"

"Donno. All she had in one piece was her coat. Her dress was all tore up and bloody, and she was black-and-blue and . . . and tore up. You know. Down there. Called a doctor for her, and Mrs. Temple sent her off again. She never come back. Not here, anyway."

He couldn't speak for a long time.

Lettie finished, got a damp towel, and brushed at his shoulders to clean off the clippings. "I'm done, Mister."

He shut his eyes. After a few minutes, the bedsprings squeaked.

"Mister?"

"Gabe," he whispered. "Gabriel."

"You want to do anything?"

He blinked clear of the empty dark. She sat on one corner of the bed, bare feet dangling, the robe hanging loose and open. "Where did Nelly go?"

Lettie shrugged. "One of the girls said she went back to her mother. They brought in a new girl and told us to keep quiet. It was like Nelly was never here to start with. Mrs. Temple won't let us talk about her, gets mad if anyone says her name."

"But she's all right?"

"I guess. You'd have to ask Mrs. Temple."

Indeed he would, but not until the cold, sick roiling in his gut eased. A drink would help, but he couldn't touch the stuff on the dresser. As for the stuff in the girl's veins . . . he was sure he could not touch that, either.

Lettie slipped off the bed. "You wanna see how I did?" She picked up a hand mirror and offered it to him. "I think it's okay, but it's your hair."

He held the mirror and checked the faded image in it. The features were vaguely familiar, but he didn't know the man wearing them. "Best I ever had."

That he could remember. He gave back the mirror.

She was pleased by the praise, and he knew he had to get away from her. Lettie was pretty, and he'd wanted her, but that wasn't going to happen. He would talk with Mrs. Temple, find out what she knew about Nelly Cabot, and get the hell out.

He stood and reached for his pants. There, that hadn't changed, one leg at a time, pull them up, button the buttons.

"You leaving?"

"Yeah."

"But . . . did I do something wrong?"

No, but I might have. "Nope."

"You can't. I mean . . . Mrs. Temple will—"

"I'll fix it with her, don't worry."

"At least stay a little longer. They're gonna think I didn't do a good job for you."

He touched her cheek briefly. "I'll say you were terrific . . ." Her confusion got to him. Love was all she had to offer, paid for or not, and rejection hurt. She'd recover. He found his wallet and pulled out a century note. He folded it into her hand.

She gaped. "But I—but . . ."

"Call it a tip," he said. "For the barbering." He pulled his undershirt on, tucked it in. His feet were cold, in more ways than one. He sat on the chair and snagged his socks. When he straightened, Lettie suddenly crowded close and parked her duff on his leg, arms around his neck to keep from falling off.

"Hey!"

She wouldn't get up. "Hey, yourself. You wanna pay for nothing, that's your business, but I gotta do at least this much."

"Or what?"

"I donno. C'mon. We're friends, ain't we?"

Well, he'd been the one to put the idea in her head. Must have been one hell of a strong suggestion.

She squirmed, and he had to bring his legs together to balance her, dropping the socks. Her robe was wide open, and everything was close and smelled good. He didn't know what to do with his hands, finally giving up and letting them hang at his sides.

"You're not making this easy," he said.

She giggled. Damn, she was cute. She squirmed some more and gave him a closed-mouth kiss. That was first-class. Yes, he'd have some of her lip color on him, more than enough proof that they'd . . .

Lettie wriggled off his lap, turned, and straddled him. Her arms went around his neck again, but now they were face-to-face. "You're a good-looking man," she told him.

She was paid to flatter, but he liked hearing it. "Lettie, I—"

Another kiss, warmer, softer, her mouth opening just a little. She pressed close, but he cringed away. He couldn't do this.

"It's all right," she said. She stood, backing off him, her hands running the length of his arms. She tugged on his wrists until he stood as well. "C'mon."

"I can't."

"What, you're sick or something?" One of her hands dipped to his crotch, lingering. "You feel fine to me."

This time she was much slower unbuttoning his pants. They slid to the floor, and he stepped clear of them, getting just that much closer to the bed. She helped with the under-shirt, too. The gooseflesh returned to his arms and thighs as she dragged his underwear off.

"That's better. Right over here."

Yes. The bed. It hadn't moved an inch.

She pushed him onto it.

Any protest at this point would be ridiculous. He made room for her, and she climbed in next to him.

"You like anything special?"

"Just you," he heard himself saying. He pulled her onto him, full length. The step-ins were in the way. She wiggled around and got rid of them. No bleach job that he could see. She was soft there, very soft; his tentative caress made her smile.

"You're beautiful, Lettie."

She didn't disagree with him.

He wanted to touch every inch of her. He could not remember how he'd been with women before his change but appreciated that he was different now. What his mind could not recall, his body did. His big hands slid over her smooth, smooth skin, and he found himself kissing her shoulders and breasts, going lower and lower. He finally rolled atop her and tasted that musky softness between her black curls. She writhed under him, and he held on to her hips.

How quiet she was, but her breath came fast, and her heart beat faster. He lifted enough to kiss the insides of her thighs. One of her hands was on the back of his head and pressed him down low again. She'd liked what he'd been doing there. He took his time, until the musk turned sweet and silky in his mouth.

She abruptly shuddered under him, which startled him until he realized what was going on. Well, anything to please a lady. He continued until she settled a little, then moved his way up, going slow.

Her eyelids were half-closed, a dreamy expression on her face. He nuzzled her breasts, then her throat. Yes, the big vein there, easy to find, too easy to damage. Just a little ways past it, then.

But first . . . there. He slipped right into her as though they truly were longtime lovers. Yes, that felt good, damn good. Her legs wrapped around his, hips moving for him.

Lettie did not quite match his rhythm, just enough out of sync to press herself against him. Her breath shortened again. Damn, the girl was going for a second helping.

He slowed, smiling when she made a somewhat frustrated moan.

"More, baby," she whispered. "Just a little harder."

His open mouth ranged over her throat, seeking that one spot. Yes . . . his corner teeth were out and had been for some time. His own throat ached. How he wanted her.

Her palms pressed against his backside. "Just a little more . . . please."

He obliged.

She arched under him again, trying to hold in her cry.

Now or never. He bit into her, not deeply, but enough. Her blood was better than the sweetness between her legs, and he drew strongly on it, tasting her climax as it whipped through her. An overwhelming release surged through his body in that moment, and he was able to draw it out in a way wholly new to him. Another taste, another crash of ecstasy for them both, over and over and over. She moved under him, hands clutching and beating against the mattress.

He held on, making it last, pushing gently inside her, drinking from her. He needed it to last, because to his wonderment he was able, for just a little while, to forget the pain of not remembering who he'd been.

In this room, and for this here and now, it was all about who he was learning to be.

Gabriel drowsed, arms around Lettie as she lay on him. She didn't mind being held. She was solid but soft weight, and he liked the feeling of her heartbeat against his chest. He'd not realized how much he missed that sensation. From now on he'd have to borrow from others. Hell of a life, but better than that grave in the woods.

A clock ticked somewhere, other people in nearby rooms laughed, murmured, or grunted with sweating effort, beds squeaking under the pressure. Sometimes he wished his hearing wasn't so sharp. He wanted to come back to this place again, but with more privacy and less distraction.

Maybe that was what had happened with Nelly Cabot. He'd wanted to take her to a better, quieter spot, had ar-

ranged for a weekend out . . . then something had gone
wrong. But it couldn't have been his fault. Mrs. Temple had
to be mistaken about him. He could never hurt a woman, it
just wasn't in him.

The driver . . . Ramsey. Gabe couldn't remember the
man's face, just the name, and then only because he'd asked
others. The people who knew him didn't know that much.
Even with hypnosis to push things, Gabe got nothing more
than that Ramsey was a tough son of a bitch who knew guns,
cars, and kept his mouth shut. Indispensable traits for a mob
bodyguard and probably why Gabe had chosen him. Certainly it meant the Gabriel Kroun of that time had secrets to
hide. Ugly ones, if Sonny's ravings had any truth in them.

Why would I bring the girl to the sanitarium?

Showing her off to Sonny? Checking his reaction to her?
Or had she been there for Sonny to play with? No . . . not
that, or the old bastard would have bragged about it and
demanded more.

I have to finish this.

Which meant speaking with Mrs. Temple.

Gabe checked his watch. He'd been here long enough to
ensure Lettie's reputation in the house was secure. He un-
willingly quit the bed and dressed. His movements woke
Lettie. She got out on her side and pulled on her silk robe
but not the step-ins. God knows where those had ended up.

He adjusted his tie by touch, but Lettie came over to
make some small change for him. He caressed the side of her
throat, close to the marks he'd left. They'd soon heal, but for
the present looked alarming.

"You have anything to cover that?" he asked. "Beads or
a collar or . . . ?" Damn, what kinds of stuff did women
wear?

She went to the dresser mirror, checking. "It's not so bad.
I've had worse."

He fixed her with a look. "Forget that I made them."

Her eyes clouded for a moment, then cleared. "You ever
come back, ask for me, okay?"

He couldn't think of anything to say to that. Maybe she liked him, or his money, or it had to do with that suggestion about being friends, but it was nice to hear.

He bent and gently engulfed her in a bear hug. He held her tight for a long, sweet, contented moment, then reluctantly eased away and departed.

The bouncer was at the foot of the stairs when Gabe came down. The man threw him a quick glare and went up, probably to check on Lettie. The madam hurried out of a back room, her face taut with a frown.

"Mrs. Temple?"

She lifted her chin.

"Got a private place to talk?"

She went pale.

Not his easiest interview. Mrs. Temple had imbibed earlier, and it was hard to get past the booze; the effort made his head ache. Gabe got the name of Nelly Cabot's mother and that she ran a diner someplace, but no address. He also got the name of the doctor and where he might be found. As for what had happened that night, Mrs. Temple simply did not know, nor had she the curiosity to find out. The hysterical girl had been turned over to the doctor, and that was the extent of Mrs. Temple's responsibility. Asking questions about the private habits of the big bosses could make you dead.

The doctor, annoyingly, had since moved to another state. She didn't know which.

Gabe persuaded the bouncer to drive him to the Nightcrawler Club. The man hadn't known anything useful, so the trip was utterly silent. Plenty of time to think.

None of the previous goings-on at the brothel had gotten back to Gordy, or Gabe would have already found out from him. But Michael knew more than a little, though. He'd been in a lather to turn Gabe away from that cabin and from Sonny. Was that from having a guilty conscience? Might *he* have been involved and have something to hide?

I should have thought to ask Sonny, dammit.

But just looking at the old bastard made Gabriel's guts spin like a mill wheel. It'd taken everything he had not to puke all over those torn-up newspapers. He'd been playing that talk wholly by ear, improvising to get any information Sonny might have. Then came a point where Gabe couldn't stand to hear another word.

The easiest path would be to talk with Michael and get his end of it.

Which would mean coming clean with him. About everything.

Gabe wasn't ready to take that road yet. It would leave him too vulnerable. The less Michael knew about the whole blood-drinking angle, the better. Anyway, he would simply discount it and believe that Gabe had gone dangerously insane like Sonny and had to be put down. There would be no lingering in a loony bin.

I could disappear myself, but sooner or later he'd find me, and he'd kill me.

Yes, that was a given.

Mike would feel really, really bad about it—

But do it all the same.

9

FLEMING

On the way over to Escott's office, I stopped at a couple
places and bought a couple things. I was unsure if they'd do
much good, but what the hell, why not?

Not knowing what lay ahead, I approached the block slowly,
on the lookout for Coldfield's Nash. It was a newer version of
the one Escott drove, armored, of course . . . and parked right
in front of the outside stairs leading up to the office.

I cruised past, circled the block, and stopped to wait far
down at the end behind another car.

Yes, I was being chicken. Coldfield had already clobbered
me this week, and I was in no mood to risk more of the same
or worse. Not so long ago I'd have tried an eye-whammy to
cool him down, but I couldn't play that card again; I'd just
have to tough things out. Besides, Escott might get in the
middle and he had to have enough on his mind already.

Just as I set the brake and cut the motor, Coldfield came
downstairs onto the sidewalk. He looked both ways but
didn't see me, got in the Nash, and drove off, alone.

Lights remained on in the office.

Not knowing how long that would last, I grabbed my parcels and moved quick.

I clumped up the stairs to the door with THE ESCOTT AGENCY painted on its pebbled-glass window. He'd have heard me, but I knocked twice before trying the knob. The door swung open easily with a soft creak.

Escott sat at his desk in the small, plain room, pipe in hand, stacks of mail in front of him, business as usual. I damn near choked at the normalcy.

"Busy?" I asked, keeping on my side of the threshold. I couldn't help but recall the first time standing there, pretending to need an invitation to enter, while he gave me a good long look to figure out if I was friend or foe.

He gave me another good long look, his lean face just as wary. By God, his bruises were gone. He looked the same as ever . . . but things were changed. Break a leg, and the bone could heal straight, and you might not even limp, but you'll still feel it, you'll always feel it.

What I'd broken was the trust we'd had.

"Were you waiting long for Shoe to leave?" he asked.

That was normal, too, him figuring things out so quick. "Just parked. You send him away?"

"I needed an uninterrupted hour to myself. Business." He indicated the mail.

"Oh. Okay."

"Jack."

I halted my turning to leave. Looked back. With the pipe he gestured at one of the empty chairs before the desk.

"Come on, old man," he said, not unkindly. "Let's get it over with."

I shoved the door shut with one foot and sat facing him. Things got quiet, and I didn't know where to look.

"Well. This is bloody awkward, isn't it?"

"Oh, yeah." I checked over the small office, avoiding his eye.

"What have you there?" he asked.

The parcels. I put them on the desk. "Peace offerings."

He pulled the paper from one, which uncovered a bottle of dark beer, cool, not cold. The others held a fresh loaf of rye bread and a quarter pound of salted butter.

His eyes went wide. "What the devil . . . ?"

"You asked for them the other night."

"I did?"

"Before the fever really took hold."

"They had me doped with some awful stuff. I don't remember."

Just as well. "You hungry?"

"As it happens, I am. This is perfect." He had a flat sharp letter opener handy and used that to cut the bread and spread on the butter.

I didn't much care for the food smells, but he was eating . . . and drinking. He knocked the bottle top off using the edge of the desk and washed down the bread with a healthy swig.

He noticed me watching. "Worried that I picked up one of your habits?"

"Huh?"

"Swilling blood instead of this excellent brew?" He tilted the bottle.

"Shoe told you what happened?"

"In rare detail. I missed the show, but he was highly impressed."

"Kroun laid us in the aisles all right. How are you?"

"Remarkably well, thank you." He brushed two fingers along the side of his face. Last night his eye had been swollen shut, his face more black than blue; not a trace of injury remained. "All better."

Jeez. I was used to that sort of thing for myself, but not for others. This spooked me. "You remember anything about that part? Drinking the—"

"Thankfully, I do not. Shoe's description was vivid, and I shall do my level best to forget even that much." He slapped on more butter.

The food smells didn't agree with me, but thank God he was eating. He was alive to do it.

Another slug of beer, and he set down the brown bottle, politely suppressing a belch. "Who would have thought such blood to be a curative? It's like some patent concoction from the back page of a dime magazine, only it clearly works."

"And Kroun knew about it. I tried to find out more from him, but he wouldn't talk."

"Doubtless he has a reason."

"We have to know if it's going to have a permanent effect on you."

Escott seemed to be at a loss there. "Hopefully, your friend might be persuaded to part with information on that point. I am understandably curious."

"You sure you feel okay?"

"Never better. Which disturbs me because I recall feeling damned rotten the last time I took stock."

"Anything else?"

He caught my meaning. "Ah. Well. I've not exhibited any extranormal strength, my vision at night hasn't improved, nor have I experienced any sanguinary cravings. My canines are their usual length, and mirrors still work for me."

I was relieved. "That covers it."

"Of course there was an alarming moment when I woke from a nap and found myself floating just a few inches short of the ceiling . . ."

"Tell me that's a joke."

"A poor one, to judge by the look on your face. Sorry."

Some of the starch went out of my spine. Then I couldn't say anything, just sit in my cold sweat feeling sick and helpless. This was how I'd been before, and it had led me to put a gun to my head. I didn't want to be like this.

"What?" he asked, his gaze sharpening with concern.

His trust in me was broken, maybe never to mend. He would *always* wonder if I'd do something stupid again. "I . . . I waited too long."

"For what?"

"I didn't know what you'd want. I couldn't think."

"In regard to . . . ?"

"Trying to save you. Whether I should have tried a blood exchange so you might have a chance—"

"Ah. Shoe told me about that as well, along with your reluctance to act."

"That's what he saw."

"You made your point that it had only a slim chance of success. We all know that."

"I wasn't sure he understood. And I couldn't make the choice for you; he did."

"But Mr. Kroun stepped in."

"Yeah. A good thing. We might not be here."

That hung in the air for a moment. Escott had more beer, looking patient.

"But I waited too long."

"Because you did not know my preference in regard to a choice between being dead or Undead?"

"God forbid this ever happens again, but what do you want?"

For the second time that night I saw a man suddenly unsure of himself, hesitating. "I have thought about it," he finally admitted. "And thought and thought. I honestly don't know."

"How can you not know?"

"Some days it seems a good idea; youth, long life, strength, all the other advantages, those balanced by certain disadvantages to which one must adjust. But other days . . . it seems like the worst thing in the world. *Your* decision was originally based on wanting to be with the woman you loved."

And lost. Yes.

"My circumstances are different. Whether I returned or not, either outcome would effectively remove me from my life as I know it now."

"You're thinking of Vivian?" If she was a part of the decision, then he'd gotten pretty serious about her.

"She's a very intelligent, knowledgeable woman, but I shall risk underestimating her and judge that she would not be at ease knowing of such matters."

"That's not fair to either of you. Just talk to her."

"Have you spoken to anyone in your family about *your* change?"

He stumped me on that one. "They wouldn't understand."

"My point exactly."

"You can't make a choice based on how another might react to it."

"Of course I can. It's done every day. Sometimes one stumbles in the process."

He was referring to my attempt at suicide. I'd gone into that with no regard for the harm it would bring to anyone else.

"Things might change in the future," he said. "For now, I just don't know. If—God forbid—another similar situation falls upon you, all I can say is use your best common sense in regard to whatever circumstance you find yourself."

"That's only if I have time to decide. What if you get hit by a truck or something?"

"Then it is my fate to be hit by a truck. But in the meantime, I shall endeavor to avoid wandering into the street."

"And if the truck jumps up on the sidewalk?"

Escott opened his mouth but hesitated again. He could read me easy, and saw that I was serious. An odd smile came and went on him, and he shifted a little. "All right, I'll tell you this and you can believe it or not. The other night some part of me was aware of what was happening. I recall that much."

"Aware of . . . ?"

"That I was dying."

Oh, God.

"Jack, let me assure you . . . it was all right. It really was."

This had to be a leftover from that time in Canada when

all his friends had been murdered. Surviving that horror had changed him, made him careless about his own life in the years that followed. I'd thought he'd gotten over it, though. "There's nothing all right about wanting to die."

"I'm so glad to hear you say that."

"It's not about me."

"Nor is it about my wanting to die. *Wanting* was not a factor. I was simply aware that I was dying, and it did not trouble me. It was . . . not being forced upon me by the ill will of another, but just something that had come to happen."

"But my fault," I said. "I'm the one who—"

"Oh, don't start, you sound just like Shoe."

"He's right."

"No, he's not. You and I sorted our credentials, and that's the end of the matter. My going septic afterward was just bad luck. That sort of thing could happen anytime and come from a paper cut. I wish to hear no more about the business. Please."

"Okay," I muttered.

"Thank you. What I'm trying to say is that if you find yourself unable to offer your unique help to me, don't be troubled too very much. I'm refusing to worry about it, though I will give more thought to the matter. For now— again—I just don't know."

"You sure? That you're not sure?"

He shrugged. "Should I make a determination one way or another, I will tell you. I promise."

The way he said it told me the discussion was closed and only he could open it again.

"Besides, Mr. Kroun's unexpected hand in my recovery may have resolved things already. We need to question him. I thought he'd be along with you. Shoe had the idea you were looking after him."

"Kroun went for a walk. He's not exactly leash-trained. I put him up at the house at first, but last night he disappeared into some bolt-hole of his own."

"Not in the literal sense?"

"Hm?"

"Bobbi mentioned his inability to vanish." Escott raised a hand. "Please, she didn't purposely break her silence about him. After Shoe told me what happened, I asked her to fill in the gaps."

"Kroun's gonna love that."

"Secretive, is he?"

"Like a safe."

"Well, he is among strangers, all of whom know how to remove him. When one is wholly helpless during the daylight hours, one must be careful."

"Yes, one must."

"I would like to meet Mr. Kroun and thank him. Is that likely to come about?"

"Oh, yeah, I just don't know when. He's up to something I can't figure, and it's got a stink to it."

"Indeed?"

It was enough of an opening. Something shifted in the air between us, and we were suddenly back on another case again, same as ever. It was a conscious thing, and if a little forced for the effort, reassuring for being familiar.

I told him everything I'd told Gordy, then what Gordy had given to me about Kroun. It didn't take long, though it felt like hours before I ran out of words.

Escott finished his bread and beer, digesting both along with my information. "That business with Sonny is something I can look into."

"You stay clear of it. Kroun wasn't happy telling me the guy was his father."

"Yet he did. Why?"

"Moment of weakness?"

"I doubt that. It's odd. No idea where he went afterward?"

I shook my head. "He was plenty upset. Maybe he did just want to walk it off."

"His friends from New York will be less than pleased with you for not keeping track of him."

"They can take a flying leap, I've got my own row to hoe."

"Tomorrow I'll see what I can turn up on them, especially Sonny."

"Charles . . ."

"Be assured I shall be most circumspect. A phone call to the sanatarium while impersonating a physician should be enough, then I won't have to go near the place."

"Good. You don't want Kroun hearing you've been nosing around. He's going to figure I talked to you anyway, but . . ."

"Yes, yes, caution, absolutely. The directions to that cabin might prove helpful."

"He's going to be touchy about it. Don't go looking for trouble, okay?"

"Very well."

"You're not driving up there without me."

"Wouldn't dream of it. Word of honor."

While Escott sorted through his stack of mail, I transcribed the smudged shorthand on my shirt cuff to notepaper, making three copies. Kroun would want one.

"Now, about the Alan Caine case—"

"It's over," I said. "There is no case. I left a false lead for the cops, and they're off and running."

"Something went wrong for you on it. It had to do with Hoyle's death."

Escott was too sharp by half.

"What went wrong doesn't matter now," I said. "I wasn't thinking straight and wound up being stupid. You showed me just how stupid, and I nearly killed you. I can't apologize enough for that."

"You don't have to, old man. It's past, my number was not called that night. I've miles to go before I sleep."

My gut gave a twist at that thought. He'd come *too* close.

"Keep whatever it is to yourself if you must, I understand that. But I am still angry with you on Bobbi's behalf."

I felt myself go red. It was shame. Out-and-out shame. It blazed through me, intense as fire. It was worse than when I'd shot myself. "I get you," I whispered. "Never again. I swear on Bobbi's life."

He grunted.

"You gonna clobber me again?"

"If I have to."

"You won't have to."

"Are you going to tell her what you did?"

I gaped in shock. "Hell, no!"

He relaxed a bit. "I'm most relieved to hear it."

"She's asked why we fought . . . I can't tell her. She'd never be able to trust me again."

"Good instinct. It would only adversely taint her affection. What she doesn't know won't be a constant reproach to you and worry for her."

That told me how he was thinking. This was going to be a long road. "She's going to keep asking, you know that."

"Tell her that *I* made you promise. Pretend I was the one in the wrong about something and began the fight. You're only protecting my good reputation with her."

That was one hell of a favor. Too much of one. He'd done enough. "She'd never buy it. I can't—"

"You most certainly can and will. It worked tolerably well on Shoe."

The implications of that sank slowly into my thick skull. He'd put one over on Coldfield? I couldn't see how Escott had gotten away with it, but if anyone could . . . "Really?"

"Best to agree before I change my mind."

"Okay, okay!" I put my hands up, surrendering. "Is Shoe going to ease off being pissed at me?"

Escott went somber. "I doubt it. Not for a long, long while. Whatever the circumstances that led up to this near disaster, and whatever the miraculous cure that averted it, he's not going to cease blaming you."

I didn't expect otherwise. But, damn, it was tough. I valued Coldfield's friendship.

"Just give him time, Jack."

"Yeah, sure."

He glanced at his watch, shuffled the mail and food leavings to one side, and tapped his pipe empty. "Well, nothing here that cannot wait until the morrow. I'll be glad to sleep in my own bed tonight."

"Uh—there's one thing . . ." I told him about the break-in at the house. "It could be Kroun's two buddies messing around. Until I know what's going on, you should stay at Shoe's hotel."

"Bloody hell. I don't want some unknown thug dictating where I sleep."

"Me neither, but you're settled in already, aren't you?"

"At Shoe's quite forceful insistence."

"Go along with him. There's no harm in it. He'll feel better."

"Where will you doss down?"

"I'll be at Lady Crymsyn. If it looks safe. For all we know, it was just a regular burglar."

"You don't believe that."

"Not these nights, no. Another thing—your Nash might not be home for a couple days. I'm having the steering wheel fixed." I thought he'd be happier not knowing about the bloodstained upholstery. "You can call Derner at the Nightcrawler about it."

"Why, thank you. I'd not given it any thought."

Well, he had been sidetracked.

A car door slammed down in the street. "I think Shoe's back."

"Somewhat early. He's giving me a ride over to see Vivian."

It occurred to me that Escott could stay with her for the night, but I kept quiet. How he conducted his big romance was his own beeswax. "You going to tell her any of what's happened?"

He gaped in shock. "Hell, no!"

*   *   *

While I stood quiet in the office's back room, Escott locked up and went off with Coldfield. The lights were out, but enough glow came through the blinds to allow me to dial the Nightcrawler.

Derner picked up on the first ring. "Yeah, what is it?"

He must have been having a full evening, too. I let him know it was me and asked how things were going. Michael and Broder had come by and were down in the club. They wanted a word with me—or Kroun, who was keeping his head low in the office. Derner gave the phone to him.

"Thought you'd be here by now. What's the holdup?"

"I had things to do. I still have things to do."

"You can kiss your girlfriend later. Come over. Quick. I'll meet you on the street in the back."

It didn't sound like an emergency, more like impatience. If so, then why wait for me? He could get a car and go off on his own easy enough. He damned well better not want to make an expedition up to that cabin. It was distant enough that we couldn't manage a round-trip in one night, and I was not leaving town without seeing Bobbi again.

Good thing Kroun waited outside, there was no parking anywhere close, including the alley behind the club. A delivery truck blocked the entry. Several large guys in dark coats (and probably up to no good) glared my way as I rolled by at a snail's pace. Stuff was being dropped off or picked up—bodies or booze, I couldn't tell what—business as usual for the Nightcrawler Club.

Kroun emerged from a shadow, stepped up on my running board, and opened the passenger door.

"Keep moving," he said before I could hit the brake.

I kept moving, feeding more gas once he was inside and had pulled the door shut. Even he had to work hauling it to, because of the armor and thick glass. "What's the deal?"

"Just head west and watch the mirror."

"What's got you spooked?"

"Broder. I think he saw me. I ducked and got scarce, but you never know with him."

"Why not just hypnotize him?"

Kroun didn't answer.

"Or maybe you tried once, and it didn't work? Crazy people are immune. Is he crazy?"

He thought that one over. "Single-minded. He's Michael's watchdog. Won't work for anyone else."

"Nice pals you got. Just talk for a minute and get 'em off your back."

"I have nothing new to say and better things to do. Michael will see it differently and waste time for everyone."

Sounded reasonable. "Why am I here?"

"I need you to drive while I figure the roads."

"Where're we going?"

"That mirror clear?"

"Seems so."

"Make sure."

I made sure. Broder was the kind of mug one should always avoid.

Kroun twisted around to watch for tails. His mood was considerably improved and more energetic, and I wondered why until an intake of breath tipped me to a faint trace of perfume clinging to his clothes.

I got uncomfortable pretty fast and opened my mouth without thinking. "Is she all right?"

"What?"

"The girl you were just with. Is she all right?"

"You followed me?" He was more surprised than anything.

"I can smell her on you. Is she—"

"She's *fine*. Cripes, can't a man have some privacy?"

"How much did you take from her?"

He didn't reply, apparently overcome by sheer disbelief for the question. "What the hell—?"

"Figure it out. The things Sonny said, the hints Michael dropped about you making trouble, and the other night you were harping at *me* about feeding from—"

Kroun cut me off with one burst of gutter language and slammed the back of his hand against the door in frustration. I kept driving, ready to hit the brake in case he took a swing. Instead, he steamed a while, shaking his head, then barked a short laugh.

"Fleming, it is no goddamned wonder that people want to kill you."

"Just doing my job."

"Now you start," he muttered. "Okay, fine. I understand. I've got a bad reputation, so I'll let this pass. On the level—the lady is just peachy. But don't take my word for it, find a phone, pull over. I'll even give you a nickel to call the joint."

He named one of the more expensive brothels under Gordy's supervision, the name of the madam, and the girl in question. A phone call wouldn't take long. My eating crow was preferable to letting him get away with something ugly. Of course, Kroun could have hypnotically primed everyone with a story.

His reaction was not that of a guilty man, but then Michael had mentioned Kroun's lack of a conscience. Gordy's accounts of cold executions backed it up. Sonny's obscene ravings—none of it seemed to fit the man on the passenger side of my car. I measured that against Kroun's saving Escott's life, getting me off the death list, and his behavior in general.

But some people were very good at hiding the dark inside.

I glanced at him. He was angry, but there was no sign of that hell-pit emptiness in his eyes. For all I knew, the same thing showed in me when I went off my rocker. Maybe it was part of our shared condition.

"I'll check on it later," I finally said.

"Lemme know what you find out."

"I have to do this. It's not connected to Michael's orders."

He thought that one through. "Yeah. I see that. You're a stand-up guy, you can't help it."

I didn't expect that response.

"But you know," he continued, "you could try, just *try* not to be such a pain in the ass while you're at it."

That was more like it. "Just part of my charm."

A few miles of twisting and turning around the Loop convinced him we were in the clear. He gave me a direction.

"West," I said. "Not Wisconsin." And I'd been braced for a fresh new brawl for refusing to head north.

"Nope. I want what you wrote down on getting to the cabin, though." He had a pencil and another Nightcrawler matchbook.

Rather than drive while reading from my shirt cuff, I passed him the copy I'd made.

He grunted a thanks, then checked the paper. "This is word for word."

"Just a knack. Again—where are we going? And how long will it take?"

"Can't say. I don't know the area." He folded the paper into the matchbook, shoving both in a pocket, brought out a map, and wrestled it open. A black circle around a thread-thin line of country road marked our general destination.

Closer than Wisconsin, but not all that close, and I'd planned to see Bobbi tonight. I pressed hard on the gas. "You need a chauffeur, not me," I grumbled.

"I'm keeping you clear of Michael."

"So he doesn't know about your visit to Sonny."

"He'll find that out on his own. This is just to keep the peace."

"How?"

"You're both used to being in charge, and neither of you likes to be bossed. He pushes people, that's how he operates. If he pushes you the wrong way, then Broder has to step in; someone could lose an eye."

"You don't trust me with your friends?"

Kroun didn't laugh but was mightily amused. "You trust me with yours?"

"I didn't have a choice. What's going to happen to Charles?"

"He's better?"

"Like he was never sick. And he's asking questions. Is he gonna become like us?"

"Why should he?"

"Because our kind of blood is different. It changes things."

He stopped smiling. "Sure as hell does."

"You knew it would help him, but how's it gonna be for him later?"

"Damned if I know."

"You *don't know?*"

"Yes, I said that. I really did. You wanna figure it out, read a book."

"There aren't any. I've read everything on what we are, and nothing mentions a word about what you did. All I've got is you."

"Then you're out of luck, because I don't know. I'll say it again if that hasn't sunk in."

That exasperated me, and I let him see it.

"I don't," he repeated. "Really."

"And why is that?"

He shook his head.

What the hell? But more questions wouldn't work; he'd pulled on his poker face. Escott might have better luck getting an answer.

Maybe—and I was disinclined to believe it—Kroun was giving me the straight dope after all.

I'd suffered a blackout about my death. I'd lost days of time, though most of the memories had eventually come back. Perhaps he had that, too, and didn't want to admit the weakness. It would explain a lot. The bullet in his skull might make his case worse, blotting out who had made his change, how he knew certain things.

I opened my mouth to throw that at him, then caught
a glimpse of his profile. His head was pressed against the
window so he could gape up at the buildings as we rolled
along State Street. His grimness was gone, and he suddenly
looked like a farm kid marveling at the wonders. Everything
would seem different because of the internal changes. Those
towers would be new, shining and miraculous under a night
sky that wasn't dark anymore.

No need to interrupt that. I turned on the radio and found
some music to distract me.

Go far enough away from Chicago, and eventually you run out
of city. It trails off grudgingly. In the last ten years a million
people had moved in—I was one of them—and while most
clustered in close to the lake, there were plenty spread around
the outer areas. Instead of tall buildings full of flats, you saw
individual houses that gave way to fields and trees with no
sidewalks running under them, no fences cutting between.

The roads turned rough, the solid-rubber tires made them
bumpy as hell, and most corners lacked a signpost. If you
didn't know where you were, tough luck. There hadn't been
much traffic to break up the last snowfall, so I had to go slow
in spots. The heavy car skidded uneasily when the solid tires
weren't trying to rattle our teeth loose. It got too noisy to
hear the radio. I shut it off to focus on driving.

Kroun scowled at his map and didn't answer questions.
Annoying, but nothing new. I played chauffeur and paid attention to the route to remember it later.

"Pull in there," said Kroun after half an hour.

Suspecting he'd lost his bearings, I did, braking near
some gas pumps standing sentinel before a run-down white
building. Dropped onto a wide patch in the road, it was
shaped like a shoe box with square windows cut into the
long sides. Faded signs informed drivers that they could buy
gas, hamburgers, and hot coffee, the latter two emphasized
by bold, inexpert artwork.

The place was open; a lone light, the only one in view, shone over the screen door. Even in the most isolated spots out in farming country you can nearly always spy a light in the far distance and know that people might be there or had once been there. This would be the joint shining that light. Nothing else but trees and wind and loneliness lay beyond in all directions. When I cut the motor, the silence crowded in like an unwelcome witness.

The muddy slush between the building and the gas pumps indicated customers had been by that day, but no sign of them now. Kroun got out and looked around, his manner telling me that this was his intended destination. Who the hell did he know here? Another crazy like Sonny?

He struck off, heading for the door. I followed, and we went inside.

Like any hunter I scented the air: the stink of old cooking grease, onions, and stale coffee dominated. I'd eaten in countless diners just like this during my newspaper days. For twenty-five cents you could get a filling meal that sometimes digested without incident and flirt with the waitress if she was in the mood for it. This country-cousin version inspired the kind of nostalgic pang that made me glad I was now drinking blood.

The woman behind the counter looked to have had a hard life, but a lot of that was going around. Her black-and-gray hair was pulled back and pinned tight, her face amiable enough despite the lines. She had to get all types in, but nothing recent that looked like us. We got the quick assessing stare reserved for newcomers, and she asked if we needed gas, food, or both.

Kroun took his hat off. "No, ma'am, thank you. I'm looking for Mrs. Cabot."

"Who wants her?"

"I'm supposed to deliver something."

"You're no mailman. What is it?"

He hesitated, then pulled out a letter-sized envelope, holding it up. "Not sure. Looks like money. They don't pay me to be curious."

"Money for what?"

"I don't know. Are you Mrs. Cabot, Nelly's mother?"

She went dead still, her eyes going flat. "What about Nelly?"

"I'm here to make sure she's all right. If I could talk to her a minute . . ."

The woman pointed toward the door. "Get out, the two of you. Now."

"Mrs. Cabot—"

"*OUT!*" she bellowed.

He moved closer instead, but she was faster. Before he could even begin to give her the evil eye she pulled a Colt six-shot from under the counter, leveling the muzzle square on his chest.

"Our mistake," I said, and backed toward the door. I caught Kroun's arm and tugged. He retreated a few steps, reluctant.

"Please, ma'am, I only want to talk, there's no need—"

"*OUT!*" Her eyes blazed wild.

"C'mon, Kroun." I pulled harder. "Haul it."

She gave a double take. "Y-you're Kroun?"

He offered a hopeful smile. "Yes, ma'am. If you'd put that d—"

The barrel roared fire, short, ugly, and deafening in the confined space.

Kroun had hellishly good reflexes and ducked a bare instant ahead of the shot. I vanished entirely, came back, and grabbed him while the smoke still billowed.

The next second we were out the door in craven retreat for the car. Mrs. Cabot was right behind, taking aim, one-handed. Shaking and cursing as she was, she missed. Kroun slammed the passenger door shut in time to stop the third round. The thick glass chipped and went opaque right where his head was; he flinched back in the seat, and in a strange, strained voice told me to get us moving.

Good idea, but under certain circumstances it takes a damned long time to start a car and work the gas and clutch just right. I managed. In the meanwhile, she slammed two more shots into his window, each making progress toward shattering it completely.

We were suddenly bouncing onto the road, the motor howl drowning out any more gunfire though I was sure something pinged off the back. I didn't slow until a sharp turn half a mile down made it a necessity.

"Pull over," said Kroun.

"No, thanks." Just because I was more bulletproof than when I'd been alive didn't mean I enjoyed getting shot.

I put another mile between us and Mrs. Cabot, and he repeated himself. I'd gotten my own shaking under control by then and obliged. An unpaved lane leading into trees opened on the left. I went far enough in so we were hidden, cut the motor, got out, and went still.

Kroun got out on his side. "What is it?"

Held my hand up. "Listen."

He did, then shrugged. "Nothing. Just wind."

"Yeah, no siren. She should have called the cops by now. Even the ones in the sticks have radio cars."

"Maybe Sheriff Hickory is on the other end of the county ticketing cows without a license."

Good point. "What did you do to that woman?"

"Nothing. I wanted to talk to her daughter if she was there."

"About what?"

But he wasn't sharing. The wind threw itself through bare tree limbs and brush, which always made me nervous. It sounded like a ghost army was prowling around us. I was born on a farm but preferred the city. The sharp angles made it easier to pick out people when they came at you.

"Back in," I said.

"What?"

"We gits while the gittin's good, before the law comes."

"We're staying."

"So they can find us? They know these back roads and can

figure where we might hide. I'd rather be a moving target. We leave now, and we might slip clear."

"Jack, calm down. I can handle any cop who comes by."

"Like you handled her? No thanks, I've had enough." I got in, and so did Kroun, but he yanked the keys out.

"We're waiting," he said.

Goddammit. A flash of anger went through me, and I understood that woman's urge to shoot him. "Just tell me what you're trying to do!"

To give him credit, he thought about it. I could see wheels spinning and gears grinding behind his dark eyes, and for one naked moment glimpsed painful indecision there. Then he shut it down. He shook his head, pressing his palm against that white streak as though it hurt. "Can't."

I thought about slamming his forehead into the dashboard a few times but decided it wasn't worth the effort. By tomorrow Escott might have the whole story. "Okay. Why are we waiting?"

"For her to settle down."

"That could take a few years."

"You see her nose?"

"Not really." All I could see was the Colt swinging my way.

"Veins."

"Veins?"

"A nose like that means she has a bottle. She'll lock up, reload, have a drink or three, and fall asleep. We go back on the quiet, get inside, then I talk to her."

"Get inside? She's going to hear you sneaking up, I don't care how asleep she is."

He nodded. "I got that. The sneaking up is your job."

"The hell it is."

"All you have to do is hold her until I can put her under. I'll calm her down, make her forget everything."

Since Escott took me on as a silent partner in his business, I'd slipped into more than one place on the sly, but always in a good cause. Trying the same gag on Mrs. Cabot . . . no. Not without an explanation. "You tell me why, first."

Kroun gave a frustrated snarl, but cut it off. "I said I can't. I'm only here to find out if her daughter is all right and where she is. That's all. Don't ask who her daughter is. I can't tell you that, either."

He made it sound as though he was working under duress for someone else, but I wasn't buying. He'd ask the lady a lot more than just two questions. From those I'd learn more about what was going on with him. I'd pass what I knew to Escott, maybe Gordy, and they might be able to fill in the picture.

"We wait an hour," I said. "That's my limit."

He scowled, then gave a nod, handing over the keys.

That was one damned slow hour. I couldn't play the radio in case it ran the battery down, and neither of us was in a mood for conversation. For something to do I turned the car around so it faced toward the road. That filled up a whole minute.

The rest of the time it was dead quiet inside except for the wind outside and the tick of our respective watches. I'd gotten used to hearing breathing and a heartbeat with other people. Kroun had neither. Now and then I'd check to make sure he was still there, just my bad luck that he was.

It got cold, too. Even for me.

I wondered about Mrs. Cabot and her daughter Nelly and what either of them had to do with Kroun. My half-formed speculations were on the dark side.

Five minutes short, he had enough. "Let's get this over with."

Finally. I returned to the main road, keeping the speed sedate, slowing as we approached the diner. The CLOSED sign was up, every light was on, and a car was parked in front, partially obscured by the gas pumps.

"She called someone to come sit with her," I said. "No deal. Try again tomorrow."

"Just as easy to hold two down as one," he said.

"No, it isn't. She could have her whole family in there waiting with shotguns. Tomorrow." Before he could object I hit the gas.

We sailed by. Kroun grumbled to himself, looking back. "He's following."

I checked the mirror. The other car had pulled onto the road, headlights off. Anyone else would have missed him, but Kroun and I had the advantage at night. I picked up speed; the other guy matched me.

"Cops?" I asked. "Unmarked car?"

"I don't see any radio antenna. Some friend, maybe."

"We'll lose him in the city. Not much I can do out here. What'd you do to piss them off?"

But he didn't answer and continued to watch the other guy. "He's catching up."

I fed more gas, but didn't gain speed. Derner's garage pals might have tuned the motor, but they couldn't make it produce more power to compensate for the weight of the armor. My once fleet and sweet Buick was now a turtle.

Our shadow's windows reflected the surrounding snow, so neither of us could see inside. All I saw of the driver was a hunched form with his hat pulled low. The other car—it looked like a Caddy—came up fast.

He bumped hard into us, and I automatically hit the brake. He wouldn't slow, and on the slick road he was able to push and keep pushing. I floored my gas pedal, but it wasn't enough to get ahead until we started down a long slope. We gained a whole inch on him.

Crump, as he bumped again, much harder.

I fought to keep control. He hit the horn, which was supposed to unnerve me, and made a pretty good job of it.

Kroun rolled down his fractured window. He had his gun in hand.

"No shooting!" I yelped.

He looked pained. "Just going to discourage him. Drive."

Dammit.

The Caddy slewed toward the left as Kroun's first shot made a hole in the passenger-side windshield. Was his eye that good or had he gotten lucky? Before he could aim again, the other car hit the gas in earnest and plowed into my left back bumper. I nearly tore the wheel off keeping us straight and yelled at Kroun to get himself inside. He was half-out the window.

"What'd you say?" he asked, sliding back down.

"Stop shooting, you just made him mad."

"Chicken."

Hell, yes.

CRUMP.

It was a bigger and uglier sound than before, and the shock of impact went through the whole car. The Caddy had darted forward and slammed us broadside. I had the weight to resist, but no purchase with those damned solid-rubber tires.

We shot off the road.

10

FLYING is better when you don't have a body to deal with the inevitable hard landing.

But instead of sensibly vanishing, I held on to the wheel and stuck it out.

We were in the air for maybe three seconds, it seemed longer, then *wham*, we hit the snowy ground at about fifty, bounding quick and rough down an incline toward some trees. They would stop us, oh, hell, how they would stop us. I pumped the brakes (not working too well), kept the wheel straight, which was pointless since the car's momentum was in charge. We hit something, and the Buick slewed majestically, rear wheels coming to the front, the landscape rushing by sideways and far too fast.

A terrible low hammering noise, an abrupt and sickening twist—the big metal body tipped and tumbled like a kid's toy.

I was thrown around for one brutal, bruising, and frightening turn before winking out like a bad light. The steel bulk of the car pummeled my invisible form, but I'd be spared a maiming or worse. Dimly, I heard Kroun curse amid the tin-can noises as we rolled.

Then it stopped, just that quick.

Re-forming, I found myself lying faceup on the ceiling. The car was upside down, a fact that was slow to creep into my rattled brain. I understood it would be a good idea to get clear—especially when I smelled gas.

Kroun was curled awkwardly on his side, still clutching his gun. He looked dead, but was more likely just stunned.

I kicked at a window to break it—forgetting it was too thick for that kind of easy escape.

The effort made me grunt. I could almost taste the gas in the air.

Squirming and in a hellish hurry, I aimed myself feetfirst toward Kroun's open window, went nearly transparent, and slipped out backward belly down. Solid again, I got purchase with my knees braced against the outside frame, grabbed his shoulders, and pulled. He weighed more than I expected. The bad angle wrenched my back, but I pulled again. Once my shoulders were clear, I was able to get a better grip. I dragged him free and didn't stop until we were twenty yards away behind a thick pine trunk.

Then I collapsed. Some nerve in my spine went off like an electric shock and had me close to screaming, but another quick vanish and return took care of it. I didn't bother getting up. Sprawling exhausted in churned snow in the woods was all I wanted to do for the next few weeks.

Kroun shifted and groaned. Yeah, things were bad all over. He sat up, wobbly, staring around.

"Over here," I said, raising one hand.

His stare concentrated full on me. It took a second before I realized something was off. His eyes had gone funny, dilated to the point of being all black with no pupil. That *thing* so carefully hidden behind them was back.

"Gabe?"

It didn't recognize me. We were complete strangers.

"Whitey?"

It still had the gun and swung the muzzle around.

Oh, shit.

I got out of there, invisibly, and not an instant too soon. I felt the bullet punch through the space I'd occupied.

No second shot, but I heard him moving, standing up. I shifted quick, trying to get behind him, but he'd backed against the pine trunk. He was silent, making no unnecessary moves.

He fired again, accurately. Unlike other people, he was able to see my amorphous form floating around.

I could wait until he ran out of bullets, but this crazy change in him sparked a matching fury in me. Hit me for no reason, and I'll hit back twice as hard; that's how it works.

He got off a shot as I rushed him, but no more when I went solid, grabbed his arms, and slammed him into the trunk. He ducked his head forward, twisted, and suddenly I was the one about to collide with the tree.

I faded, shifted, went solid, and hit him in the gut. He doubled over, but brought the gun up again. I stepped into his reach, knocking his arm wide, backhanding his jaw on the return with my fist.

He should have dropped, damn it. I'd gotten too used to dealing with regular guys. Kroun was a match for my own strength and speed and also knew how to fight dirty. He swiped his gun hand quick as lightning toward the side of my head. I had to fade again, coming up behind, but he was ready for that, so I wasn't solid for long. A glimpse of his face threw me; cool, purposeful rage distorted his features into that of a wholly different man. What in God's name had come over him?

He wasn't anyone I wanted to meet in the dark woods at night. I floated back some yards, hoping he'd waste bullets, but he wouldn't take the bait. Going solid, I cast around for something useful. The ground snow hid any rocks the right size for throwing. Tree limbs? Nope, those were hidden or still attached. I had my own gun in a coat pocket, but hadn't reached the point where shooting him was a prudent option. I was mad, but not that mad. He, on the other hand, looked—

Shot.

That one missed my nose by a fraction. I disappeared and rushed upward. Much as I hated heights, that was my best place to get a weapon. The plan was to break off a dead limb for a club, except this time of year they all looked dead. I shifted to another tree, going higher. Soon as I judged the branches thick enough to take my weight, I had a quick look, made a grab at one that might work, and yanked hard. It snapped off with a crack as loud as a gunshot—which I heard a second later. I made myself missing, dropping the branch. It was too big to vanish with me.

Moving to another tree, I skimmed down on the side away from Kroun, going solid just enough to get my bearings.

We were about twenty feet apart. He stood over the fallen branch, looking right at me as I held to a semitransparent state. I couldn't talk; there wasn't enough of me formed up yet to push air. He kept his gun aimed point-blank at my chest. From his coat pocket he drew out another gun, the one he'd taken from Michael the other night.

Kroun—or whatever it was that was running him—pointed the second muzzle my way. He seemed ready to hold out all night like that.

We traded glares, catching our mental breath since neither of us had a need for the other kind.

He held himself tense, but his features began to gradually relax. That crazy blank-eyed rage ebbed, replaced by wary puzzlement.

He tilted his head, eyes going narrow. "What the hell are you doing? What's going on?" he asked, sounding annoyed. He looked like himself again.

But I wasn't taking chances. He had a beaut of a stare as I floated across the space between, going solid at the last second.

I busted him as hard as I could.

Damn, that hurt my fist. But this time he dropped and

stayed down. I pocketed his guns, then leaned against the tree. The woods got quiet again.

We were miles from anyplace except the diner. I'd had my fill of Mrs. Cabot's country hospitality and figured to take a stab at hitchhiking back to town.

Provided the road was clear of the guy who'd rammed us.

Of course my efforts were bound to be hampered by Kroun's unconscious body slung over my shoulder. He was goddamned heavy to haul uphill, too. I took it at a long easy angle almost parallel to the road, but the vanishings had tired me out. Halfway along I gave up, put him on the ground, and grabbed a handful of snow, mashing it against his face.

He came awake, snarling and struggling. Since I'd tied his arms together with his coat belt, I was in a better position to keep him from doing much damage.

"What the hell is this?" His outraged roar echoed through the trees.

"You're *nuts*, that's what it is," I said in a calm voice, which was surprising. Part of me wanted to bust him again.

Other guys might have done a lot more yelling, but he clammed up, giving me a second look and maybe a second thought to my statement. He could see neither of us was in a neatly groomed state. "What happened?"

Since he asked in a civil tone, I obliged with an answer in kind, filling him in.

The last thing he remembered was the car going off the road. He unexpectedly thanked me for pulling him clear, but shook his head over the rest, not believing it. "Why would I want to kill you?"

"Bad driving?"

That netted me a "go to hell" glower.

"Why do you think you wanted to kill me?" I asked.

He shrugged as best he could with his arms restricted. "Undo this, would you?"

"You going to go crazy again?"

"I've had two bad turns in cars in less than a week, how the hell am I supposed to know? C'mon, my head's killing me."

He did look bad, but his eyes were as normal as they could get—for him. I began to work the knot from the belt . . . and heard something.

Kroun caught it, too, and tried to stand. I shoved him back, signed that I'd check things, then moved toward the sound's source. Someone was working through the broken brush of the slope, following the trail my Buick had plowed. He was a distance away; only my hearing and the wind being in the right direction scotched his chance of going undetected.

The trees prevented me from seeing him. Between the trunks I caught a blur of a shadow heading toward my wrecked car. An innocent Samaritan might have seen the skirmish on the road and be checking for survivors, but my money was on its being the maniac from the diner come to finish us off. I was in a mood for dealing with the latter and crept closer. A little mayhem, followed by robbery, would suit me fine. Thump the guy to a pulp and take his car, yeah, that sounded good. Maybe I could persuade him to tell me why Mrs. Cabot had a grudge against Kroun.

The shadow far ahead was not careful about keeping quiet. The wind still restlessly stirred things around. He might have been counting on that to cover his own noise.

I could be absolutely silent, though. It just required going invisible.

Which I did, after fixing a direction in my mind and holding to it. I'd get to the car ahead of him, pop out of nowhere . . . yeah, a good old-fashioned bushwhack.

I streamed down the slope, flowing between trees, compensating for the push of the wind, going at a good clip. A partial re-forming showed that I was only five yards off course. I checked toward the road, hoping to spot him.

Lot of trees, black trunks stark against unbroken drifts

of snow except for the wide gash the car had carved. My poor Buick was banged up, but not nearly as crumpled as it should have been. The armoring had held the frame intact, preventing it from pulping Kroun during the fall. He'd have probably survived, but he wouldn't have been happy.

Footsteps . . . up there. The man was too far away to see. Just another black shape concealed by the woods. Damn, but I preferred the straight lines of the city.

He paused a moment, probably checking things out. He might have smelled gas and was keeping a prudent distance. The wind was wrong for that, but the stuff was all over.

Something as big as a goose egg arced through the air. I could only track the movement and general size for a split second, then instinct took hold, and I vanished completely.

Damned smart of me. I'd have probably survived, but I wouldn't have been happy.

He'd lobbed a grenade at the car.

I figured that out afterward.

The explosion—despite my muffled hearing—was impressive. Shrapnel and God knows what else tore into the space I'd occupied, violently and quick as thought. I felt each one, but had no real physical reaction. Stuff like that and bullets pass right through, disrupting a relatively small area.

Wind, on the other hand, can throw me around like a son of a bitch.

The grenade combined with the gasoline displaced a hellish amount of air in very short order. I didn't know what was going on, but the hurricane lasted entirely too long and was a few notches past unnerving. Abruptly going solid, I rolled downhill, no breath left in me but cursing a blue streak even when I picked up a mouthful of snow. I spat and rolled and cursed and vanished again, then popped back solid before coming to a halt.

It was another damned tree that did the halting. My

upper legs banged against it, my body folded, and I finished up wrapped around the base of the trunk like a damp sheet of newspaper.

After all that I didn't feel like moving for a good long while. Except for a terrible roaring somewhere upslope, my world was fine just like this. I was tired. A nap would be nice. I couldn't have one, but it would have been nice.

The roar died, and the red lights dancing on the other side of my eyelids faded. By then I'd worked out what the goose-egg object had been and what the consequences of dropping one of those things close to a ruptured gas tank were, and that I'd gotten lucky.

Footsteps slogged my way.

Odds were the Caddy driver would miss me in the dark. He'd thrown his toy at the car, not me, probably unaware I was so close. I lay still and . . . well, it's not called waiting when you don't give a damn about what comes next.

The steps got closer, walked wide around the tree, then slowly approached.

Kroun crouched on his heels and squinted into my face. "Hey. You in there?"

He looked normal and had somehow recovered his hat. Mine was gone and my head was cold. I hated that he had a hat and I didn't. "Go 'way."

"Love to, but someone blew up your car, then lammed it. I might have stopped him from leaving if you hadn't trussed me like a turkey."

Yeah, I'll keep that in mind the next time you go nuts and start shooting at anything that moves. I wanted to say it, but all that came out was something sounding like, "Rrrer-nugh."

Kroun straightened, hands unencumbered by the belt that I'd tied tight enough to keep him out of trouble. He rethreaded it through the loops on his overcoat then bent again to peel me away from the tree.

That hurt, and I got even colder rolled out flat in the snow.

"You're a mess," he said, taking back the two guns I'd

taken from him. He checked each for bullets and put them away. "Looks like you were right. I must have blacked out or something. Sorry."

"You do that a lot? Blacking out?"

"I wouldn't know now, would I?"

Good point.

"Come on, let's get clear before someone spots the smoke."

Oh, jeez. My car. I boosted up in stages after finding out just how dizzy my downslope tumble had made me, using the tree for support. I hung on to it like a drunk and gaped at what was left of my Buick. She lay belly-up, dead and strangely poignant. The gas had burned away; smoke from the still-burning seat covers and smoldering tires rose high into the night, making a terrible stink. The fire hadn't spread. The recent snowfall had discouraged that, thankfully.

Eventually I got close enough to throw snow on the tires to kill the smoke. It was a lot like dropping clods on a coffin after it was in the ground. She wasn't my first car, but had been the first one I'd paid for without help, even if I had taken the money from a gangster; I had a right to mourn.

"So . . ." said Kroun. "You got insurance?"

Hitchhiking at night in the winter on a country road without your hat is terrifically boring. I don't recommend it, especially when you have to duck from sight to avoid grenade-throwing maniacs. Every time we spotted headlights, we dodged clear, so we weren't exactly hitching. My shoes and socks started out soaked through and icy and never improved despite the exercise.

Neither of us talked much. I was mad, and Kroun again mentioned that his head hurt, then shut down. At one point he made a snowball and held it against the white streak on the side of his skull, and apparently that helped. Sometime later he threw what was left of the ball at a fence post ten yards away, hitting it square. He grinned briefly and kept walking, taking on a cheerful gait. The way he could shift moods was both annoying and disturbing, and I wondered if that was a personal quirk or something to do with the bullet he carried.

We progressed a couple miles toward the city glow far ahead before hearing the low grumble of a truck motor coming east and decided to chance it. I stuck out a thumb; Kroun held up a ten-dollar bill.

The truck, a big one with a covered load caked with snow, slowed and stopped, the driver bawled down at us. "I'm goin' to Detroit. You?"

"Chicago," Kroun yelled back over the diesel noise. "Buy you gas to get there?"

"That's enough to pay for my whole trip. Climb in!"

I didn't get his name, but he and Kroun had a fine old chat about the weather, bad roads, lousy drivers, and who did what for a living. Kroun and I were stranded insurance salesmen whose car had died in a lonely and inconvenient spot. The driver was hauling machine parts and usually drove at night because there was less traffic.

The night-driving business bothered me, and I wondered if he was in the club, too. But he took a swig of coffee from a Thermos jug, and it smelled like coffee, not blood. He offered us some, which we turned down, and Kroun asked him about trucking jobs since it seemed a good way to make a living. That set me to wondering if he was just passing the time or really interested in the work. Though monotonous, it was one way to earn money without having someone looking over your shoulder.

"Your friend okay?" the trucker asked.

"He's just tired."

Nail on the head for that. I wanted to stretch out in a warm bed and ask Bobbi to rub the sore spots even if I didn't have any. If I turned up this late in her room, she was more likely to bounce a lamp off my noggin.

The driver was agreeable enough from the talk and the

money to take a route through Chicago's North Side, dropping us at a hotel two blocks from the Nightcrawler Club. Kroun added another ten to the first, pumped the delighted man's hand, and wished him good luck on his haul. He sounded absolutely sincere, as though he'd made a new friend. When the truck was gone, he turned to look at me, his smile amiable. If he felt good, then the whole world should feel it, too.

"What?" he asked, when I just shook my head. "Is it the car?"

"You could say."

"I guess that was sort of my fault. We should have taken one of Gordy's. Tell you what, pick whatever you like, and I'll have Derner put your name on it."

"I don't want one of Gordy's cars."

"You're right. You should have something new." He pulled out one of the wads he'd taken from Michael and counted off a grand in hundreds. "This should set you up."

I took the money. The car was Kroun's fault, and that much cold cash did ease the sting. I was still mad and shaken that he'd shot at me, though there wasn't much I could do about it. As for what led to it . . . "Someone wants you dead and anyone with you. Why?"

That took his smile away.

"Nobody followed us out there. Your Mrs. Cabot called for help, and it came fast and packed grenades. Not a lot of farmers keep that kind of stuff in the toolshed. I wanna know what's going on. Everything."

Again, visible indecision as his mental gears spun and finally stopped. "Not now. I don't know when, but later."

"Why?"

"You'll know when I tell you."

It would be bad news, not that I expected any different, but he had a reason for having me along, and it wasn't just so I could tell tales to Michael.

With the wind freezing my ears and the street slush soaking my already wet shoes, I was in no mood to walk. The hotel had a taxi stand. I crossed to the first cab and got in. Kroun followed, and I gave directions. We got out again behind the Nightcrawler, and I tipped well since the drive was so short.

The delivery truck and mugs who had been in the alley were gone, but other mugs stood in their place. Soon as one of them saw us, he hurried inside.

"We're expected," said Kroun. He ran a hand over the white patch of hair and settled his hat in place. "Dammit."

Before we reached the back steps to the kitchen, Michael slammed the door open and came down. He was hatless, with no overcoat, evidently impatient.

"Where the hell have you been?" he demanded. He stopped and pushed his glasses up, giving us a once-over. "And what happened?"

"You tell me." Kroun put his hands in his pockets, apparently ready to stand outside all night and discuss it. "Where's Broder?"

"Back at the hotel. Why?"

"You sure he's at the hotel?"

Michael looked at me. "What's happened?"

I shifted in my soggy shoes. My feet were damned cold. "Somebody ran us off the road, then blew up the car. Does it bother you we got clear?"

He digested the news pretty quick. Smart guy, unless he'd known already. "You think it was Broder?"

"Unless it was you." I checked his shoes and pant cuffs—dry—but he'd had plenty of time to change from walking in knee-deep snow. "Give me proof to think otherwise."

"You—" Michael shut himself down. "Inside. We'll talk there."

"Mike," said Kroun. "Did you send Broder after us?"

He glared at me—I had the same idea, and it showed on my face—then he turned to Kroun. "No, I didn't."

"And you think he's at your hotel?"

"That's what he told me."

"Did you come after us?"

Michael shook his head. "I've been here all night waiting for you to turn up. Derner and half the dancers will tell you—"

"Only half?

"Never mind. Are you okay? You look like hell."

"I'm just peachy. Word to the wise, Mike: if it was Broder, you keep him out of my way. If it was some other mutt you let loose, you keep *him* out of my way."

"Are you done?" The wind was getting to Michael. He'd hunched in his suit coat, fighting off an initial bout of shivering.

"I'll tell you when I'm done."

"What'd the old bastard say to you?"

If the question was meant to surprise him, it didn't. Kroun took a moment, apparently considering his answer. "Not a damn thing. He's crazy, you know that?"

I got the sense that Michael was being careful not to look at me. He'd want to hear my version of tonight's fun and maybe hope Kroun wouldn't figure it out. I was tempted to vanish and let the wind carry me clear, but had a more prosaic option to take. "I'm leaving. See ya tomorrow."

"Not yet, you stay put," said Michael.

"I've punched my card for the night, I'm going home."

"And I need to talk to Derner," Kroun said. He stepped around Michael and went up the stairs, banging the door shut.

Michael started after him, then turned back to me. I picked up that he was worried, grimly worried.

"If you'd tell me what the problem is . . ." I said, slowly and calmly, though inside I was kicking myself. This was officially sticking my neck out. Or putting my foot in, I wasn't sure.

"Whitey didn't?"

I missed my hypnosis gag. It made many, many things a lot easier. "I think he means to."

"What happened with the old man? You were there, right?"

Kroun had allowed me into the small room with that two-legged snake, knowing I'd talk to Michael. Maybe it was why I'd been there. "The old man's crazy."

"Yes. But what did he say?"

"Whitey tried to get him to talk about that cabin, going up there for the fishing. The old guy seemed to think that would be a lot of fun. The rest of the time he was cussing us out or tearing pictures of women from a newspaper." I threw out the last bit to get Michael's reaction.

He pulled in on himself just that much more, nothing to do with the cold.

"That's why he's in the booby hatch, because of how he treats women?"

He kept his gaze fixed, unreadable.

It had long past come to me that if I showed too much interest, then dire consequences could follow. It might already be too late.

He gave me a long, assessing look. "About this car trouble—what exactly happened?"

"We were taking a drive in the country . . ." I made out that Kroun hadn't told me our destination, gotten us lost, and when we finally turned back to Chicago, the guy in the Caddy tried to kill us. It was a risk. If the guy was Broder, then Michael would learn his end of it and know I was lying for Kroun.

I wasn't exactly siding with him, but I did owe him for saving Escott's life. Besides, it might goad Michael into telling me something useful about whatever feud he had going. "If your boy Broder's behind this—"

"He won't be," Michael said quickly.

"You don't know that. He could have his own operation running, like the late, unlamented Mitchell. If that's the case, you may need a friend."

"You?"

"Uh-uh. Derner." I let that sink in. "I'm just a saloon-keeper. Soon as you guys leave town, I'm going back to my bar and keeping my nose clean. That's all I've ever wanted, it's no secret. For now I'm getting out of the cold, that was a hell of a long walk."

I turned to look for another cab, but he caught my arm. "Your car's wrecked?"

"Grenade, tank of gas—what do you think?"

"Here . . ." Damned if he didn't dig out a wad of cash and peel off ten portraits of Ben Franklin. "Get another on me."

He shoved the bills into my hand, then hurried back to the club, hunching low against the cold.

"Thanks!" I called after him. He raised one hand to show he'd heard, shot up the steps, and hustled inside.

I looked at the money. It was real. I would keep it. That Kroun had already bought me a replacement didn't matter. After tonight's excitement, I deserved a tip.

KROUN

Gabe took the stairs to Gordy's office one at a time, but quick-stepping it. He wouldn't have much of a respite before Michael finished with Fleming and followed.

Derner didn't stare too much. "Have some trouble, Mr. Kroun?"

"You could say. I need a car. A good one, gassed up and with some heavy blankets in the back. No one's to know about it. Especially Michael."

"Uh . . . okay. Now?"

"Sooner."

That done, he crossed to the bathroom and shook out of his once-new coat. It wasn't a total loss, but the slush and mud stains annoyed him. No time to have it cleaned or get another.

He checked his faint reflection in the mirror and scrubbed the scrapes and dirt from his face. The hot water warmed his hands. He'd not realized how cold they'd been. Aware of the problem, he checked his shoes. Yeah, soaked and freezing, no wonder Fleming looked so miserable.

Gabriel gingerly touched the ridge in his skull, bracing

for pain, but nothing blazed up. Holding that snowball against the damage had killed it. He'd have to buy an ice bag sometime.

He emerged, coat over one arm and a pistol in each hand. Derner was on the phone giving orders about the car and only looked a little curious when Gabe dumped the coat and put the guns on the desk. Gabe opened each, removing the empty cartridges from the revolver and checking how many bullets were left in the semiauto. He opened his hand in a "gimme" gesture. Derner pointed to a chrome-trimmed liquor cabinet against one wall and mimed opening a drawer.

The second drawer held boxes of ammunition of various types. Kroun found what he needed in the jumble and loaded his guns. He thought about packing extra bullets, deciding against it. If he couldn't turn a problem in his favor with the loads he had, then it was unturnable.

It griped that he'd had no chance to resolve matters with Mrs. Cabot, but the woman had surprised the hell out of him. Fleming should have done something then, damn him. He could have gone invisible and gotten the drop on her while they were there.

Instead, he hauls me clear.

But to be fair, Gabe hadn't argued the point. Though more or less bulletproof, he had no desire to go through another night coughing his lungs out and feeling that burning inside as he healed. But what was Fleming's excuse? On the other hand, any man with sense would have run from Mrs. Cabot and her six-shooter. The look she wore could scare granite.

What the hell had happened to her daughter in that cabin?

And was it my fault?

He felt cold sweat along his flanks, his usual reaction to the not-knowing.

"Got your car, Mr. Kroun," said Derner. "It'll be out back in five minutes with a driver."

"I won't need the driver."

"Oh. Okay."

"You remember my last visit here? When was that?"

"Uh, yeah. August."

"August. Not December?"

"No, sir. I had to get you tickets for Wrigley Field, and it was hotter 'n hell you said."

Gabe put his fists on the desk and leaned in; Derner blinked under the pressure but filled out the details. He had no idea who Ramsey was or where he might be. He did not know anything about a girl named Nelly Cabot or her mother. Gabe told him to forget and eased back.

A couple nights ago, Gordy had given the same story about Ramsey, didn't know about Kroun's December visit, and chances were he was ignorant of the Cabots. Whatever business had brought Gabe to Chicago two months ago had been very much under the table.

"Gabriel," said Michael from the doorway. He always used that tone and that name when he thought things were truly serious.

He turned, on guard as always with Mike, which was a shame. He wanted to like the guy. He *did* like the guy, but couldn't trust him. "You look cold. Why don't you get one of those chorus girls to fix that?"

Michael scowled and couldn't suppress a shiver, and it clearly irritated him. "Where did you go tonight?"

"You already know."

"Besides seeing *him*."

"I got a haircut."

"A haircut?"

Gabe brushed the side of his head and put on his hat. "I got 'em all cut for that matter. The barber talked boxing, and I didn't listen." Gabe pulled on his damp overcoat and slipped the semiauto in the shoulder holster. As he reached for the revolver, Michael beat him to it.

"That's mine," he said. The gun rested lightly in his grip, not pointing at anyone, but ready for use. He had long strong fingers, and they reminded Gabe of Sonny's hands.

"It's reloaded," he said cheerfully.

"Who did you shoot?" Michael's tone matched the cheer.

"Doesn't matter. I missed."

"You?"

"It was a new gun."

"Who'd you shoot?"

"Black Cadillac, last year's model. It'll have a damaged front bumper, a lot of scrapes along the passenger side, and a bullet hole in the windshield. Ask Broder. Let him explain."

Derner, who had gone very quiet as soon as Michael walked in, made a soft sound from the back of his throat. It had to be involuntary, the man was trying his best to be invisible.

"What do you know?" Michael asked him.

"Uh, I got a call about that. One of the club Caddies was stolen earlier. The boys were hopping mad about it. No one saw anything. They figured some kids hot-wired it and drove off. Anyone else wouldn't dare. We don't know where it is."

"Have them look within walking distance of Mike's hotel," Kroun suggested. "Was it stolen at about the time Broder left here? No, don't tell me, Mike will deal with it. I have to go." He pushed past, aiming for the door and hoping things were off-balance enough for him to make a clean getaway.

"Where?" Michael demanded.

"Wrigley Field. I heard it's an ice rink now."

Mike didn't follow. Gabe had raised enough doubts to make him think twice about Broder.

Seems pretty obvious.

Gabe hadn't been a hundred percent on it, but the timing worked out right.

Mrs. Cabot had called for help, and while he and Fleming waited in the woods, Broder came rolling up in his stolen car. He had no reluctance about running them off the road and dropping a grenade on the wreck. He was not concerned about consequences. That was Broder all over.

Was he on his own or working for Michael? How did the

woman even know to call Broder? Or had she wanted Michael, and Broder answered instead? She'd have had to call New York first. No one there would have given up the name of Michael's hotel, but they'd have passed on the message. How did she rate that kind of service?

Or had it been Ramsey? Maybe he's still involved.

Michael wouldn't lie to him, but neither would he tell him everything. Gabe was tempted to go back, put the eye on Mike, open up his head, and find out what lay inside.

Not here.

Not at the Nightcrawler. He'd need someplace more private. He needed better questions to ask, too. Gabriel didn't *know* enough yet to ask the right ones.

The car was a new Hudson, painted a snappy green. It was warmed up, the tank full, and four thick wool blankets lay neatly folded on the backseat. What had Derner made of that request? Probably something to do with body disposal. He wouldn't be too far off.

The waiting driver was a young, friendly, chatty sort, with a mouthful of chewing gum. Gabe thanked him and got rid of him quick.

Once behind the wheel, Gabe went easy for a block to get the feel of the gears, then headed toward Fleming's house. He still had his crumpled and damp Chicago map in one pocket and only had to pull over once to get his bearings.

The lights were on, but no one answered the bell. He let himself in and listened. The house was empty, the only noise coming from the electric icebox. Good, else he'd have to put up with a bunch of questions from Fleming.

Gabe thought about tracking down the doctor who had treated Nelly Cabot. The man would have questioned Nelly and very probably called someone else for help with the problem. Not anyone in Chicago, or Gordy would have heard something. The disappeared doctor had apparently been high enough in the pecking order to have a number direct to New York. If so, then some word of what had happened must have reached Michael.

Who doesn't want me anywhere near that cabin.

That is, if Mike and Broder had been there . . . or had it been only Ramsey's doing?

The lack of memory was a different sort of pain than the physical kind that often hammered at Gabe's skull, but just as intense.

Gabe cracked open one of the suitcases and pulled on fresh clothes. The dry socks were the best improvement; he wore three pair since they were the fancy silk kind and thin. Wool would have been better for this trip. He wanted woodsmen boots, too, but had only the one pair of shoes. Wet, of course. None of the clothes he'd bought during that ten-minute shopping jaunt were suitable, but he'd survive. He left his discards draped on the stair rail for Fleming to marvel over and snapped the suitcase shut. He thought of taking it, but decided against. Better to travel light and make everyone think he'd be back for his stuff.

He *planned* to return, after all.

Thoughtfully, he relocked the door when he left.

The Hudson ran a little rough, but he got used to it. He checked his map again, compared its routes to the directions Fleming had so accurately copied down. It seemed simple enough: get out of Chicago, head north, follow this line, then that one.

Depending on the roads, he could make pretty good time before dawn.

11

FLEMING

I GOT one of the friendlier mugs at the Nightcrawler to give me a lift home and to take the long way so I could hear the club gossip. He filled me in, carefully not inquiring about my own state of scruffiness. Things in the trenches were copacetic, considering. Some of the guys were edgy about the Alan Caine murder, but only because the cops had hauled a few in for questioning. Chicago's finest were looking for Mitchell, but they'd have to hold a séance to get him now. He'd had a summons to a higher court, and good riddance to the bastard.

When I asked about my called-off hunt for Gilbert Dugan, the mug didn't have anything that could be called cheerful. Half the guys who'd wanted the reward money felt cheated, and the other half thought I'd just blown smoke to make myself look important. I shrugged it off as booze talk. Some of the boys were smart, like Derner and Strome, the rest couldn't beat a monkey at checkers.

Our ramble around the Loop turned up an unexpected

bonus: a butcher shop that was open. Lights were on, and they seemed to be taking a delivery via the side alley door. Open late or up early, it would save me a trip to the Stockyards. My last meal had been interrupted, and tonight's exertions left me tired and in want of fuel, fresh or not. What they had couldn't be worse than the stuff I stored at home. I had the guy pull over.

My order got me a predictably fishy look from the hired help. He couldn't have had many customers stopping in at this hour in need of a pint of beef blood, but the crisp dollar bill I put on the counter must have reminded him the customer was always right. He put the stuff in a thick cardboard container, passed it across, and I told him to keep the change. He told me to come back soon, adding a smile that looked genuine.

I emerged, signed for my driver to wait, strode purposely off to the next alley, turning into its shadowed cover. Human eyes had no chance in this darkness, so I eased the top from the container and sniffed the contents. Not fresh, but better than anticipated. One sip, then another. Not bad. Though cold, it raised a nice heat in my belly that spread to my limbs. I'd taken a lot of abuse; it was good to feel warm again.

Only after I'd eagerly and with much relish drained off the last ounce did I realize I was not in the throes of frenzied compulsion. I'd taken in enough and was satisfied. The thought of going back to the shop for more raised no impulse within to do so. I gave it a few minutes just to be sure, then got bored with the waiting. Tossing the cardboard into a dented trash can, I left, revived and hopeful about . . . well, everything.

I took care not to look at my driver, knowing my blood-flushed eyes were something he wouldn't want to see. He asked no questions about our stop, seemed utterly incurious about it, and I liked that. Strome would have also not asked questions, but he'd have wondered.

My driver dropped me at the front door of my home and settled in to wait again. Apparently he didn't know I lived in the old pile. I tipped him a magnanimous five and told him to spend it in one place. He told me I was a card and rumbled away.

I unlocked the door and listened, but the house was quiet. A quick check proved that I was alone. The only intruder must have been Kroun, to judge by the discarded clothing thrown over the stair rail. His suitcases were here, so he'd return.

Maybe. He'd be off making another try at seeing Mrs. Cabot, I was sure of it, and if he wasn't quick enough, she'd put a second bullet in his skull. He could do his own damned sneaking around, though, I'd had enough. Michael could find someone else to babysit.

Upstairs I washed and changed into dry clothes, which improved my mood. I hid the two grand inside a hollowed-out book in my room and felt even better. That much money could buy a lot of car with plenty of change left over.

For insurance. Yeah. This time I would get insurance.

I phoned for a taxi, scrounged a dry overcoat from the hall closet, and had sorted through the day's mail just as my ride pulled up. A lot of them had radios just like the cops, and it made things faster. I gave the driver directions rather than say outright the address. Some guys were reluctant to go to the Bronze Belt, daylight or dark.

I spared this one and paid him off in front of a drugstore in a border area, going inside to phone Bobbi. She sounded awake and yes, she still wanted me to come over. Just as I'd done earlier, I walked within sight of Coldfield's hotel, then vanished, skimming the rest of the way unseen, eventually slipping inside. It took a few minutes to find Bobbi's door, but I figured it out.

When I was solid again, it was in a room very similar to Gordy's. Just one light by the bed was on. Newspapers and a couple of magazines lay on the floor by a reading chair. The radio played softly. I heard water running in her bathroom. She finished brushing her teeth and came out, stopping short with surprise.

"Wow, that was quick," she said.

"You complaining?"

"Nope."

The next little while was very pleasant for us.

It had been an ice age since I'd last held her, and this time it wasn't about hanging on to life and sanity or shared grief for a dying friend. If she sensed that, it didn't show. Tonight was about us being together.

I wasn't sure how things would go. If I felt the onset of a seizure, I'd have to leave, whatever the consequences. Better that I hurt her feelings than do something much, much worse.

When those fits began ambushing me, I'd not dared to go near Bobbi. While feeding at the Stockyards, I'd taken in more than was needed or wanted by my body. I'd fed until it was agony, then fed some more. Now I understood it was connected to how starved I'd been for blood when Hog Bristow had been carving on me. Some part of my mind was trying to take back that lost blood, unable to accept that the crisis was past.

The gorging had terrified me. If it took over at the wrong time, I could kill Bobbi.

My taking from her when we made love was a very delicate process; I *had* to be in control. Too deep a bite, too great a flow, too long a drink, and she could die.

Since the fight with Escott, though . . . I felt different. Much had changed that night and since.

"I talked with Charles," I said. "We're still friends."

"He told me when he came back. He's in his room if you want to see him again."

"No, thanks." She had to be kidding. I wasn't about to leave. However things went, I just wanted to be with her.

So far as I could tell through the smooth fabric of her silk robe, she didn't have anything on under it. I breathed in the scent of her hair while kissing her temple and tried holding her even closer. My body reacted to this in an entirely normal manner, which was damned reassuring.

"Ho-ho," she said, pressing against me down there. "Isn't this nice?"

"Oh, yeah." I felt my corner teeth budding—from arousal, not hunger. There's a big difference between the two.

But she pulled back a little. "Are you all right, Jack? I mean it. You've been—"

"I know what I've been, baby. And I'm sorry. I didn't . . . I wasn't ready."

"You sure you are now?"

"Pretty sure. Be gentle with me?"

She snickered, pressing close again. "The walls here . . . I'll have to be quiet."

"Both of us." After a moment, I took off my overcoat and suit coat, just to start things.

She liked to undress me and began with my tie, working her way down. In short order my tie was off and shirt open, and she stopped, stopped cold.

"Oh, Jack . . . oh, my God, sweetheart . . . I didn't *know*." Oh, *hell*.

I'd forgotten the scars. A wave of mortification started up from God knows where, but I smothered it, quick and with absolute finality. They weren't my fault. I had nothing to be ashamed of; she'd have to see them sooner or later. "It's all right. They don't hurt."

Bobbi was a woman who didn't cry much, hated to cry, but she gave in to it now, silently, tears brimming, then streaming from her eyes. "I'm sorry," she whispered.

I couldn't think of anything to say. Might as well get it over with and let her have the worst of it. I removed my shirt and turned slowly so she could see them all, see every last square inch of Bristow's brutal handiwork—chest, arms, and back covered with thin white threads where he'd stripped away the skin with his knife. Ugly.

But I'd survived. I'd earned them.

She rushed back to the bathroom, shut the door, and sobbed.

I waited her out. When she was ready, she'd emerge

again. It was how we did things. While I was prepared to offer her a shoulder to soak, that wasn't what she wanted this time.

The wait was hard, but I felt strangely patient. I thought about putting the shirt on again, but decided against.

Bobbi blew her nose, splashed water, and returned. She'd smoothed her expression out, but I didn't think she was finished with the high emotions just yet.

"They don't hurt," I gently repeated.

"Why don't they heal? When you vanish, shouldn't they—"

I shrugged. "I don't know." Maybe the damage had been too great or I'd come too close to death or bled too much or it was all in my head. Pick one, pick them all. "They might fade with time. Just have to wait and see."

"Is it all right if I . . ." She faltered, staring.

I took her hand in both of mine. "You don't have to. We can wait."

"What?" She broke off her stare. "Wait? What are you talking about?"

"Uh . . ."

"You think I don't want to be with you because of this?"

"I'll understand if you—"

The blazing glare she shot shut me right up. "Jack Fleming, stop being an ass."

"Yes, ma'am."

We didn't say anything for a while. She looked at my scars; I didn't know where to look. The mood was shattered. We'd been together long enough to not try forcing things back into place. It was there, or it wasn't.

She tentatively put her hand on my chest. "Is that okay?"

"Yes." I was not going to push her. She had a lot to absorb, and it could take days, weeks. However long, I would wait.

"You're so cold."

I didn't feel it. "How 'bout you?"

She made no reply, still getting acquainted with the changes, touching me. "I'm fine. I'm so sorry."

"It's all right." I wasn't sure what she was sorry about, that I'd suffered so much or that she'd not fully understood the extent of it. It was pointless to dwell, though.

She took my hand, tugging just a little. "Come on."

"Wha . . . ?"

"Let's just take this slow. Get to know each other again." She backed toward the bed.

"You sure?"

No reply, unless unbuttoning my trousers counted.

She tenderly stripped me, shed her robe, and we slipped between the clean white sheets. Kissing, lots of kissing. I'd missed that.

"We can shut the light off if you want," I suggested when she paused for breath.

"You'll still be able to see me. I want to be able to see you."

"So I really should stop being an ass?"

"Uh-huh."

She rolled on top, straddling me. I sprawled, arms up, fingers grasping the head rail of the bed. She moved over me, scarred skin and all, and at some point murmured that I was feeling warmer. Then she was too busy to talk, her beautiful mouth doing other things.

I didn't usually breathe, but could certainly gasp and call on God when inspired to do so.

Bobbi threw me a quick smile at my reaction and went back to driving me crazy. I remembered to keep quiet, but there was no helping the squeaking bedsprings as we rolled around, and I turned the tables. With my confidence restored, I pushed her legs apart and gave as good as I got. She stuffed a corner of a pillow in her mouth and bit hard on it as I kissed and teased and tasted.

"Jack." She had the softest whisper. That tone meant she was close to a release. I pulled away and moved up.

"You bastard," she said, grinning, reaching. I didn't move

and let her play some more, but there was only so much I could take.

Rolling again until she was on top, she guided me in. She eased forward, her neck taut, brushing against my lips. I didn't take the invitation, though my teeth were out.

"Soon," I said.

She rode me, and I looked on her face in delight, wonderment, and awe as she climaxed. It was as intense as hell but all too brief, and she did not quite succeed at keeping quiet. As the last of it passed, she slumped forward, and I caught her shoulders, easing her on her side, then her back. I was still erect and hard and in need of my own release. I'd seen where she'd gone, my turn to take her there again . . . for a longer visit.

The vein in her neck pulsed, her heart pumping strongly, her blood rushing swift. I kissed her there for a long moment, this time teasing myself. She pressed the back of my head, urging.

But I moved down, nuzzling her breasts for some while before going lower, pausing at the velvet-smooth skin just below her navel, then biting just deep enough and no more. A very tiny flow beaded up, just enough to taste and trigger my own climax. Her response was immediate and strong, and she smothered her cry with one hand. I drew hard, seeming to feed as much from her reaction as from the small wounds in her sweet flesh. Her pleasure was mine, while it lasted. This was no slow rise and fast fall of sensation; I had us both at a peak and could keep us there for hours.

We had the time.

As requested, I took it slow.

She slept in my arms for a long while afterward. I kept still and held her until my muscles burned, and I was thankful for it. A sweet feeling that I eventually recognized as absolute contentment saturated me through and through. We had no past or future, the present was everything and more than enough. Those moments never last, of course, but while this one was upon me I would enjoy it. I wanted to sleep as well, but the closest I could get was this sense-swamped doze.

However thin the walls, no one had bothered to investigate the noise we'd made. This was a real hotel, and doubtless others were here tonight who had indulged themselves in a similar manner. Eyes half-closed, I drowsily regarded the shadows on the ceiling, and even at this late hour heard activity in the various rooms. Snoring was the main sound, distant, originating from several individuals on this and the other floors. A night owl's radio played far down the hall. The one in our room was tuned to a station that had signed off for the night a while ago; only low static came through the speaker. I pretended it was rain. In a few more weeks, if we were lucky, the first spring rains would fall and eat away the snow. That would be good.

Bobbi stirred, murmured something, and left our bed. She went to the bathroom still half-asleep, but returned woken up again.

Those moments . . . never long enough.

She turned the bedside light out and snuggled close for warmth. "Can we talk?"

Women. Always talking. Gordy had that right. "Aren't you tired?"

"Wonderfully tired."

"But things have been happening?"

"A lot of things."

"What's the matter?"

"You are such a pessimist."

"Which is how I can always be pleasantly surprised. On the phone you said there's more. This is the more?"

"A big bunch of more." Her tone indicated it could be a good thing.

"I'm not going anywhere."

She held her breath, then let it out. "It's to do with Roland and Faustine and Lenny Larsen going out to Hollywood."

"Yeah, he fixed them up with a movie you said."

"Not all of it. They want me to come out, too. Lenny can get me a screen test."

At that I went very, very still. With no breath or heartbeat, it's easy.

"Jack . . . ?"

"You serious?"

"Yes. This is what—"

"I know what it is."

She'd been working, dreaming, and praying for this. She had the talent and at long, long last the door had opened for her. I'd known that it would happen sooner or later, but had hoped for later.

"Jack?"

"Well, this is great." I tried to sound happy for her, but it didn't work. It failed miserably.

"You hate it."

"No, baby. I'm . . . getting used to the idea." I couldn't let her see that she'd pushed me off a cliff. Good thing the light was out. If she saw my face, she might start crying again. "When?"

"Not right away. Roland's in no shape to travel."

We had a couple weeks then. Plenty of time for me to get used to things.

Maybe.

"Look, this might not work out. I could take the test, and they might not want me."

"Of course they will. They're not dopes."

"Jack—I want you to come with us."

We'd discussed this angle before. We knew it by heart. I didn't want to go to sunny California. My job was in Chicago, my friends, everything. I wouldn't know what to do with myself surrounded by movie people and orange groves. The one thing I could not do at this moment was to give her a blunt *no* or the coward's no of a weak and limping *I'll think about it.*

"Will you think about it?" she asked, and I wondered for the umpteenth time if she could read minds.

"Of course. This is a lot." Like getting gut-punched, only I couldn't vanish and heal from it.

"Your nightclub. I know what it means to you."

And I knew what this meant to her. The one sure way to lose her forever would be to try holding her back. She'd had this dream long before we'd met. She loved me but wouldn't put up with me being an unreasonable, selfish ass.

I thought of another angle that we'd never discussed. I had one hell of a lot of time ahead of me, decades, centuries of it. Bobbi had only a short span, and not just her lifetime. She had precious few years left of still being young enough for the merciless cameras to find her interesting.

"I'll think about it, baby," I heard myself saying, but it sounded sincere. "I mean that."

Dammit. She started crying again.

And kissing me.

Okay, I liked that part.

I left well before dawn and walked in the cold for a while, head down, trying to think.

Solutions to my problems came easily to me during that walk—what I wanted was some way to quash them.

Yes, I could hire a general manager to look after Lady Crymsyn. Gordy could help there and keep things aboveboard, no gambling, good acts, plenty of business, and someone mailing me a check each week. Hire the right people, and the place could run itself.

But I didn't want that easy a fix. I wanted a way to stop it, stop her, and it just wasn't coming to me.

There was no reason why I shouldn't go with Bobbi and the others when the time came. None at all.

So why did this feel like the end of the world?

That sweet contentment was gone. In its place . . . yeah, something familiar and dark had flooded in.

When Maureen—my lover, the woman who gave me her

blood, who changed me forever—when she vanished with no word, no explanation, that was a world-ender for me.

She'd never returned.

That too-familiar dark was the fear that I would lose Bobbi, too. Not in the same way, but just as permanently.

Damned stupid to feel like that, but there it was.

It had been a hell of a night. I needed a day's rest and would figure things out later. The situation would be there when I woke, but my mind would be clear. I'd think of something brilliant then.

Making my way to an el platform, I waited for one of the early trains. It took me to the stop close to Lady Crymsyn. I passed the drugstore where Kroun had bought the cigars. He was a problem that could wait as well.

The club's outside lights were off. I let myself in and locked up behind.

"Hello, Myrna," I said to the empty lobby. The light behind the bar remained steady. I listened, but the place was eerily quiet. That was wrong. It should be full of people and music, with Bobbi on the stage singing under the spotlights. Why couldn't that be enough for her?

I climbed the stairs. My office was dark, the radio off. I changed that, wanting sound and illumination, if only in this small space.

While the radio warmed up, I dropped in the chair behind my desk and had an unsettled moment noticing that things had been changed around. The mail wasn't in its usual spot, items were lined up, pencils sharpened. In the middle of the blotter was a thin stack of writing paper. The sheets had been crumpled, then spread flat. They bore my handwriting. My hand was usually hard to read—the years in journalism had degraded it—but the lines I'd put down were strangely neat, almost mechanical. In them I had tried to explain the inexplicable. I'd given up and left them unfinished.

Escott had spent hours sitting here. He'd walked in, found me on the couch with a hole blown through my skull, seen the gun, and in the trash found the notes I'd attempted. He'd have read them, over and over.

I couldn't imagine what he'd gone through in those hours before sunset waiting to see if I would wake up. For distraction he'd cleaned things, made order from the chaos, enforced some form of control in the room despite the cold presence of my corpse. He had sat in my chair, thought God knows what thoughts, and . . .

How could I have done that to him?

And how had he ever been able to forgive me?

Feeling sick, my face hot with fresh shame, I crumpled the papers again, took a big glass ashtray from a table, and burned them in it. The fire flared and died, the smoke lingered a bit longer. I used the blunt end of a pencil to crush what was left to gray powder. No one else would ever know about this.

The radio now played dance music, but when an announcer came on he was replaced in midword by a polka tune. Myrna was up and about. Of course I'd missed seeing the radio dial move. The polka ended, and some guy spoke enthusiastically in German or Polish. Another polka started. Who on God's green earth would be in need of such music at this hour in the morning?

"Hi, Myrna," I said again. "I've had a rough night."

Maybe I could tell her about it, but where to begin?

The less sprightly dance music returned. I didn't see the dialing knob move then, either.

"I'm spending the day here, if you don't mind."

I stared at the long leather couch against the wall opposite my desk. I'd planned to lock the door and sleep the day through on that couch, having done it many times before.

Not tonight. I couldn't go near the thing now.

At the far end was a hole in the leather back, and a messy spray of dried blood, visible evidence of my attempt to kill myself. The wooden slug I'd carved was probably embedded in the stuffing someplace.

It seemed like some other man had gone through that horror, suffered with, and then caved in to despair. How could I have been that man?

I wasn't.

He'd been Hog Bristow's awful creation. Some portion of him was still inside, but no longer able to influence me. Maybe with time he would fade completely. I wanted that.

I should leave the couch there as a reminder never to be stupid again, but Bobbi would see the damage and ask questions. She wouldn't be fobbed off with a lie, and knowing me as well as she did, might even figure things out.

That couch was the scene of an attempted murder. Looking at the bullet hole and stains made me feel like I was my own ghost. No way in hell was I going to keep that hunk of furniture here one more minute. It had to go.

After removing several oilcloth packets of my home earth from under the cushions, I considered how to move it out. It was too big to push through the window. While I had the strength to lift it easily, I was short on space and leverage. The thing was almost too wide to get through the door and had to go in stages, pushed through until it wedged against the wall opposite. I had to crawl over to pull, then crawl back to push, and was sweating by the time I got the awkward bastard clear. How anyone had gotten it into the office in the first place was beyond me.

I manhandled it down the hall and regarded the stairs with aggravation. Certainly I could pitch the whole thing down, not caring if it broke apart, but the marble-tile floors below were of some concern. I didn't know how much abuse they could take before shattering.

In the end I took the hard road and worked the couch gradually down the steps into the lobby and outside. Once there I carried it toward the parking lot, placing it on the edge of the curb, where it would not block foot traffic. I had every confidence that some scavenger would take it away before the day had passed. The bloodstains and that hole might make someone wonder . . .

To hell with it. I couldn't be bothered with "what ifs" and went inside, locking the front doors with a sense of relief.

My office looked considerably larger now. Perhaps I could leave it this way with no couch, bringing in a couple of chairs instead. But the old caveman inside reminded me that sometimes Bobbi and I found a couch to be a very convenient and comfortable place for reclining.

I'd get a new one—but what was the point if she was leaving for Hollywood?

I sat behind the desk and scowled at its tidiness. There was always something that needed to be done, my club kept me damned busy. I always had paperwork, mail to answer, supplies to order; even with the place closed there was work needing attention, and I *liked* that work. But tonight I had absolutely nothing to keep me from thinking about Bobbi leaving.

Damn it.

Getting hot under the collar, pacing, grumbling about how unfair the world was, eventually speaking aloud, eventually shouting, it came rushing out, all the stuff I couldn't say to her face.

Just as some tiny bit of normality began to creep back to my life, *this* had to happen. I didn't want it. I wanted Bobbi to stay here and for things to be like they'd been. My job was to run a fancy nightclub, glad-hand happy customers, and her job was to be onstage singing to them. Her job was to be my girl, not go running off to be a movie star.

I got louder as what churned through my head got worse. The depth of anger surprised me, and I gave in to it. By God, she wasn't going to do this to me. How dare she? After all the crap I'd been through, I needed her *here*. I'd put my foot down—

The glass ashtray flew off the desk. The damn thing *launched* itself, crashing against a wall, landing hard on the wood floor, scattering ash from the burned notes, making a hell of a noise—yet not breaking.

I yelped and jumped about two miles.

As I stared at the ashtray, it slid half a yard toward me. It was as though someone had kicked it along. The glass grated loud over the wood. It moved again, half as far, then stopped. The place was silent. Even the radio was turned down. I seemed to feel a kind of pressure around me, like a pending storm.

Myrna.

She'd scared the hell out of me. All the anger, too. I would never have cut loose like that had anyone been here, but had forgotten about her. She must have gotten fed up. Dames. Always sticking together.

"Sorry," I said.

The lights remained steady. The radio music came up. Dance music.

She was getting stronger, I thought.

In a much calmer tone—and feeling like a fool for talking to what might well be an empty room—I told Myrna what was going on and the problems they'd brought and the fears I had. Whether she hung around to listen was unimportant, I let it pour out until nothing remained.

The room was quiet, but it was different from that earlier angry silence. At some point the radio had switched off again. The only sound was the desk clock ticking and the distant hiss of traffic in the waking streets below.

I'd not made a decision, nor did I feel any better, but the worst was past. Thankfully, Bobbi would never hear any of it.

Maybe things would be more clear tomorrow.

A glance at the clock told me to get moving if I wanted to beat the dawn.

I went downstairs into darkness. The light behind the bar was off. Myrna always liked having it on. Maybe the bulb had burned out again; it often did. No time to check and change it. I continued through to the main room, crossing to the larger bar at the far end.

The three tiers of platforms for tables and booths arranged in an ascending horseshoe shape created a lot of dead space

below, but it wasn't wasted. A small access door led under
the seating, and we used the area for storage. Usually I spent
the day up in the office when I didn't feel like driving home,
but this bolt-hole was more secure. I'd taken pains over it.

The storage section was sizable, stacked with bar supplies
and extra chairs, with an unremarkable plywood wall that
blocked access to the rest of the dead space. The wall looked
solid, but with Escott's help I'd put in a hidden door. You had
to know it was there, and even then you had to look hard for
the trigger to get it open. The door was partially blocked by
boxes; I usually entered by sieving through. Inside was a sliding bolt lock so I could seal myself in. I wouldn't have bothered with a door at all, but Escott pointed out that sometime
or other I might have need of one should there be an emergency. The only drawback was that the place wasn't fireproof.

I vanished and went inside.

The concealed area was roomy, plenty of space for an army
cot with a layer of my earth under an oilcloth sheet, a box,
and a lamp on the box. It was a near duplication of the basement sanctuary at home. I re-formed in darkness and fumbled quickly to switch the lamp on. Nothing had changed
since my last visit, just a little more dust than before. On
the cot were several spare oilcloth packets of my home earth
and a months-old *Adventure Tales* I'd forgotten. Well, something to read before the day took me. I had been thinking
of writing a story for . . . maybe I could get back to that. In
California, with no nightclub to distract me, I'd have plenty
of time to write.

I snarled again. That was too much like giving in.

The cot-side lamp flickered.

"Not now, Myrna. I'm too tired, and it's too late."

It went out completely.

Damn her. What was her problem? Probably still mad
about me yelling to myself up in the office.

I hated the dark, but had come prepared. On the way
down, I'd pocketed one of the many flashlights scattered
throughout the building. I took it out, snicking it on.

"So there." I slid the bolt, officially shutting myself away from the rest of the world for the next several hours.

Stretched on the cot, I opened the magazine and its half-remembered stories, flipping to an editorial page. Nothing like out-of-date opinions for numbing the mind.

The lamp came on again, very bright. I cut the flash and checked my watch. Not long now. No more than a few seconds. I felt the sluggishness sweep over me. It was a sweet lethargy. Things would look after themselves while I got a good day's rest. I fell gently toward that stupor, carefully not thinking about Bobbi leaving me.

The lamp went off-on-off-on.

Oh, hell.

Something was *wrong*. My internal alarm finally got the message and shrieked a belated warning. I struggled to stay awake, but was too far over the edge.

At the very last instant before slipping away, I heard the destructive crash as the hidden door was forced open, lock and all, then a shadow blocked the lamp's light from my now-sealed eyelids.

Too late. Much too late.

I'd made a terrible, terrible mistake—

12

KROUN

THE lines on the map and the written directions bore no resemblance to the actual lay of the road, Gabe decided.

He'd planned to be patient, aware he was exploring unknown territory, knowing it might take a while to find the right turnoff, but after a futile hour of cruising up and down, backtracking, and finding one dead end after another, he was justifiably irritated.

Somewhere he'd missed something. That, or Fleming had written things down wrong.

Or Sonny had given the wrong—

Gabe allowed himself a snarl of disgust, then hauled the wheel around in yet another U-turn. He went back three long miles in the country darkness to the last intersection, where a crooked sign pointed the way to the nearest town. The name held no meaning for him; it was ten miles distant and not on the route.

He stopped the Hudson, letting it idle, and got out to look at the sign.

As he thought, it was loose in the ground. Some fool had knocked it over and put it back, pointing in the wrong direction. A swell joke to play on a nonlocal, yessiree, that's a real knee-slapper.

Gabe slammed the wooden post into the ground so the sign was parallel with the road, then checked the written directions against the map.

Okay, *that* made sense.

Back in the car, he turned left from the intersection and covered five empty miles, counting them off and slowing. The trees were thick and grew close to the road, their black branches arching over and meeting high above, making a skeletal tunnel. Snow, unbroken except for animal tracks, lay heavy over humped shapes that marked brush and stumps. Plenty of deer were about; he'd seen a few dead ones on the way up. No roadside bodies mangled by hurtling machines were here, though. If Farmer Jones hit one with the old truck, then it would be fresh venison for supper that night. Country folk knew better than to high-hat a free meal.

The tires crunched a new path through the snow. No one had been up this way at least since the last fall, however long ago that had been.

Some flash of memory had him hitting the brake without benefit of thought, and the Hudson slewed and skidded to a reluctant halt.

He stared at three oak trees on the left, each more than a foot thick and planted so close that the trunks were fused together for about fifteen feet before separating into different directions. Some of their upper branches had twined as well in the struggle to obtain more sunlight. The thing was one huge, ungainly knot. The ground was distorted on one side where the roots were exposed, poking up from the snow in a black tangle, their fight continuing on under the earth. Rot had set in on one of the trees, and in the course of time it would spread and kill the others. Though not in the directions, this was a landmark he recognized; he could not recall details, only that it was important.

Just past the oaks was a break in the woods lining the road, no more than eight feet wide and overgrown, very easy to miss. The snow looked deep, and not even animal tracks crossed it. This was the turn he wanted, the one that would lead to the cabin.

He worked gears, fed the car gas, and urged it in. The Hudson rocked and slid over ruts hidden by the snow until it bumped something that scraped alarmingly along the undercarriage. It pressed gamely on, but Gabe judged that was far enough; no point in breaking an axle. He was well out of sight from the road. Anyone driving past might notice the tire tracks, but he doubted there was much traffic at this time of year. This area was disturbingly isolated.

He cut the motor and got out, feet sinking deep into a drift. There was less snow under the trees, so he floundered toward their cover, then threaded cautiously forward. Ahead, he heard the murmur of flowing water, lots of it.

The cabin was a few hundred yards in and dark. He expected as much, but studied the area carefully, looking for fresh prints in the snow as he made a wide circle. No recent visitors. Good.

The structure was about twenty feet to a side, with a stovepipe piercing a roof that extended out over a porch that ran the width of the front. Its one door faced a gradual downward slope that led to a wide black river. The far bank was a thin gray line covered with unbroken pine and beeches.

Gabriel couldn't remember its name but knew that he had fished there, his legs hanging over the edge of a boat dock, bare feet in the water, a blue, blue sky above, and sweet summer sun pleasantly baking the top of his head. In the mornings and late afternoons, the sun would spark on the water, the reflected light dazzling him.

Very unexpectedly he choked and felt chill, wet trails from his eyes. He swiped at them, embarrassed, ashamed . . . and suddenly afraid. Men don't cry. Especially if . . . but he couldn't carry the thought further than that; his memory failed yet again.

He'd fished in that river, but not here. No dock was in sight, nor the remains of one. The solitary picture from a long-ago summer vanished from his mind's eye.

When Gabe refocused, he took in the cabin and grounds in more detail, hoping the sight would kindle some other recollection to explain his bad dreams.

Nothing was familiar. The old wooden building had been constructed God knows how long ago. It needed paint but seemed sturdy, the walls and roof solid. A pump stood in the middle of what served as a front yard, and about a hundred feet to the right, downstream and built out over the river, was an outhouse, the door hanging open. No prints marred the snow between it and the cabin.

The wind kicked up. The place had been silent except for the river and his footfalls. Now he heard the soft whirring song that only pine trees sang, sounding exactly as it did in the dreams—only this time there was no peace to it. He thought of graveyards and ghosts. He didn't think he believed in ghosts, but if he did, then that was the kind of noise they'd make. Gooseflesh shot up his arms, spread over his spine, and down his legs. He wanted to put his back to something, anything, and had to quell the urge to pull out his gun.

When no invisible beast from the beyond leapt out, Gabe shook off the fit, if not his apprehension. He was sensibly afraid of what he might find here.

And more afraid that he might not find it.

He had to know what had happened in December, the why behind his very quiet trip to this lonely place, what had happened to the girl, what had happened to his driver . . .

And who put the bullet in my head.

He trudged toward the cabin, mounting an ice-coated wood step to the shallow porch. A small, uncurtained window on one side of the door gave a limited view of the interior. Nothing fancy, plank floor, some basic furnishings, no electricity or plumbing, but once upon a time it might have been someone's idea of a good place to live.

Gabe pushed the door open. It had no lock, just an old metal latch to hold the panel shut. After a moment, he went in.

His night vision was such that the ambient glow from outside was enough to see by. Even so, he made use of a candle stub shoved in a holder on a shelf across from the door, using his new silver lighter to bring it to life. The action reminded him of lighting Sonny's cigar, leaning in to the old bastard's ravaged face, smelling his breath, and hearing the creak of his finger joints. Gabriel had felt uncomfortable being so physically close, but he'd taken care not to show it.

He pushed away the memory and turned his attention on the rest of the cabin. It was depressingly plain. A sagging bed leaned in a corner next to a rusting potbellied stove, a narrow table, and two simple benches made from planks took up space under the front window. More planking formed a waist-high shelf that held battered cooking gear—and a dusty white fedora.

He looked it over carefully before picking it up. It was his size, and the label matched that of identical ones in his closet back in New York. No doubt of it now, Whitey Kroun had been here. This was the source of his nickname and a damn-fool thing to wear at any time of the year. The bold white made him a walking target in a crowd. Maybe that was part of his bravado: Whitey Kroun, afraid of nothing and nobody, just try starting something.

Clearly someone had, or the hat wouldn't still be here. He put it back.

I must have been an idiot. He touched the dark brim of his new hat, reassuring himself that he'd grown more sensible in the last couple months.

Shelves above the counter had a store of canned goods so old the labels had faded gray. Below was a stash of wood for the stove and several booze bottles, empty or nearly so.

All very innocuous—except for the splashes of dried blood on the floor by the bed. A rumpled and moldy blanket on top was also stained with the stuff.

He first took it for black paint that some vandal had splattered there; breathing in, he caught the thick, rusty scent.

After a long, long time of staring, he realized the stains were also from his bad dreams. In the dreams the stuff was fresh, red, and he'd been laughing for some insane reason.

He felt his throat tighten again.

Was that his blood? His head wound would have bled . . .

He felt physically sick as possibilities slithered through his mind. He'd seen blood before, damn it. He *drank* the stuff, for God's sake.

He still wanted to vomit.

Or had it come from the girl? What had happened to her?

The left side of his head throbbed wearily. He swept off his fedora and gently touched the ridge in his skull. The nascent pain bloomed into something truly awful, as though his brain had swollen too large for the surrounding bone.

Gabriel stumbled outside, slipping on the steps, grabbing at a support post to stop his fall. He forced his legs not to buckle.

He clawed for a handful of snow and pressed it against his scalp, biting off a cry. The agony was so bad that for a long, terrible moment he couldn't see. He held hard to the post and waited for the torture either to fade on its own or kill him.

Such vulnerability was foreign to him. He shouldn't be like this. It wasn't going to happen. He wouldn't allow it. He blinked until the black veil dissipated.

The compress of snow helped, really helped, but it was slow. Minutes crawled by, then bit by bit the pain reluctantly ebbed.

Breathing in icy river-tainted air helped, too. He made his lungs pump until his guts settled. It took longer for his brain to clear. Speculation about what had happened in the cabin could wait until he was calmer. He shut that part away for the moment, like closing a door. Out of sight, out of mind; he was good at forgetting, after all.

Gabe straightened, brushing snow from his hand. His fingers looked blue, but didn't feel cold. He cautiously put on his hat. No internal explosions sparked. He should have bought earmuffs at that store; fedoras weren't right for woodland expeditions.

Once he was sure his legs could manage the labor, he made another slow circuit of the area, this time facing outward.

He struck off, moving away from the river. No conscious memory prompted him, only some wisp of dream that made him think the area was familiar. The snow confused and concealed things, though. The place would look very different after the thaw in a couple months; he should come back then . . .

Like hell. He couldn't live with the not-knowing for that long. He *had* to get this over with—

The wind started up again, making the surrounding pines sing louder. He paused and knew he was close to something important. Looking back, he judged himself to be about fifty feet from the cabin. The candle glow through a side window seemed about right. Oh, yeah. Very close.

The glow flared and died, and he had to work to keep from twitching.

The nearly spent stub had finally guttered, that was all. No one had blown it out. He'd have heard company long before seeing them.

Unless Fleming followed me.

Not likely, but not impossible. The loon might have somehow managed to tag along; his ability to vanish was damned handy. He could have hidden in the trunk and—

Gabe held still and waited, but no ghostly gray shapeless *thing* floated between the trees. That was how Fleming looked while in that form, though Gabe had the understanding that regular humans couldn't see it. Just as well, too; it was hellishly creepy.

He wondered what it felt like: being bodiless, able to go through walls, instantly heal. Damned useful, all of it.

The snow layer thinned. The pine branches above had prevented serious drifts from forming. He picked out animal tracks: deer and rabbit, and several kinds of paw prints. He couldn't tell wildcat from wolf, but took for granted that four-footed observers might be lurking in the silent woods. Those he didn't mind so much.

An unevenness of the ground, a mound hidden by the snow, nearly tripped him. He backed off and studied things. The snow lay smooth, softening the irregular surface beneath. He crouched and brushed until reaching old leaves and earth. Nothing to get excited about, probably just a covered-over garbage pit dug for whatever wasn't burned or tossed in the river.

But the mound was grave-shaped.

And leaning against a pine trunk, only a few paces away, was a shovel.

Its wood handle was aging fast in the weather, the metal rusted. Someone had left it there, but had he simply forgotten it, or was it to mark a special place?

Gabe's hands closed on it, and *that* felt familiar. He dragged it free and used the blade to clear the snow away.

The pine tree . . . he looked up, hoping for a clue, but nothing came to him. Still, this had to be the place. The wind in the branches sounded the same.

He began to dig.

The frozen ground was not as solid as it should have been, but he had to work at it. His improved strength was a great help, though a few times he had to go easy as the handle threatened to break if he applied too much pressure. He slammed the blade in, cut deep, loosened, then cleared, his movements machinelike, giving him to understand that he was used to such labor. He felt like he was accomplishing something.

About three feet down, the shovel hit something that was not dirt, and he stopped.

By now he was sure of what would be there. The scent of the turned earth had done the trick, had merged what lay before him with what he'd dreamed.

He hated it, but continued, slowly.

The stink of decay rose and mixed with the pine, snow, and river air.

Soon he uncovered the man's face. There was enough left to recognize features, but Gabe's patchy memory failed him again. He had to dig farther to reach the rest of the body to check the pockets, finding a wallet. It held a few hundred in twenties, the tough paper still intact as legal tender. A New York state driving license was readable, identifying one Henry Ramsey, born July 15, 1912. Date of death? Sometime in December, 1937. Just a kid. His friends probably called him Hank.

Cause of death? Less certain, though Gabe thought the damage and stains on the front of the clothes might have been caused by bullets. There was a leather shoulder rig similar to his own on the body, but no gun in it. That lay in what remained of the corpse's right hand, fingers curled around the grip, index finger against the trigger. It was a .32 revolver, rusted and caked with dirt.

Gabe carefully worked it clear of the dead man's grasp. Four bullets were still in the cylinder. He wondered if one of the two missing slugs was lodged in his brain. Where had the other gone? Since Ramsey was holding a gun, chances were good he'd not been caught unawares. He might have gotten one shot off before dropping. Then what? The killer had dug a long hole and rolled him in?

The grave was too shallow. Come the spring thaw, animals would find, dig up, and scavenge the remains for food. Sooner or later a passing hunter, curious about the cabin, might discover it. It was a miracle that hadn't already happened. Was the hole deeper . . . yes . . . someone had dug a much deeper grave.

Mine.

Instinct, not memory, provided that conclusion.

With a bullet in his skull and all signs of life gone, someone had buried Gabriel Kroun a few yards from the foot of the pine. The first shovelful of wet earth had covered his face and, quickly after, the rest of him.

And at some point along the way, Ramsey had been dropped in as well.

Did we die together? Or was I first, then Ramsey?

In the dream-memory, Gabe had clawed his way toward the sky, pushing aside some heavy obstacle that lay on him. The rounded thing he'd touched, recognized, and recoiled from had been Ramsey's head. What happened afterward Gabe could not recall. His resurrection was a hazy, disjointed, painful event. The agony in his skull from the bullet wound had kept him thoroughly distracted. After dragging free from the grave, he must have reburied Ramsey before moving on. That didn't seem too likely, though.

Gabe straightened, the wallet and its contents in hand. He put the license back and, after a moment, the cash as well. It made little sense not to keep and use the money, but with some surprise he discovered within a profound loathing for robbing the dead. He returned the wallet to its pocket and went to work with the shovel, burying the man again.

The sky had changed by the time Gabe finished. He'd not be able to make it to that town before the dawn overtook him but had allowed for the possibility.

He was exhausted and half-frozen by the time he got to the car and folded himself into the backseat. The four heavy blankets wrapped around him would block the weak winter sun and keep in his remaining body warmth. He chose not to worry about anyone finding him during the day. No one had been out to the cabin in months, after all.

He lay still, eyes closed, listening to the wind beyond the rolled-up windows. It whirred between the pine needles and hissed through the bare branches of other trees. Rather than being at peace, he felt lonely . . . and afraid.

Gabe sensed the sun, the change it forced upon his body, the slowing of his perceptions and thought as conscious control slipped away. This day's bout of dream torture might be the worst yet. He'd have to get through it somehow; he had to *know*.

He shifted to a more comfortable position, arms and shoulders stiff from the recent exercise. It didn't work. He'd be creaking around like an old man when he woke. He should have ordered up a small panel truck. He could have stretched out in the back . . .

Why hadn't he dropped off yet?

He should be out by now, not grousing to himself for picking the wrong kind of vehicle. What the hell . . . ?

He sat up, pushing off the blankets.

Yes, he was sore and cold and creaked, his muscles cramped from staying in one position for far too long—the whole damned day as it happened. One sniff of the damp air, one glance at the painfully bright sky with its last gilding of sunset, and he understood he'd slept right through the day, no dreams, no memories at all.

He'd been *cheated*.

He *needed* that internal hell. With the things he'd just learned, he had to dream again to find out what had happened. Awful as they were—

Damn it. God *damn* it.

He pitched from the car, looking around as though to find someone to blame. The woods were as empty as before and silent; the wind had died.

How was it that, after all this time, he'd finally—

Gabe looked down. His shoes and pant legs were caked with dried-out mud from his grave, enough to do the job. He knew from his talks with Gordy that Fleming kept packets of his home earth in his sleeping areas. He even carried some in a money belt should he get caught away from those shelters. Until now Gabe had been dubious about the idea of the stuff providing true rest during the day. It struck him as just being another kind of superstition associated with his condition. The sight of a cross and the touch of holy water didn't bother him, so why should grave dirt have such an effect? What a damned stupid thing *that* was. It had robbed him of that day's progress toward what had gotten him killed in the first place.

He grumbled and stretched out the kinks, which weren't too bad, considering. He *did* feel rested, far more energetic than he'd been in weeks. Okay, there was a good side to his mistake.

Gabe followed his tracks back to the cabin, wanting another, much more thorough search before leaving.

The dried blood still very much in place, he lit another candle and checked every corner, every stick of furniture, tapped each board, looking for anything resembling an explanation.

He soon found a six-shot .22 revolver, bullets spent, blood-smeared, rust creeping over its surface. It was behind one of the benches, not hidden, just not in plain sight. Perhaps the shooter had dropped or thrown it there. The numbers were filed away, and it had the kind of checkerboard grip that didn't hold fingerprints. A feeble weapon for some, but mob soldiers who favored the caliber liked the gun's small size and low level of noise. Fold a pillow around it or hold it directly against a target and it sounded like a balloon popping, if that much.

Gabe didn't know how he knew that, but was not surprised such details lurked in his mind.

Maybe Nelly had brought the gun, unless a fourth person had crashed the party.

Complications, he thought. They annoyed the hell out of him, but Gabe had to keep them in mind.

He left the bed for last. Gingerly, with thumb and forefinger, he pulled the top blanket off and spread it out on the floor. There was no pattern to the bloodstains; it was a mess. Someone had bled there.

A mildew-eaten gray sheet beneath was also bloody, most of it in the middle. He recalled what Lettie had said about Nelly Cabot's injuries and fought past a bout of nausea. He lifted the sheet to reveal an ancient stained mattress that also stank of mildew. The stuff was all over, dormant from the cold, but still disgusting. Touching as little as possible, he dragged the mattress away from the bed, which was made from simple planks nailed across a box frame, nothing store-bought about that operation.

In the spaces between the planks, the floor beneath was visible, and something shiny caught the light.

He tore a plank away and got it. Got *them.*

Should have looked there first.

He closely examined a small, empty amber vial and a syringe. Whatever had been inside them was long dried and gone.

Michael.

The fourth person.

A complication. A damned big one.

Maybe *he'd* hurt the girl.

And maybe he killed me. Or had Ramsey do it, then killed him to keep him quiet. But when I came back Mike thought the job had been botched and that I didn't suspect him. No wonder he didn't want me up here.

Upon his return to New York, Gabe had been very careful not to let on about his loss of memory. It was easier to do than he'd hoped. He was in a position where no one questioned him. You could get away with a lot using a stern look and not saying much.

Michael had been out of the country at the time, or so he said. Distracted by his own problems, Gabe hadn't thought to check.

He peered through the side window into a very silent night. The woman weeping in his dream-memory—had it been from terror instead of grief? While Ramsey filled in the grave, Mike could have been in the cabin with her, doing God knows what to ensure she would keep quiet.

Then I get the blame since she was last seen with me.

He put away the items. They clinked against the rusted revolver. He shifted the gun to a different pocket and found that his hands were shaking.

Rage. Yeah, he had plenty of that.

Soon as I see Mike again . . .

He pinched out the candle flame.

Grabbing the white fedora, he let the latch fall on the door and walked to the pump. Its works were frozen for the winter. The bucket next to it meant to hold priming water was topped with snow. He went down to the riverbank, loaded the inside of the hat with a few rocks, using a handkerchief to tie the brim tightly over them to keep them in place. He flung the hat far out over the water. It splashed once and vanished in the black flow.

Next he scooped sand and icy water and scrubbed his hands until the mildew smell went away, all the time regarding the dark cabin and what was inside.

He wanted to burn it.

Tempting, but a bad idea. However secluded, flames and smoke could draw the wrong kind of attention to this place. Someone might feel bound to track down the property owner . . . Gabe realized *he* could be the owner. He just didn't know.

Better to leave it for now. He could always return with a few gallons of kerosene.

That would cleanse the place . . . every square inch of it.

The miles back to Chicago seemed to have stretched themselves. He had too much to think about and wished for company. Even Fleming, with his endless questions, would have been welcome. Gabe turned on the car's radio, and the noise of a comedy show helped.

Michael would not be in a good mood tonight; he was probably making Derner's life miserable. Half of the muscle at the Nightcrawler was probably out looking for the green Hudson and its missing driver. Fine. Let 'em earn their keep.

Gabe took a wrong turn, tried correcting at the next street, got lost, and pulled over to study the map. He wondered if getting lost was part of his lack of memory or if he'd always been like that.

His clearest postdeath recollection was waking in a cold barn loft where he'd hidden from the sun behind stacks of hay bales. From there he'd gone groggily down, washed off blood and grave dirt in an ice-crusted water trough, and taken his first feeding from one of the milk cows. That had awakened him fully, though the agony in his head kept him from indulging much in the way of thinking. He seemed well able to look after basics like getting food, of knowing how to deal with his change if not the how or why of it.

The circumstances—his blood-drinking, the bad dreams during his daylight sleep, lack of memory of how he'd gotten into such a spot, and all that came before—didn't really bother him. It seemed normal to be different. Not knowing himself was just how the world ran, and his instincts told him he'd be fine, just fine. He had a wallet with a driving license that provided a name to use, an address to go to, and more than enough money to get there.

A few nights later, first hitchhiking on country roads, then taking a train, then a taxi, he used a key from that wallet to get into a hotel flat in New York. Though he couldn't remember it, he assumed it to be his. Old mail scattered over a desk bore the name on the license. The flat was nice, and the clothes there fit. He moved into a stranger's life.

Pretty soon friends turned up.

Well, acquaintances.

They showed him respect and something he later came to recognize as fear. A very few asked about the white streak in his hair. He found a smirk and a shake of the head to be sufficient reply.

Mike had walked into the flat as though he'd been there many times before, looking uncomfortable and on guard. In retrospect could it have been guilt? He was the only one who met Gabe's eye and stood up to him like an equal, though.

They had a business meeting, which required going to a bar and sitting in a booth across from a tough-looking man.

Michael talked a lot of business that didn't make sense. The man challenged him on a point. Mike looked at Gabe. At a loss for what to do, Gabe looked at the man, who abruptly backed down, agreed to something, then left, sweating. Mike said *thanks* in a flat voice and departed as well.

From that point Gabriel decided he'd better learn what the hell kind of job he had.

It didn't take long. He killed people. He was good at the work.

He wasn't sure how he felt about that. Not then. Later, he decided that cold murder wasn't something he wanted to do to anyone.

The roughhouse when he and Fleming had taken on Mitchell didn't really count. Heat-of-the-moment shooting was one thing, but to walk up and coolly put a bullet into a stranger . . . that was just wrong.

There had been a couple of times when he'd felt angry enough to do violence, such as when he'd thought Fleming responsible for blowing up the car. But Gabe had wanted to punch him in the nose more than anything else. The gun had been a tool, little more than window dressing to get attention.

On the other hand, Fleming had been pretty clear about what had happened after the car crash last night. Gabe couldn't remember anything after their car left the road, but *something* had upset the kid. The lapse was disturbing, but there was damn all to be done about it.

In that first month in New York, Gabe worked out how to hypnotize people. They told him a lot he didn't like and much he didn't believe. He decided the whole crowd, including Michael, were considerably crazier than he and far more dangerous. The only way to keep from being consumed by them was to maintain the long-established outward front.

Strangely, no one noticed anything different about him. They all had certain expectations as to how he should behave, and, when he drifted outside those expectations, the mugs simply stretched their limits to accommodate. It was their fear of him. They put on their own fronts, acted friendly, shook his hand, laughed at his jokes, but were still pissing-in-their-pants terrified of him.

Yeah, crazy.

Gabe observed carefully and from them learned how to impersonate the man he'd been. It wasn't perfect; he'd sometimes surprise an odd look from Mike, but the guy never said anything.

Down deep he had to be terrified of Whitey Kroun, too.

That covered *who* he had been, next came the *what* he had become.

He eventually went to the big library with the lions out front and looked up stuff about vampires. It was crazy as well, but since some of it seemed to apply to him, he shrugged, accepted, and moved on, keeping his lip shut.

Gabe had yet to find out exactly how he'd come by the condition.

Somewhere out there a woman—he was sure it was a woman, Fleming's reckless dig notwithstanding—had done something quite out of the ordinary to Gabe. The details were lost, taken away when the bullet had ripped into his brain.

Very damned annoying, that.

Once the dust was settled on his current problem, he might have to try finding her.

Gabriel navigated the gradually thinning traffic, pulling up in front of Fleming's brick house a little after midnight. No lights showed, just like the cabin. He pushed the thought away, strode up the walk, and used his picklocks to get in.

That was also a skill he could not recall learning. Useful, though.

He listened before shutting the door, noticing that the broken window at the far end of the hall had been replaced. Hand it to Gordy, he ran a tight ship.

The place was empty, but Gabriel checked through it before turning on any lights. He didn't need them, but they'd let Fleming know company was present should he return. If the kid had any sense, he'd be cheering up that sweet blond girlfriend of his. Bobbi. Funny name for a dame, but it suited her.

Gabe got both suitcases and went up to the third-floor guest room. The rumpled bed was as he'd left it, and it almost looked like the one in the cabin, but without the blood.

I gotta stop that kind of thinking.

He straightened the top spread, opened the cases, found a crisp new shirt and the second suit he'd bought. It was identical to the one he had on, black with a charcoal pinstripe, very sharp. He didn't like to fuss over clothes, just pick good quality and forget about it.

Stripping and taking a shower-bath was a little piece of heaven. He stayed in until the hot water ran out, but emerged clean, shaved . . . and still feeling well rested. That grave dirt . . . well, clearly it worked. He'd have to start sleeping with a bag of it in the bed. What a luxury to be dream-free once this was over.

He thought he should save the residue on his discarded clothes and bundled them into a pillowcase and put it in the small wardrobe. Was it too close to the bed?

Only if he slept here for the day. He would use that abandoned store again. Broder and Michael didn't know about it.

Gabe dressed slowly, liking the feel of new clothes. Fresh and ready for anything, he went downstairs to phone the Nightcrawler.

Derner sounded harried. "Mike's on the warpath and wants to talk to y—"

"Give him a Bromo-Seltzer and a blonde."

"I would, I really would, but he's in Cicero."

"Well, that's his hard luck. What's he doing in—no, forget it." It would be business. With Mike it was always business. He could do half a dozen things at once and give each his full attention. Smart guy. Very smart. "Where's Broder?"

"With Mike."

Interesting. Broder must have spun one hell of a story to get himself off the hook for the grenade job—unless Mike had lied and faked his surprised reaction. If Broder's task had been to kill Gabe, then it made sense for Mike to keep him around.

But why does Mike want to kill me? Was it on general principles or for a specific reason? Why wait two months for another try?

"When will they be back?"

"Didn't say, but I've got a number you're to call."

Gabe wrote it down on a notepad by the phone. Cicero wasn't that far. He was reasonably sure he could find it, but a local guide would be better to have along. "Has Fleming turned up tonight?"

"Huh? Uh—no. Probably at his club. He usually calls in before now. You gonna talk to Mike?" Derner seemed worried. More so than usual, that is.

"In about two minutes." He pressed the hook long enough for the connection to break, then tried the new number. It turned out to belong to a hotel. He asked for Mike and got put right through.

He picked up on the first ring.

"Hello, Michael." Gabe used a friendly, cheerful tone, intending to be as irritating as hell. "Problem?"

"Where have you been?"

"Are you going to tell me to go back to New York again? Because the answer's no. Now that that's settled, how long will you be in Cicero?"

Mike made some strange choking noises. "A couple of days."

What the hell . . . ? Gabe continued the good cheer. "Fine. I'll keep busy. The old bastard wanted to get some air. I thought I'd take him fishing in the morning. It'd do him good to get out, have a little fun."

Dead silence. Lots of it.

Well, I wanted to stir things up.

"Whitey . . . please."

Pleading? That was a surprise, though Gabe wanted him off-balance and scared. "I've been to the cabin. The place looks great. You should see it."

"What have you done?"

"Nothing yet. You think I should do something?"

"No games . . . let's talk first."

"Sounds good."

"When can you get here?"

"I've had enough driving. We'll meet at Gordy's club." Mike would think twice about getting frisky in front of witnesses and be more likely to keep Broder in line as well.

"Okay. I'll get there soon as I—a couple hours."

"Why so long?"

"Business."

Gabe snorted and hung up. *Must be some business.* From keeping company with a girl to calling in extra muscle. Or arranging an exit.

For himself or for me?

Mike had agreed too readily. That could mean a lot of things. Gabe started to list the possibilities and how to counter them, then abruptly let it go. He'd find out soon enough and deal with it then.

Broder would be along, somewhere in the background, watching. Gabe knew how to keep his back to a wall, but Broder was nearly a ghost himself. He moved fast, quiet, and was a dead shot. If Fleming could be talked into helping out . . . but did he really need to know all this?

Yes. Better to have him as a friend than not. He'd want an explanation for the sickening things Sonny had said.

Both of us want that.

Waiting around the Nightcrawler held no appeal. Derner would be trying too hard not to ask questions. Gabe wanted a couple hours of not being watched like a zoo animal. He looked up the number for Fleming's club but got no answer. He would wait there; Broder and Michael wouldn't expect him to go to a closed club, and maybe Fleming would show. It would also be quiet. You could hear if someone tried to sneak in.

He snagged a newspaper from the pile on the front porch, kicked the rest inside, and relocked the door, then drove to Lady Crymsyn. Funny name for a club. Maybe Fleming had gotten the idea from his girl and her funny name. He could have spelled "crimson" right, though.

Gabe recognized enough landmarks on the trip to avoid getting lost. The club's inside lights were on, including the one in the upstairs office. A little glow escaped around the drawn curtains. Fleming must not be answering the phone or had just arrived himself. The parking lot was empty. He'd have walked or cabbed over, what with his car being all blown up and burned.

The street was clear of stray cops; Merrifield and Garza apparently had other duties tonight, leaving no one to watch as Gabe let himself in the front. He left things unlocked. It was always a good idea to have an escape route ready.

The light behind the lobby bar was on, and something was odd about the bar itself. As he drew closer he saw that dozens of matchbooks with the club's name on them had been propped open and set on end. Little red inverted Vs marched every which way, covering the whole length of the bar. What the hell . . . ? If Fleming had been here, he had some pretty odd ideas about how to fill the time.

The bar light flickered, not quite going out.

Gabriel stared, then called Fleming's name loud enough to reach upstairs.

No one replied. Why had he left all the lights on? Spendthrift.

The building was empty and dead silent. And big. Big, silent, and . . .

The light steadied.

Then the lobby phone rang. Louder than should be normal.

He didn't jump, but jerked around, stopping in midreach for his gun. He debated whether to answer or not.

The ringing was continuous, and then trailed off as though the bell had exhausted itself from the effort.

He waited, but no second ring came. Wrong number or a phone-company hitch.

The bar light flickered again. Fleming had said there was a short.

His problem, not mine.

Gabe went upstairs to the deserted office. It wasn't as fancy and large as the Nightcrawler's but had the usual stuff except for a gaping space opposite the desk. From the dust pattern on the floor some large piece of furniture had been removed from the spot. A couch, maybe.

On the desk were several oilcloth packets. They were heavy and smelled of earth.

Well. Damn. What was Fleming doing? Moving house?

He checked the lock on the door. It was a particularly sturdy model: wood panels over thick metal. The windows— bulletproofed, with heavy curtains—confirmed that this was one of Fleming's daylight bolt-holes. Not bad. He did all right for himself.

Gabe shed his coat and hat and sat behind the desk. The chair was comfortable; you could tilt back and put your feet up. Not bad at all. He dropped the packets out of the way into one of the drawers, opened his paper, and settled in to read. It had been a busy day. New pieces had effectively edged out further mention of the car explosion in the Bronze Belt, the Alan Caine murders, and even that movie actor and his flashy foreign wife.

Those were all that interested him; the rest just didn't mean anything. He looked for and found the funnies. Hey, a crossword puzzle—he liked those.

The radio came on. All by itself.

He looked at it for a good long while, considering a variety of causes. The elusive electrical short seemed the most likely. Someone leaves the radio on, when the power returns, it warms up, then surprise: dance music.

He didn't mind, but wouldn't be able to hear anyone coming in. He shut the radio off.

While trying to work out if the clue to seven down was "gable" or "table," the front door downstairs opened and closed. Gabe listened, following the progress of the ensuing footsteps . . . a man's shoes by the sound. He got partway across the lobby and paused.

Bet he's wondering about the matchbooks, too.

The newcomer started up the stairs. "Jack?" he called.

Gabe didn't know the voice. He shifted his gun from its holster to the desk, slipping it under the paper.

The visitor pushed in and froze at the halfway point, his body partially shielded by the door. He was surprised for a moment at seeing Gabe, but clearly recognized him. The man was tall, lean, and angular. His face was all angles, too, with bony cheeks, a big blade of a nose, and needle-sharp eyes. He looked familiar . . . the dying man from the hospital. Gabe's last recollection had him flat on his back, unconscious, black-and-blue, and with a death stink rising from his skin. He'd been in bad shape then, the worst.

"Hey, pal, you're looking better," Gabe said.

"Thanks to you, Mr. Kroun."

English accent. Fleming hadn't mentioned his partner was from that far out of town. The way he spoke, this bird apparently knew everything. Until he had come to Chicago *no one* had known about Gabe being a vampire. Fleming might as well be broadcasting on the radio.

The man continued. "I'm very grateful for what you did. It can't have been easy. Thank you for saving my life."

"So long as it worked."

"Was there any doubt?"

He didn't know how to answer that one. "It's Escott, right?"

"Yes. Charles Escott. Jack said you were staying at the house."

"Only part-time." Why didn't he come the rest of the way in? Why the stony expression? Usually people relaxed after introductions. *He probably knows my reputation.* "I'll be leaving soon."

"Indeed?"

"I can leave tonight if you want."

"No need to trouble yourself." He took a quick look around the room, his gaze pausing on the empty space on the floor. "Why are you here?"

The man's tone was off. He had things on his mind. "Catching up on my reading. Yourself?"

Escott made no reply, but glanced at the paper on the desk and must have made a fast guess about what lay beneath the pages. He moved, smoothly, with much confidence. He'd been hiding one hell of a big damn revolver behind the door. He aimed it at Gabe's chest. "Raise your hands. Now."

"Hey, just hold on a minute . . ."

"Now."

Gabe hesitated, throwing an involuntarily glare. He didn't know what he looked like, but the outward change always took the starch out of the toughest mugs in New York.

Escott, however, seemed immune. "I know how fast you are, but I *can* get one clear shot. It may not kill, but it will hurt. As you cannot vanish, you will require time to heal, during which interval I can inflict a great deal more damage."

Gabe assessed his options and reluctantly concluded the man was right. And certainly insane. He was breathing a little too slow for the situation, and he looked ready to follow through on his threat. Did his gun also have a hair trigger? "Come on—this is a new suit."

"Don't give me cause to ruin it."

Gabe slowly raised his hands. "What's this about?"

"Jack Fleming." Escott watched him, not blinking, holding the gun dead center and rock-steady.

He finally shook his head. "Still don't understand."

Apparently that wasn't the right answer. Escott cocked the gun.

Gabe felt a small jolt in his chest in response, as though his dormant heart tried to jump out of the way. "Hey! Slow down, pal, I'll help if I can. What do you *want?*"

"Jack Fleming," Escott repeated through clenched teeth. His eyes were the same color as steel and not nearly as soft. "Where the hell is he?"

Gabe thought his first reply—along the lines of *How the hell should I know?*—would get him shot. His second—*What? You lost him?*—was idiotic and would also result in gunfire. He did his best to read the stranger before him and decided that now would be a good time to cease being Whitey Kroun.

"Tell me what's happened," said Gabe.

"It's about what has not happened."

"Okay . . . tell me that, then."

Escott continued to study, probably trying to read him right back. Something changed behind those hard eyes. He took the revolver off cock, but otherwise kept it ready and centered. "Every night, without fail, as soon as he's awake, Jack calls his girlfriend or she calls him. That may seem trivial to you, but it is not. For him it is cast-iron habit. Also, without fail, he contacts a certain Mr. Derner at the Nightcrawler Club—"

"Yeah, he stays in touch 'cause of the business. So he's late on a couple calls, that's enough for you to want to shoot me?"

"A few minutes late, even an hour is acceptable, but not *eight* hours. That's much too long. Something's happened to him."

"And you've tried to find hi—"

"Of *course*! I've called everyone and been everywhere. The

previous evening he went to visit Miss Smythe, and no one's seen or heard from him since. That is highly atypical behavior. He is not to be found. His car wasn't here, but I saw the lights on and hoped—"

"You talk to Derner?" Now was not the best time to let the man know the fate of Fleming's car.

"He wasn't forthcoming with information. He did admit that Jack had not checked in tonight."

"How about I call and straighten this out? Will that make you put the gun down?"

No reply.

"Look, I don't know where he is, either. Last I saw he was behind the Nightcrawler talking to one of the guys; after that, I couldn't say."

"Aside from myself and Miss Smythe, the only person he's spent any time with has been *you*. Mr. Derner did impart that you and Jack went on an errand for several hours last night."

"We did, but came back to the club, and I don't see how it could have to do with him taking off tonight. A man's got a right to keep to himself if he wants t—"

"No. There's something wrong. Seriously wrong."

That was uncompromising. "You know him better than I do. You say he's missing, okay, I'll help you find him. Lemme use the phone. I'll see what I can get from Derner."

Escott nodded, just the once.

It took Gabe a moment to remember the number for the Nightcrawler's office phone. Having a cannon aimed at his chest made him that nervous. You learned something new every night.

The connection went through. "Yeah, what is it?"

"This is—" Damn, what was he calling himself to this guy? "Whitey."

Derner got more respectful. "Yessir."

"What's going on with Fleming? Where is he?"

"He hasn't checked in is all I know. Did you call Mike?"

"Yes, but forget that—I need to speak to Fleming. Now."

"Bu—"

"Hang up, make calls, find someone who knows where he is. Five minutes, then you ring me back here." Gabe read the number off the dial and dropped the receiver back on the hook.

"You enjoyed that," Escott observed. He seemed slightly less on the edge—by at least a quarter inch.

"It's good to be top dog, yeah." He'd bought five minutes, but didn't know what to do with them. Trying to sit still with a crazy man ready to shoot if he heard the wrong word was not a good way to fill the time. He gave Escott a serious appraisal and thought about hypnotizing him. That would bring on a headache; Gabe couldn't risk a reprise of the blinding skull-breaker he'd had at the cabin. "Look, I've been on the road since I left him in the alley last night, you can believe that or not. He could have had a fight with his girl, gone to a movie, be holed up in a pool hall. That guy Coldfield is pissed with him, maybe—"

"I've asked. He's not seen Jack. He's angry, but he'd tell me . . ." Escott paused, assessing. "You've been up to that cabin." Statement, not a question.

His mouth went dry. "What?"

"You heard. What did you find there?"

"Nothing I want to talk about." Gabe wasn't sure that was his voice.

"Something important, then." Escott showed a tiny glint of satisfaction.

How did he even know about . . . oh. Yeah. "Your partner talks too damn much."

"He was only expressing his concern about certain aspects of your visit to the sanitarium. He could not understand why you allowed him along on so private an interview. Perhaps he heard things he should not have known, thus giving you a reason to keep him quiet."

"In which case I'd have knocked him off after we left."

"And you would certainly know how to do that."

Gabe held his most intimidating gaze on Escott, who failed to react at all, much less show fear. The man knew how to focus. "Only I didn't."

"Your original purpose for coming to Chicago was to kill him."

"Funny, but that didn't happen either. I've got no motive."

"Then perhaps someone with you does. This Michael or Mr. Broder."

"I'm gonna do you a favor and ask—I just said *ask*—you to back away. If they're involved, I'll handle 'em. The worst thing you can do is let them know you exist."

"The best thing you can do is tell me the why of it."

Gabriel considered, then shook his head. "I'll pass. What's going on with them has nothing to do with Fleming."

"Michael sent him to watch you. That, sir, is not to be ignored."

He had a point. Maybe Fleming hadn't delivered enough details to satisfy. Michael could have gotten fed up and finally turned Broder loose to do something. Broder might well have turned himself loose without telling Mike. That would be bad for everyone.

The phone rang. Before Derner could speak, Gabe interrupted. "Hold on a minute. Whatever you have on Fleming, I want you to say it to this guy first." He held the receiver out.

Escott reached to take it, still keeping the gun level. "Yes?" Apparently Derner did not have good news. Escott fired off questions, but the replies were clearly not to his liking. He said thank you and hung up. "Very well, no one at the Nightcrawler has seen or heard from him. That leaves you."

"Only I wasn't around to do anything." He'd finally got that the man with the gun was deeply afraid and only barely able to keep himself from flying apart.

"Yes. You were at the cabin. What did—"

"It's a fishing cabin. I went up there to fish."

"In the dead of winter?"

"I never said I was good at it."

Escott wasn't amused. "That . . . that is the most bloody stupid thing I've ever heard."

Gabe shrugged. "The night ain't over, pal."

Another change—lightning fast—shifted everything behind those steel gray eyes. They somehow got harder and abruptly blazed with a lunatic fury. He raised the gun until Gabe found himself looking right down the barrel.

No . . .

Gabe tore his gaze from the gun and stared at Escott. No chance of hypnosis pushing through those emotions. He was too far gone.

Escott's heart pounded loud in the silent room, and now his hand shook. But at this distance he wouldn't miss.

"Why?" Gabriel blurted out the word.

Escott blinked once. Better than shooting.

"Why?"

He trembled all over, visibly slipping.

"Tell me, dammit!"

A thin crack in the man's intent. He blinked rapidly now, like a sleeper waking. "W-what?"

"You're not mad at *me*—who then? Why?"

The crack widened, and the moment stretched, and gradually Escott's pounding heart slowed. The gun lowered by an inch. Then another. It was a long progression, but Escott finally sagged and put the cannon away in a shoulder holster.

Gabe felt like falling over, but resisted.

"Mr. Kroun, I apologize for this." He spoke in a strangely neutral tone that sure as hell didn't sound right for the situation. "I shall not waste any more of your time." Escott turned and left, just like that.

It took a few seconds for Gabe to find his feet and lurch from behind the desk. Escott was halfway down the stairs.

"Hey! Stop!"

Amazingly, he did.

"Get up here."

Escott wavered, then turned and trudged back. He walked past Gabe, not meeting his eye, and on into the office. He went to the window, standing before the closed curtains, hands at his sides, shoulders down.

Gabe came around and peered at his face. There was a lost soul if he ever saw one. He went to the liquor cabinet, picked something strong at random, and poured. He had to fit the glass into Escott's hand and lift it to get him started. He drank without reaction, and the glass slipped from his fingers. Gabe caught it, not spilling a drop, and guided him toward a leather chair in a corner, making him sit.

The radio blared on, the volume all the way to the top.

This time Gabe jumped. He crossed the room in two strides and shut the damned thing off again. When he looked back, Escott was slumped forward in the chair with one hand over his face.

"Oh, Myrna, what's happened?" he whispered, very, very softly.

Myrna again. Who the hell is Myrna? "What do you think has happened?" Gabe asked aloud.

Escott glanced up, surprised, perhaps, that he'd been heard. He shook his head.

"You've got an idea, or you wouldn't be like this. So give."

He opened his mouth, but nothing came out. Gabe put the glass in his hand again. Escott eventually finished the rest of the drink. He still looked lost.

"You're scared," Gabe said. "But Fleming's a tough bastard and can take care of himself. Why are you so worried?"

"Things." Escott cleared his throat. He sounded like a strangling victim. "Things have been . . . difficult, because of what he went through with Bristow."

Gabe frowned. "Yeah. Go on."

The man stared at the empty space on the floor where the

furniture piece had stood and didn't speak for a long time. Then, "Here the other night . . . Jack tried to kill himself."

"What?"

"And . . ." Escott's face worked as he fought to keep control. "And I'm afraid he might have tried again . . . and succeeded."

13

FLEMING

MY first moments at waking were the worst I'd ever had in a long parade of bad times, and it went downhill from there, headlong into hell.

The trip was in stages, like Dante's ten-cent tour, and not nearly as nice.

It began with a bewildering dream.

I became dimly aware of being dragged, carried, and awkwardly shoved into a cramped space. My eyes shut, my brain gathered information but was unable to take meaning from it. A single question floated through the shadows—*Where's my earth?*—then drifted out again, getting no answer.

After that, the space was in motion, bumping and roaring over pavement for an unguessable time.

Another bout of being carried and set down. I was dead, my body not responding to anything, unable to move. My limbs were arranged flat on something, not a bed. My arms were stretched wide, palms up, knuckles hanging.

Then my earth must have been returned, for the dream ceased.

Sunset.

Eyes wide, internal alarm bells on full, I shot awake in absolute darkness. I *hated* the dark. After my change, my eyes could make use of the least little sliver of light—if it was there to be used.

This kind of dark was cold, damp, and rock solid. I tried to reach for the cot-side lamp, but something kept my arm from moving, and at the same time hot, sickening agony shot from a spot below my elbow and straight into my brain like a spear. It was so intense that I yelled, tried to pull away, and that made it ten times worse—for both arms.

Things went cloudy for a long, terrible stretch as my body fought against whatever held it. The more it fought, the greater the pain, until I howled nonstop like a trapped animal.

When exhaustion set in, it was a blessing. The pain remained, but did not increase so long as I kept still.

When I was able to think—and that was a struggle—I wondered why I'd not vanished away from the pain. Even as the thought came I tried slipping into the gray oblivion that had always healed me.

But *nothing* happened. I remained anchored in flesh, and the effort exhausted me fast, like racing a car in neutral.

Panicking did no good. I knew that, but still failed to stop a choking wave from sweeping over me. I heard myself bellowing God knows what until the fit passed.

This wasn't like the seizures. I could escape them by vanishing, and that had been unaccountably made impossible.

I forced myself quiet, pushing the fear to one side, trying to find out . . . anything.

Flat on my back on something hard, arms spread wide, and hellish pain if I moved either of them, yes, that was pretty damned bad. Whatever rope or chain bound me in place was too tight, and gouging into me in a way I couldn't figure out.

The hard surface ran out a few inches from my wrists. My hands were over free space. I could move them, but it hurt.

The room, cave, whatever, was empty and silent, but . . . someone was nearby . . . in another room. There was a little distance and a wall or floor between, but I heard a heartbeat and the quick saw of breath and imagined him listening in turn.

Of course I yelled for help, but none came, and no one replied. Was he in the same boat? Was he the one who'd brought me here?

My next wave of panic was more subtle, not as noisy, but there was no coherent thought going on. I struggled, fresh agony stabbed through my arms, and soon the physical pain pulled me clear of the fit.

Eventually I lay quiet, and again tried to work out what was around me. My other senses failed to provide much help. Arms held in place, pain if I moved them, and the sharp smell of my own blood and terror. Whatever was wrong with my arms . . . dammit, they were *bleeding*. A lot, enough to flow over the edge of something and drip to the floor. I heard the soft regular patter as it hit a hard surface, sounding like a faucet leak you can't shut off. Oh, hell. Too much, and it would kill me.

I held perfectly still. I had fed well last night but could not afford to lose any of it. Couldn't tell how much I'd already lost, only feel it as a cooling wetness beneath my forearms.

They began to itch. Annoying, but a good sign, it meant healing. Whatever wounds were there would seal up quickly enough, even without vanishing. Let them be and . . .

I was hungry again. God, it *hurt*. Not as bad as my arms, but given time and no replenishment it would worsen. I never allowed myself get so starved. Too dangerous. The last time . . . yeah . . . the damned meat locker.

Okay, one thing at a time: what the hell had happened?

I was no longer on the cot under the seating tiers at Lady Crymsyn. Someone had invaded that sanctuary and taken me elsewhere. Poor Myrna had tried to warn me.

He'd come softly and cut the timing fine. Had he been in the building earlier, I'd have heard him. In those last moments before sunrise, he must have crept in, and only Myrna had known.

I had a choice of suspects: Kroun—or rather his cronies, Michael or Broder—near the top of the list. He could hypnotically control them into doing whatever he wanted. The *why* of it . . . I couldn't guess. Maybe he wanted to be the king vampire of Chicago. Great, fine, he could have the job, I'd leave, no fuss.

Next up was Strome. He'd seen me walking around just fine after having much of my skin stripped off and might have gotten curious over that improbability. Just a couple nights back he'd seen me appear out of thin air, which surprised the hell out of us both. I'd popped him unconscious and been fairly sure he'd not remembered the Houdini act, but he could have faked it. With his stone face, he was the perfect liar. Again, the *why* escaped me.

Number one choice—and I hated it: Shoe Coldfield.

I didn't want to believe it. The idea made me sick, but he'd shown his violent side by pounding me flat the other night. Standing over Escott's dying body, he'd promised to kill me. Escott's recovery might not have been enough to change Coldfield's mind.

He had a serious grudge on and knew my weaknesses.

He was more than capable, but—and I grabbed hard onto this one—it wasn't how he worked. Coldfield would look me in the eye and slam me through a wall, but hold me prisoner?

I went back to Kroun again. When he fell into those blackouts where his eyes went strange . . . but that was also direct and short-lived. *Why* would he do this? Had he gone back on his decision not to execute me for Bristow's death?

There was a long list of mob guys I'd annoyed. While some might take a shot if they thought they could get away with it, none would know how pointless it would be. Whoever had done this knew how to deal with me.

Back to Strome . . . but I just couldn't see it. Back to . . .

What if Michael and Broder were acting independently of Kroun? Michael might have made a guess about my nature. Hell, he could know all about Kroun as well. There was no guarantee that he'd been able to keep his big secret. Michael could learn that I survived Bristow and a lot more besides—it was cheap talk at the Nightcrawler's bar; if you knew what clues to look for . . .

But I couldn't see the why of it, either—unless he was keeping me on ice in order to gain some kind of control over Kroun. Of course it would only work if Kroun was concerned about my welfare. I had no confidence in that.

However bad the thoughts, the thinking steadied me. I noticed more about my surroundings and myself. I lay on, perhaps, a long and very sturdy table. It had held out against my struggles without shifting. Maybe it was bolted to the floor or just exceptionally heavy.

I was dressed, so far as I could tell, in the same clothes, but the lower part of the sleeves were gone on my coat and shirt, cut away. What remained covered my chest; even the tie was in place. I longed to loosen it and undo the collar button. My legs seemed to be tied down to something. The restraints there gave a little and could be rope rather than chain. Strong, though. I wasn't moving, no leverage. I was under a heavy blanket or tarp, implying someone was either concerned for my comfort or wanted to be able to conceal me if needed.

The air was chill, but not freezing; there was an earthy scent to it, and my voice had bounced off hard surfaces. I heard no traffic or other outside noises. My best guess for location was a cellar with no ground-level windows. The utter silence—except for the heavy breather keeping his distance—indicated a deep and private hole.

Which was strangely familiar.

And threatened to bring on another wave of panic.

I crushed it. Quick. Giving in to more mindless fear was not going to help. I had to stay in control. Whoever had done this had kept me alive, had gone to considerable effort over it. He wanted something from me or would use me to get something. Maybe he was just waiting until I calmed down.

Okay. Why the hell not?

"Ready to talk now?" I bellowed. I sounded a lot braver and more confident than I felt. "Let's start the lodge meeting!"

No reply.

I chose to think he was mulling things over. I chose to think that I was not down here to starve to death in the dark.

"*Hello!*"

No reply. I waited a good long time.

I did hear something during the wait. Footsteps from the floor immediately above as someone paced around, unhurried. He was free to stroll, not tied up.

"*Hey!*"

The steps halted, probably in reaction to my yell. Good. I needed a way to get his attention.

A lunatic part of me with nothing to lose took over. I started singing "Happy Days Are Here Again" in an offensively loud bawl.

I have no vocal talent and limit my musical outbursts to the car or the shower when I'm alone. What isn't flat is off-key, or my voice just doesn't reach certain notes or cracks like an egg. It's a shame, because I like music.

In this case I hoped the racket would prompt a reaction. Even if all he did was come down to gag me, I'd at least get a look at him.

Nothing on the first chorus. I didn't know the other words, so I repeated it, putting in a remarkable amount of cheer and gusto. Maybe he'd think I'd gone nuts. Whatever it took.

Halfway through a third repeat a light came on.

The brilliance was too much after the darkness, lancing into my eyes. My lids hammered shut on their own, but I stubbornly kept singing. I tried to force them open and couldn't. I wanted to rub them—they were dry. After a bit I was able to squint past a veil of red and black sparklers and take in quick glimpses of the place.

Basement, as I'd guessed, gray concrete walls, low ceiling with dusty support beams for the floor above.

I was indeed on a table, broad, long, and sturdy, a Victorian behemoth built to withstand anything except modern times. Someone had shunted it down to the basement to age in solitude . . . until someone else came along and tied me to it.

My legs, not moving at all. I was bound like a mummy.

My arms—what the . . . ? No, that couldn't be right.

I blinked, desperate and disbelieving. The song died on my lips.

Both arms—no—that was goddamned *impossible.*

My fingers twitched when asked, but it hurt. There was something between them and my order-giving brain, something that went miles past mere horror and straight into stomach-turning grotesque.

I couldn't see for a moment; a gray mist settled on my eyes. I thought I was at last vanishing, but my body held solid. My mind simply didn't want to accept the straightforward cruelty of it.

Vision clearing . . . cleared . . . and the awfulness was still there.

My arms stretched out—and midway along below the elbows was a vertical piece of threaded metal rod.

The steel was half an inch thick and *in my flesh*, piercing right through, passing between the two bones of my lower arms.

The tops of the rods were at a right angle like the flat handle of a walking stick. If I pulled my arms straight up the L-shape of the angle would stop them. Presumably the rest of the length went through the table. I was held fast. I'd seen miniature versions of this used to pin insects to display boards.

It was too much. I couldn't help but struggle. This wasn't happening to me. The panic flooded back, full force.

Flailing against the immobile steel was useless, but I couldn't stop, not until exhaustion overtook me again. I finally collapsed, shivering from head to toe.

You're not supposed to be able to faint lying down, but I went blackout dizzy, and my guts wanted to turn themselves out. There was no waking from this nightmare.

"It's just going to get worse."

I looked around for the source of that voice. He sounded familiar.

Oh. It was me.

I was standing right over myself: cleaned up and in a sharp new suit, I looked sympathetic, but clearly unable to offer more than an opinion.

That other me usually turned up when I was right out of my mind.

Good timing.

Still, I was company of sorts. However crazy I got, I didn't have to be alone in the pit.

"Any ideas?" I asked in a shaky whisper.

"Try singing some more."

What the hell, why not?

Couldn't bring myself to do it just yet. No energy. My struggles had me bleeding again, and every drop falling to the floor weakened me. I'd lost a lot, and the hunger would continue to grow. My corner teeth were out, I was in all kinds of pain, hallucinating, and there wasn't a damned thing I could do.

Helplessness. I'd been here before, hanging in a meat locker, convulsing in the throes of a seizure, standing at the foot of Escott's hospital bed while he lay dying . . .

I imagined him rising to look at me, his face distorted by the bruises I'd put there, but still recognizable, wearing a sardonic expression.

"You're the strongest man I know," he told me.

I didn't feel it, but he was a good judge of character. I could put up a front, fake a courage I did not possess. If some bastard wanted me to die like this, then I'd go with a little pride.

Howling a fourth chorus, I sounded absolutely insane, even to me. That was scary, but I kept going.

"I know you can hear me," I called. "I can do this all night."

The me in the new suit smiled and nodded, giving a thumbs-up, and looked across the room.

A door opened. I couldn't see it but heard the drawing of a bolt and creak of hinges. Footsteps on wood stairs, descending, one-two-three-four . . . I counted sixteen steps, storing the information.

He crossed into my field of view. He was also in a nice suit and also smiled, though that was the natural expression of his pale face. It was how his mouth was shaped, giving him an air of smug perpetual amusement. He held a .45 revolver in one hand and seemed very confident.

My short list of suspects failed to include this man. The familiarity of a basement prison had been a clue from a hidden corner of my mind. Not so very long ago I'd chained Hurley Gilbert Dugan to a wall in a very similar place.

He'd gone me one better with this variation.

I stared, and Dugan smiled back, and damn, but he was enjoying the situation.

No reason why I shouldn't as well. I began to laugh again. The laughter was odd; I'd never laughed like that in my life. The me standing opposite Dugan approved, grinning as well. This was goddamned funny. It really was.

And it spoiled Dugan's moment.

He must have anticipated some other reaction from me, anger or fear, cursing or begging, but not this. His intentional smile soured, replaced by a flash of irritation. The man had no sense of humor, not the normal kind. He liked feeling superior to others and relished a good gloat, but take it away, laugh at *him*—he hated that.

I was in no position to be antagonizing, but there was little he could do to me that Hog Bristow hadn't done first. If Dugan found a way to improve on *that*, well, I'd die a little bit quicker.

And I would die.

I wasn't getting out of this one. I saw it in his eyes, knew in my heart that for him it was a practical necessity. This was where it would happen, no coming back from this lonely grave.

But if there was *any* way I could take him with me . . .

In the short time since my change, I'd killed. I was a murderer. There were deaths I'd caused indirectly and others that were without question my own doing. To one degree or another each had a measure of regret attached, not that I would have changed things in a couple cases, but taking a life lessens your own. It leaves a wound on your soul that never quite heals.

But sometimes . . . it's worth it.

Hog Bristow, yeah, I'd kill him again and no problem. There would be a certain physical disgust for the act itself, like stepping on a poisonous spider and leaving a mess. But you do it anyway.

Hurley Gilbert Dugan was different. I would take a great deal of pleasure in the act of killing him. I might even prolong it to give him a taste of the terror he'd given to others. As a kid he was probably responsible for at least two deaths: a governess and another kid. As an adult he was the brains behind a girl's kidnapping and the murder of a harmless old couple whose isolated farmhouse he wanted for a hideout.

There might be more, and I wondered about the fate of the owner of this place. Dugan lied, manipulated people for fun, and wrote countless essays arguing the merit of executing those he thought to be inferior specimens of humanity. He was genuinely puzzled when anyone disagreed with him. Clearly they were just the sort of shortsighted fools he would have culled from the herd.

He'd been in that meat locker, too, running loose in the

background, not important enough for Bristow to bother with, and witnessed my torture. It had made him sick. He had no belly then for violence, not when he could get someone else to do the work. But he'd learned much in that hour. He knew things about me that I didn't want to know myself; for that alone I wanted him dead.

He would be dead if not for the rods holding my arms. That was why he'd not been present at my waking. He wanted to be sure I was safely pinned in place. Everything in me wanted to tear loose and rip him in two. But if I'd been unable to get free by now, then it wasn't going to happen. I was just too weak.

That was a hell of a lot of frustration, more than enough to make a man crazy.

So I laughed in his endlessly smiling face and sang off-key and laughed some more.

Until he gently pressed the muzzle of that revolver against my temple.

I trailed off but kept grinning. If he shot me in the head under these circumstances, it just might do the trick. I'd be dead without finding out what he wanted, though. If he'd simply meant to kill me, that would have happened back in the nightclub. He'd gone to a lot of trouble to get me here.

Dugan examined the threaded rod on his side, poking at the area where the metal went in. It hurt when he did that. From what I could see from my angle, the skin was healed tight around the metal, red and puffy, like an infection swelling around a splinter.

He abruptly grabbed the handle part of the rod and gave it a full twist all the way around. My skin parted from the metal, blood welled, and I couldn't stifle a gasp. When a small portion of the red-hot haze in my brain receded, he twisted the thing back again. I was almost prepared for it, but not really. I squirmed in vain to get free.

He watched with a calm detachment.

Well dressed, well fed, and yes, that complacent expression was starting to return. But I'd seen him puking and terrified. That gave me one up on him. Anything to boost my morale.

He'd made his point, though: this was his show.

He reached out of my view and drew up a chair, settling in. He seemed to be ready to spend a good long time with me.

God, what had I done to deserve this?

"I've been following you," he said.

No greeting, no preamble, he spoke as though continuing a conversation begun hours ago. Some people do that, usually the most self-absorbed.

"You never once looked over your shoulder. You made it easy."

I felt no need to reply, resigned to what promised to be a lengthy recitation of his life and hard times since our escape from the meat locker. He loved himself more than anyone I'd ever met, and he assumed others also found him fascinating.

He'd taken ten grand from a misguided lady friend and disappeared himself, a difficult task what with every mobster in Chicago looking for him on my say-so. I'd tentatively concluded that he'd left the city and hoped he'd departed from the country altogether.

Optimism can be a very, very evil thing.

Dugan must have been preparing his little speech for some while—there was a rehearsed quality to it as he told his story. I didn't give a tinker's damn how clever he'd been at watching me from afar. Nor could I work up any interest for his account of how he'd learned to use firearms. The .45 made him dangerous, not tough.

It was clear he cherished the sound of his own voice, and it was a nice voice: educated, articulate. He reminded me of Michael that way, but Michael was someone I could deal with; Dugan was not.

"Every night I've kept a close eye on you, Fleming," he said. "You never knew."

"You need a better hobby."

"Watching and studying and learning exactly how you waste your abilities."

"Should've gone to the movies. They have cartoons."

Dugan was very proud about how he'd broken the window and gotten into the house. He thought himself to be very slick, indeed. He'd found my basement shelter eventually, for he had reasoned I must have something like that.

Only my own caution had spared me from being kidnapped that night. He'd returned during the day, intent on hauling me out, but I'd slept safe in the neighbor's attic. Had I done so again instead of staying at the club, I'd still be free.

Dugan broke into Crymsyn that day, covering his tracks better, and scoured it for hidden sanctuaries. I'd been smart to have one someplace other than the basement; but being such a genius, it was inevitable he would discover it.

He'd been watching from afar when Kroun and I had gone to the Stockyards the other night. Good thing Kroun hadn't left the car. Dugan gave no hint of knowing there was another bloodsucker in town. He complimented me for later buying blood at a butcher shop, and it was unsettling to learn he'd been so close behind. How could I have not noticed?

I was sick of him. "You want applause? Undo my arms."

"Please, I went to too much trouble setting this up. I remembered what you told me when that two-legged animal had you hanging from the ceiling. You couldn't escape because a piece of metal lodged in your body prevented you from vanishing. That's fascinating. I'm delighted that my experiment to keep you here was so successful."

Some experiment. But I had to admit, it worked like a son of a bitch.

Dugan twisted the rod again, so the healing skin parted from the metal and fresh blood appeared. The sight of it and my pain didn't bother him tonight.

In one of those infrequent flashes that usually occur just a little too late to do any good, I began to get a glimmer of what this was about, and the bottom dropped out of my belly.

I could not show fear, hell, I couldn't even tremble. I was absolutely petrified.

He saw that, and it pleased him.

He rose from the chair, going around and behind the head of my bed, out of sight. I heard odd noises, a rustle and slither like stiff fabric shifting, a metallic click, his step as he returned.

He'd put on a butcher's apron. It covered the whole of his front.

And he'd traded the revolver for a scalpel.

My thinking he'd go one better than Bristow and kill me that much faster . . . I'd been crazy. Even if death was at the other end, I couldn't go through it again. I just couldn't.

I closed my eyes. In a safe and well-sheltered part of my mind there was a single perfect hour from a perfect summer day. I'd floated alone in the cool water of a stock tank, master of the world and content. In memory, I breathed sweet, hot air, felt the still water holding me up, and the lazy wind whispering over my skin.

It was fragile protection against what was to come. Far stronger was the memory of Bristow stripping my skin off. I'd done all I could to blot that out, but Dugan brought it hurtling back.

Unable to run, I trembled, head to toe.

My scars began to burn.

If he wanted me to beg, I would.

I'd do anything, say anything.

I had no pride, no courage.

He owned me.

KROUN

GABE went to the desk, reached for the phone, changed his mind. Derner wouldn't know any more about Fleming's whereabouts than he had a few minutes ago.

The number for Michael . . . well, he was on his way in. Gabe would grill him then.

He checked Escott, who had not moved from the chair, though he'd straightened a little. He looked sick, but in a different way than the other night in the hospital. He continued to stare at the empty space on the floor.

"Hey," Gabe said. "Let's go."

It took a moment, but Escott found his feet. "Where?" His voice was flat, drained.

"Outside. I want air."

If Escott appreciated the irony of that, he gave no sign. Gabe pulled on his overcoat and hat and made sure Escott didn't fall down the stairs as they descended. They paused in the lobby; something had changed on the bar.

"Were those all propped on end when you came in?" Gabe

asked. The dozens of matchbooks scattered about were flat now, the covers neatly tucked back into place.

"Yes. They were." Escott's eyes flickered.

"Who else is here?"

"That would be Myrna. She's a ghost," he said, deadpan as hell.

Gabe considered the circumstances and Escott's state of mind. He was crazy, but not that crazy. "Ghost. You got ghosts?"

"Just the one. She plays with the lights. I wish to God she could tell me what's happened."

The lobby phone rang. The bell went on for far longer than normal, then faded. Escott broke away and picked up the earpiece, listening, but apparently nothing came through. He returned it, disappointed. "She's never played with the phone before." He stayed put, apparently prepared to wait for it to ring again.

"Air," said Gabe. "Now." He wasn't afraid; it was just damned weird, and he didn't want to think about stuff like that tonight.

Freezing and windy, nothing new about the weather, though he hoped the shock might clear Escott's head. Gabe paced up and down the front a few times, the exercise working off adrenaline generated by having a gun pointed his way. He also checked the area for anything that shouldn't be there, like Broder or Michael. Nothing caught his attention; and no one shot at him, so far so good.

Huddled under the canopy of the club's entrance Escott tried to light a cigarette, but the wind kept blowing out his match. Gabe offered his lighter, noticing that Escott had gotten his shakes under control.

As good a time as any.

"So . . . what did Jack do? Jump off a building?"

Escott threw him a short glare, then looked away. He smoked the cigarette halfway down before replying. "He made a wooden slug, fitted it to a cartridge, then shot himself in the head."

Gabe winced, experiencing an uneasy sympathy mixed with disbelief. "Cripes. And he survived that?"

"At sunset he vanished and healed. I didn't know if he would, I—"

"What, you found him?"

He nodded. "On the couch in his office."

"What couch?"

"The one that's not there. I suppose he got rid of it. There was blood . . ."

No kidding.

"He'd survived, but I was so damned angry with him. That's why we got into a fight. It got out of hand, went too far . . . but he promised . . . he swore on Bobbi's life he'd never hurt himself again."

"Does he keep his promises?"

"I thought he did. He always has."

"Then lay off the worrying."

"What do you mean?"

"Ever think that something *else* happened to make him take off?"

"He'd phone—"

"Unless he's tied up somewhere against his will."

Escott snorted. "That's impossible. He'd just vanish and leave."

"Listen, the other night the cops tried to hustle us right over there in the parking lot. I made them forget, but they could have shaken it off and grabbed your pal. If they're throwing him a blackjack party in some station house, he wouldn't dare vanish, and he couldn't make a phone call. He can't hypnotize people anymore, right?"

"But they—"

"Please, tell me every cop in this town follows the rules, and I will personally apologize to each one and his dog."

With new hope on his face, Escott threw away his smoke, went into the club, and beelined for the lobby phone. He pushed nickels into the slot, making one call after another.

Gabe stood by the bar and watched the scattered matchbooks. Not one of them moved.

Emerging from the booth, Escott shook his head. "I've contacted everyone who would hear if Jack had been picked up."

"Things like that can be kept quiet."

"Of that I am aware. It could even be the FBI taking an interest."

"Why would they do that?"

"Why not?"

Damned if I know. Gabe had mulled over the possibility that Michael or Broder might have stepped in. Fleming might be tied up somewhere in Cicero, getting questioned. He might put up with it, but not indefinitely. "You know how to get to the Nightcrawler Club from here?"

"Of course."

He handed over the keys to the Hudson. "C'mon. Maybe Derner can work faster if I'm looking over his shoulder."

The suicide attempt had surprised the hell out of him. Fleming had given no sign—but then Gabe didn't know him. That twitching fit at their first meeting . . . Fleming had been in bad shape then, but he'd pulled out of it. A couple of times he'd acted odd, though: down in that garage basement and in the hospital, but anyone would be upset. He'd steadied up.

But shooting himself?

Damn.

No wonder Escott had been nuts enough to pull a gun. Gabe wasn't sure he should overlook that. On the other hand, the man had apologized. That was nuts, too.

Aren't there any sane people in this town?

Long odds against that. Just have to make the best of things. Find Fleming, deal with Michael, then what? Go fishing? Maybe not.

Escott parked the Hudson on one side of the building rather than in the back alley of the Nightcrawler. It was too soon yet for Michael to show up, but Gabe didn't mind waiting now that he had something to do and other things to think about than his own problems.

The mugs on watch got scarce soon as they saw him getting out. Apparently his reputation was as bad here as in New York, and he was not above exploiting it. That was how he'd survived those early days without people noticing anything was wrong.

He used it now, leading the way up to the office, aiming a grim face at Derner, who was at the desk.

"Haven't found him yet, Mr. Kroun, sorry," he said, correctly interpreting the reason behind the personal appearance.

Gabe stood over him. "Don't give up on that, okay?"

"No, sir." Derner spared a quick, curious glance at Escott and grabbed the phone. "Heard you were sick, Mr. Escott."

"I was. Much better now, thank you."

"Cops," said Gabe. "See if he's been picked up by any of 'em."

Derner winced. "Uh . . . there could be . . ."

"What?"

"Oh, you know—guys listening in. Some of those G-men . . ."

"So? You're just looking for a missing friend who might have been taken in by mistake. Nothing wrong in that."

Derner didn't seem too convinced on the point but went back to dialing.

Gabe gave Escott a critical once-over. The man was ragged at the edges. He must have been running without stop all night.

"You look like hell," Gabe observed. "Eat anything lately?"

Escott shook his head and sank into one of the overstuffed chairs facing Derner.

Dropping his coat and hat on another chair, Gabe went

to the door and gave orders to one of the mugs loafing in the hall, who hurried off. In a wonderfully brief time, two of the club's waitresses—very cute in their short, spangled skirts—came in with covered trays. Gabe pointed them at Escott.

"Really, now . . ." Escott began, startled as they swooped on him.

"You need your strength," said Gabe. "Girls—give 'im the works."

He retired to a couch opposite the main desk, partly to watch Derner and partly to remove himself from the heavy smell of the steak-and-potatoes meal. Gabe found entertainment in the show, though. A clearly nonplussed Escott enduring the torture of two cooing, smiling Kewpie dolls cutting his food and hand-feeding him one bite at a time . . . the club photographer should be up to take a picture.

Gabe's smirk lasted until he saw Derner's face. The man had gone dead white as he stared at the fun. Gabe went to the desk, leaning in close. "What's wrong?"

"Nothing, Mr. Kroun," he said, voice very low. "It's your business."

He'd stepped in something, he just wasn't sure what. "Look at me."

Derner reluctantly did so.

It was risking another headache, but he had to know and pressed in. "Have I done this before?"

"Yessir."

"What happens next?"

"You take 'em down to the basement. They don't come back."

Oh, hell. He had no memory for any of that, but the stories . . .

He'd not understood what had suddenly prompted him to look after a guest; it just seemed like the right thing to do. This macabre twisting of hospitality was yet another ugly remnant of the man he had been. The more he found out about himself, the less he liked.

His head hurt now, a hot drill was burrowing into the bone. He frowned as he leaned over Derner again. "This isn't a last meal. We clear?"

"Yessir."

"This guy is our friend. From now on he gets treated with the same respect as I do."

"Yessir."

"Back to work."

Derner obeyed, no questions, no comment, just the way Gabe liked it.

In the last two months he had made a few such unpleasant discoveries. He'd do or say something innocuous and find a nasty surprise attached. More than once he caught himself questioning an impulse that came out of nowhere.

But second-guessing everything was no way to live. Better to keep his eyes open and catch the reaction of others, as he'd done with Derner. It had worked well enough so far.

Gabe went into the bathroom, wet a folded washcloth through, and pressed it to the knot of hot pain under the white streak. He peered at his ghostly image in the mirror but found no clue to that earlier life.

"Damn . . . you must have been one hell of a crazy bastard," he muttered.

The arrowhead-tipped hands of a black-and-chrome wall clock made their slow circuit into the next hour, and there was still no news of Fleming. Gabe wasn't worried, but Escott took Derner's place at the desk and used the phone, rechecking with various people. Things got sticky when he called Fleming's girlfriend. She'd not seen or heard from him, and Escott had to do some quick talking so she wouldn't worry. With a fine disregard for the truth, he told her that Kroun was likely responsible for keeping their friend busy. She bent Escott's ear for a time, and whatever she said had his full attention.

"Oh . . . I didn't know that," he said. "Congratulations.

Really. I'm delighted for you. Overdue and much deserved. Well, yes, I suppose he might not be too pleased, but he'll get over it, not to worry. Yes, of course I'll tell him to call you."

Escott hung up, looking flummoxed.

"What?" Gabe prompted from the couch. He'd stretched out to work on a more difficult crossword puzzle from a different newspaper.

"Miss Smythe informed me that she's soon to leave for Hollywood to take a screen test."

That explained the congratulations, though his delivery had been lukewarm. "Sounds good. A pippin like her should be out there. Better weather."

"Yes, well, Jack won't think so. They've had some considerable discussion on that topic. He wouldn't stop her, but neither is he willing to go with her. His job is here."

"He's choosing a nightclub over his girl?"

"Perhaps."

"He's nuts. You can open a club anywhere and make good, but a dame like her is once in a lifetime."

Escott shot him an appraising look. "Mr. Kroun, I think you should repeat that within Jack's hearing. It might sort him out. Miss Smythe imparted the news to him last night, and he did not take it with any great enthusiasm. It could explain his dropping out of sight."

"His girlfriend's leaving town so he goes off to sulk? Does that sound like something he'd do?"

"The more I think about it . . . yes, it does. He can get himself fairly deep into the dumps, though his club kept him happy until . . ." Escott didn't finish.

"Hog Bristow. Yeah. My fault. I know. None of that was supposed to happen."

"Yet it did."

Gabe felt himself get warm in the face. Shame was an unfamiliar feeling. He didn't like it much. "Where does he go to sulk?"

"No place special. His club, but I've been all through it,

been to my office and—oh, hell." He grabbed the phone and dialed again, giving his name to someone on the other end. He scribbled on a pad, then stopped, his eyes going sharp as he listened. He gave a terse thank you, slammed the receiver down, got up and paced, looking exasperated.

"Yes?" Gabe asked after a suitable pause.

"Bloody idiot," Escott snapped.

"Him or me?"

"Neither. This is my doing—bloody *hell*!"

"What?"

"I never once thought to check my own answering service. He left a message earlier tonight."

Gabe put down the paper and sat up, the better to enjoy things. "A message?"

"To quote: 'I need to do some thinking, don't worry, be back soon.' Bloody hell, I'll flatten his skull for this."

"For what—leaving a message you didn't check?"

Escott responded with a few ripe and expressive words. For all that, he looked hugely relieved. He dropped into his chair, rubbing the back of his neck. "Once again I apologize, Mr. Kroun."

"Remind me—is that still for nearly blowing a hole in me after I saved your life? Think nothing of it. Could happen to anyone."

"You're too kind." Escott met the sarcasm with a dry tone, but evidently got the point. His ears had turned red.

Oh, yeah, it'll be a while before he lives that one down.

"This is being unconscionably inconsiderate to Miss Smythe. He could have phoned her. He could have phoned me. Why leave a message?"

"Probably just didn't want to talk." Gabe started to pick up the crossword again, but the office door banged open, startling Derner. Escott twitched, going alert.

Michael was early.

He wore his best poker face. The glasses helped. They reflected the lights, concealing half his expression.

Gabe remained seated and smiled just enough to annoy Mike. Strangely, he didn't react, just stood there.

Waiting.

Mike glanced at Derner, then Escott, and apparently dismissed him as one of the club's many hangers-on. "We'll talk in the car. Private."

"And cold."

"You can take it. Come on."

This was a new side. Maybe he'd learned something about Broder that had gotten him thinking. Reaching for his coat and hat, Gabe shot a surreptitious look at Escott, who seemed incurious and inclined to stay put. Smart of him.

The club's last show was in full swing out front, but the kitchen staff was gone, and most of the lights were off. The alley was also dark and empty except for Mike's Studebaker. Gabe emerged cautiously. Broder could be just around the corner at either end or even on one of the surrounding roofs, biding his time to take a shot.

Keeping his back to the club's wall, Gabe went down the stairs and did not cross to the car. Mike seemed to expect that and turned to face him midway between, hands in his pockets.

"It's safe," he said.

The wind was still up, masking sound. Gabe didn't like it; but if there was a bushwhacking in his near future, his reactions were a lot faster than before.

He looked at the man standing solid before him and once more tried to see something in his face that would spark a memory.

Mike was a familiar stranger, hostile, wary, more so tonight than before. Had he always been that grim? Had they ever been friends? Gabe had not seen a hint of that so far, but it must have been there once.

Of course there was the eight-year age difference. Growing up, Gabe might have been too busy to bother with a little brother, especially a half brother. He knew that some could end up hating each other, but at some point in their childhood, he and Michael must have played together, looked out for each other.

Gabriel had no memory of any of it, and no one he'd spoken to from the old neighborhood could tell him what had gone on behind the closed doors of the Kroun family flat.

Michael knew though.

Gabe had been tempted many times to pull the facts out of him hypnotically but never acted upon it.

For one thing, you just don't do that to family.

For another, he was afraid of what he might learn. The little that he had already gleaned was ugly.

Even without the slug in his brain, Gabe would not have remembered his own mother; she'd died a few months after his birth. He'd looked it up in the court records. Sonny had come home drunk one night. He claimed that beating his wife to death had been an accident. Since he worked for a neighborhood boss, a big shot who had influence with a judge, Sonny got sent up for manslaughter instead of murder.

Gabe went to a state orphanage, but no one adopted him. Eight years later his supposedly reformed father came to claim him, a second wife and a baby named Michael in tow.

What had that been like? An orphan all his life and suddenly young Gabriel gets a family. Had a brutal father like Sonny been better than no father at all?

Whatever had happened during his upbringing had turned Gabe into a killer. Chances were good that lightning had struck twice, doing the same for Mike, twisting him a little differently.

Until now there hadn't been a good enough reason to make him talk. The evidence up at the cabin changed that.

"So . . . how's Cicero these days?"

"Shut up, Whitey." Mike looked ready to burst, there was so much inside him wanting to get out. Give him time . . .

But the minutes went by. Nothing. Michael's hands worked inside his coat pockets, making fists, forcing his hands open. It was a mannerism he only ever fell into when they were alone.

He thinks he's still dealing with the son of a bitch he's always known. Not me. Who do I need to be to get answers?

"Where's Broder?" Gabe asked, checking both ends of the alley again.

"Maybe he's pounding the bullet dents out of that car he took the other night."

That was unexpected. "He told you."

"Yeah. He told me."

"After he drove us off the road things got a little hazy. What'd he say?"

But Mike clammed up.

"Oh, come on. What kind of arrangement have you got that someone like Momma Cabot can call Broder whenever she wants?"

"You stay away from her."

"Why?"

Mike shook his head.

"Is that why you gave Fleming the green light to keep me in line and no reprisals?"

"He told you that?" He stopped making fists and took his hands from his pockets.

"Your voice carries. Why do you want to kill me, Mike?"

No reflections on the glasses now, Michael's blue eyes were wide open and for an instant showed a mix of anguish and guilt. He shut it down. "I don't want to."

"But you wouldn't much mind if someone else did the dirty work. What problem gets solved if I'm gone?"

Michael shook his head again.

"I know it has to do with that damned cabin. You were there."

"I was never there," he stated, voice like a razor.

Gabe had hit the nerve he'd wanted. "I went up. I saw the blood, and I found Ramsey's body." He searched for further reaction, but Mike had turned to stone. "I'd like to hear your side."

He was taking a different kind of risk now. The man Gabe had been before his death would never have said anything like that.

"My side?"

"What happened there." Gabe pulled out the .22, holding it flat on his palm so it wouldn't be mistaken for a threat. "Is this yours? Or Ramsey's?"

"What is it?"

He can't see in the dark. Gabe crossed now, opened the driver's door, and put the headlamps on. Mike followed him to the front of the car, staring down at the rusted weapon in the harsh glare. They made fine targets, the pair of them.

"Not mine," he said. "That's your kind of gun."

He was probably right. There was every chance that Gabe had been in the habit of carrying a small-caliber shooter with the numbers filed off. He could throw it away after a kill. Okay, that just meant someone had taken it from him.

"And this?" He drew the amber vial out next, holding it between thumb and index finger.

Mike looked and dismissed it. "What do you want from me?"

This wasn't going the way it should. What had been conclusive up in the woods seemed ridiculous here. Michael should be angry and defensive for being caught out, not like this. Unless . . .

"Then it was Broder. He'd planted stuff. What was his angle? Kill me and Ramsey, then move up the ladder? Is that where that bastard Mitchell got the idea? Or did you order it from the start?"

Mike showed his lower teeth, eyes blazing. He raised one hand, fingers skyward as though to grab something. His fist finally closed on air.

"Well?"

"I'm sorry, Whitey. I promised Ma I'd look after you, but it's too much now. I can't do it anymore."

In the last two months, Mike had never spoken of his mother. All Gabe knew about his stepmother was her name and the official records concerning her death. Sonny had made such a vicious job of his second wife's murder that they'd thrown him into an insane asylum instead of hanging him.

Mike had been fifteen at the time; Gabe had become his legal guardian. Why was it that—

"No more," Mike whispered. Hands in pockets again, briefly. He pulled a gun out, the one Gabe had reloaded himself the previous night.

"Hey, wait!" Gabe backed clear of the lamp glare. He didn't know his brother that well, but this was completely wrong for him.

Mike fired. His aim was off, and Gabe dodged. The bullet noisily took a chunk from the wall behind him.

Instinct said to run, but insanity took over. Gabe dove forward and tackled him before he could get in a second shot. They hit the pavement and rolled in wet filth. Mike fought to win, was quick as a snake, not pulling a single dirty punch.

But the fight was finished in seconds. He just didn't have the same speed and strength. Gabe made his one hit count, and that was all she wrote.

He pushed himself off the dazed Mike, cursing a blue streak for the situation. He'd had enough. It was time to haul the kid into the club, put a light in his face, and bust his brain open.

He heard someone grunt, and after a moment realized he was on the ground again, facedown. What the hell—?

Gabe tried to get up and the movement set off a fireball in his head. Hideous blinding agony struck him flat.

Dimly he heard heavy footsteps, Broder's deep voice asking a question, and Michael's faint and groggy reply. Scraping sounds, a groan, the slam of a car door.

More steps. This time Gabe heeded instinct and went perfectly still. Not difficult; the pain had paralyzed everything but the urge to scream. He choked it off.

Pressure on his throat. Broder was feeling for a pulse. Getting none, he pushed up the back of Gabe's overcoat and suit coat, grabbing his belt. One-handed, he lifted and pulled Gabe's limp body along like a heavy suitcase, the man was that strong.

A gun went off. It made quite a roar within the confines of the alley. Three shots at least, so close together that they could have been from a machine gun.

Broder dropped his burden. Gabe forced his eyes open. Filling his view was one wheel of the Studebaker, inches from his face.

Another shot.

Broder was in the car, gunning it to life. The wheel slipped, grabbed, and spun away. The Studie departed, its open trunk lid bouncing, then slamming into place as the car screeched out of the alley.

Gabe dragged himself upright. He hurt too much to be doing anything so stupid, but anger was running the show by then. He staggered, using a wall for support, working his way toward the street. If they knew he was alive, they'd come back. He wanted a shot at Broder.

Behind him a car horn honked an irritable warning.

Now what?

He pressed out of the way as the Hudson tore past in pursuit. Escott was at the wheel. Eyes impossibly bright, he glanced once at Gabe, showing the mirthless grin of a crazy man, and kept going.

15

FLEMING

DUGAN held the shiny-clean scalpel rock steady between his fingers, looking down with that damned permanent smile that had never before reached his eyes. They glinted now. He was a truly happy man.

You know what comes next," he stated.

I had no way to brace against it. I'd been to the brink and over. I couldn't go there again.

Eyes shut, I gave up.

My mind slipped away and hid in that perfect summer hour, adding more detail. The cool water contrasting with the hot breeze, shade tree overhead, sunbeams streaming through the leaves, birdsong . . . good, good, but I needed company.

Leaning against the tree was Escott, coatless, shirtsleeves rolled up, waistcoat unbuttoned, no tie. He sipped lemonade from a tall glass, his attention on the green fields around us. He looked surprisingly at peace.

Bobbi was in the stock tank. She held me, kept me from

sinking. She wore a skin-hugging swimsuit . . . I couldn't fix on the color. It kept shifting from red to blue to yellow, sometimes black. None of them seemed right on her, but this was the first time I'd ever seen her in sunlight. It made her blond hair glow and set off the green sparks in her eyes.

She smiled like it was the world's first day and bent to kiss me. I felt her lips and knew if she stayed with me I would be all right.

Something stung my left wrist, kept on stinging, harsh as a wasp.

I held fast to my illusion for a few more precious seconds, then had to see what hurt.

It was and was not what I'd expected.

My wrist hung out past the edge of the table, and Dugan had sliced into it, but not to strip away flesh. He was hunched over holding a glass under the wound, collecting the blood.

My initial shock and disgust were overwhelmed by elation. He wasn't going to skin me, just drain me dry. That wasn't as painful. In the end I'd just fall asleep.

As deaths went, it was the best I could expect.

I smothered my relief, but while one part of me celebrated an easier passing, another part seethed with blind fury for what he was doing. I tried to pull away, but of course the metal held. The hot shock was more remote this time. My body was slowing down in reaction to the blood loss. I could feel my strength literally rushing out.

Dugan's smile was genuinely warm. "Things got so very interesting the other night, didn't they? The hospital. Your friend was so sick. I was there."

How . . . ? One of the reporters? But they'd left. The only other one . . .

"You are quite the catalyst for calamity, aren't you, Fleming? First that actor shot, then your partner hurt. What a terrible beating he had. I troubled to get close to your little group, and it was just too easy. You're all so tidily wrapped up in your concerns. You looked right at me once, but didn't really see. No one notices a humble janitor with his bucket and mop."

He had that right. Too late now to feel stupid over it. The wig, thick glasses, and a big mustache to hide his distinctive mouth had done the trick.

"Such a *remarkable* event transpired that night. The whole hospital was gossiping about the dying patient who was made to drink blood, then had a miraculous recovery."

The cut inside my wrist healed shut, leaving a welt that would fade if I lived long enough. The glass he held was a laboratory beaker with measurement lines up the sides. He'd drawn off at least a cup of my blood. Much more than that had dripped to the floor when I fought to get free. I was dizzy from the loss.

He straightened, sniffing the contents of the beaker.

"How generous you were to save his life—and letting me know for certain how to change mine for the better."

I wanted to smash his smile to the other side of his head. Underestimating him . . . not smart . . . damned stupid in fact.

His self-absorbed ramblings . . . I'd not paid them the proper attention. Now they made sense; he hadn't been lecturing just to hear his own voice. I understood now.

He wanted to turn himself into a vampire.

Dugan correctly interpreted my revulsion. He leaned in close. "Remember when we first spoke in your office? I told you then I wanted you for a very simple experiment— nothing that would offend your sense of morality. You should have listened." He thumped a finger sharply against the rod. It made my arm twitch, tearing the skin again, and more of my life leaked away. "All I wanted *then* was for you to get into one of the larger banks for a modest withdrawal. They wouldn't have missed it, and it would have been of considerable help to me. But you had to be difficult."

God, I was so hungry. Bloodsmell was everywhere, and I couldn't touch it. I had to fight to stay focused.

"I realized there would be no effective way to control you;

therefore, my best course of action was to acquire your abilities myself. I did a bit of research, but there is appallingly little information available, and much of it is suspect. However, your friend's misfortune gave me all I really needed." He lifted the beaker. "I'm estimating that it will take three nights to effect the full transformation. The folklore is in general agreement on that point, though it's mixed up with religious nonsense. Now you know how long you'll be here. Once I'm like you, I will let you go—I know you don't believe that. You dealt me some very shabby treatment, but really, I was never your enemy."

I'll carve that on your gravestone.

"Be assured, I'll have a long head start before you're set free. I know you won't be persuaded to a sensible neutrality toward me, but I truly have nothing against you. You're no different from any other animal succumbing to instinct. You lack the capacity for—"

"Ya want in the union?" I asked. My voice had turned reedy. It was hard to draw in enough air to speak. "Why dint ya say so? I'da put th' word in."

"You waste yourself."

No doubt. I needed him to underestimate me.

"And you can't even see it. But you have my word: three nights, and I'll let you go. Oh—your friends won't miss you. I repaired the damage made when I broke into your little lair. I also left a suitably misleading message with that detective fellow's answering service. They're under the impression that you've gone off to do a bit of thinking. Exasperating, perhaps, but they won't look for you."

Would Escott question that? Or Bobbi? The way I'd been acting lately . . .

"This won't be pleasant for either of us, but I will be civil to you for the duration. Once this is over, you'll never see me again, and that should be some consolation."

Dugan raised the beaker to his lips and took his first taste. It must not have been to his liking, to judge by his expression. He had to force himself.

He drank all of it, which was more than was needed. A sip would do the job—if it worked. I stared the way you do at a car accident. It's bad, but you can't stop until you see the worst. What would it be, a dead body or a dying one? I was the one dying, though. I'd lost so much life, and he was drinking away the rest.

Yet as I lay there, weak and starving, I began to laugh, very softly.

He's got it wrong.

I used up what little strength remained, laughing.

If he thought me insane, well and good.

His eyes were strange, very bright. It would be hard getting him to think I was crazy. He was so far gone himself.

"What is it?" he asked. Suspicion from him now. I had to be more careful.

"You . . ."

"What?"

Huh. Had to finish it, give him a reply. Something to mislead. "You . . . look funny, Gurley Hilbert." I trailed off drowsily. Not an act—I was shutting down the same as I did at dawn.

He disliked the distortion of his name, but his smug smile returned. I hoped that meant he thought himself to still be fully in control of this two-legged animal. Hell, he *was* in control, but it wouldn't last. He'd made a big mistake letting me get so weak.

"That pettiness doesn't matter to me. You don't see that I . . . I don't—"

Then he abruptly broke off, falling from the chair, whooping and gagging.

Drinking blood is not something people just *do*. There's only so much an ordinary human can take before getting sick. Even with my change making the stuff taste good, it had taken months before my mind got used to the idea itself and accepted it. How much worse was it for this fastidious, fancy-pants society swan. You can't think too much on the process, and Dugan was obsessed with his intellectual superiority. Whatever was going through his mind . . . he'd have to quash it thoroughly. Odds were he'd find it impossible. Minds like his had no off switch.

But was his reaction a result from taking blood in general or *my* blood in particular?

Until that miracle in Escott's hospital room, I'd have bet on the former. Not so sure anymore. A vampire's blood had saved a sick man from dying, but what would it do to a well man? Make him healthier?

No matter. The bastard's got it wrong.

This had happened to me before, but the woman who'd forced me to change her had gotten the ordering right. If Dugan had somehow made me drink his blood *first*, and then taken from me, I'd have been worried. He'd left out that step. We were both in strange waters with this variation.

I wasn't going to tell him about it, either.

Pyrrhic victory to Jack Fleming, maybe.

He moaned, but it sounded more like ordinary disgust than physical pain. Escott hadn't reacted, but he'd been unconscious.

If I could just lift up a bit to see what was—

Then my eyelids suddenly closed on their own.

Death's own silent chill seized my body.

A relentless progress, feet, legs, trunk, it was like being buried in snow, very snug, very final. I'd been through this before, too. Didn't like it, but better than getting skinned.

I'd expected this, but still felt a hurt surprise.

My death would mess up Dugan's plans. Cold comfort, but serve him right. He didn't understand how vulnerable I was to blood loss. He'd ignored things while I bled. He had literally talked me to death.

I sought that summer day, and it flooded around me, sweet and warm. Bobbi held me safe until it was time to drift free.

It was very like those moments when I went invisible, but even that formless state had weight, keeping me bound to a physical world. Now I shrugged it off, lifting above myself, wonderfully light.

The clay I'd left behind was in poor shape. The face had gone terribly gaunt, fingers curled into grasping claws, outstretched arms so desiccated that the shape of the bones showed through the gray flesh. He'd been through much pain, but that was finished now. No more suffering for him, the poor bastard. The me that floated above him was unsure of what to do next now that having a body was of no further importance.

The other man in the room finally got off the floor and went to check on the remains. No amount of shouting or slapping of the face would animate that corpse.

The man rushed out of my field of view. I kept staring at me, reluctant to say good-bye. Once I left, that would be the end of it. No more ties to this world. No more . . .

Bobbi—she won't know what's happened.

That wasn't anything I could fix. What was done was done. I had to go soon.

I can't just leave her.

I hesitated. And thought. And thought some more.

And came to see what lay ahead.

What she'd go through—I couldn't do that to her. I'd carry the remorse with me forever. But weren't you supposed to shed that at death? Apparently not. I could deal with my private failures and mistakes, but not the wrongs I'd inflicted on others. Added up, they were worse than my time in hell hanging from the meat hook.

But this was out of my hands. Someone had taken my life and all chance to make things right with anyone. Bobbi would never . . .

The helplessness returned again. My regret had weight like a thousand anvils, and it dragged me toward the empty shell below. I hovered close to what had been familiar features. His mouth sagged, and his eyelids were at half-mast over dulling orbs. That was a dead man's face. I didn't want to sink into it and pushed away, just a tiny distance.

Bobbi will look for you and cry and wonder and worry and never know . . .

She deserved better than that. I couldn't let her go through what I had endured when my lover, Maureen, had disappeared. For years I'd searched, always wondering; the grief and anger and the not-knowing had eaten me hollow.

I brushed against the cold, leaden husk and recoiled. How could I possibly take up its burden again?

I couldn't. That wasn't for me anymore.

It was over; I had to leave.

At the end of the day, at the end of life, it's the same for us all. We get the answers we've always sought. Things are finally clear. Everything would turn out all right. Bobbi would go through a bad stretch but get past it. Decades from now, at some decisive future point, her time would come, and she would hover like this over her body. I'd be there waiting for her—

Unless she made the change and became Undead.

A small chance, but possible.

Then she would live on and always wonder and never know and perhaps blame herself, just as I had. Only she'd never find me. She would *never* find me.

I couldn't allow that.

I had to get *back* to her.

Desire and will added weight, and I sank lower. There was an invisible barrier between me and my cooling flesh. It seemed permeable, but I sensed that would not last long, growing thicker and more difficult to breach the longer I delayed.

With hard effort, I pushed past it and instantly felt the awful press of gravity dragging me into agony and blackness.

Reluctantly I came to, the taste of cold animal blood on my tongue and clogging my throat. I gave in to a convulsive choking swallow and got most of it down. Whatever reviving magic it possessed began spreading through my starved body. Everything woke up at once: the constant pain, the helplessness, the rage, and especially the hunger. That hurt the worst.

Someone held my head at an awkward angle and had a cup to my lips. He cursed as the stuff sloshed past my mouth. I got another gulp down and another, and then it was gone. I still hurt, still needed—

"More," I whispered.

Dugan stared. There was a smear of my blood on his cheek. "It's disgusting."

"You're the one . . . who wants this."

He didn't move. He seemed to be having second thoughts.

"More . . . or I die."

"You won't. You're immortal."

There's no arguing with an idiot. My eyes shut again, and I didn't respond when he slapped me.

That worked. He hurried away and returned with more blood. I didn't want to gorge, but couldn't stop. My previous out-of-control overfeedings had been to sate an addiction; this was pure survival. That was what I told myself, and from the way the stuff gusted through me, sweetly filling out the corners, it was the truth. I'd come that close.

After several trips upstairs and back, Dugan must have run out of stock; he stood over me for a time, watching and asking variations of "Are you all right?" at intervals until I mumbled at him to shut up.

That seemed to reassure him. He went up and didn't return. He left the basement light on. An oversight, perhaps. What had happened must have spooked him badly.

That made two of us.

I kept still, resting, recovering, thinking of ways to kill him. None seemed a brutal or painful enough payback.

My brain cleared; I listened to his movements, heard the splash of water. Yeah, things had gotten very messy; he'd want to clean up. Wish I could. This place had running water, electricity, I'd not yet heard a phone. It was information, perhaps useful, perhaps not.

Then he paced. Restlessly, uneven, up and back in a not-very-large room, to judge by the number of steps he took.

Then things went quiet. I thought he'd fallen asleep until a very faint scratching sound came through the floor to me . . . a pen on paper. The son of a bitch was writing.

What would it be? A harrowing and heroic account of his first feeding? Perhaps another essay arguing the social practicality of killing off inferiors or maybe a scientific record of his reaction to my blood. How about a grocery list? *Memo to self, stop at butcher shop for another gallon* . . .

I'd recovered enough to laugh again, softly.

The other me turned up again at last, walking into view the same as a real person. He looked sad now. He was right, I'd had my opening to escape and chose to return. Neither of us had reason to believe Dugan's promise about freedom on the third night. He would kill me and put what was left where it would never be found. Bobbi would still never know . . . *No, dammit. Stop thinking like that.*

I would figure out something. I would get back to her.

Things had improved, such as they were. I'd taken in enough blood to ease my belly pain and allow me to think. I didn't feel very smart at the moment and looked to my benign doppelgänger for suggestions.

He shrugged. "What would Kroun do?"

That one was easy: not get caught in the first place.

His extra caution, not letting even me in on where he spent his days, had worked well. Of course, Dugan didn't know the man was a vampire, having assumed I'd been the one who saved Escott.

Unless Dugan *wanted* me to think that. No, let's keep this simple. He would have said or asked something by now. He had a trapped audience; there was no way he could resist crowing about his cleverness.

Had Kroun been here, he'd probably have tried hypnosis. It wouldn't have worked. Hurley Gilbert should be locked in the booby hatch down the hall from Sonny. Even if I'd been free and clear of giving myself a fatal headache from the attempt, the old evil-eye whammy didn't impress members of their club.

"Anything else?" I muttered, confident that the other me had the benefit of my internal reply.

"What about Escott? How would he get out of this?"

He'd be dead if his arms looked like mine did now. Otherwise, he would listen, learn, and use any little shred of information to his advantage.

Dugan's pen scratched away, fast and without pause. He was just bursting with thoughts tonight. He liked dark green ink on thick notepaper. When done writing, he used his handiness with origami to fold the paper into whatever shape he wanted, which was a very unique way to file things. Was the upstairs of this place filled with little paper sculptures, each one bearing his thoughts? He could make cranes, giraffes, boats, and once left a small paper coffin where I would find it. He'd not written on it, but I got the message that he would be back. Too bad for me I'd let other concerns crowd it out.

"How about Dugan himself?" asked the walking-around me. "What would he do?"

Manipulation. That was his specialty: getting people to go along with him against their better judgment. No one even thought to disbelieve him, such was the effect of his brand of charm. He exploited their weak points. He had plenty of his own I could use against him, but he would be suspicious of anything I said.

On the other hand he knew he was a genius, while I was little more than a talking animal. I'd already played on that. Giving him what he expected shouldn't be hard.

I winced. I wasn't good at that kind of thing.

"Better learn quick, then," said my friend who wasn't there.

16

KROUN

GABRIEL blundered his way clear of the alley before the nightclub's muscle turned up to deal with the noise. He ducked behind a parked car for cover and kept going until his legs decided they'd had enough. He ended up sitting on a curb, holding his head, in too much pain to even groan.

It was almost as bad as his first waking. The main improvement was that he wasn't covered with earth, blood, and Ramsey's body.

Broder must have used a blackjack, not that his fist would have caused less damage. He'd hit the perfect spot on the left-hand side.

Gabe found a patch of mostly clean snow, balled some up, and pressed it to his skull. That helped, but he felt sick throughout his body, not just his head. He wanted to hole up somewhere and, if not die, then sweat through this agony undisturbed until he healed.

After the snowball melted to nothing, he was able to stand without wobbling too much.

The next street over had a few other night owls prowling about, but no cabs in sight. He dug out another ten-dollar bill, stood under a streetlight and held it up at passing cars. As it represented over a week's wage for the lucky ones with jobs, it didn't take long for someone to pull over. The risk for this kind of hitchhiking was being found by a mug looking to take the rest of the money. Gabe was in no mood for games.

The man at the wheel checked him over. "You inna fight?"

Perceptive of him. "Yeah, can you get me out of here? My wife's on the warpath and—"

"Hop in!"

The driver was cheerfully drunk, in a let's be pals mood, and happy to commiserate about matrimonial tribulations. Gabe turned down an offer to share booze from a pocket flask and talked him into driving clear of the Loop, all the way to Fleming's house.

"Sure about this?" asked the man when they got there. "Won't she be waitin' for you?"

"Home's the last place she'll look," he assured his bleary Samaritan, who thought that to be extremely funny. He drove off laughing, ten bucks richer.

Gabe had trouble with the picklocks. He couldn't get his fingers to work together. It took nearly a minute to break in. He was well aware that he wasn't thinking too clearly, but willing to risk that Mike wouldn't come nosing around. He had a pounding to recover from himself, and Broder might still think his assault had been fatal.

As for Escott, well, he was supposed to be smart and good at his job, but his choice to follow them . . .

"Nuts. Everyone in this town is goddamned *nuts*," Gabe muttered to the empty house as he trudged upstairs in the dark.

He made his way by the faint glow coming in around the window curtains. It was brighter than before, too early for dawn, he thought, until checking his new watch. Damn. How long had he been sitting on that curb? It had seemed only minutes. Maybe he'd blacked out. He'd lost time after the car crash. Wouldn't that just be the pip if Fleming turned out to be right?

Gabe dug his earth-crusted clothes from the bottom of the wardrobe, grabbed blankets from the bed, and went hunting for the attic.

Behind a hall door he found a narrow stairs that ended in a ceiling trap, which at first seemed to be locked, though there was no mechanism, just a handle. He gave a hard push and the door lifted when something heavy fell away on the other side.

Somehow a trunk had been left on top of the trap. How the hell . . . ?

Oh. Fleming's disappearing trick. He'd pushed the trunk on the door, then slipped down past it. He probably used the attic for refuge, and this was how he locked himself in.

Gabe shoved the trunk back and cast around for a place to flop. There was a dusty window at one end; he found a spot far from it and curled up around the wad of clothes, covering himself completely with the blankets.

Just in time. His adrenaline gave out. He couldn't move another inch. Even fresh blood wouldn't have helped. He needed absolute rest to heal, and the earth would give him that. He cushioned his head on one arm, gritting his teeth until the rising sun brought oblivion.

No dreaming today, but this time he didn't mind.

He was only aware that he'd slept by the fact his pain vanished between one blink and the next.

Damn. That was . . . good.

And disorienting. One second it's dawn and the next full night. He didn't like that. Unpleasant or not, the dreams gave some sense of passing time. Without them, Gabe felt as though those hours had been stolen from him.

Michael would have had a whole day to get himself out of town to—where? He had friends in Havana . . . but why should he leave if he thought Broder had—

Take it slow and in order. Mike tried to kill me. He managed to miss. On purpose?

Probably not. That he'd botched it said something for his ultimate reluctance, but he had been serious. The look on his face . . . that was real. He'd attempted the murder of his brother.

He'd have felt bad afterward, though.

Mike then lost the fistfight, Broder stepped in with his cosh, then gunfire from a third party cleared the playing field. Chances were good that lunatic Escott was behind the noisy interruption. Who asked him to horn in?

Maybe Fleming was back by now. He sure picked a rotten time to run off and sulk about his girlfriend—or else was showing sense by keeping himself clear of the mess. There was a first time for everything.

Gabe pushed upright in stages, cautious about sparking another fireball behind his eyes. He was rumpled and stiff, but otherwise felt fine. He checked his head and so far so good.

Someone was moving around below. Gabe froze. The sounds, muffled by the floors between, were too indistinct to follow. Perhaps the burglar who'd broken the window had returned.

Hell, it's probably Fleming.

But there was no harm in being careful. Gabe left his makeshift bed, quietly moved the trunk off the trap, and edged his way downstairs.

His gun was still in his overcoat pocket. He pulled it out on the second-floor landing. The other person was in the front room playing with the radio. Static and music, then it steadied on Bergen and McCarthy trading quips. Trusting that the program would cover the sound of his footsteps, Gabe made it to the ground floor and looked in.

Strome was comfortably ensconced in a chair that faced the hall. His feet were up on the low table before the sofa, and he was just raising a beer bottle to his lips. He noticed Gabe right away, nodded a greeting, and drank deep.

Thankfully it was real beer.

"What's up?" Gabe asked, not putting his gun away.

Unconcerned, Strome reached over to turn the radio down, cutting Charlie McCarthy off in mid wisecrack. "I was told to wait here in case you showed."

"Why?"

"That English guy asked Derner, Derner told me. If you showed, I was to drive you over to Fleming's club."

"You sure it was Escott?"

Strome shrugged. "I'm goin' by what Derner said."

"Is Fleming back?"

"Didn't know he was gone."

"What do you know?"

"Nothing, Mr. Kroun. Not one thing."

"Good way to get along."

"Yessir." He drank more beer.

As Strome didn't seem to be in a hurry, Gabe went back up to change his shirt and shave and felt better for it. He was out of suits; the one he was wearing would have to do, though it was creased, and the knees were muddy. The overcoat was past salvage, but Fleming wouldn't mind loaning him another. The one left folded over a chair in the kitchen was still there; Gabe pulled it on, and the fit was pretty good. He thought he could ignore the bloodsmell since it was his own.

Strome had nothing to say on the trip to Lady Crymsyn. He wouldn't know anything useful, so it was pointless to ask him stuff like "Does Michael know I'm alive?"

Once again, Gabe pushed away the urge to plan against the unknown. He might have done that in the past, but at the moment it seemed a waste of time. Actuality was always different from one's expectations. Better to see what's there, then figure out how to deal with it.

If Escott had arranged this trip over, it meant he'd have news.

If Michael was behind it, then Gabe wouldn't have to spend the night hunting him down.

The green Hudson was the only car in the Crymsyn parking lot. Gabe had Strome circle the block, but there was no sign of the Studebaker. Strome stopped at the canopied entry, leaving the motor running. Gabe got out and looked things over, ready to duck, if need be.

Escott opened the front door. Lights were on in the lobby behind him. "Ah. Very good. Thank you, Mr. Strome."

Strome lifted one hand to sketch a salute, shifted into gear, and rolled away.

Escott frowned. "That's my coat."

"Mine needs a clean. Why'd you want me here?"

"In the event that Jack turns up. When he does, it will be here, my office, the Nightcrawler, or with Miss Smythe. If he knows what's good for him, he will have an apology ready for her."

"What if he turns up at the house?"

"Mr. Strome left a note where it would be found." He stepped back inside, and Gabe followed, checking the room. They seemed to be alone.

Escott went to the lobby phone booth, thumbed in a nickel, and dialed. "Mr. Derner? The prodigal's returned, all's well. Mr. Strome is on the way back. Thank you so much for the help." He hung up. "Excellent fellow. Very well organized."

"I noticed that, too. You answered why you're here, not why I'm here."

"Sorry, I've rather a lot on my mind. I thought you'd want to know what's happened since we parted company. You're much improved from last night's misadventure. I thought that large fellow had split your skull open for sure."

"Me, too." Gabe removed his hat, brushing one hand over the white patch. "When did you get to the party?"

"Just in time, apparently."

"What did you hear?"

"I was too distant to follow your conversation. When things went against you, I decided to make a nuisance of myself."

"Are you a bad shot?"

"Not at all, but causing injury to your attacker was not

needed. Do sit down." He nodded toward the bar, which was clear of matchbooks. There was no telling if Escott or the supposed ghost had cleared them away. Myrna. What kind of a name was that for a spook?

A light was on behind the bar. It went out while he was looking at it. There was no popping noise from an expired filament; it dimmed and went dark just like the ones in theaters.

Escott was nowhere near a wall switch. He saw it, too. "Myrna? Perhaps you would rather wait in the office with the radio on. If Jack returns, he will go there first." Again, he spoke with a completely straight face as though someone was there to hear him.

Wary, Gabe put his hat down and eased onto one of the stools, angling so he had the lobby door in sight. He decided to ignore Escott's digression. "What the hell were you thinking taking off after them like that?"

"I wanted to see where they went."

"Could have told you."

"They might have changed their locale. As it was, I enjoyed a drive to an unremarkable hotel in Cicero."

"Broder didn't spot you?"

"Right away, as it happened—traffic was very light at that hour. I let him lose me, then resumed tailing at a more prudent distance. He's a relative stranger here, whereas I know the streets quite well."

"Good for you."

"They seemed to settle themselves in for the night. I returned to find you long gone and the staff at the Nightcrawler considerably mystified about the contretemps in the alley."

"You always talk like that?"

"Like what?"

"Never mind, go on."

"I drove around and found you only a block away sitting on a curb like a vagrant. I tried to get you in the car, but you took a swing at me, used some foul language, then sat down again."

Impossible.

Escott searched his face. "You don't remember. Not any of it."

"Because it didn't happen."

"Of course it did. One can hardly blame you for wishing it to not be so. It's terribly disturbing to have a lapse like that."

Much too disturbing, Gabe didn't want to accept it. "What did Fleming tell you?"

"I've not heard from him since that message. What would he add, were he present?"

"He—" Gabe bit it off. No need to get started about the car wreck. He couldn't deny that he'd lost some time afterward, same as last night. "You left me there?"

"You were in no temper to be helped. On my second attempt you drew a gun, threatened to shoot my nose off, made a crude observation about its size, damned me to hell, and sat down again to hold a snowball to your head." He paused as though waiting for a reaction, then went on. "You did not recognize me at all."

What's he want, an apology?

"You have a serious problem, Mr. Kroun. It is most certainly to do with the bullet in your brain."

"Ya think?" Gabe thought hypnotizing Escott into a lapse of his own might be worth the headache. But the man knew where Mike was staying and had a car.

On the other hand he doesn't need to know about my business to play chauffeur.

Escott went behind the bar and built himself a short gin and tonic, heavy on the tonic. "Let's put that aside for now. You've recovered and seem to be yourself again. Perhaps if you simply avoid further injury—especially to your head— you can get by without threatening bodily harm to others."

Or shooting people in the woods. *One minute the car's leav-*

ing the road, the next I'm tied up and Fleming's talking crazy.
Gabe's face felt warm.

"In regard to your visit to the sanitarium . . ." Escott paused again, but Gabe remained silent. "Why did you let Jack come along? You must have known there was a possibility he would learn things you would prefer to keep private."

"It just happened. I'm not happy about it."

"Please, Mr. Kroun, I respect your intelligence. If you needed to exclude him, you'd have found a way of doing so. You wanted someone to hear your father. Certain details about your previous visit—"

"The old man is nuts. It doesn't matter what he says or who hears him."

"Indeed? Then what occurred at that cabin two months ago?"

Good question. "I hired a girl to keep me company up there, that's all. She was in the wrong place at the wrong time. I'm just trying to find out if she's okay."

"Then let me alleviate your worry. She's well enough."

"How do you know? Where is she?"

"I spent a portion of the day finding out things."

"Such as?"

"The reason why Michael wants you dead." Escott drank half the gin and tonic, then hauled his cannon of a revolver from its shoulder rig and aimed it at Gabe. "And I agree with him."

Gabe took in the gun and the gray ice of Escott's gaze and whatever expectations he might have planned against would never have included this. "Why is it you keep pulling a gun on me?"

"The first time was a mistake on my part."

"So's the second."

"Be so kind as to remove my overcoat."

"Don't want bullet holes in it?"

"Certainly not, but I'd rather the weapon you have in the right-hand pocket remained in place. If I asked you to surrender it, you'd be fast enough to risk a shot at me. Neither of us would be pleased with the outcome. It's best if you just put the coat on the bar."

Gabe undid the buttons and shed the coat. He thought about throwing it as a distraction, but Escott would be wise to that one and shoot first. "What's your game?"

"Justice, whenever possible. In this instance, justice for a young woman named Nelly Cabot."

There was only one way he could know that name. "You talked to Michael."

"Not easy, but I managed."

Gabe snorted. "What'd he tell you?"

"Many things. Now I want to hear your version of events at the cabin."

Well . . . he was the one with the gun, why not? "It's just over the state line. I went up for a look the other night. There was blood and the body of a man named Ramsey, who'd been my driver."

"That's what you found. What happened?"

"Someone shot us both and buried us in the woods. Only I didn't stay dead."

Escott had a good poker face, but his eyes widened at that news. "So that's when . . . you are new at this, aren't you? Who shot you?"

He shook his head. "Ramsey, I think."

"Don't remember? Jack had a similar problem. Bit of amnesia about his death, but the memory came back after a week or so."

Yes, Gordy had mentioned that. Fleming had thrown his weight around in a big way trying to find his killers. Not smart, but effective.

"Miss Cabot was the girl you hired?"

"Yeah. I think Ramsey was supposed to kill me, and she witnessed it." Gabe's mouth was dry.

"That sounds reasonable."

"I'm sure Mike was at the cabin, too, but last night he started shooting before I could get him to talk."

"He was in a calmer frame of mind today—as you will shortly see."

Cripes. He palmed the ace right in front of me. "That call wasn't to the Nightcrawler. Okay, I get it, fine."

"He'll be here soon."

"Good." It was last night all over again. Escott had his facts wrong and needed proof from a third party to straighten him out. Before it had only taken a call from Derner. This time . . . "Look, you want the truth here, the real truth, right? I can get it for you."

"Via hypnosis?"

Sharp guy. "If you let me."

"What do you propose?"

"I put Mike under, and you do the talking. Keep the gun on me the whole time and ask him anything you like."

"I expect Mr. Broder will be along."

"You can tell Mike to order him to go outside. You'll be in control. I won't do anything."

"That sounds . . . reasonable as well."

"This is too easy," Gabe muttered.

"It's an excellent idea, Mr. Kroun. We'll see how it works out. Before he arrives, perhaps you can clarify a point or two. If Mike was at the cabin, why did he allow Miss Cabot to leave?"

"He's soft on dames."

"And why was he not surprised to see you alive later?"

"He thought I'd gotten away."

"But this was a clandestine excursion. How did he even know you were there?"

"Broder can track anyone, anything, without getting noticed."

"Why would Mike want you dead?"

"You tell me." Gabe nodded at the gun. "You said you agreed with him."

Escott's mouth thinned. "Yes. I do."

"What'd he tell you?"

Outside, a car pulled up, the motor cut, and doors slammed. Gabe turned from Escott and toward the entry.

Broder barged in first, his gun out. He was hard to read at the best of times, but tonight was different. He looked ready to kill. Though used to Broder and his ways, a jolt of pure terror lanced through Gabe like an electric shock, leaving his fingers suddenly numb. Until now he'd always felt himself unquestioningly in control of everything. The look on Broder's face told him otherwise.

So did the look on Mike's face when he came in. The usual impatience, frustration, anger, apprehension, and all the shadings in between were gone, replaced by straightforward disgust. He stopped just inside, holding the door open.

A woman in a dark winter coat, a thick headscarf tied under her chin, reluctantly came in. Mrs. Cabot glared at Gabe with undiluted loathing.

"It's okay," she said. "They got him covered. He ain't movin'."

A younger, prettier version of her crept forward and paused on the threshold. She was paler than paint and visibly trembling head to toe. When she saw Gabe, she jerked and looked ready to run out again.

Can't blame her, seeing a dead man back on his feet would shake anyone.

"Nelly?" said Gabe.

She made a little choking noise and tottered into her mother's arms. She began sobbing.

Gabe closed his eyes. For an instant he was in his grave again, drifting in that brief moment of absolute peace and calm despite the sound of a woman weeping her heart out. He listened to the echoes in his tattered memory and matched them exactly to what he heard now.

"It's all right," he whispered. "It's all right."

When he opened his eyes, they all stared at him as though expecting him to say more.

Except Nelly, who continued to cry. Her mother opened a

big black purse on her arm and groped for a wad of tissues. The girl soaked them through.

No one moved. Taking it slow, he reached toward his breast pocket for the silk handkerchief there. He held it out. The mother hissed and pulled back, dragging Nelly along.

"You don't touch her!" she snarled.

"I'm just trying—"

"Shuddup!" Mike got between them and suddenly plowed in with a vicious sucker punch. Gabe caught it under the ribs and dropped back, surprised as hell. Mike loomed over him a moment, then turned away, angry, but keeping himself in check.

For once, Gabe decided to listen and made no comment. He glanced at Escott for some clue, but the man was coldly hostile.

Whatever it was had them acting crazy. Gabe wasn't running things now, couldn't order them to tell him what was going on. If he waited long enough, one of them might talk; but the tangible fury hanging in the air was just short of catching on fire.

Mike was the key. Gabe focused on him, putting effort into it to get him under, make him calm.

"Mike, I need you to listen to me . . ." Usually that was enough. Catch their attention, throw a hard look, and they got cooperative.

Instead, Mike faced the Cabot women. "You don't talk, Whitey. Not another word."

Gabe next tried Broder, who was staring right at him. It should have been easy, but nothing got through. As he suspected, the man was too focused, and that was better than armor.

As for Escott? No point in trying; he was little better than a bystander now.

"I didn't think you'd bring the ladies along," said Escott.

Mike gave a small shrug.

"My girl should see him," Mrs. Cabot said. She made

Nelly straighten up. "You look at him. You look at that son of a bitch and see how afraid he is."

Gabe went still. He was indeed afraid. He's stepped in something again, and there was no bluffing his way clear. He looked at the girl, but absolutely nothing sparked in his memory about her. Her face and form were unfamiliar, though he liked what he saw. She was dark-haired with a soft, rounded figure . . . but Lettie had described her as being blond. A trip to the beauty parlor would change her quick enough.

Lettie had mentioned other things, but Gabe had dismissed them.

She's wrong. She has to be.

Only one person could set things straight.

He focused on Nelly, and it was nothing to break through to her. She was too vulnerable. She ceased crying and stared blankly back. Once he was sure she was hooked, he shot a glance at Escott.

"Ask her," he said. "You want to know what happened, *ask* her."

Escott looked startled.

"He's already heard," said Mike.

"Well, I haven't. Nelly—tell them what happened at the cabin."

Despite his influence, she was slow to speak. Mrs. Cabot stepped into the gap.

"No! You don't put her through that again!"

Gabe moved forward, stopping when Broder shifted his bulk in the way. "Let her talk, dammit!"

"Mr. Kroun," said Escott, "do not continue with this. She's been through enough."

"I got a right to hear what you have against me."

The sound of his voice startled Nelly awake. She scrabbled one-handed at the black purse. Instead of tissues, she pulled out a revolver, the same one her mother had used the other night, swinging it around.

Gabe made himself a moving target, but there wasn't space for it. He threw himself to the side away from Escott just as the gun roared. Something kicked his left arm, hard. His legs went out from under him, and he smashed back-first against the tile floor. Rattled, he tried to roll and get upright, but Nelly stood over him, the gun's muzzle right in his face. She was shaking and crying too much to hold it steady.

He was fast enough to grab it away, but unable to move. The rage in her face stopped him.

What did I do to you?

The answer was there, and he could not accept it. It was impossible.

I'm not like that!

Not now, but two months ago he'd been a murdering bastard capable of doing anything. And what he'd done to Nelly . . .

No. That was wrong. That kind of horror just wasn't inside him.

Broder yanked the gun from Nelly's hand and bodily pushed her toward Mrs. Cabot. The woman grabbed her daughter, her own anger shifting to fear.

"You can't hold that against her!" she yelled. "You know what he did!"

Michael went to her, and they held a short, intense exchange, which Gabe was too distracted to follow.

He was bleeding. It wasn't like that chest wound, but by God it hurt, and he couldn't afford the blood loss.

The bullet had torn a chunk from high in his left arm and out again, and even as he pressed a hand over the wound, it began to burn with hell's own fire. He snarled and cursed and couldn't see straight. The pain didn't fade so much as he made himself ignore it. He forced himself to his feet, trying to get a look at Nelly, but Mrs. Cabot put herself in the way, protecting her.

Escott was still behind the bar. He seemed unfazed by the gunfire. He found a towel and slid it over to Gabe. "Put some pressure on it."

Nodding a silent thanks, Gabe did so. The least movement made it burn worse. His blood was all over the place. It was stupid, but he found himself annoyed about his ruined suit. That lasted two seconds, then Broder was dragging him over to a chair and shoving him down. His big paws lay heavy on top of Gabe's shoulders, holding him in place.

Mike went from Mrs. Cabot to talk with Escott. "We have to keep this quiet."

"I am no representative for the police in this. Punish him as you see fit, but take him elsewhere when you're done. Mr. Fleming will be none too pleased to have his club so ill-used. I'll clean up."

"And keep quiet?"

"So far as I am concerned, this is a family matter between you and your half brother and none of my business. Once you leave, I shall do my best to forget this entire day."

"What about Fleming? He was supposed to keep an eye on things."

"As I said, he had some personal affairs to look after, but be assured, he will say nothing."

"Gordy said he was stand-up."

"You may have complete confidence in that assessment. What about the ladies?"

"The old girl said she wants to see it through. Thinks Nelly will sleep better at night, but there's some things you just can't make up for."

"Indeed not."

Mike came to stand before Gabe. "I didn't think I could hate anyone as much as the old bastard, but you . . . you're sick-crazy like him, and your kind of sick doesn't get better. You've gone too far."

"Doing what?" Gabe asked. "Say it."

"You're not worth the breath." Mike reached into his overcoat's inside pocket for a leather case, not the one he used for his glasses. He opened it, revealing a clean glass syringe and compact amber vials within, setting them out on a table.

What the hell? "Escott?"

But Escott put his back to him. He began cleaning blood from the bar top.

Mike loaded the syringe with the contents of all the vials.

"That's too much," said Gabe. "You'll kill yourself."

Mike ignored him. "Broder?"

Broder ripped away the towel and smashed his fist against Gabe's wound three times with bone-breaking force. Blood went everywhere. The pain exploded into a white-hot firestorm, unbearable. He tried to bite off the scream and failed. He dropped from the chair, consumed by it, unable to move. Someone grabbed his right arm and pushed the sleeve up. He didn't feel the sting as the needle went in; the other agony simply blotted it out.

"I don't know how you got through the day without this stuff," said Mike from somewhere above him.

No, this is wrong, it's not me, no, no, no . . .

Gabe felt the poison go up his arm, spreading throughout his body. It was a delicious cold balm to his wound. One second the pain's so bad you want to die, then the next it's gone. A dark miracle, almost like sleeping on his earth.

The chill slithered through him, curling around his brain, pressing against the spot on his skull and winding down to his feet. They lost feeling immediately, as though they'd somehow detached themselves and drifted from his body.

The cold flooded and filled him, and for a few moments he saw everything with bewildering clarity . . .

And it was beautiful.

The people stared at him with such unconditional hatred, but he couldn't hate them back. They were too wonderful. Every detail of their faces, the depth in their eyes, how they stood, each little movement—they had no idea just how *perfect* they were.

The room with its clean lines and stark colors was only the antechamber to a wider space of concrete and starlight and motion and more and more perfect people. There were so many to see and meet and cherish, so many bright marvels waited for him beyond these walls.

He loved them, loved it all; the whole goddamned world was his, and he loved it passionately.

A stranger used his voice to laugh for him.

Not a stranger.

It was one of the monsters that hid in the shadows of his mind, only emerging during his day sleep. One of the countless tormentors within that knew the truth but refused to make it clear was now awake, aware of him, and amused.

Looks just like me.

The poison inside lit it up like an actor onstage. It was handsome and confident, though possessing no substance, no more solid than the shadows it hid in.

But it was in charge now.

17

FLEMING

HOURS later the scratching of Dugan's pen finally stopped, springs squeaked, and shortly after he was snoring.

I was grateful, spared from listening to his voice, able to rest and think, though neither moved me closer to a way out.

I bled as I lay there. Even when trying to be motionless, you can't help but move. The muscles in my arms cramped around the rods and twitched involuntarily, opening the wounds again. Other times I just shivered, though still covered by the blanket. My bound legs ached, giving off sharp twinges when I flexed them, the long muscles cramping.

Despite the influx of blood, I was exhausted. My body was constantly trying to make itself vanish clear of the pain. Race a motor long enough without going anywhere, and it eventually burns out.

I tried to remember exactly what I'd seen while hovering over myself, but the impressions were general and fuzzy, no more than what I already knew. Nothing else had been important to me then.

The little I could see was of no help: low ceiling and off to the right a stairway of sixteen steps leading up to what? A house, barn, warehouse? The cement walls were bare of any clue, though Dugan would probably prefer a house. I couldn't turn enough to see what was behind me but guessed there might be another table for holding a scalpel and the .45.

When I tried to rise, nothing shifted but my flesh, and that made more pain. Everything was too secure, given my weakened state. Perhaps I could marshal enough strength to rip free, tearing muscle, breaking bone—but my bones were different since the change, denser, heavier. They would prevent such an escape.

Dozing, never quite going to sleep, I let myself drift into summer again. Bobbi and Escott weren't there this time. My arms were stretched wide, mirroring my current posture. Though free of the rods, there were holes in my flesh, and they bled into the stock tank's water.

A wasp sting on my right wrist startled me. I snarled, tried to jerk away.

Dugan was back and held the beaker to collect the blood flow.

It was a physical effort to shove my rage down, and when I collapsed, it was not pretense. I'd never been this tired or hopeless. Now I understood why an animal will chew off its own limb to escape.

How much time had passed? Was this the second night already? "Sprout fangs yet?" I asked.

He shook his head. He seemed very intent on the job, frowning.

There was damn little to read from his face. He seemed to be in the same clothes, minus the butcher's apron, and his skin was shiny as though from fever. I could smell his sweat. There was a taint to it I couldn't place, but it lacked the rankness that comes with time. Same night then, he'd just come down for a second helping. Crazy bastard.

The slash he made with the scalpel healed. He cut another, holding the beaker until he'd collected a cup's worth of red. Then he pressed a handkerchief to the wound, applying pressure. How thoughtful.

"I know this isn't terribly nice for you." He was not apologetic, just stating a fact.

"It's killing me, you son of a bitch."

"You recover quickly enough. I've made a note to lay in a fresh replacement supply. It ran short tonight, but there will be no repetition."

He took my blood in three big drafts, like a thirsty farmer downing a beer. This time he did not gag and collapse. Only when finished did he give in to a deep involuntary shuddering that was slow to pass. That reaction was too similar to my own after a feeding. Something was definitely happening to him, then. Maybe the ordering was not as crucial as I'd thought. Maybe the change was taking him regardless. There was too much I did not know about my own condition.

When he recovered, he smiled at me.

I wanted to pull his face off. "I'll bleed to death before the next sunset."

"I won't allow that to happen."

"Going to anyway."

"If you've a way to hasten the transformation process, I will release you that much sooner."

"The metal has to come out, at least during the day when I'm dead. You can put them back in before I wake at sunset."

He thought that one over, then shook his head. "I'd rather not take the chance. You lost more than this in the meat locker and survived, but you've given me an idea. I'll make sure to catch the lost blood, and either take it myself or give it back to you. A very practical symmetry."

I held off from telling him what to do with his symmetry.

His reaction informed me that the rods could be removed. He'd used the threaded kind for a reason. Perhaps twist them enough by the handles, and they'd come right up and out.

I didn't want to be awake for that.

He pulled the blanket down and lifted a packet of my home soil into view. It had been on the table next to my waist. "What significance does this have for you?"

"Read *Dracula*, figure it out."

"Actually, I saw the play in New York some years ago. Such a ridiculous melodrama. It makes no sense to keep earth about one or sleep in a coffin. It's superstition, nothing more."

"You'll find out different."

"There must be some scientific reason behind it. Have you given it no thought at all?"

Plenty, and I didn't give a damn. I felt myself slipping away. The sun was rising. Did he sense it, too? I ignored him until my eyelids were too heavy to hold up, then froze for the day.

He said my name several times, tried to wake me, but got no response.

I was aware that he stabbed my wrist again. The pain was a distant thing compared to the horrors just beginning to march before my mind's eye. I was back in the meat locker again, hanging upside down, but instead of Hog Bristow, it was Dugan skinning me alive.

He must have put my home earth back against my body, for I was suddenly fully conscious and blinking in the dark. The small packet had abrogated the whole of the day to an instant; I was wide-awake and still in hell.

And weaker than ever.

And hungry.

It hurt. The hunger goddamned *hurt*.

Where was Dugan? I hated being dependent on him, but that was how things were, and I'd just have to find a way to use it.

Pushing aside the initial wave of distracting pain, I listened and heard him stirring on the floor above. Springs squeaked, and he cleared his throat several times. Had he been sleeping, too? What was my blood doing to him?

Dugan took his time coming downstairs, his steps heavy. When he flicked the light switch, I shut my eyes and only sluggishly responded when he lifted my head, holding a glass to my lips.

I drank, of course. Cow's blood. Cold, but easing the pain in my gut. He'd gone out during the day to get more then. Hopefully, he'd brought back enough to keep me alive.

When finished and full, I continued with the listlessness act and didn't so much as flinch when he cut into my wrist, though I watched, hoping my eyes looked dull and vague.

He was focused on the task, paying no attention to me.

His hand shook as he held the beaker. A lot.

What did that mean?

He drank his dose straight down, then came that long, shuddering reaction.

He seemed to *enjoy* the blood now. Christ in heaven, that could not be a good thing.

When the last tremor passed, his eyes were bright, the pupils dilated like Kroun's. His heart thumped strong and too fast, as though he'd been running.

"Was this how it began for you?" he whispered.

I did not reply. I had to appear lethargic, and it was hard going because this new turn was scaring the hell out of me.

"I feel so alive. Your friend reacted very rapidly to your blood; no wonder he got well again so quickly."

If Escott were here he'd open your skull with a dull spoon.

My well-dressed twin leaned into view. "You're not going to get free without help," he said.

He was right. I was sure I could get Dugan to bring Escott here, but chances were one of them would get killed in the process—most likely Dugan. Escott had his own scores to settle and would shoot him on sight, which would leave me stuck here to starve to death. I went down the short list of people able to help me, but was not willing to risk their lives to save mine.

Not yet. Time and desperation could change that.

"Will he become like us?" asked Dugan. "Fleming? Answer me. Will your friend—"

"You won't make it," I mumbled.

"What do you mean?"

"Takes longer than three days. I'll be dead before then."

"How long does it take?"

"Weeks."

"I don't believe you."

"You'll see."

"Why so long?"

"Body has to adjust. Took me two weeks."

"The books said three days."

"Books . . ." That disturbing laughter bubbled on my lips again. "You're an idiot, Gurley Hilbert."

"I'll simply feed more often . . ."

"I'll be gone. You won't change." I let myself relax, eyes closed.

That shook him. He went upstairs and returned with more blood. I drank all that was offered and continued with the dying act. It didn't require much acting on my part.

"You've taken in more than you've lost," he told me. "You should be better."

"Dead blood," I whispered. "Not as good."

"That's what you drink. You buy it at the butcher's. I saw you."

"Can't live on it. Not for long."

"What do you mean?"

"'S gotta come from a living body, heart still beating."

"Don't be ridiculous."

"'S why we got the fangs."

His mental wheels were visibly turning. I couldn't explain my need to have soil by me during the day, but the extralong teeth . . . Animal predators had big canines to grasp and hold struggling prey. Since he seemed to think people were another kind of animal, Mr. Genius just might make the right kind of connection.

"You expect me to free you for a trip to some farm?"

That's it, figure it out. "Living blood . . . human. Keeps me alive."

"You can't expect me to donate."

"Your blood's poison to me now. Won't work."

"Poison? What do you mean?" He sounded alarmed.

"'S no good to me . . ." I wanted to remove the risk of taking any of his in. Otherwise, his harebrained plan might have a chance of working.

"Why is that?" When I didn't answer, he shook me.

"Human. Best."

"Why?"

"Donno."

"I suppose I could find one of your friends . . ."

He was fishing for a reaction with that threat. I gave none. "No good. Poison, too. Can't touch 'em."

"Well, then, who hasn't tasted your blood?" Skeptical, but he'd asked the right question.

I mumbled something and seemed to drift off. It took him longer to wake me. I made him work for it. That told me he was buying at least some small part of the bullshit I was dishing. My hovering twin seemed hopeful, nodding encouragement.

"Who?"

"Whitey," I finally whispered. "They won't miss 'im."

"Who's that?"

"From hospital."

"The man with the patch of white hair?"

"Healthy. Clean blood." I closed my eyes, relaxing into stillness again.

Dugan made no attempt to wake me now, probably thinking.

Kroun was the best choice. If Dugan got the drop on him, Kroun would want to know the reason why and play along. He might even recognize him as the janitor. Though Dugan was immune to being hypnotized, he was laughably vulnerable to an old-fashioned strong-arming. It wouldn't take much for Kroun to break him.

That was my *hope* on how things could go. Kroun could fall into one of his black fits and kill him.

Just have to chance it.

Out of nowhere my body began shivering, violently. No act, I was really that cold.

"Fleming? What is it?" Dugan backed away, startled.

The shaking made things bad for my arms; I didn't fight it, knowing it looked damned ugly. I wanted him scared and off-balance.

The fit passed, leaving me exhausted and bleeding, but the involuntary dramatics had done some good: he brought me more to drink, and I took every drop. It gave me a stockpile of strength to fight the constant reflexive effort of trying to vanish.

"Your color is better. You're not dying just yet, Mr. Fleming."

"Ever eat paper?" I whispered.

"What?"

"Fills you, but you can't live on it."

Dugan thought that over, apparently, since it shut him up for a good long time. I listened to his heartbeat, which was still too fast.

Lying there and resting, my belly full, I noticed my skin had not knitted itself to the rods again and I wasn't bleeding as much.

Maybe my body was actually getting used to the torture. Dear God.

He finally gave a small grunt and stood. "In three days— well, two now—I'll know whether you're telling the truth. Should that be the case, then I'm sure I can arrange to bring you what you need. A healthy human is not that difficult to find in a city of this size."

He went upstairs, my heart dropping a mile for every step he took.

Damnation, I should have seen that. Why try for Kroun when Dugan could pluck just anyone off the street? Chances were too good that he'd grab someone more easily managed, someone he'd see as expendable, a woman, or God help us, even a kid.

Once the door closed, I checked over my situation once more, desperate to find a weakness.

The L-shaped ends of the rods were at right angles to my arms, each pointing toward the wall behind the table. It was effective for holding me, but it would have been better to have them parallel, the ends toward my hands.

But that would have interfered with his being able to easily cut my wrists, though. If the ends were swung toward my head, I might be able to get free by pulling my arms inward. This was as good as it would ever get.

Before I could think about it first, I jerked my right arm up along the rod, twisting.

Flesh tore and I swallowed, literally swallowed my scream. It burrowed into my gut and tried to claw another way out. My body bucked, and my legs tried to kick, and some of whatever bound them came a little bit loose.

Collapsing flat again, I sucked air with my mouth and throat wide open to keep from howling.

Then I couldn't move for a long while. My arm burned so badly I kept looking to see if it had actually caught fire. The skin around the rod was cherry red under the seeping blood. Not much feeling in my hand; both were looking clawlike again.

The burning got worse. In weak moments I whimpered like a dog, and tears seeped from my eyes. Neither made the pain go away. The more I worked to ignore it, the worse it got, until I started moaning. I shut it off quick because it was too close to how things had been in that meat locker.

Dugan came down hours later, hurrying, clutching a milk bottle full of blood. He poured some into a glass, then lifted and held my head up so I could drink. I eventually drained the bottle. He was sweating, and I picked up that strange taint again, stronger now, acidic, like rotting fruit.

"You never had this much while I was following you," he said, sitting.

"I wasn't pinned to a table and bleeding, idiot." I hoped he wouldn't notice the fresh damage. He'd not cleaned me up; new blood was well mingled with the old.

"I'll get you more then, but it won't be human, not for a few days, yet. Such an expedition will require careful preparation on my part."

That was something. He liked to plan things out in detail. "Go to the Stockyards."

"But the butchers . . ."

I had to keep up the lies, hope to waste his time, and buy myself more. "Fresh stuff will keep me alive longer."

He didn't want to hear that but offered no argument. "I suppose I'll have to learn how sooner or later. It's the price one must pay."

I gave in to maniac giggles, the sound eerie as it bounced off the cement walls. Was his hair going up on the back of his neck? Mine was.

I laughed until he jabbed the scalpel into my wrist.

18

KROUN

WHITEY felt himself relaxing for the first time in what seemed like months. It was as though he'd been holding his breath and could finally let it out.

He laughed. God, he felt great.

Sprawled on the floor, he grinned up at Michael, who looked sick. Stick-in-the-mud Mike had no time for real fun. This kind of euphoria would be wasted on him. Broder? Forget it. What about that skinny bartender?

"Hey, you, c'mere." He tried to wave him over. "Set 'em up . . . drinks are on me."

The man only stared. He must be able to see the monster, and it scared him.

That was damned funny. Whitey tried to explain it to him, but the words tumbled out too fast, slurring and blending into each other. There were so many words in his head that he couldn't say them all. That many crowding in there would make his brain explode. He kept talking to get them out.

And his head was . . . not hurting, but something was

muddled within, verging on dizziness. A thousand bees buzzed behind his ears, swarming and spinning, banging against the inside of his skull, trying to escape. Noisy bastards.

He tried to get up, but Broder slammed him flat. Must have forgotten who was boss here. Whitey suddenly rolled clear and stood, rounding on him, still grinning. The man seemed surprised, but pulled out his gun.

That was funny, too.

"You should go on the radio," Whitey told him. He swatted at the gun, slapping it from Broder's grip; it spun across the room, cracking heavily on the marble tile.

"Whitey?"

He pointed at Mike. "You, too." He aimed himself at the bar and somehow his feet got him there. "Set 'em up. Beer for everyone." He fumbled for money, fingers clumsy. He snapped the money clip like a dry twig. Fifties and hundreds exploded across the bar top.

The bartender seemed not to notice the expensive mess. His mouth shaped itself into a brittle smile. "Mr. Kroun, your table is ready. Please take a seat, and I'll bring you your drink."

Whitey liked this one. "You've earned your tip, boy. Where izzit?"

"Just over there, sir." He pointed to a chair.

"Don't like it. Too far away from company. Serve 'em up here." He slapped the bar with the flat of his hand. Look at all the money. "You play poker?"

"Yes, sir. Would you like me to arrange a game?"

He took in the others. "We got enough players . . . but I want some fun first. Li'l dancing, some laughs, where's my damn drink?"

The man hastily drew a beer.

"Escott," said Mike, addressing the 'tender, "what the hell are you doing?"

"Humoring him. Please stay back."

Whitey wrapped both hands around the glass. He couldn't

feel them, had to look to be sure they closed. He downed half his drink. It was cold, but the taste . . . he doubled over, retching.

"What kind of rat piss you serving here?" he demanded after spitting out the last disgusting drop. He threw the glass, but Escott ducked. The shelving behind him shattered as though struck by a bullet.

Someone grabbed Whitey from behind. Broder again, but he seemed to be moving in syrup. Whitey avoided his fist, and gave him payback with interest. Broder staggered drunkenly and toppled.

How about that? Barely tapped him.

"Mike, you need to hire a better class of—"

Escott quit the bar, going to the two women behind Mike. Whitey hadn't noticed them, they'd been so quiet. One of them was pretty. A real humdinger. Escott seemed hell-bent on hustling them out the door.

"No need to get greedy. There's plenty to go around," Whitey told him, and suddenly he was between them and the exit. Now they all seemed to be suspended in syrup, moving so slowly—that was funny, too. The looks they had . . . Escott had gone dead white, and Mike was outright dumbfounded.

The girl, well, she needed cheering up. Her face was blotchy, tears brimming and falling from red, swollen eyes, but still a humdinger of a twist. You didn't need to look at what was on top to enjoy the rest.

"C'mere, cutie. Let's go someplace else, we can have a good time."

Mike had *his* gun out, sighting down the barrel at him.

"No need to be like that. C'mon, Mikey. *Look* at me." Whitey spread his arms, smiling at his too-serious little brother. "Put that away."

Very strangely, Mike did just as he was told. His blue eyes were wide open, yet at the same time he looked asleep on his feet.

Whitey glanced at Escott, but he was busy hauling the women backward, urging them on. He sure was intent on getting them into the main room of the club—and the place wasn't even open.

Whitey put himself in their way again, gave Escott and the old bat a shove, cutting the little cutie out of the herd. She screeched, but a hand over her mouth shut that off quick enough. He hauled her easily along the curving hall into the dark, where they could have some privacy. The others were moving so slow it'd take them hours to catch up.

No more dark. Every light in the place abruptly blazed on.

"We're in time for the show," he told the girl. One sweep of his leg was all it took. She was on the floor, he dropped on top of her, and, damn, she smelled *good*. Especially there on the side of her neck . . .

She wasn't interested, kept squirming and fighting. She tried to knee him, but he shifted and slapped that out of her. Women just didn't know what was good for them. He'd have to show her. A little of this and that, and she'd settle down; they all did. First, get that coat open, now push up the dress, see what this one had for him.

She hissed and clawed his face, and the sharp burns from her nails cut through his haze of good feeling. He pulled away, startled.

Get off her!

Who was that? He looked around, but no one was near.

"Nelly, get away—*now*!"

Someone had used his voice to yell at the girl. What in hell—?

She slipped out from under him. He tried to grab at her, but something slowed him down. He was only able to catch her ankle. He twisted and pulled and was on top of her, this time pinning her hands. He could smell her terror and his blood and by God, it was *good*.

A sudden stab of pain on the left side of his head came out of nowhere.

Get off her, dammit!

His vision fluttered, and for a moment he couldn't move. The girl pushed her way clear, rolling.

He shook off whatever it was, found his feet, and got in front of her again, keeping her from running. She was within reach, but he hesitated.

Let her go.

"Why should I?"

Because this is wrong.

"What the hell's that mean?"

Back away. Let her go.

"Who are you? Ramsey?" It didn't sound like Ramsey's voice, and it was close, as though someone were speaking right in his ear. Where were they? This wasn't the cabin.

She darted past him, and that seemed to break the spell. He caught and dragged her close, her back pressed to him. She bent forward, fighting, but he wrapped one arm around her body to hold her tight and pulled her head to one side with the other. He nuzzled her sweet throat. He heard her blood roaring, felt its thrum with his lips. He wanted to bite into that taut flesh and just *taste* her—

"Whitey!" A man's bellow cut across the room.

He paused, annoyed. Escott was just coming in, but stopped short, one arm raised, something in his hand.

What is it with all the guns?

Whitey threw him an exasperated look. Before he could speak, Escott fired.

The bullet went high and wide, but Whitey recoiled at the sound. The girl squealed, getting away.

Escott took her hand, and they retreated up the hall. Whitey wavered over who to deal with: the little humdinger or the shooter who needed to be taught a lesson. Never pull a gun unless you can kill on the first shot.

Might as well take care of him. Chase off the distractions, then he could show the sweet thing how to have a real party.

The lobby was a mess: blood on the floor, broken glass, what a sty. Broder, shaking his head like a punchy boxer, was only just picking himself up. He'd be trouble once he got rid of the cobwebs. Mike seemed to be waking, too, blinking, confused. What'd happened to him?

The girl was back in the arms of the old lady; Escott was in front of them both, gun pointed squarely at Whitey.

This was ridiculous. Whitey tried to tell him as much, but it was hard to talk. Those damned bees were buzzing so loud a man couldn't hear himself.

Escott yelled at Mike, his words distorted.

"Not done with you yet," Whitey promised the girl, winking.

Yes, you are.

He heard that clearly, despite the bees. It sounded like his own voice, but that was crazy.

"Whitey!"

My name's Gabe.

But he turned his head.

Mike was fully awake, his gun aimed and steady.

Whitey knew he could stop him again. A quick glance, a single sharp order, and he could—

No more.

He looked steadily into his brother's eyes. Mike could only see the monster, though. Gabriel *made* it hold still and used its voice.

"Do it, Michael."

"I don't want this," Mike whispered.

"I know." The monster forced Gabriel to take a step forward, then another. "But it's all right."

"Stop."

"I can't." One more, and he'd grab that gun and feed it to Mike the hard way. "Now, Michael."

"I—"

"Now, dammit!"

Mike's gun roared. In midreach Whitey felt another kick—this one much harder—against his chest, but he fooled them all and kept standing. He had a new hole in his suit, high on the right side. Fresh blood spilled out, and there was a corresponding flow down his back.

He threw a grin at Mike. "What you got in that thing? Rock salt?"

He coughed. It hurt.

He thought to draw a breath and couldn't quite fill his lungs. Must be a cold coming on. Another cough. A knot of blood splattered on the floor. He stared at it, wondering how that had happened.

The air was too thick, that was all. Too thick to breathe. He didn't need to, anyway. Good party trick, impress the girls.

There was a pressure around his chest like a steel ring; it was shrinking tight against his ribs. That wasn't right . . .

"Mike?" He was smart. He'd know what to do.

Whitey felt feverish. Sweat popped out over him. His body was baking inside his hot skin.

He clawed at his tie, dragging it off, tore at the top buttons of his shirt. Still too hot. He fumbled with the suit-coat buttons, but his fingers weren't working. Tremors jerked through them and up his arms. One of them was bleeding. What the hell? He couldn't feel it. There was that awful pressure squeezing his chest, though. What was happening?

"Mike?"

But his brother didn't speak, didn't move.

"I forgot something. What is it?" He'd spoken clearly. Mike had to have heard.

Whitey felt another coughing bout coming on. A bad one, so bad that his legs couldn't hold him. He awkwardly folded to his knees. Then the floor came at him. He tried to push it away and only ended up on his back again. The ceiling spun, the lights there too bright.

Broder started in on him, kicking him. That was what it felt like. But he kept well clear. Whitey's body thrashed and spasmed all on its own. Convulsions. They were tearing him apart.

He bit his tongue, tasted blood, heard gagging noises. His body stopped flailing on the floor, but the poison was still in him, oozing through his blood. The growing pressure around his chest would crush him from the inside out.

He became aware of the others, one in particular, the shivering girl with the dark hair. He reached toward her, though she was too far away.

She whimpered, clinging to the other woman.

The monster was scaring them. That was wrong. He pulled his arm back. His clutching hand turned into a fist, and he drew it tight against his aching chest so there was no chance of accidentally touching her. He nearly echoed her whimper, but shut it down. Show weakness, and Sonny would beat it out of him. The bastard could *smell* it.

Gabriel couldn't remember the beatings, but the monster did. The monster *loved* Sonny.

The steely pressure on his chest worsened, slowly crowding out his lungs. He had to say something, say it quick before his air was gone. He gasped like a fish, trying not to cough.

Where was she?

His sought her eyes, willing her to—

Look at me!

He managed to croak her name. She looked up, and he put his last effort into it; desperation got him past the surface mask to the soul inside. Vital, but damaged, trying to heal, hardly able to limp from one day to the next—how could she live like that?

I hurt you. I'm sorry . . . I'm sorry.

But his lungs were crushed flat.

He couldn't get the words out. He never would.

He stopped moving altogether. The feeling was much like his day sleep, his active mind trapped within a dead body.

He heard weeping. That would be Nelly Cabot, crying in her mother's arms.

"It's over, honey," the older woman murmured. "It's all over. He can't hurt you anymore."

It was true. The monster was gone.

Gabriel was alone.

He drifted in the red shadows behind sealed eyelids.

People were nearby, but he was detached from their concerns like a stranger overhearing a private conversation. It was interesting for the moment, but he had no real care for the goings-on around him.

Someone put a hand on his throat, fingers resting on the pulse point for a long time.

"He's dead," said Broder.

Michael muttered a curse and walked away a few steps. His shoes crunched against broken glass, then there was the slosh of liquid. He choked on his drink and cursed again, and it almost sounded like a sob.

No one spoke for a time. Gabe had the impression they were in some kind of shock.

Mrs. Cabot broke the silence. "What was the matter with him? He go crazy? How could he move so fast?"

"The drug did that," Escott promptly answered. "Cocaine can be a very powerful stimulant."

"He used the stuff," said Michael, his voice thick, "but not all the time. He kept it quiet. If you didn't know to look, you just didn't know. But the last year . . . he got bad. He'd go off on 'fishing trips' to shoot dope. That's what he called them."

Mrs. Cabot snarled in disgust.

"Ma'am, I'm sorry. I thought he was only hurting himself. I swear, I did not *know* about your daughter. Broder should have told me."

"Why, so you can blame my girl?"

"No, I—"

"We don't want nothin' more to do with you. Just leave us alone."

"Yes, ma'am. I promise."

"One of you get us home, and that's the end of it."

"I'll drive them," said Escott. He was over by the bar now.

"What are you doing?" Mike asked.

"Your brother has no need of it." There was a rustle of shuffling paper. "I'm sure the ladies won't mind a small monetary compensation for the hell they've been put through tonight."

Mike grunted.

The door was opened. "Ladies, if you would? The green car just around the corner."

They shuffled past Gabe's body. Cold outside air flowed over him.

"Will you have sufficient time before I return?" Escott asked.

"He'll be gone," Mike said.

"You've made arrangements?"

"You could say."

The door closed. Shortly after, a motor turned over. A car rattled past the front entry and faded.

Mike must have been holding his breath. He choked out another curse and had another drink.

"It had to be done," Broder rumbled.

"Why'd I have to be the one to do it?"

"Just how things work. Stay here, get drunk. I'll deal with him."

"It's a two-man job. He's my responsibility. You shouldn't have kept quiet about this. Should have told me."

"Seemed like the right thing to do at the time."

"Him shooting the dope I could deal with, but not him hurting women like the old bastard."

"I kept an eye on him. If he stepped out of line, I was gonna—"

"Kill him?"

"Tried to. Would have saved you from it."

"But . . . he seemed to want me to do it. Did you see? At the end?"

"Yeah, Mike. He knew. He was crazy-sick like you said. No cure for that kind of thing. It's over now."

Neither spoke after that. Broder went outside briefly and returned, then Mike shut the lights off. The red shadows went black.

They lifted Gabe's body and carried him into the cold, dropping him heavily into . . . he wasn't sure what until the trunk lid slammed down. The car grumbled to life, and they began moving. Start-stop, start-stop, they must be hitting every signal between here and . . . where were they going?

Gabe couldn't bring himself to worry about it. He floated within the boundaries of his skull and decided being dead wasn't too objectionable. At least he wasn't having those dreams. That might change when the sun came up, but again, it just wasn't important. They hit a smooth road, and he drifted off.

The car began to jolt and jounce, sometimes skidding.

It was enough to wake Gabe from his long doze.

His chest itched. So did his left shoulder. He couldn't move to scratch either annoyance, though he tried hard to do so.

Damned drug. He was bogged down in its sluggish flow.

A sharp turn, and, though the car crawled along, the jouncing increased. His inert body slipped about in the trunk, unresponsive.

They stopped, the motor died, its growl replaced by the sound of wind sighing through pine boughs.

He was back in that dream of absolute peace and calm. He was safe. Here there were no monsters wearing his face to trouble him or anyone else.

After an indeterminate time, he was taken from the trunk and carried a distance. They left him on his back on raw, bare ground. He floated in cold shadows while the others got on with their own concerns.

None of it had to do with him, even when the first heavy wedge of damp earth slapped over his face.

19

FLEMING

THE third night I awoke weak, cold, and shaking, with the hunger like a gunshot wound in my belly. It had never been this bad before.

Dugan was upstairs snoring, a short, heavy rasp, as though even in sleep he breathed faster than normal. When I yelled his name, the snoring abruptly ceased. After a minute the springs squeaked, and he paced unsteadily back and forth.

Last night he'd fallen into a pattern of first feeding me, draining away my blood to drink, followed by another feeding—four or five times. He kept up the assurance that this would speed his transformation, and it was clearly having an effect on him. Toward dawn he was unnaturally restless, with so much energy thrumming through him I thought his heart would give out. He took that as evidence his procedure was succeeding.

I'd continued my dying act and hoped it would remain an act. He was careful to replace my lost blood, so when the sun rose, I was in reasonably good shape considering the situation.

Plodding down the stairs, he put the light on, and it took time for my dazzled eyes to adjust. What I saw scared me.

Now I looked at my left wrist, which was covered with many more thin welts where he'd cut me. The son of a bitch had been drawing off blood while I slept. That was why I was so sick.

Dugan looked the way I felt. He was unshaved and drawn, his sweat-sheened skin had a yellow tinge, and that rotten-fruit smell was more pronounced. I wondered if he'd noticed. Though his wide-open eyes were not flushed wholly red the way mine got after feeding, they were bloodshot and muddy. His movements were jerky, hands shaking, fingers nervous. He looked exactly like an alky caught short on booze.

My blood had to be killing him, consuming him.

"I've kept up my end," he said brightly, holding another milk bottle within my view. "Straight from the Stockyards— less than an hour old."

My corner teeth were out. I was hurting for it. I'd have taken anything then, including human blood from an un-willing donor.

Solicitous as a nurse, he lifted my head, allowing me to drink from the glass he'd filled. I finished it quick, but the belly pain didn't cease.

"You're draining me during the day," I said.

"Only to speed my transformation process. Have more, have all you want. I went to considerable trouble to obtain this for you."

I shut up and finished that bottle and the second one he fetched.

Dugan had been careless, letting me know we were less than an hour's travel from the Stockyards. That covered a lot of area, of course, but I filed the information away with other details I'd gleaned about my location, which was definitely the basement of a house. I was able to pick up certain noises unique to a home: the hum of a refrigerator, the rumble of an oil heater, the plumbing, and sometimes the click of an electric light.

I heard no traffic, but being belowground might have to do with that. Earth and concrete make for great insulation from the outside world.

Throughout the previous night, I'd paid attention to each sound, trying to distract myself from the constant pain, sometimes succeeding. Once he put on the radio to listen to a news show, giving a snort of disdain whenever he didn't like what was said. The rest of the time he paced back and forth or was writing, to judge by the frequent scratch of his pen. If he had so much to say, why didn't he just get a damn typewriter?

As the blood saturated my body, the sickness slowly faded, but I demanded more.

"Where are you putting it?" he asked, surprised.

"Losing ground."

"What?"

I glanced toward my mangled wrist. "You don't give me time to heal. I need more than you take just to recover. More than that to stay alive."

He almost sounded defensive. "I didn't do it that often."

The day feedings terrified me. If his thirst got the better of him, I might not wake up tomorrow night. "Enough to kill me if you don't . . . oh, God . . ." I trailed off into a groan and submerged into my dying act.

"I'll get another bottle," he said and left. He stumbled on the stairs on the way up, caught himself, and shot a quick, self-conscious look back. My eyes were mostly shut, so he was a blurred figure through my lashes, but I'd seen. This flash of insecurity was good. I had him worried.

He let me empty the third bottle with a fourth standing ready before doing his little cut-and-drain operation. Tonight, he gulped the beakerful with alarming speed and relish. When his shuddering subsided, his eyes were fever-bright and much redder than before. The whites were nearly gone.

Maybe he *was* turning into a vampire, just no kind I'd ever heard about. I fought to maintain listlessness.

"I'm feeling so much stronger," he said, swinging his arms around. "I've never been so energetic. I'd been looking forward to acquiring the ability to influence weaker minds, but it never occurred to me that my physical being would be so greatly augmented."

He sniffed at the untouched bottle of cow's blood, took an experimental sip, and grimaced. Apparently it wasn't to his taste yet.

"I should be fully changed by now," he said. "Perhaps you were right about it taking longer. I'm very sorry, but you'll have to remain here. But I'm optimistic—today I had to go out, and though it was cloudy, I wasn't at all comfortable in the light. That's progress, though it is rather short of the comalike state you fall into."

How much of that was self-suggestion, I wondered.

I mumbled for more blood. He cheerfully complied, chatty now, telling me about his goals once his little experiment was completed. He was excited about leaving Chicago and moving up in the world. First he'd have to deal with his criminal record. He was a wanted fugitive, and that had to be fixed.

"The police and court papers should be easy enough to destroy. Then I shall talk with everyone concerned with the case. I'll persuade them to completely forget me—even your English friend won't recall anything of it. Neither will that woman whose deficient offspring I kidnapped. She'd be better off without such a burden, you know." He sounded speculative. "So many things to do once I have your abilities. I shan't waste them, though. The world is going to improve significantly because of me."

Oh, brother.

But he could be right. Say he went to Washington and started doing an evil-eye whammy on anyone he chose. Though its influence wasn't permanent, I'd read enough history to know that one man in the right place at the wrong time could change things. For good or ill was up to the man. In Dugan's case, I couldn't really imagine how bad things could get.

How I hated his voice. I looked around for the other me. He was out of view. Dammit, I wanted his company. *He* could listen to the idiot; I wanted to hide in that summer day again.

Maybe Dugan was only blowing hot air to entertain himself, but his plans were too detailed.

Without referring once to it, I also understood he would kill me despite his promise to the contrary. I'd known that from the moment he first showed himself; this simply disposed of any lingering delusion. He couldn't set up anywhere and feel secure with me running loose.

I had a black moment, wondering how he'd carry it out. He could drain me completely by accident or do it on purpose. Or would he resort to the traditional stake and hammer, followed by a beheading just to be sure?

Bobbi would think I'd walked out on her because of her going to Hollywood. She'd never know.

Escott would think I'd gone off my head again and run away to kill myself.

They'd never find me.

My friendly doppelgänger appeared just then, scowling down. "You going to feel sorry for yourself or do something?"

I'm open to suggestions.

"You know what to do." He talked right over Dugan's blather.

A better hint, please.

He pointed at my right arm.

It's hard to pretend to be at death's door while at the same time trying to observe what's going on around you. I kept my eyelids at half-mast, looking straight ahead and unfocused, but still managed to see plenty whenever Dugan turned his back. Not that there was much to notice at the moment; my view was blocked by another glassful of blood, which I drank. I was feeling full now, but made no objection as Dugan poured another. While he was busy, I let my head loll to one side.

The L-shaped rod was still in place, the handle pointing in the same direction, my arm a ragged mess around the wound. A glimpse was enough, then I straightened back so he wouldn't notice.

I finished the next glass. The milk bottle was empty.

He gave me a long, considering look. "Tell me about that female of yours. How do you feed from her?"

What the hell? "None of your damn business."

Dugan's eyes flashed amusement, and I instantly regretted speaking. I shouldn't have reacted at all. Dear God, if he went after Bobbi . . . I wanted to rip free and strangle him. At the last second I changed the expression of the impulse and out came that maniac laughter again. There was no humor in it, and it sounded even more disturbing than before.

He backed away. Good, I'd scared him.

I let the laughter die and shut my eyes. Let him think I'd passed out.

He trotted energetically upstairs and slammed the door. Soon water was running, a lot of it, as though for a bath. The sound just might be enough to cover things if I ended up screaming.

I checked my right arm again. Sometime during the day a miracle had happened.

Healing had taken place, and the dried blood had concealed it. The skin was no longer adhering to the metal, trying to mesh to it, but had shrunk back from the rod. Not by a lot, just a fraction. It fit snugly enough, almost exactly the same as an earring wire through a woman's pierced ear, but larger in scale.

The important thing was that the wound had closed, and I was no longer bleeding.

I'd had the right idea last night when I'd tried to rip free, just not the strength or a reserve of blood to draw on. It had been too soon. My body needed time to figure out that the metal wasn't going away and had to be accommodated.

Now I slowly lifted my arm, working it along the threads a little at a time. It was awkward, and my muscles cramped. I told them to shut the hell up.

My arm couldn't twist to the point of getting the bone over the angle, but I got enough leverage to start bringing the end of the rod around. It came reluctantly, one inch, two, then it gradually swiveled into place, pointing at my head.

More twisting, and it burned like blazes, and suddenly I was pulling my arm off the damned thing.

No need to breathe, but I was panting, half from pain, half from triumph. I kept looking at my freed arm, fearing it was another hallucination. The hole was ugly as sin. I wasn't crazy enough to make up anything that bad; it had to be real.

Moving was painful. I'd not done much more than shiver and twitch the last two nights. Every joint was brittle and popped, but I made myself roll over to the left. My other arm was still pinned, the skin sealed to the rod, but I had momentum going, mental and physical.

I grabbed the handle and pulled it sharply straight up. The threading provided friction for my grip. Back, forth, back—the thing snapped and came away. I yanked my bleeding left arm up, unaware of my howling until I smothered it. That would bring Dugan running.

As soon as flesh lifted clear of the metal, I tried to vanish.

Nothing.

Goddammit. Now what?

I threw the blanket off and tore at the ropes binding my legs. The muscles burned at the sudden movement.

My hands no longer clawlike, the fingers were now swollen and clumsy. The rope was too thick to break casually unless I got some slack to work with, but Dugan didn't know anything about knots. He'd coiled the rope around and around, wrapping me like a mummy, immobilizing to a man lying flat, much less effective when he was vertical. All it took was to push everything down to my feet.

It was more painful than it should have been.

There were spots of blood along the length of my trousers, making the material stick to my skin. Then I looked closer. It was just too easy to put myself in Dugan's place and figure out what he'd done. I didn't have time to fix it; the basement door swung wide.

He was partway down, a bottle in hand. My yells must have made him think I needed another feeding.

The shock on his face when he saw me lurching toward him was sweet to see—then that smug smile came back. He'd planned for this. If I'd somehow gotten free on the first night, he had prepared for it.

He threw the bottle, missing me. The glass broke; the contents splashed everywhere. He whipped around and up, and I was right behind him. He was in time to slam the door in my face. I spent a couple seconds yanking it open. That gave him what he needed, the opportunity to get to his revolver.

I ducked back, and he wasted one of his six bullets when it struck somewhere to the side of where I'd been. Like Kroun, I couldn't vanish. Getting shot now could truly be fatal.

"I can stay here all night, Mr. Fleming," Dugan announced. "Until the dawn comes." He tried to sound bland and bored, but couldn't pull it off. He was breathing too hard.

My view from the basement was limited: an unadorned wall within arm's reach, part of a hallway. I had no idea how far it went in either direction. He sounded close, only steps off. I could charge him blind and collect a bullet, hopefully not in the head. Satisfying as getting my hands around his throat would be, I could not risk the damage.

I slipped back down the stairs, looking for anything to even the odds. My legs complained with vicious sharp pains, but those were nothing compared to being pinned to that table.

Which was indeed a huge Victorian thing, too large to get up the stairs and throw. I grabbed smaller stuff: empty milk bottles from the floor.

"Fleming, I don't expect you to be reasonable, but if you would just think a moment, we can easily revolve this. We can come to an arrangement that will be mutually beneficial. I have a great deal of cash . . ."

He'd stolen it from that misguided girlfriend. No thanks. He was moving, edging closer to the door. I reclaimed the stairs, and keeping all but my arm inside, blindly flung one of the milk bottles down the hall. It crashed and shattered, I immediately followed it up with the second, then risked a look. He was in the act of dodging, but fired at me and struck the ceiling. Two bullets wasted.

He knew how to shoot, but aiming is a skill. Some naturals can point and hit the bull's-eye; most need hours of practice. His planning hadn't taken into account that I'd hit back. I hurled an empty at him like a cannonball.

He dodged that one, but not the second. By then I was halfway out in the hall and able to put some pepper on it. The heavy glass container got him square in the chest. He staggered back, and I took the opening.

I was wobbly and hurting, but made a solid tackle that rattled his teeth. We rolled in broken glass and pummeled each other, and I heard a maniac laughing and cursing. I shut him up once I realized it was me. Dugan still had his gun, but I had a grip on that hand, keeping him from firing.

He threw some good punches, and their force was a surprise. Drinking my blood had improved him. He'd gotten stronger and faster, but he was unprepared for frenzied desperation.

However much thought I'd put into how to kill him, I wasn't thinking now. Brutal instinct to survive was running this show. He was a threat, I had to make him harmless.

I slammed pile drivers, one after another, to his gut, and that broke him. He couldn't draw breath and sagged in place. I wrested the gun clear, pushed away, and scrambled upright. He gasped, clutching at me, but I made sure he saw where the muzzle was pointing, which was right in his face.

Eyes wide, he stopped; it must have penetrated that I wasn't going to shoot him immediately.

I was tempted.

We stared at each other, me unnaturally still, Dugan puffing like a runner, his face sweaty and more yellow than red from exertion. I let him catch his breath, listening to his heart as his lungs sawed air. It was going too fast even given the circumstances. Whatever benefits he'd taken from my blood, it was devouring him from the inside out.

"Pliers," I said, my voice uncannily gentle, but then I wasn't what could be called winded from the fight. I was pissed as hell and working to keep in control.

The remnants of his ingrained smile gradually distorted into a confused expression.

"You'll have tools. I want pliers."

He must have thought I planned to yank his fingers off—not that it hadn't occurred to me—and hesitated. He was visibly thinking.

I roared "pliers" at him, and he got moving.

We were in a small room, perhaps meant to be used as a parlor or for dining. It had a long and ancient sofa, a table and chair, a radio, and on the floor, an open suitcase of jumbled clothing. He'd picked this room closest to the basement door to set up camp.

I was not surprised by the large collection of origami animals spreading across one corner of the floor like a lost herd. He'd been very busy with his fountain pen and green ink, so many profound thoughts to record.

This room opened directly to a kitchen, with a box of tools on a counter by the sink. They were new, as though he'd bought them all at once from a hardware store. He'd likely gotten the threaded rods at the same time.

With me keeping him covered and giving specific instructions, he gingerly got the pliers. His hand shook so violently he dropped them. He glanced at me and bent to pick them up again, getting a better grip.

That rotten-fruit smell had taken on a more familiar tang that I knew to be fear. He had no idea what was coming next. I was tempted to keep him hanging, but this wasn't the time or place.

I sat on the sofa, grunting as I stretched my legs out. The blood spots on my pants were more than simple stains.

He was a grating, insane, self-important bastard, but give him credit, he'd planned this one through. If I somehow freed myself from the table, this was his insurance to keep me anchored in flesh, allowing him time to either escape or wound me enough to restrain again.

The spots on the trousers were nail heads, not bloodstains. While I'd been in my day sleep, he'd pounded the metal into my legs right through the cloth.

I pointed to one of them, then at the pliers in his hand. "Pull it out."

"Wh-what?"

"You put 'em in, you pull 'em out. Make it fast, and I'll let you keep your ears."

He knelt, made an effort to still his shaking, and did as he was told. He gripped a nail head with the pliers and pulled hard.

I hissed, and made an effort not to shoot him. The damned nail was a good two inches long. And I'd been able to *move* with all those in me? Jeez.

"Next one," I said, my voice thick and harsh.

He repeated the operation, faster. I hissed again, and once more did not shoot. That was moderately encouraging to him. "Mr. Fleming, I'm sure we can—"

I suddenly grabbed his hair with my free hand, twisting his head around almost to the breaking point, and shoved the gun hard against his nose, the muzzle half an inch from his left eye. "You say another word—*one more goddamned word* . . ."

No need to finish. He got the idea and continued in sweating silence.

The next few minutes weren't fun for either of us. I had to endure his ham-fisted surgery, and he had to not talk. Suffering was likely equal for both parties.

When the last nail came free, it was better than Christmas.

I wasn't there anymore. My poor body vanished into that sweet, gray, healing nothingness.

Dugan gave a surprised yelp, falling back. I could imagine him looking around in confusion, wondering what would come next.

He bolted.

I heard a door jerked open, there was one in the kitchen, and swooped myself that way, following his panicked breathing as he pelted toward some goal.

A car, as it turned out. I went solid right behind him as he scrabbled at its door handle. He screeched in panic as I caught his collar and spun him to the ground.

My mind was very clear now that the pain was gone. In a glance, I took in the back of a small, plain house, trampled snow, the little yard surrounded by tall, overgrown holly bushes. They blocked the view of whatever lay beyond and worked better than a brick wall for concealing everything within.

This included two holes in the middle of the yard, one long enough to hold a body, the other smaller, located several yards from the first. Both were deep. I was surprised Mr. Genius had applied himself to so much physical labor.

Dugan's legs weren't supporting him, but he tried to run anyway. His version of instinct was trying to get him clear, but I wouldn't allow it. I dragged him toward the larger hole and let go just at the edge. He sobbed and rolled around to face me, hands pawing the air, begging. I still held the revolver.

He was not a pretty sight, his groveling made it worse. I'd been here before, on the edge of murder, and there is no satisfaction to killing a man, however deserving. Dugan's death would just create another dark burden for my tattered soul to haul around for however long I walked the earth. I had too many of those. No need for more.

I'd throw a good scare into him, tie him up, remove all trace of myself from this place, and drop him at the nearest police station. He had to pay for all those deaths. A judge and jury were needed, not me.

"Please . . ." he said.

Then again . . .

"That——" I told him "——is another goddamned word."

20

KROUN

A SLOW, dull pounding awakened Gabriel. The vibration of each impact thumped against his cold, cold body, irritating him to no end.

Can't a man get some sleep?

Apparently not. The heavy, regular thumps continued, getting louder. He tried to roll away from it, pulling a pillow over to cover his ears, but was unable to move. That was when he became aware of the weight pressing him. Evenly distributed so he had no sense of being crushed, it held him solidly in place, like a bug suspended in amber. Strangely, he did not find that to be alarming.

Thud. Thud. Thud. Like God knocking on a malleable door, coming closer, closer.

Gabe was unsure whether that was a good thing or not. After some thought he leaned toward the more negative assessment, certain that God had debts to call in. Better not keep Him waiting. Gabe pushed against the weight, man-

aging to wriggle a little. He tried to take a breath to speak
and got a mouthful of dirt.

Oh, cripes, not again.

The pounding stopped when he made a sudden frenzied
shove that caused earth to shift above him. The weight fell
away from one of his arms, and he clawed free air.

A hand grasped his wrist and pulled.

He emerged spitting and blind, frantic to escape his second grave. He shook off the help, scrabbling up and over the
sides, not stopping until he was yards from it. He rubbed his
eyes clear, catching impatient glimpses between blinks.

Snow. Trees. River. Sleet. Wind. Lead gray sky. A flashlight
on the ground, its beam toward the disturbed grave. A man
standing by the hole. Lean and angular body. Dour face.

Despite the bone-freezing sleet, he was in shirtsleeves,
sweating. A shovel lay discarded on the broken ground. The
man held a large revolver now.

Gabe rubbed his face, his fingers gritty, and stared at the
company.

"What—what *is* it with all the guns?" he asked.

Escott aimed down the sights like a duelist. "That de-
pends, Mr. Kroun. Who are you tonight?"

What a damned stupid question. "Who do you think?"
He spat more dirt.

Escott picked up the flashlight and pointed the beam at
Gabe's face.

"Hey!"

"Open your eyes," he snapped.

He made it sound important. As Gabe found himself un-
armed, he complied as best he could. The light seemed to
pierce right through his skull—which began to thunder inside. He grabbed a clump of snow from a drift and pressed
it against his head.

"You done yet?" he growled, squinting.

"Normal as can be expected." Escott switched off the
light.

"Huh?"

"Your eyes. Last night what little iris you had vanished entirely. I don't think the others noticed, not that it matters to them now."

Gabe stayed put, applied another snowy compress, and began shivering in the wind. "You wanna fill me in? 'Cause I'm thinking you're nuts."

Escott slipped the gun into its shoulder rig and retrieved his suit coat, which he'd hung on a low branch. "You're correct in that assessment. It can be the only explanation for why I'm here." Next he drew on his overcoat. He left both unbuttoned, his revolver within easy reach. "What do you remember of last night?"

"You pulled a gun on me again. That's pretty vivid."

"And?"

Gabe shied away from more, but couldn't ignore the holes and blood on his mud-covered suit. "Mike shot me," he muttered.

"What about your actions leading up to that point?"

He wanted to put off thinking about that until his head pain eased. At this rate it might never happen. Sleet flecked his face, and the wind flayed his exposed skin. "Where the hell are we?"

"A place familiar to you."

Cripes. This was his lucky night. "How'd you know they'd take me here?"

"I asked Mr. Strome to wait within sight of the club and follow your brother and Mr. Broder when they departed. He tracked them to this dismal spot, then phoned me when he could."

"You set me up. You knew they'd kill me."

"Yes—though I did not foresee the method. I suppose your brother was trying to make it painless for you. Injecting an overdose of cocaine should have rendered you unconscious. Instead, there were some unexpected and singularly unpleasant consequences before you succumbed."

His memory on that was disjointed. Someone else had

been running the show except toward the end. He'd asked
Michael a question and gotten no answer.

"You set me up," he repeated.

"Because it was the right thing to do." Escott had an edge
in his tone that stated he was immune to reproach. "There is
a terrible darkness in you. We saw Whitey Kroun last night,
and he is a monster. Have you any control over him?"

He winced at the word *monster* and that someone else used
it so accurately. "If people left me alone, I'd be just peachy."

"You can't, then."

"I—"

"Yes?"

"I did. A little."

"Indeed?"

He rubbed his numb hands. "I was scaring the girl. Tried
to tell her I was sorry."

"For scaring her? Just for that?"

What more do you want? "It wasn't me. I'm not like that.
The dope pulled that out. It's over."

"You're certain?"

"What kind of proof can I give you for that?" Exasperated,
Gabe looked around. The hole he'd crawled from wasn't his
original grave. This one was much closer to the river.

"Where's Ramsey?"

Escott nodded toward the right. Farther into the trees
was the mound of black earth. There had been changes
since Gabe's visit. Someone had tamped down the top
and arranged large river stones over it into the shape of a
cross.

"How'd you know which one to dig up?"

"Yours was unembellished." Escott grabbed the shovel,
bracing it upright against a tree. "I suppose your brother
thought God wouldn't have you."

"He was right."

"Come along, Mr. Kroun. I've not yet decided what to do
about you."

That made him pay attention. "What do you mean?"

"Pick yourself up." Escott said it the way someone else might say, "Time to settle the bill."

I hate this place.

With less effort than anticipated, Gabe got to his feet. His day's rest in the ground had restored him. His scratches were gone, and the chunk torn from his shoulder was filled in, no longer hurting. There was a scar, but it was well healed. Another day, and it might be gone entirely; the same went for the hole in his chest. His head continued to throb, probably a hangover from the dope.

Following a well-trampled path in the snow, Escott trudged toward the clearing and the dark cabin. Gabe did not want to go there.

The hinges creaked, and Escott left the door open. Inside, he lit a few candles. Shadows jerked and quivered, as though surprised by the intrusion.

I should have burned the dump when I had the chance.

Gabe forced himself up the step and in. The wind followed him, carrying the whirring sound of the pines singing to themselves. He slammed the door on it.

The cabin looked smaller and meaner. The bloody, mold-eaten blanket and mattress had been thrown back on the bed. Gabe scowled and sat on a bench as far from it as possible. A fire in the potbelly stove would be good, but take time to start, and he didn't want to linger any longer than necessary. Escott obviously had some things to say. Let him get it out, then they could leave.

"You talked to Mike," prompted Gabe. He tried to not look at the bloodstains by the bed. Escott had to have noticed them.

"At length."

"He pay you off?"

"He did not. After a call to Gordy to establish my bona fides, I persuaded Mike to accept my help and silence in exchange for the truth of what happened in this cabin."

"What'd he tell you?"

"It was Miss Cabot's story that convinced me you needed

to be dealt with. She and her mother were present. Broder had been hiding them from you in Cicero. What you did to that girl . . ."

Gabe made a cutting motion with his hand. "Never mind that."

"No, I will not." Escott's voice lowered, taking on a harsher tone. "You crossed a line."

"*Shuttup.*"

Surprisingly, he did. Escott used a candle to light a cigarette, smoked it to the filter, and stubbed it out.

During that pause, Gabe tried to fit things together with this new information. He couldn't. "Ramsey was supposed to kill me, thought he had, and the girl was in the way, a witness. All I wanted was to find out if she was okay."

"She's as well as can be expected. Perhaps her mother is right, and she may find some shred of peace now that you're dead to her."

"But I *couldn't have*—"

"Mr. Kroun, you don't remember your death or what led to it, not one moment of it. Please have the courage to face the truth: Ramsey had no orders from anyone to kill you; he just couldn't stomach what you'd done to that poor girl."

"I did nothing! There's *no* way I'd have hurt her. You got that yet?"

Escott was silent for a long moment. "You absolutely believe that."

"It's true."

"It is not true, yet you believe it. Were that not so, you would never have hypnotized her last night and demanded she tell her story again. That would have damned you on the spot, but you tried anyway, thinking she'd exonerate you."

"Listen to me . . ."

"No." Escott cut his gaze away and pulled out his gun. "None of that. Try to put me under again, and I will shoot you. Look at the floor. Now."

That was stupid. He did as he was told. He was fast enough to rush the man, but it would put a stop to learning anything else. Escott would fire, and that might bring the monster out. Gabe was angry, but he didn't want to risk killing Escott.

He put a hand on the side of his pounding head and wished for more snow. "All right . . . what did she say?"

"You're ready to hear the truth?"

"Just tell me."

"Very well. Two months ago you did hire Miss Cabot's services as a companion for what you termed a 'fishing trip.' She understood that much and went willingly as the money was good. Ramsey drove and turned a blind eye; that was his job. You stopped at the asylum to show her off to your father, then continued on to Wisconsin."

Gabe's shivering abruptly ceased as heat crept up his neck and face. He was ashamed of what he'd done even if he couldn't remember it.

"This cabin was not the warm winter lodge she'd been led to expect. Soon as you arrived you gave yourself an injection of your chosen poison, then gagged her to keep her quiet. I shall not repeat what followed, only that it was brutal and went on for some while. Ramsey waited in the car as ordered, but when she managed to get rid of the gag, he heard her screams and came running. He burst in, did not like what he saw, and shot you dead."

Sickness rolled through him; Gabe shook his aching head. "You're wrong. I could never do that to a woman."

"Why would she lie?"

"I don't know." God, it hurt. "Keep going."

"Along with an hysterical girl, Ramsey had the problem of how to explain your death to your brother. Fearing the reception of that news would result in his own swift demise, he decided to get away and make himself scarce. He said as much to Miss Cabot, telling her she should do the same."

"Did she kill Ramsey?"

"Yes. Miss Cabot was in a bad state, fearful for her life. She knew how things worked in your world and had little trust that Ramsey would just let her go. By then she really was a witness to murder or at least a justifiable homicide. Perhaps he said something to make her doubt him. She said it was self-defense. She took the car back to the brothel."

"Why not to her mother?"

"Didn't know where to find her. The girl had fallen in love with some man when she was fifteen, run away, and some years later wound up working in that house. The madam there called a doctor for Miss Cabot, and since you were involved, he, in turn, called your brother."

Gabe risked looking up. "Then Mike knew all along?"

"No. It happened that Mr. Broder answered the phone. He took the next train to Chicago to sort out the mess. It was he who eventually found Mrs. Cabot and got her daughter home again. He paid her a sum to keep quiet. If she had any trouble, she was to phone him, which she did when you arrived unannounced at her diner. Her trunk call to New York got her message passed on to him here, and he came running."

That explained the car crash and grenade-throwing. "Why help her? What's his stake in this?"

"Because he is at heart a decent man."

"Decent? The man's a piece of walking granite."

"Who still had pity for the girl and wanted to spare your brother from having to deal with you." Escott let that sink in. "He found the broken grave and Ramsey, but you were missing. He buried Ramsey and left. Thereafter, he was careful to keep an eye on you. Broder accepted the story you yourself put about—that you'd been grazed by a bullet."

"Okay, some of that adds up, but not the rest. Not what happened here. Nelly was hysterical, she mixed things up. Or she was afraid of what Mike might do to her. She figured out a story that would keep her alive. She's not the first dame to accuse a man of—look, just *get* me to her. If I can put her under for five minutes, you'll hear the truth."

Escott stared, thinking maybe. One-handed he pulled out another cigarette and lit it with a candle. He kept the gun's aim steady. "It's truly lost to you, isn't it? Not just what happened that night, but everything. Otherwise, you'd never say that."

A hot spike hit that spot on his skull. Gabe flinched.

"You insist on your innocence because you don't remember who you were."

Gabe managed a snort despite his pain. "What gave you that idea?"

"I also had a long talk with Gordy. Jack mentioned you'd been getting information from him, then making him forget. I found that a little prodding on my part brought back some recollection of your conversations. It was clear to us both that you had no memory of who you used to be before that bullet hit your brain."

"That's crazy."

"Why deny it?"

Because it was weakness. Show that, and they ate you alive.

"You wanted details concerning your death, but with it came the ugly facts about the life you led. That's why you let Jack know certain things. You craved the truth but knew there might be consequences. If at some point you remembered and turned back into what you'd been, then you'd need someone who could keep you in check. Who better than another vampire?"

Gabe stood and walked out of the cabin, his knees shaking. He scooped more snow and pressed it to the white patch, but the agony wouldn't stop. His head felt too full. Sleet ticked down steadily, freezing, leaving a crust on everything. It stung his face, clinging to his eyebrows and lashes until his vision blurred.

He sank onto the icy step, holding tight to the porch support post. He wanted the cold to take him, freeze him solid so he wouldn't have to think or feel. Maybe Escott could simply bury him again, let the earth cover and blot him out forever.

He heard Escott's step behind him. The man passed by and stood in the blowing sleet, finishing his cigarette, let-

ting it fall to the snow. "This way," he said, heading toward
the trees.

Gabe felt too dizzy to walk, but made himself move.

Escott stopped on the other side of the black mound,
looking down at its cross. "You weren't even meant to be
here."

"Why is that?" Trying to distract himself out of the pain
he searched for anything familiar, anything that would spark
his memory.

"Miss Cabot said Ramsey scavenged the place for something with which to weigh your body, planning to sink it
in the river."

"Not bury me?"

"He changed his mind when he found this grave ready
and waiting."

Gabe looked up. "What?"

"You heard."

"But who put it here?"

"You're being unnecessarily obtuse, Mr. Kroun. You dug
it yourself."

He just couldn't see. "Why?"

"For *her* body when you were finished with her."

That was too much. "No. Absolutely not."

The wind swept his words into empty darkness. Bare
branches clacked around them, sleet hissed, and the pine
boughs made sad music.

But from his last visit he recalled the familiar feel of a
shovel in his hands. The blade cutting into the earth, regular as a machine, he was used to such work, took enjoyment
from it.

Now he knew why.

Just as Sonny had murdered his wives, Whitey Kroun
would murder his little hired humdinger . . .

He sagged, unable to deny, unwilling to accept. Ice crept
down the back of his neck. He didn't want to know any
more. This was too much.

Shivering, he turned toward the cabin.

Escott stood blocking the path. "Not yet. There is still a debt to pay."

Gabe spread his hands. "But I don't *remember*!"

"If you did, I'd kill you myself."

"*How* can I be responsible if I don't remember?"

"Your victims do."

That hit Gabe as hard as one of Sonny's slaps. "Wh-what?"

Escott pointed.

He rubbed sleet from his eyes. Peering, half-expecting to see Ramsey's ghost drifting between the tree trunks, Gabe only saw more snow. There were footprints wandering here and there in the clean drifts. Escott had been exploring, but his tracks were filling in.

"There and over there and that one . . ." Escott said, still pointing.

Gabe couldn't see anything but trees and snow and—

God . . . no . . .

The many layers of white fall covered several low mounds scattered over a wide area, softening their lines, but their shapes were unmistakable.

No . . . no, no, no . . .

Gabe staggered back, blundered against a trunk and held on to keep from falling. He turned away, doubling over. There was nothing in his cramping belly, but it twisted inside out regardless. He retched and gagged, staggered a few more steps, then doubled over again, unable to stop. He coughed bloody spittle, choking.

"Kroun!"

No more. He had to get away from that voice, that name, away from this hellhole.

Sleet blinded him. He kept going.

His legs seemed on fire as he slogged through deeper and thicker snow. The burning surged upward, tearing into his chest. It closed with a rush over his head, cutting off the wind. He leaned into the flames as they started to tug him down. Blistering hot, yet exquisitely cold. He was going to hell where he belonged.

Then something strongly grabbed one of his arms and, half-pulling it from the socket, hauled him back from the flowing abyss. He had no strength to fight. His feet tangled, he tripped, and abruptly body-slammed against rocky ground.

He lay stunned, blinking sluggishly, eyes swimming. Tears or melted sleet, he couldn't tell.

Escott stood over him, panting from some recent exertion. He was soaking wet and cursing, the invective aimed at Gabriel.

"On your feet, you idiot," he finally snarled.

Gabe dragged himself upright. He was soaked, too. He'd run himself straight into the river. "Why'd you stop me?"

Escott pointed again, up the easy rise, past the cabin, toward— "Those women—they had families, friends, people who need to know what happened to them. *That* is your debt. You will pay it before you leave this life."

It was insane . . . how could Escott expect him to—

"We'll sort something out."

Was he a mind reader? "You're gonna help me?"

"I'm helping *them*."

"Why?"

"Someone has to. Whitey Kroun was a very sickening fellow, perverted, dangerous, without conscience, and thoroughly deserving of his fate when it overtook him."

Dizziness washed though him again. *No more, please . . .*

"He died far too quickly and easily for his crimes."

He scrabbled for more snow, pressing it to the spot of agony on his head. It burned, gradually cooled, and left his fingers white and numb.

"Then you rose from the ruins. *Tabula rasa*—a clean slate."

"Not so clean." With flaws. So many dangerous flaws.

"But I believe you want to do the right thing. You just don't know how."

" 'S crazy."

"You saved my life, Mr. Kroun. If you will allow, perhaps I can help save yours."

Gabe had forgotten the hospital, what he'd done for a stranger. Things made better sense now. He began shivering again, more violently than before. His clothes were freezing to his skin. Escott looked no better, but still waited for a reply.

Gabe didn't know what was expected for a moment, then understood. "You're crazy, you know that?"

Escott gave a nod and held out his hand.

But I can leave. He could do that. Just walk away. He could bolt and disappear himself quick enough. Leave the state, leave the country.

But maybe . . . maybe this would make the pain go away.

He had to chance it. No plan. Deal with whatever came, whenever it came, and hope for the best.

He put his hand out and sealed his deal with another madman.

"It's cold, Mr. Kroun, we should leave."

"Don't call me that. I'm not him anymore, never again. Gabriel. Gabe's fine."

FLEMING

DUGAN'S hideout was the last of four similar small houses on a narrow road that continued south through empty fields; in the distance were enough lights to indicate a town. The two farthest houses showed lights, the nearest was dark. He'd picked a great spot for privacy.

To the north was Chicago, its glow against the clouds unmistakable and reassuring.

Mindful of how Dugan had acquired his last lair, I looked for graves and was thankful when nothing obvious presented itself. There was a rickety shed in back, empty, dirt floor undisturbed, a faded FOR RENT sign leaning against one side. The house itself was empty of furnishings except what he'd apparently brought himself. He must have gone legit to better keep his head down.

Putting the revolver on a kitchen counter, I gave myself a preliminary wash in the big sink, getting most of the blood and grime off my face and arms. The water was even hot.

He'd been intent on bathing, too, before my interruption. The bathtub had water in it, but it was draining away around a leaky plug. I quelled an urge to fill the thing and dive in.

His shaving things were balanced along the edge of the sink. I felt my beard, considered for less than a second, and left. I didn't want to touch any of his stuff if I could help it.

First things first, I found the rest of the blood supply he'd brought for me in the fridge: a dozen quart milk bottles filled to the brim. I snagged one and drank it straight down. My healing and the fight had taken it out of me, and even after my drink I still felt a general weariness.

That, I told myself, would fade with time. He'd given me his worst, and I'd beaten him. Maybe tomorrow night I'd get the shakes or cringe at a bad memory, but I'd worry about it then, not now.

Next I had to clean things other than myself, and it wasn't easy going back down into that damned basement. It stank of blood and terror. I made an effort not to breathe the rusty sweet stench.

The table must have been brought down in pieces; it was that big. He couldn't have managed it on his own otherwise.

The two rods stuck up as I'd left them, one with the handle broken off. I looked underneath to see how he'd worked it and saw that there had been a reason for the threading.

The lower part of the rods extended about a foot and a half below the table, and he'd filed the ends to points, the easier to pierce my arms. There were two thick metal squares with half-inch holes drilled in their centers firmly screwed to the underside of the table. Each rod went through that hole, held firmly in place with thick nuts and washers. Without the plates to spread the load, I might have been able to pull the rods out from the wood. Hideous, simple, and it worked.

I wanted to burn the table, but that would not be practical. Instead, I removed the rods, leaving the table with the holes and reinforcing plates as a mystery for anyone who happened to come down here next. The rods, rope, and my packet of earth went into the car. I kept the butcher's apron out.

The basement had a cement floor with a drain and over in a corner was a faucet. Cold water, but it did the job once I found a bucket and an ancient mop. I threw water over the table and swabbed it down, on top and underneath. My blood had soaked into some spots, but given time would turn into unidentifiable stains.

After the table I threw water on the stairs and floor, mopping them down. The porous cement would not scrub clean, but most of the red stuff went down the drain, and the place looked less like a slaughterhouse. The mop head remained bloody however much I rinsed it, so it would also go in the car.

Upstairs, I swept up the broken glass and put it in the bucket. I carried his radio, toolkit, and the bottles of animal blood to the car. He had a crate in the trunk, and the bottles fit neatly into it with no chance of spilling. This must have been how he'd carried them in the first place.

I searched his suitcase, finding bundles of money, spare clothes, newspapers, and most of a ream of writing paper, but nothing to indicate his identity.

On his writing table was a bottle of his favorite green ink ready to refill his favorite fountain pen.

In his neat, machinelike hand, he'd covered one sheet of paper with personal observations about his experiment—me. I didn't care to read more, and found matches left forgotten in a kitchen drawer. I crumpled his latest thought into a ball, and gathered up all the origami animals, carrying them to the kitchen sink.

They made a nice blaze for a few long minutes. I unfolded and fed them in one by one until the green was consumed by black, then crushed the ashes to dust. Running water flushed the last of his poisonous thoughts away for good. The sink had a scorched area, but that would be someone else's problem.

I squashed his clothing into the suitcase with his shaving

gear, the paper and ink—everything he'd brought—and put it in the car, keeping one of his shirts. I used it to rub down every surface in the house I could remember touching and a few more besides just to be careful. I used it like a glove to pick up the revolver again, wiping it, too, then thoughtfully switched off the lights. The doorknobs got a final swipe as I went outside.

My arms were still bare, what with the sleeves having been cut away, but I didn't feel cold. I'd worked up a good sweat from all the work.

There was one last job to do, and I'd allowed for the fact that I might not be able to finish it.

Dugan lay flat on the ground next to the grave he'd dug. I'd shot him. He was dead.

For now.

I didn't know if he would stay that way.

After all the blood he'd drained from me, I sure as hell wasn't going to take any chances.

I looked at his corpse, and all I could feel was relief. Guilt, regret, fear of being caught, even satisfaction—all the varied emotions that people experience when they murder another human being weren't there for me. I was only relieved that it was over.

Maybe that meant another piece of my soul was gone, burned away like his writing. Or maybe I was in some kind of shock.

Then it was a *relieved* kind of shock.

I dropped the revolver into the hole and tossed the shirt aside in case I wanted a rag for later.

His shovel was on the ground next to a pick he'd used to break up the tough earth. He was no expert at grave-digging, but he'd made it and the smaller hole very deep. All the energy and strength he'd taken from me had had to go somewhere.

I stooped and got the shovel. It still had the price written on the handle in grease pencil.

Last job.

It was a bad time to stop and think, but I realized I didn't know just how to do what needed to be done.

One short moment of consideration later, I turned him on his face. His body was flaccid and oddly heavy. Was it already repairing that bullet hole in his heart? I had no sense that there was anything left of him. There is an awful emptiness to the dead. You expect them to notice and react to your presence. It's unsettling that they don't.

Of course, it's even more unsettling if they do.

Two-handed, I raised the shovel and brought it straight down like a guillotine blade on the back of his neck. It sheared through the bones and flesh, biting into the earth beneath. His head did not roll away. Appalled that I'd even thought of it, I had carefully banked snow around him to prevent any such motion.

There was, not surprisingly, a great deal of blood. Much of it leaked into the ground, but a lot splashed onto me. I'd put on the butcher's apron, though, tying it low to cover my legs and shoes.

I kicked his body into the longer hole. It landed chest up.

Snapping the pick handle in two over one knee, I vanished, went down in the hole long enough to ram half of the splintered length of wood into his heart, took off the heavy apron, and shot swiftly clear.

Solid again, I quickly stumbled away and threw up.

My legs gave out. I fell on all fours in the snow, heaving and whooping and finally sobbing, though my eyes were dry. The emotional reaction caught up to me sooner than expected. I rode it out like a storm, letting my body have its way so I could eventually function again. On an intellectual level I'd done what was necessary, but certain horrors are harder to deal with than others.

Nausea anchored me in place for some time, blotting out even the cold, wet snow as I lay curled on the ground, groaning and miserable.

Once more I conjured that perfect summer day, but it

was less perfect now. The stock-tank water was uncomfortably cool, and gray clouds crowded in, dulling the blue sky. Bobbi and Escott were nowhere in sight.

My doppelgänger loafed under the shade tree, hands in his pockets, his expression sympathetic.

For the first time it occurred to me that doppelgängers in legend were supposed to be evil things. They brought calamity, chaos, and worse to those unlucky enough to see theirs.

Maybe he was the real Jack Fleming, and I was *his* doppelgänger.

The other me gave a sardonic snort, shaking his head, showing a brief grin.

"Don't be a pill," he said, then walked away.

I blinked awake. What the hell did that mean?

Ah, crap, I'd think about it later. I was freezing.

I scattered snow over the mess I'd made and went back to the long hole. Dugan's body was still in it, showing no signs of resurrection. I shoveled dirt in, enough to discourage scavengers, then regarded the smaller hole.

Clearly he'd dug it as a place to bury *my* head when the time came. It would be easy enough to toss his in, but I felt a reluctance to do so. There was no excuse not to use it, but from there I went up against an unexpected streak of superstition.

I had a nightmare picture of Dugan's body blindly lurching from its grave to go digging up its head.

That would *not* happen . . . but sometimes it's okay to give in to a mild case of irrationality. If it makes you feel better, why not?

My irrationality was sufficiently strong that it gave me the stomach to slam the sharp end of the pick through the back half of Dugan's head. Can't say I felt better, as the nausea returned in force, but the action removed all doubts that Dugan would somehow revive. His ghost might haunt me, along with the sound his skull made when the bones shattered, but everyone else was safe.

I shut the impaled remains in the rickety shed along with the swabbed-down shovel. In a couple days I'd call the cops and complain about intruders in the house and a bad smell coming from the shed. Of course they would be revolted by the headless corpse and the obvious violence that had taken place, but that couldn't be helped. They would eventually identify Dugan from his prints or what was left of his face and unofficially close a few files.

Someone would have to make an effort to find his killer, of course. That was of no concern to me so long as they didn't come knocking on my door. If that happened, well, I had plenty of friends who would provide me with an alibi, no questions asked.

Keeping my head low, I drove his car past the two occupied houses at a sedate, everything's normal pace, and continued north.

The city gradually embraced me, fields giving way to sidewalks and houses and traffic; I made brief stops to clear the car of evidence. Most of it went into an incinerator near the Stockyards that I'd used before for getting rid of incriminating things. Dugan's suitcase and that goddamned bottle of green ink went into the fire, along with the mop.

I left the small radio on someone's porch. Did the same again for the box of new tools. Happy birthday.

The blood went into a gutter drain. It seemed to take a long time to pour out, but only because I was worried someone would catch me at it. Though it was wasteful, I wasn't hungry. The empty bottles and threaded rods I shoved into trash cans behind a closed diner along with the bucket of broken glass.

The car emptied bit by bit until only the bundles of cash remained. In a few weeks I'd mail the money back to the woman it belonged to with the hope she'd wise up about her choice in boyfriends.

Cleaned out, my prints wiped away, I left the car across from a police station and slunk off into the shadows before anyone noticed.

I was still in a scary-looking condition and avoided peo-ple. A beat cop noticed me and started coming in my direc-tion, but I vanished into an alley and sped along for a block before re-forming again.

Needing clothes and a cleaning up, I slipped into a closed men's store and helped myself to one of everything, leaving the tags and more than enough cash on the counter.

A few streets over I found a hotel. Not wanting to startle the night clerk, I floated up the outside wall and sieved into an empty room on the top floor. There I stripped and scalded clean in the shower bath.

With much relief I noted that there were no permanent scars on my arms or my wrist where Dugan had cut me. The old ones left by Bristow were still present, but they didn't bother me as much now.

I had no shaving gear, but the rest of me was clean and grateful for the new clothes. I shoved my rags down the hotel's own incinerator chute and left five bucks in the bath-room for the maid to find.

Doing a plausible impersonation of a respectable citizen, I hired a taxi from the hotel stand, and got a quick ride to Lady Crymsyn.

The lights were on. Myrna must be awake. I paid off the driver and strolled across the street, checking both ways for anything more dangerous than myself.

The front door was unlocked. I listened a moment. A radio played, and a woman was singing along with the music.

I pushed in. Bobbi was at the bar with several stacks of paper scattered over it. She was in deep study over some-thing but looked up the moment the door opened.

Her eyes widened as she stared me up and down, but I couldn't read anything of what she was thinking. I let the door shut softly behind and stepped in, unsure of my recep-tion. She shut off the radio.

"I'm back," I finally said, just to break the thick silence.

"No kiddin'," she replied. "You get your thinking all done?"

Oh. Dugan had left a misleading message on my behalf.
May he rot in hell or at least in that pit he'd dug for me.
"Yeah. All done."

"Good."

I wanted to *hold* her, make sure she was real, but sensed
she was in a prickly mood. "What's that?"

She rested her fingers lightly on the papers. "Head shots,
clippings, and my credits list. It was in the files upstairs. I
want to get everything in order. Lenny Larsen said I'd need
to have new photographs, but that I should wait and have
them done in Hollywood."

"He'd be the expert. How are Roland and Faustine?"

"They're fine. He's getting better. So's Gordy."

I nodded, forcing a brief, wooden smile.

God, I felt as awkward as a kid at his first dance. After
three nights of surviving hell's antechamber it was disorienting to be back in my normal world. It and the people
there had no idea of what I'd been through. I had no inclination to tell them, either.

"What is it, Jack?"

"I . . . I'm just glad to see you. I missed you."

"Missed you, too."

She was waiting for me to work up to the delicate topic of
her going off to make that screen test. I'd promised to think
about it. And I had. At length. It was one of the things that
had kept me alive.

It had to wait, though. A car pulled up out front. Probably some late drinkers hoping the club had reopened. I went
to the door to lock it, but not in time.

Escott, looking like he'd been dragged through Lake
Michigan and hung out to dry in the rain, barged in. He
stopped in surprise, glaring.

"Well, it's about damned time you got back," he told me,
and bulled past.

Behind him was Kroun. "Where the hell have you been?"
he said.

He didn't wait for an answer but trudged to a chair and

dropped heavily into it. He'd been dragged through the lake, mudflats, *and* some kind of obstacle course.

Bobbi didn't know who to stare at the most. That made two of us. "Charles?"

"May I have a whiskey?" he asked her. He peeled out of his damp overcoat.

She played barmaid. "What happened to you?"

"Minor escapade. Quite stupid and wholly boring."

She shot a glance at me. Neither of us believed him. "Mr. Kroun?"

He held up a grubby palm and summoned some charm for her. "Gabe, please."

"Gabe. What happened?"

He grimaced and brushed his hand over the white patch. "I had some business problems to work out. Got a little messy. I need to lie low for a while. Escott said this joint would be all right." He looked at me.

I gave an I-don't-mind shrug, trusting Escott would explain later.

Something shook inside my chest, fighting its way out. I tried to suppress the urge, but nothing doing, it was too strong.

I started laughing.

Thankfully, it wasn't that scary, maniacal kind, but the three of them stared until I got it under control.

"Sorry," I said.

"We were worried about you," said Escott sourly. He downed his drink.

Bobbi poured him another and growled agreement.

"I wasn't," said Kroun. "But you picked a hell of a time to run off."

"Sorry," I repeated. "Won't happen again."

That stood on its own for a while. I took off my new coat and hat, putting them on one of the stools. No one seemed disposed to start a conversation until the light flickered behind the bar.

"Hello, Myrna," I said. "Good to see you, too."

Kroun muttered something I didn't catch.

"Figuratively speaking," I added.

The flickering stopped. I thought that later, when I was alone, I'd tell Myrna what I'd been through. She wouldn't mind. It wouldn't change things between us.

"What's with the beard?" asked Kroun, rubbing his own unshaved jaw.

"Forgot my razor."

"Jack . . . is that a new suit?" Bobbi came around the bar for a closer look.

"Like it?"

"It's nice."

At the clothing store, the only double-breasted in my size that I could halfway tolerate had been a pale gray number. I felt like an overdressed street sweeper.

"It's kind of light for the season, isn't it?"

"Well . . . uh . . . I heard it's warmer in California."

Her eyes blazed impossibly bright; she gave a laughing shriek and jumped into my arms.